APPLIED WELFARE ECONOMICS

Applied Welfare Economics

CHRIS JONES

OXFORD

UNIVERSITY PRESS

OXFORD

UNIVERSITY PRESS

Great Clarendon Street, Oxford OX2 6DP

Oxford University Press is a department of the University of Oxford.
It furthers the University's objective of excellence in research, scholarship,
and education by publishing worldwide in

Oxford New York

Auckland Cape Town Dar es Salaam Hong Kong Karachi
Kuala Lumpur Madrid Melbourne Mexico City Nairobi
New Delhi Shanghai Taipei Toronto

With offices in

Argentina Austria Brazil Chile Czech Republic France Greece
Guatemala Hungary Italy Japan Poland Portugal Singapore
South Korea Switzerland Thailand Turkey Ukraine Vietnam

Oxford is a registered trade mark of Oxford University Press
in the UK and in certain other countries

Published in the United States
by Oxford University Press Inc., New York

British Library Cataloguing in Publication Data
Data available

Library of Congress Cataloging in Publication Data
Data available

Typeset by Newgen Imaging Systems (P) Ltd., Chennai, India
Printed in Great Britain
on acid-free paper by
Biddles Ltd., King's Lynn, Norfolk

ISBN 0-19-928197-1 978-0-19-928197-8

1 3 5 7 9 10 8 6 4 2

For John Logan and Ross Parish

Preface

Applied Welfare Economics is a graduate course taught to economics honours students in the Department of Economics at the Australian National University. It was initially taught by Ted Sieper, who over two decades moulded the course into one that played an important role in the training of students who passed through the program. While drawing the material together in a coherent framework, he uncovered many challenging propositions and puzzles that occupied the minds of many colleagues within the Department and at other institutions around Australia and overseas. After his departure I was given the responsibility of teaching the course, whereupon it became abundantly clear how important welfare is to economics. This realization made it much easier for me to teach introductory economics to first year students in a way that captured their interest and attention.

Many people have made contributions to this book. Foremost among them of course is Ted, whose lectures provided a large portion of the material in the first two chapters. I have also benefited enormously from conversations with George Fane over many years. His thorough comments on earlier work and the patience he displayed when confronted with another of my propositions is greatly appreciated. There are many others who have assisted me with their valuable time and insights, and they include Akihito Asano, Scott Austin, Matt Benge, Simon Grant, Peter Hartley, Mark Harrison, Alex Robson, and Albert Schweinberger. I am also grateful for the beneficial interactions with students in the honours course, in particular, Declan Trott who kindly agreed to read the final draft and Lucy Rees who provided helpful comments. Their enthusiasm and diligence motivated me to work harder at giving better intuitions and explanations for the material.

I would especially like to acknowledge the assistance received from two recently departed colleagues, John Logan and Ross Parish. John's enthusiasm for economics gave me the interest and desire to learn more about the subject. While I had limited personal contact with Ross Parish, I benefited considerably from his written work. He has, in my view, made important contributions to applied welfare analysis over the years and his wisdom and insights were greatly appreciated by those lucky enough to have known him. As is always the case, however, I am solely responsible for any errors, generalizations, or oversights that undoubtedly remain in this book.

Finally I would like to thank everyone at Oxford University Press who contributed to this book. In particular, Andrew Schuller, who kindly agreed to consider the first draft, and Jennifer Wilkinson, Jenni Craig, Carol Bestley, and Virginia Masardo, who guided the manuscript through its many different phases. All were a pleasure to work with and were thoroughly professional.

Chris Jones
Canberra, Australia

Contents

List of Figures

List of Tables

Introduction

The actions people take are determined by potential welfare gains. Everything we do is motivated by some form of expected net benefit, including the gifts we give to others. People make sacrifices, often anonymously, to improve the well-being of others they care about. Gains from voluntary trade are what bring buyers and sellers together in markets, and individuals take actions in isolation if it makes them better off. Unfortunately, however, not all private activity raises social welfare; there are circumstances where individuals take actions that do not account for spill over effects on others, both good and bad. Outcomes of this kind depend very much on the institutional arrangements—or rules of the game—that establish the environment within which we function. For example, laws establish the way property rights are allocated in every economy. In some circumstances they are established by traditional custom, and in others by government policy. There are a variety of reasons for wanting to measure welfare changes. Individuals make assessments about the well-being of others, particularly the less well off in society, and governments look for guidance on policy choices, which unfortunately are not always driven by altruism. While politicians and bureaucrats establish institutions within which private individuals can make welfare improving choices, they also take actions to benefit themselves. Indeed, private interest can at times be a better explanation for some policy choices, like tariff protection and farm subsidies. By measuring the welfare effects of public policy decisions it is possible to advertise and monitor any social costs.

In practice, the task of quantifying welfare changes is greatly complicated by our inability to measure individual utilities. A Harberger cost–benefit analysis is the standard approach used in project evaluation. It separates the welfare effects of each component of a project with lump-sum transfers, which is useful because policy evaluation can be divided across specialist agencies. This book formalizes the conventional Harberger analysis in a general equilibrium setting. A welfare decomposition in Hatta (1977) is generalized to separate equity and efficiency effects for marginal policy changes. Also, a number of important results in the applied welfare literature are used to simplify a standard cost–benefit analysis. While conventional shadow prices are normally used to evaluate public sector projects, they can be applied generally to any marginal welfare analysis. This is demonstrated by computing shadow prices for private sector projects and a range of government regulations like production quota, price caps, and taxes. Throughout the book welfare expressions are solved as functions of the structural form parameters in the economy (i.e. demand–supply elasticities) to provide measurable welfare expressions for policy analysts to use in applied work, and it is in this sense that the book is about applied welfare economics.

Chapter 1. Measuring Welfare Changes—A Brief Overview. This chapter provides an informal summary of the properties of welfare measures used in later chapters.[1]

Due to the absence of cardinal utility measures the welfare effects from policy changes are computed indirectly. A conventional Harberger analysis does it by valuing changes in final consumption demand at market prices and summing them over consumers, where this provides an aggregate dollar measure of the changes in utility. But dollars are not normally a reliable proxy for utility when there are discrete changes in real income. Moreover, consumers are unlikely to derive the same utility from extra dollars of income so that lump-sum redistributions of income will have aggregate welfare effects. The Hatta decomposition finds dollars are a reliable proxy for utility when policy changes are incrementally small. Marginal welfare analysis, which is used in following chapters, can be justified when governments make policy changes as a sequence of incrementally small steps, for example, tax and tariff reforms. It also provides information about the gaps between private and social valuations under existing policies, thereby highlighting areas where policy reform is most urgently needed.

Perhaps the most contentious issue in applied welfare economics is how to aggregate welfare changes over consumers, particularly when policy changes make some better off and others worse off. One approach assigns different distributional weights to their dollar changes in utility and then sums them. However, it is based on subjective assessments about the marginal social valuation of income for each consumer. Another approach avoids this problem, at least partially, by using the compensation principle to test for Pareto improvements. The compensation tests will be summarized with explanations of the problems that arise when they are used to evaluate second best policy changes. In following chapters a decomposition by Hatta will be used to isolate income effects from policy changes as an independent scaling coefficient on the aggregate efficiency effects. This chapter demonstrates the decomposition in a partial equilibrium setting.

Chapter 2. Conventional Shadow Prices.   The formal analysis begins here, and it is an important chapter because it lays the foundation for all the welfare analysis in following chapters of the book. A standard Harberger cost–benefit analysis is formalized in a competitive general equilibrium model of a tax-distorted economy with non-traded goods. Initially the distributional effects are removed by adopting Harberger's *dollar-is-a-dollar* assumption. In following chapters the analysis is extended by including distributional effects, internationally traded goods, externalities, non-competitive behaviour, price–quantity controls, public goods, and other market distortions.

Conventional shadow prices of goods are derived in the presence of tax distortions, and the role of lump-sum transfers is explicitly examined. Very often these transfers take place in the background of a cost–benefit analysis and their role is not explicitly acknowledged. However, they are important in a general equilibrium setting where prices change endogenously. Whenever the government balances its budget it must decide how consumers will be affected by its revenue transfers. Since different patterns of transfers across consumers can lead to different equilibrium outcomes, the government can determine the distributional effects of its policy changes by choosing the transfer shares.[2] Distributional effects are examined in detail in Chapter 3, and the analysis is extended to allow revenue transfers with distorting taxes in Chapter 6.

Lump–sum transfers play the important role of isolating welfare changes for individual policy instruments in a conventional welfare analysis. This is extremely useful from a practical point of view because policy evaluation can be divided across specialist agencies. For example, government finance departments can estimate the marginal social cost of raising revenue with distorting taxes without knowing how spending departments will use the funds. The reverse applies when spending departments measure the social benefits that flow from their programs.

Sieper (1981) proves the conventional shadow price of any good is equal to its compensated shadow price multiplied by the generalized Hatta coefficient. The inverse of this coefficient is the shadow value of government revenue which isolates income effects. Since it is independent of the policy change in single (aggregated) consumer economies, income effects will play no role in a conventional Harberger analysis. Shadow prices are also derived for privately produced goods and services to extend the welfare analysis beyond just public sector projects.

Chapter 3. Distributional Effects. Once consumers are assigned different distributional weights a policy with potential losses can raise social welfare by improving the distribution of income. There are two ways to account for distributional effects. The first is recommended by Dréze and Stern (1990) where dollar changes in utility are multiplied by the distributional weight for each consumer then summed. Clearly, if there are winners and losers a policy change can be socially profitable using one set of weights but socially unprofitable using another set. Many analysts are uncomfortable about their subjective assessments being so influential in the evaluation process.

Bruce and Harris (1982) and Diewert (1983) recommend an approach which avoids this problem by using the compensation principle to convert efficiency gains into Pareto improvements. In this chapter, the shadow prices are obtained using both approaches. Distributional effects are included in conventional shadow prices using the approach recommended by Dréze and Stern with distributional characteristics defined in Boadway (1976) and Slemrod and Yitzhaki (2001). The approach recommended by Bruce and Harris and Diewert is applied using the generalized Hatta decomposition to isolate the welfare effects of transfer policy choices. With heterogeneous consumers the shadow value of government revenue, which isolates income effects for any marginal policy change, is the distributional weighted sum of the personal shadow values of government revenue. When transfer policy choices make the personal shadow value of government revenue positive for every consumer, aggregate dollar gains in utility will be strict Pareto improvements.

Chapter 4. Non-Tax Distortions in Markets. A range of important non-tax distortions are examined in this chapter. They include externalities, non–competitive behaviour, and price and quantity controls. These are important and topical extensions to the basic analysis, and are useful in applied work, particularly in developing countries. A number of non-tax distortions apply in labour markets, and since labour is a significant input to production, both private and public, they have important welfare effects. Shadow wage rates are derived in the presence of minimum wage laws and other labour market interventions to demonstrate these effects. The analysis in this chapter demonstrates how welfare effects from policy changes depend crucially on the types of distortions in markets. While market outcomes in the presence of non-tax distortions can be replicated by an appropriate set of taxes and/or subsidies, the welfare effects from policy changes are quite different. For example, increasing the supply of a good that is subject to an effective price floor will not expand activity because it is demand constrained. In contrast, activity rises when the distortion is a tax instead of a price floor.

Chapter 5. International Trade. Welfare measures are examined here in the presence of taxes and quantity controls on international trade flows. Traditionally, the shadow exchange rate has played an important role in project evaluation. Harberger (1968) uses it to compute the shadow prices of fully traded goods by converting their foreign prices into domestic utility. The shadow and official exchange rates normally diverge when there are taxes and other distortions in domestic markets. Most derivations of the shadow exchange rate account for tax distortions on international trade flows, but not taxes and other distortions on non-traded goods. A more general expression of the shadow exchange rate is derived to account for these additional distortions under both fixed and floating exchange rate regimes.

The generalized Hatta decomposition will be used to provide intuition for the important Little and Mirrlees (1969) shadow pricing rule for fully traded goods in small open economies. Then the domestic resource cost ratio is compared to the effective rate of protection, where both welfare measures are widely used by international aid agencies like the United Nations Development Program, the International Monetary Fund, the World Bank, and the Asia Development Bank to review the effects of trade policies in developing countries. Firm data will be used to make these comparisons.

Chapter 6. Revised Shadow Prices. Governments rarely raise revenue with lump-sum transfers. Instead, they use distorting taxes, and this must be reflected in the welfare measures. The conventional welfare analysis in previous chapters is extended by including changes in tax inefficiency on the revenue transfers made to balance the government budget. This involves a simple revision to the conventional (lump-sum) shadow prices, where the revised shadow price of any good is its conventional shadow price plus the change in tax inefficiency on the (notional) lump-sum transfers used to isolate it. This adjustment is used in Chapter 7 to identify the role of the marginal social cost of public funds (MCF) in project evaluation. Finally, the Hatta decomposition is extended to revised welfare changes where income effects are isolated in the revised shadow value of government revenue. It will be used in Chapter 7 to measure the distributional effects of policy changes when government make revenue transfers with distorting taxes.

Chapter 7. The Marginal Social Cost of Public Funds. In public economics applications the MCF is frequently used to cost government revenue. Perhaps the most common example is provided by the revision to the Samuelson condition using the approach of Pigou (1947). The literature on the MCF can at times be quite confusing. There are a range of different measures for a variety of different taxes, and analysts are unsure how to interpret and use them in policy evaluation. The analysis in Chapter 6 provides a good foundation for reconciling these different measures of the MCF. It is not normally used, at least explicitly, in the applied welfare literature to compute shadow prices. This chapter rearranges the revised shadow prices in Chapter 6 using the MCF to show it is not the shadow value of government revenue. Rather, it is the cost to private surplus of transferring a dollar of revenue to balance the government budget. The shadow value of government revenue is the welfare gain from endowing another dollar of revenue on the economy. Thus, it is a gain from expanding the economies resources. In contrast, the MCF is the welfare effect of transferring given resources between the private and public sectors of the economy. Since compensated welfare gains are equivalent to gifts of surplus revenue the shadow value of government revenue, and not the MCF, is used to convert them into higher utility. The relationship between the MCF and the shadow value of government revenue is used to reconcile the many different measures of the MCF used in the public economics literature.[3]

Chapter 8. Time and the Social Discount Rate. Most policies impact on intertemporal consumption choices, where taxes on capital income are perhaps the most obvious example. This chapter extends the analysis in previous chapters by studying the welfare effects of linear and non-linear personal income taxes, as well as taxes on corporate income, in a two-period setting. The analysis in Harberger (1969) and Sandmo and Dréze (1971) is extended by deriving personal shadow discount rates in the presence of progressive marginal tax rates. When consumers have different marginal personal tax rates they use different discount factors on their future consumption flows.

The welfare effects of a classical corporate tax are analysed in the Miller (1977) equilibrium where consumers specialize in holding debt or equity based on their tax preferences for the two securities. Since the classical corporate tax favours debt it drives equity from the capital market, (in a certainty setting). Miller explains the presence of equity by recognizing the favourable tax treatment of capital gains in the presence of progressive personal income taxes. Once again, there are personalized shadow discount rates, but now the corporate tax appears in the discount factors for shareholders.

In the presence of uncertainty the discount rates include a risk premium, where the most popular way of computing it is with the capital asset pricing model (CAPM). However, it relies on a number of important assumptions which may not hold in practice. A further consideration is whether public sector projects should have a lower risk premium than the same projects funded by private borrowing. The Arrow–Lind Theorem argues that this is the case when the government can diversify risk more efficiently than the private sector. These issues will be examined in this chapter.

Chapter 9. Optimal Commodity Taxation. Ramsey optimal commodity tax rules are derived using the conventional welfare analysis presented in Chapter 6. When they apply, Diamond and Mirrlees (1971) and Stiglitz and Dasgupta (1971) prove the producer prices can be used as shadow prices in project evaluation if private profits are eliminated from consumer incomes. This occurs when private output is produced with constant returns to scale technologies, or there is a 100% profit tax. Both are demonstrated using shadow prices to value the changes in economic activity from marginal tax changes. It provides economic intuition that can be used, together with the generalized Hatta decomposition, to extend a number of familiar optimal tax rules.

Chapter 10. The Optimal Provision of Public Goods. The government provision of a pure public good is a popular application in public economics because it combines public spending and taxation in a single project. As such, it provides an excellent opportunity to apply the welfare analysis developed in previous chapters. The effects of distorting taxation on the optimal level of government spending are included by using the revised shadow prices in Chapter 6 to obtain a revised Samuelson condition, and the distributional effects are included using welfare analysis in Chapter 3. The generalized Hatta decomposition is then used to show why income effects have no impact on the Samuelson condition in a single (aggregated) consumer economy. Finally, Lindahl prices are obtained for government provided public goods when prices and incomes change endogenously in a general equilibrium setting.

Chapter 11. Problems. A set of questions are drawn from material presented in previous chapters of the book. Most are designed to emphasize important points, and to illustrate practical examples of applied welfare analysis.

In summary, this book formalizes and extends the standard Harberger cost–benefit analysis to integrate important results in two separate strands of the literature; the shadow pricing rules derived in applied welfare economics and the standard cost–benefit analysis used in public economics.

NOTES

1. A more detailed presentation of this material is available in Boadway and Bruce (1984) and Myles (1995).
2. Consumers will in general have different marginal propensities to consume extra income. When they do, transfer policy choices will impact on equilibrium outcomes.
3. Excellent summaries of the different measures of the MCF are presented in Snow and Warren (1996) and Mayshar (1990).

1

Measuring Welfare Changes—A Brief Overview

Welfare gains from voluntary trade between individuals are the invisible hand that drives resource allocation in private market economies. For an initial distribution of income, and in the absence of externalities and other price distortions, these gains are maximized in competitive markets. This is captured by the First Fundamental Theorem of Welfare Economics that states:

> *The allocation by trade of a given initial distribution of resources is Pareto optimal in a competitive general equilibrium.*[1]

At a Pareto optimum it is not possible to make one consumer better off without making at least one other worse off. Thus, there is a Pareto improvement from a reallocation of resources if it makes at least one consumer better off and no others worse off. An example is illustrated using the Edgeworth box diagram in Figure 1.1 for a two-good two-consumer economy with initial endowments at point E.

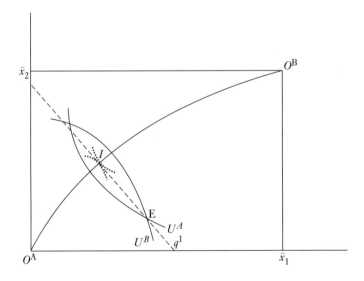

Figure 1.1 *A competitive equilibrium*

When trade takes place at the market clearing price q^1 the equilibrium outcome at I is on the contract curve $O^A O^B$, where the move from E constitutes a Pareto improvement by making both consumers better off. The new allocation is also Pareto optimal since no further Pareto improvements are possible. Thus, it is *efficient* in the narrow sense of exhausting the gains from trade. But there are an infinite number of other potential equilibrium allocations that are Pareto improvements relative to E. Indeed, all the bundles inside the lens formed by the initial indifference curves that pass through E possess this property, where the bundles along the contract curve inside the lens are both Pareto improvements and Pareto efficient.[2] With different market structures the final equilibrium outcome may not lie on the contract curve. For example, one of the consumers could be a single-price monopolist who sets a price that takes the equilibrium allocation inside the lens but off the contract curve. While this outcome is a Pareto improvement it is not Pareto efficient. However, if perfect price discrimination is possible the equilibrium outcome will be on the contract curve where the monopolist takes all the gains from trade.

Not every reallocation of resources between consumers is driven by Pareto improvements. Governments frequently adopt policy changes that make some consumers better off and others worse off, and this poses an obvious question—how can equilibrium allocations be compared when there are winners and losers? One approach redistributes income between consumers to convert new equilibrium allocations into Pareto improvements relative to the initial equilibrium. But there are normally a large number of Pareto improvements to choose between when lump-sum income redistribution is possible, where by the Second Fundamental Theorem of Welfare Economics:

> *Every Pareto optimal allocation can be realized as a competitive general equilibrium with lump-sum redistributions of the initial endowments of resources.*

Since bundles along the contract curve involve utility trade-offs, interpersonal utility comparisons are required to rank them, and that involves subjective assessments about changes in utility. In some respects this theorem creates the misleading impression that the distribution of income is an independent policy variable. In reality, aggregate income is endogenously determined by market outcomes and will be affected by income redistribution. One example is the way individuals allocate their limited time between labour and leisure, where income from labour supply funds consumption of marketed goods and services. Some income is saved for future consumption, where the extra wealth generates additional income. If revenue is transferred in a lump sum from high to low income consumers it reduces their incentive to supply labour and to save, with a consequent fall in aggregate income. This loss is likely to be larger when income is redistributed by distorting taxes. Ultimately, income redistribution diminishes private ownership claims to resources by restricting the benefits that flow to them. Some resources are endowed by nature, and when they are unique to particular individuals they can attract rents. Although taxes on rent do not affect the allocation of resources, a redistribution of income may, at least partially, be undone by voluntary private trades. For example, income transferred from Tiger Woods may be spent by recipients on tickets to watch him play in golf tournaments, or on the goods he endorses. Thus, when income is endogenously determined by private actions there are efficiency effects from redistribution, and to some extent at least, the distribution of income is itself endogenous.

The exposition of the two fundamental theorems in the Edgeworth box diagram provides a good summary of the efficiency and equity effects that arise in applied welfare economics. There are a variety of reasons why market outcomes do not realize all the potential gains from trade (i.e. there are potential Pareto improvements). The single price monopolist mentioned earlier provides one example, and external costs (or benefits) that move the equilibrium outcomes off the contract curve are another. A cost–benefit analysis measures the foregone potential gains and then estimates the efficiency costs of implementing policies to realize them. There may also be distributional effects, and once they are included in the welfare analysis a broader definition of efficiency is being used; one that seeks to maximize the gains from trade and achieve an optimal distribution of utilities. In other words, it seeks to maximize social (or aggregate) welfare.

It is difficult to quantify welfare changes without a cardinal utility measure that is common to affected consumers. The standard way to overcome this problem is to measure dollar changes in surplus underneath demand schedules as proxy measures for changes in utility. But there are two problems with this approach—first, dollars do not generally convert into utility at a constant rate underneath consumer demand schedules, and second, each consumer has a different marginal utility of income. When the marginal utility of income changes along demand schedules, dollar changes in surplus are path dependent, that is, they depend on the way they are ordered. Thus, it is possible to influence policy decisions simply by reordering them. But even when the marginal utility of income is constant, it will not normally be the same for all consumers. Thus, we cannot sensibly compare dollar changes in surplus let alone aggregate them over consumers.

A partial solution is to measure compensated welfare changes, where an efficiency gain is the surplus revenue a policy change will generate for the economy after transfers are made to hold consumer utilities constant; it is therefore free of any distributional effects. When this surplus revenue is transferred to consumers it becomes their actual dollar changes in utility. This is the Hatta (1977) decomposition which is used later in the chapter to separate the welfare effects for marginal policy changes. Before that, however, welfare changes will be measured using price–quantity data and revealed preferences, and then demand schedules derived from consumer preferences.

1.1 MEASURING WELFARE CHANGES USING PRICE–QUANTITY COMPARISONS

Consumers typically adjust their consumption bundles in response to changes in real income, and it is possible to rank some of these changes using observed equilibrium prices. They cannot all be ranked due to the limited information this data provides. That is why price–quantity comparisons provide welfare measures that are approximations for the true welfare changes.

1.1.1 Welfare Changes for Single Consumers

Consider an individual who chooses the consumption vector x^0 at the vector of old relative prices q^0, and consumption vector x^1 at the vector of new relative prices q^1. If the two consumption bundles satisfy specified conditions they can be ranked without knowing the consumer's utility function. These conditions are illustrated for the two good case using Figure 1.2.

All the consumption bundles on or inside the old budget constraint are revealed as being less preferred to x^0. They could have been purchased but were not. Thus, whenever the new bundle x^1 lies in this region the consumer must be worse off. Conversely, all the bundles with more of at least one good are strictly preferred to x^0 when non-satiation applies. If x^1 lies in this region the consumer must be better off. There is ambiguity about the welfare change when the new bundle x^1 lies inside the cross-lined regions of the diagram where there is more of one good and less of the other. Some of this indeterminancy can be resolved using the Laspeyres and Paasche quantity indices.

The *Laspeyres quantity index* provides a *necessary condition* for the new bundle to be revealed preferred (P) to the old bundle (which is denoted as $x^1 P x^0$) of:

$$q^0 x^1 > q^0 x^0.$$

It simply requires the new bundle x^1 to lie outside the initial budget constraint. In other words, it is a bundle which the consumer could not afford to buy at the old vector of prices q^0. But that does not guarantee a welfare improvement because the new bundle

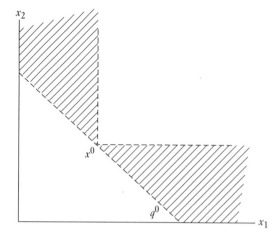

Figure 1.2 *Ranking consumption bundles*

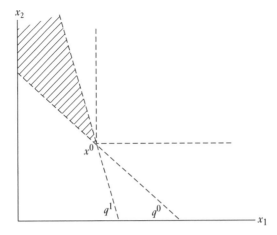

Figure 1.3 *Ranking consumption bundles using quantity indices*

could lie in the cross-lined regions of Figure 1.2. The *Paasche quantity index* provides the *sufficient condition* for $x^1 P x^0$ of:

$$q^1 x^1 \geq q^1 x^0.$$

When this condition holds it reduces the zones of indeterminancy to the cross-lined region in Figure 1.3.

If bundle x^1 costs more to purchase than the old bundle x^0 at new prices q^1, then x^1 is revealed preferred. This test is based on Slutsky compensation which overcompensates consumers for the price change. By providing consumers with sufficient income to purchase their old bundles at new prices (with $q^1 x^1 = q^1 x^0$) they can move onto higher indifference curves. Thus, there are bundles inside the cross-lined region of Figure 1.3 that are preferred to x^0 even though they fail the sufficient condition.[3] When the sufficient condition fails and the necessary condition holds it is uncertain whether $x^1 P x^0$. That is why quantity indices provide welfare measures that are approximations for the true welfare changes obtained using indifference curves. This is demonstrated for two goods in Figure 1.4 by raising the price of good 1 with money income and the price of good 2 held constant.

The higher relative price (q) reduces the demand for both goods when they are complements (which is the case illustrated). The true welfare loss for the consumer is illustrated as DA units of good 2 in the commodity space diagram, and $x_1^1 S Q x_1^0$ plus $x_2^0 - x_2^1$ in the quantity–price diagram.[4] It is the extra amount of good 2 the consumer would need to move from bundle A to bundle D, which is on the initial indifference curve (u_0). This welfare change can be estimated using quantity indices to value the changes in consumption demand at market prices. The Laspeyres quantity index values them at initial prices where the welfare change (with good 2 chosen as

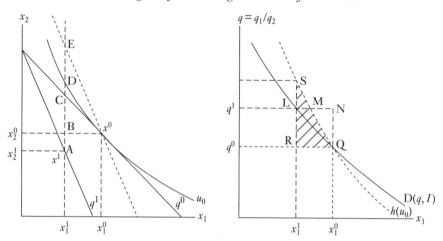

Figure 1.4 *Welfare changes using quantity indices*

numeraire) is:

$$L_Q = q^0(x_1^1 - x_1^0) + (x_2^1 - x_2^0).$$

It provides an estimate of the consumer's welfare loss from the higher price as distance CA in the commodity space diagram in Figure 1.4, which is smaller than the true welfare loss by DC units of good 2.[5] (In the quantity–price diagram the welfare loss is smaller than the true loss by area RSQ.)

Alternatively, the Paasche quantity index values the changes in consumption demand at new prices where the welfare change (with good 2 chosen as numeraire) is:

$$P_Q = q^1(x_1^1 - x_1^0) + (x_2^1 - x_2^0).$$

It provides an estimate of the welfare loss of distance EA in the commodity space diagram in Figure 1.4, which overstates the true welfare loss by ED units of good 2. (In the quantity–price diagram the loss is area $x_1^1 LN x_1^0$ plus $x_2^1 - x_2^0$, which is larger than the true welfare loss by area MNQ-LSM).[6]

From this example it is easy to see why the quantity indices provide approximate welfare measures. Not every unit of the change in demand is valued by the consumer at the old or new prices. Instead, a consumer's marginal valuation for each good rises as demand falls. Thus, old prices understate marginal valuations while new prices overstate them.

Notice how welfare measures are computed here as changes in the value of final consumption demand. In other words, as areas underneath the demand schedules. A much more common approach, however, measures welfare changes as areas to the left of demand schedules. This is approximated using the Laspeyres and Paasche price indices to estimate changes in private surplus, where the *necessary condition* for $x^1 P x^0$ is obtained from the *Paasche price index* as:

$$q^1 x^1 < q^0 x^1,$$

and *sufficient condition* for $x^1 P x^0$ from the *Laspeyres price index* as:

$$q^1 x^0 \le q^0 x^0.$$

The necessary condition tells us that the consumer could not afford the new bundle x^1 at old prices q^0. Thus, it must lie outside the old budget constraint. The sufficient condition guarantees higher private surplus when the old bundle costs as much or more to purchase at old prices as it does at new prices. That is, when $q^1 x^0 = q^0 x^0$ (and there are different elements in the new and old price vectors) the consumer can move from the high to low priced goods and be better off. Once again, the price indices can be used to approximate measures of the true changes in private surplus for the price change illustrated in Figure 1.4. Since the analysis closely follows the changes illustrated using the quantity indices the task is left to the reader.

There are two ways of measuring welfare changes—as changes in the value of final consumption demand or as changes in private surplus—and they are related through the consumer's budget constraint ($I = qx$) when money income (I) is constant, as $q\,dx = -x\,dq$. The two measures are illustrated for a marginal price rise in Figure 1.5 where the individual consumes two goods, which are assumed for illustrative purposes to be gross complements.[7]

With fixed money income the change in expenditure in each market must sum to zero, with $(a) - (b) - (c) = 0$. Thus, the fall in consumers surplus in $(a) = x\,dq$ is equal to the dollar value of the fall in final consumption demand in $(b) + (c) = -q\,dx$.

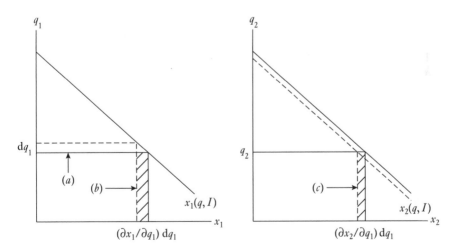

Figure 1.5 *Relating changes in surplus to changes in activity*

Any change in money income (dI) will impact directly on final consumption demand ($q\, dx$) by shifting the demand schedules for the two goods without affecting the change in private surplus in (a). Thus, to compute welfare measures using changes in private surplus we must add any changes in money income to them.[8]

This relationship also applies to welfare measures obtained using price–quantity indices. It is confirmed by using the budget constraint to rewrite the sufficient condition for $x^1 P x^0$ using the *Paasche quantity index*, as:

$$P_Q : q^1(x^1 - x^0) = q^1 x^1 - q^1 x^0 + q^0 x^0 - q^0 x^0 = I^1 - I^0 - x^0(q^1 - q^0) \geq 0,$$

which is the sufficient condition for $x^1 P x^0$ using the *Laspeyres price index* with constant money income ($dI = 0$). Similarly, the budget constraint can be used to convert the necessary condition for $x^1 P x^0$ using the *Laspeyres quantity index* into:

$$L_Q : q^0(x^1 - x^0) = q^1 x^1 - q^0 x^0 + q^0 x^1 - q^1 x^1 = I^1 - I^0 - x^1(q^1 - q^0) > 0,$$

which is the necessary condition for $x^1 P x^0$ using the *Paasche price index* (with $dI = 0$).

By recognizing this relationship between the welfare measures it is possible to understand why the general equilibrium welfare measures obtained in later chapters will solve as changes in the value of final consumption demand, that is, as areas below demand schedules. Economists are much more familiar with welfare changes when they are measured as changes in private surplus. But a large portion are simply transfers between consumers, which are not welfare losses for the economy as a whole. In a general equilibrium setting these transfers are included through the economy wide budget constraints, which is why they disappear from final welfare changes in the absence of distributional effects. Ultimately, welfare changes are determined by changes in final consumption because that is what enters the utility functions of consumers.

1.1.2 Welfare Changes for Many Consumers

Most governments collect and report aggregated price–quantity data on a quarterly basis. They measure changes in national product and its major components, as well as the consumer and producer price indices. There is considerable interest in knowing whether this data can be used to isolate welfare changes. In particular, whether consumers are better off when GNP rises. Hicks (1940), Kuznets (1948), Little (1949), Pigou (1932), and Samuelson (1948) undertake a thorough examination of this question. In *Evaluation of Real National Income*, Samuelson (1950) reviews the literature and relates it to the Pareto criterion and the Hicks–Kaldor compensation tests. Recall from the previous section how price–quantity comparisons for single-consumers could not isolate all possible welfare improvements. There are additional problems at the aggregate level when some consumers gain and others lose. This is illustrated in Figure 1.6 for a 2-good (x_1, x_2) 2-person (A, B) general equilibrium endowment economy.[9] Both agents are price takers who trade at a (single) market clearing price from the initial allocation at $0'$ onto the contract curve. The new equilibrium can be any of the Pareto optimal allocations along the contract curve $O^A O^B$ if private trade is also

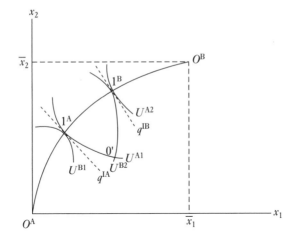

Figure 1.6 *Ranking equilibrium outcomes*

accompanied by a (lump–sum) redistribution of income. For example, policy 0 could be a ban on internal free trade, and policy 1 internal free trade with income transfers. How can bundle $0'$, which lies off the contract curve, be compared to the Pareto optimal allocations? Clearly, the optimal allocations between 1^A and 1^B make both consumers better off relative to $0'$ (see Figure 1.6). But how are optimal allocations compared either side of them between $O^A - 1^A$ and $1^B - O^B$ where one consumer gains and the other loses?

The utility possibility frontier (UPF^1) illustrated in Figure 1.7 summarizes the combinations of consumer utilities along the contract curve.[10]

It conveniently isolates new allocations under policy 1 that are Pareto improvements relative to $0'$, and the allocations where one consumer loses and the other gains. Each of the allocations on UPF^1 can be supported by a lump–sum redistribution of income.

A number of *welfare criteria* can be used to rank policies 0 and 1, and they include:

1. *The Pareto Criterion.* This identifies Pareto improvements where at least one consumer is made better off and no others worse off by the policy change. They are the equilibrium allocations between (and including) 1^A and 1^B along UPF^1 in Figure 1.7. Formally, policy 1 is socially preferred by the Pareto criterion to policy 0, which is denoted as $_1\mathrm{SP}_0^P$, if and only if $u(x^{h1'}) \geq u(x^{h0'})\ \forall_h$ and $>$ for at least one h; $x^{h1'}$ is the vector of consumption goods for consumer h under policy 1 at the new equilibrium allocation $1'$. A test for Pareto improvements using price–quantity data, with $_1\mathrm{SP}_0^P$, is:

$$q^{1'}(x^{h1'} - x^{h0'}) \geq 0 \qquad \forall_h.$$

But, as noted in the previous section, this is based on Slutsky compensation that makes every consumer better off. Thus, when it passes we must have $u(x^{h1'}) > u(x^{h0'})\ \forall_h$, which means some Pareto improvements are not identified by this test.[11]

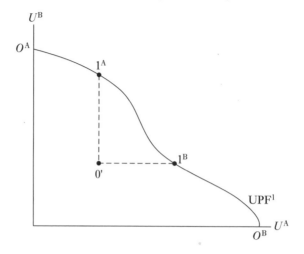

Figure 1.7 *Ranking consumption bundles using quantity indices*

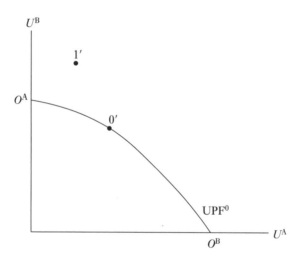

Figure 1.8 *Welfare comparisons using compensation tests*

2. The Compensation Tests. They rank policy changes when some consumers gain and others lose by using a lump-sum redistribution of income to convert new equilibrium allocations into Pareto improvements. An example is provided in Figure 1.8 where consumer A is worse off and consumer B better off at the new equilibrium allocation $1'$.

There are two ways of testing for a potential Pareto improvement. One looks at redistributing income between A and B after the policy change to see if $1'$ can be converted into an allocation along UPF^1 where both consumers are better off relative to $0'$. The other redistributes income before the policy change to make sure there are no equilibrium allocations along UPF^0 that makes both consumers better off relative to $1'$. Clearly, both tests will pass when the utility possibility frontier for policy 1 (not illustrated in Figure 1.8) lies wholly outside UPF^0, which is the case when policy 1 is first-best. In practice, however, most comparisons are between second-best policies with UPFs that normally cross each other, and when they do, there can be contradictions using the compensation tests. Four compensation tests are provided in the welfare economics literature and each will be considered in turn using aggregate price–quantity data.

(a) *The Kaldor (1939) Criterion.* This is a test for Pareto improvements where gainers from a policy change can compensate losers and still be better off.[12] In effect, lump-sum transfers are used to redistribute income after the policy change to find an equilibrium allocation that is a Pareto improvement relative to the initial allocation $0'$. Let $1''$ be the bundle of utilities when income is redistributed after the policy change, then policy 1 is socially preferred to policy 0 by the Kaldor criterion (denoted as ${}_1\text{SP}_0^K$), if:

$$q^{1''}(x^{h1''} - x^{h0'}) \geq 0 \qquad \forall_h.$$

An example is provided for the two consumer economy in Figure 1.9 where the equilibrium allocation at $1'$ is moved by income redistribution along UPF^1 to $1''$ where both consumers are better off relative to $0'$. Clearly, this test passes if the initial equilibrium allocation at $0'$ lies inside UPF^1.

(b) *The Hicks (1940) Criterion.* This is a sister test for the Kaldor criterion that looks for potential Pareto improvements by redistributing income prior to the policy change to rule out the possibility of losers being able to bribe winners to block the change. Let $0''$ be the bundle of utilities when income is redistributed before the policy change,

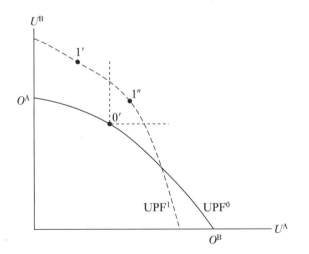

Figure 1.9 *The Kaldor criterion*

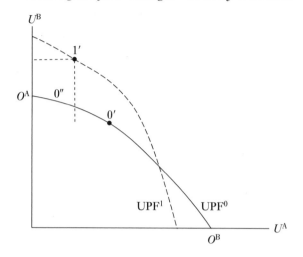

Figure 1.10 *The Hicks' criterion*

then policy 1 is socially preferred to policy 0 by the Hicks' criterion (denoted $_1\mathrm{SP}_0^{\mathrm{H}}$), if:

$$q^{1'}(x^{\mathrm{h}1'} - x^{\mathrm{h}0''}) \geq 0 \qquad \forall_{\mathrm{h}}.$$

An example of this test is illustrated for two consumers in Figure 1.10 where the initial allocation at $0'$ is moved along UPF^0 by a redistribution of income. It passes when UPF^0 lies below the new equilibrium allocation at $1'$.

Both illustrations of the Kaldor and Hicks tests in Figs 1.9 and 1.10, respectively, were carefully chosen to avoid contradictions identified by Scitovsky (1941) when utility possibility frontiers cross. There are circumstances where one test passes and the other fails, and they are illustrated in Figure 1.11. A Kaldor contradiction is illustrated in Figure 1.11(a), where the new equilibrium allocation $1'$ lies inside UPF^0. Income redistribution after the policy change makes both consumers better off relative to $0'$ so that the Kaldor test passes. However, the Hicks test fails here because income redistribution prior to the policy change would make them both better off relative to $1'$ (see Figure 1.11(b)). Thus, the winner can compensate the loser after the change but the loser can pay the winner to block it.

A Hicks contradiction is illustrated in Figure 1.11(b) where the initial equilibrium allocation at $0'$ lies outside UPF^1. Income redistribution prior to the policy change cannot make both consumers better off relative to $1'$ so the Hicks' test passes, but the Kaldor test fails because income redistribution after the policy change cannot convert $1'$ into a Pareto improvement relative $0'$. Thus, the loser cannot block the change, but the winner cannot compensate the loser after it takes place. The next compensation test provides a way of avoiding these contradictions for a single policy change.

(c) *The Scitovsky (1941) Criterion.* This requires the Kaldor and Hicks tests to both pass for a socially preferred policy change. If one passes and the other fails

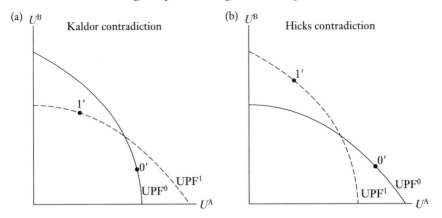

Figure 1.11 *Contradictions using Kaldor–Hicks tests*

the change cannot be evaluated by the compensation principle. Formally, policy 1 is socially preferred by the Scitovsky criterion, with $_1\mathrm{SP}_0^{SC}$, if $_1\mathrm{SP}_0^{K}$ and $_1\mathrm{SP}_0^{H}$. However, this test cannot rule out contradictions when more than one policy change is being evaluated. An example is provided in Figure 1.12 where $_1\mathrm{SP}_0^{SC}$, and $_2\mathrm{SP}_1^{SC}$, but $_0\mathrm{SP}_2^{SC}$.

(d) *The Samuelson (1962) Criterion.* This criterion overcomes these contradictions, but it is a much stronger test. It requires the UPF after the policy change to lie wholly outside the initial UPF, which is the case when first and second best policies are being compared. Samuelson proves international free trade is socially preferred to no trade using this test. It will be demonstrated here in an economy with a large number of price-taking consumers and firms.

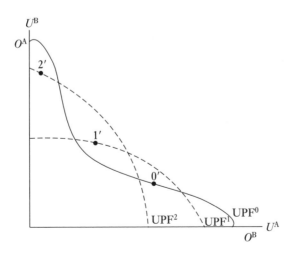

Figure 1.12 *A Scitovsky test contradiction*

Let consumers choose a vector of goods x to maximize utility when aggregate expenditure (E) is constrained by:

$$E \equiv qx = q\bar{x} + py + L \equiv I,$$

where I is the aggregate income; q the vector of consumer prices; p the vector of producer prices; y the vector of private net-outputs with $y_i > 0$ for outputs and $y_i < 0$ for inputs; py the profit from private production that consumers receive as shareholders in firms; $\bar{x}$ the vector of primary factor endowments which are assumed to be non-traded internationally; and, L is the lump-sum transfers from the government.

In total there are $N + T$ goods, with N non-traded and T traded internationally under small country conditions. The elements of the consumption vector x are the summed demands for these goods over consumers, with $x = (\sum_h x_1^h, \sum_h x_2^h, \ldots, \sum_h x_{N+T}^h)$. The net demand for each traded good is defined as: $m_i = x_i - y_i$, with $m_i > 0$ for imports and $m_i < 0$ for exports. And they have world prices measured in units of domestic currency (p_i^w) which are foreign currency prices (p_i^{w*}) multiplied by the official exchange rate (e). To facilitate welfare comparisons in tax-distorted economies we include specific production taxes (and subsidies) that drive wedges between domestic consumer and producer prices, where:

$$q_i = p_i + t_i \qquad \forall i \in N, T,$$

where

$$t_i > 0 \begin{cases} \text{is a tax when } y_i > 0, \\ \text{a subsidy when } y_i < 0, \end{cases}$$

$$t_i < 0 \begin{cases} \text{is a subsidy when } y_i > 0, \\ \text{a tax when } y_i < 0. \end{cases}$$

Clearly, production taxes are equivalent to consumption taxes in the non-traded goods markets, but this is not the case for traded goods in small countries when they take world prices as given. In these circumstances an additional tax instrument will be needed to accommodate separate taxes on domestic consumers and producers in these markets. To this end the net demands for internationally traded goods can be subject to specific taxes that make their domestic producer prices:

$$p_i = p_i^w + \tau_i - t_i \qquad \forall i \in T,$$

where

$$\tau_i > 0 \begin{cases} \text{is a tax when } m_i > 0, \\ \text{a susbidy when } m_i < 0, \end{cases}$$

$$\tau_i < 0 \begin{cases} \text{is a subsidy when } m_i > 0, \\ \text{a tax when } m_i < 0. \end{cases}$$

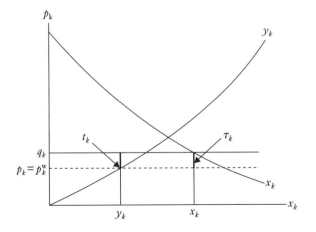

Figure 1.13 *An importable good k*

This set of taxes will generate government revenue of $T = ty + \tau m$ which is returned to the private sector of the economy as lump-sum transfers. As a way to illustrate the tax structure employed consider the importable good k in Figure 1.13 which is subject to a consumption tax. It is achieved by combining a tariff τ_i and production tax t_k set at the same rate, where the production tax undoes the implicit subsidy in the tariff, with: $p_k = p_k^w$.

Now consider the non-traded good labour (n). It is a net input with x_n being leisure consumed, $-y_n$ labour employed by firms, and $\bar{x}_n$ the endowment of time. A competitive equilibrium outcome is illustrated in Figure 1.14 with a tax on employment.

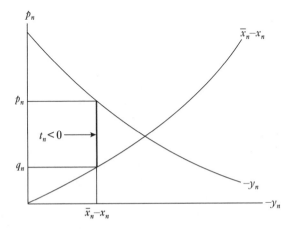

Figure 1.14 *A non-traded input—labour (n)*

Finally, in a competitive equilibrium non-traded goods prices change endogenously to satisfy the market clearing conditions $x_i = y_i + \bar{x}_i \; \forall_{i \in N}$, while the exchange rate adjusts to maintain balance of payments equilibrium, with $\sum_i p_i^w m_i = 0$.

In this setting, international free trade (1) is preferred to autarky (0) by the Samuelson criterion (with $_1 SP_0^{SAM}$) when $q^1(x^1 - x^0) \geq 0$ for all possible equilibrium allocations of x^1 and x^0. They are allocations along the utility possibility frontier for each policy change and are realized through lump-sum redistributions of income between consumers. By using the market clearing conditions the test requires:

$$q^1(x^1 - x^0) = \underset{(T)}{q^1(m^1 - m^0} + y^1 - y^0) + \underset{(N)}{q^1(y^1 - y^0 + \bar{x}^1 - \bar{x}^0)} \geq 0.$$

It can be decomposed using the price–tax relationships (and the balance of payments condition, with $p^{W1} m^1 = 0$) as:

$$q^1(x^1 - x^0) = \underset{(T)}{-p^{W1} m^0} + \underset{(T)}{\tau^1(m^1 - m^0)} + \underset{(T+N)}{p^1(y^1 - y^0)} + \underset{(T+N)}{t^1(y^1 - y^0)}$$

$$+ \underset{(N)}{q^1(\bar{x}^1 - \bar{x}^0)} \geq 0.^{13}$$

In autarky (0) no goods are traded internationally ($m^0 = 0$), while in free trade (1) there are no taxes ($t^i = \tau^i = 0 \; \forall_i$). Thus, in the absence of growth, the Samuelson criterion requires:

$$q^1(x^1 - x^0) = p^1(y^1 - y^0) \geq 0.$$

This test passes because $p^1 y^1 - p^1 y^0 \geq 0$ by profit maximization for all possible (lump–sum) redistributions of income under each of the policies 1 and 0. Clearly, it is much stronger than the other compensation tests as there are relatively few policy comparisons where the utility possibility frontiers do not cross each other, particularly for comparisons between second-best policies. Once they do cross the Samuelson test fails. Like the other compensation tests, it relies on lump-sum transfers to move the equilibrium outcomes along the utility possibility frontiers. But most governments use distorting taxes to make revenue transfers, which rules out first-best policies. In Chapter 3 the compensation principle will be used to isolate Pareto improvements for marginal policy changes. They are welfare gains that cannot be overturned by assigning different distributional weights to consumers. When all consumers benefit from a policy change the distributional weights can affect the size of the aggregate welfare gain but not its sign. This test is extended in Chapter 7 by allowing revenue transfers with distorting taxes.

Before proceeding it seems appropriate at this point to summarize the main properties of welfare measures obtained using price–quantity data. First, they cannot isolate every welfare improvement since they are based on Slutsky compensation which is not exact. They are also subject to contradictions when the utility possibility frontiers cross, which is much more likely in practice when income is redistributed using distorting taxes. In the next section the welfare measures are refined using demand schedules.

1.2 MEASURING WELFARE CHANGES USING DEMAND SCHEDULES

Demand schedules provide us with more refined welfare measures than price quantity data because they are mappings from consumer marginal valuations for goods. When consumers maximize utility they purchase commodities until their marginal valuation for each good is equal to its market price. That makes areas underneath demand schedules dollar measures of the benefits consumers derive from the goods they purchase. However, before changes in these dollar benefits can be aggregated over consumers, some decision must be made about the distributional weights to place on them. In this section we will examine the properties of welfare measures obtained from demand schedules. This will be done for individual consumers before looking at ways to aggregate them over consumers to account for any distributional effects.

1.2.1 Welfare Changes for Single Consumers

There are two ways of measuring consumption benefits, and they are:

(1) dollar measures underneath ordinary (Marshallian) demand schedules; or,
(2) willingness-to-pay measures under compensated demand schedules.

They each provide different but related information.

Marshallian consumer surplus is the area underneath the ordinary (or more generally, uncompensated) demand schedule, and it is unreliable whenever the marginal utility of income changes with relative prices and money income. This makes them path dependent, where reordering a set of price changes yields different dollar measures of the final change in utility. Their main advantage, however, is that they can be estimated empirically using observed price–quantity data.

Consider the representative consumer (h) who chooses a vector of consumption goods (x) to maximize utility:

$$u(x),^{14} \tag{1.1}$$

subject to the budget constraint:

$$I = qx, \tag{1.2}$$

where I is money income and q the vector of consumer prices. At an interior solution the marginal utility for each good i is equated to its marginal cost, with $\partial u/\partial x_i = \lambda q_i$, where λ is the Lagrange multiplier on the budget constraint. By totally differentiating the utility function in (1.1), and using the first-order conditions for optimally chosen consumption, we have:

$$\frac{du}{\lambda} = \sum_i q_i \, dx_i = q \, dx. \tag{1.3}$$

Since λ is the *marginal utility of income*, du/λ is a dollar measure of the change in utility. It is the sum of the value of the changes in consumption demand as areas underneath ordinary demand schedules. This welfare change can also be solved using the budget constraint in (1.2) as changes in consumer surplus (S), which are areas to the left of ordinary demand schedules, where:

$$dS = \frac{du}{\lambda} = dI - x\,dq. \tag{1.4}$$

With constant money income (with $dI = 0$) this simplifies to $dS = -x\,dq$. Unfortunately, however, dollar changes in utility are unreliable when the marginal utility of income changes with relative prices, which is in general the case as it is a function of consumer prices and money income, with $\lambda = \lambda(q, I)$. When it does change, the welfare measures in (1.3) and (1.4) are path dependent for discrete price changes. This can be demonstrated by raising the prices of two goods, x_1 and x_2, holding all other prices and money income constant, where the change in consumer surplus is:

$$\Delta S_g = -\int_g \sum_i x_i(q, I)\,dq_i, \tag{1.5}$$

with g being a specified path for the price changes.[15] There are two potential price paths here:

(a) g_{12}—where q_1 rises before q_2:

$$\Delta S_{12} = -\int_{q_1^0}^{q_1^1} x_1(q_1, q_2^0, \ldots, I)\,dq_1 - \int_{q_2^0}^{q_2^1} x_2(q_1^1, q_2, \ldots, I)\,dq_2,$$

(b) g_{21}—where q_2 rises before q_1:

$$\Delta S_{21} = -\int_{q_2^0}^{q_2^1} x_2(q_1^0, q_2, \ldots, I)\,dq_2 - \int_{q_1^0}^{q_1^1} x_1(q_1, q_2^1, \ldots, I)\,dq_1.$$

The difference between them is:

$$\Delta S_{12} - \Delta S_{21} = \int_{q_1^0}^{q_1^1} \{x_1(q_1, q_2^1) - x_1(q_1, q_2^0)\}\,dq_1$$

$$- \int_{q_2^0}^{q_2^1} \{x_2(q_1^1, q_2) - x_2(q_1^0, q_2)\}\,dq_2.$$

For path independence it must be zero, and since it must also be zero over every sub-interval between q^0 and q^1, it is possible to consider small price changes (with $q_1^1 = q_1^0 + dq_1$ and $q_2^1 = q_2^0 + dq_2$), where:

$$\Delta S_{12} - \Delta S_{21} = \frac{\partial x_1(q_1^0, q_2^0)}{\partial q_2}\,dq_1\,dq_2 - \frac{\partial x_2(q_1^0, q_2^0)}{\partial q_1}\,dq_2\,dq_1. \tag{1.6}$$

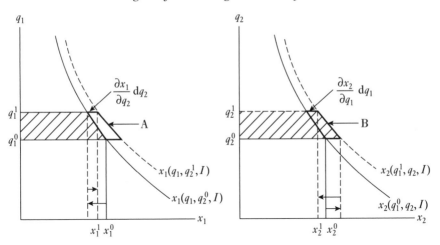

Figure 1.15 *Changes in ordinary consumer surplus for multiple price changes*

Thus, there is path independence when the cross-price changes in demand are equal, with: $\partial x_1(q_1^0, q_2^0)/\partial q_2 = \partial x_2(q_1^0, q_2^0)/\partial q_1$. This is illustrated in Figure 1.15 for price path g_{12} when the two goods are gross substitutes.

When q_1 rises the demand schedule for good 2 shifts to the right thereby increasing the loss in consumer surplus by the heavily lined area B after q_2 rises. If q_2 rises first, however, the loss in consumer surplus on good 2 is smaller by area B, but the loss in consumer surplus on good 1 is larger by the heavily lined area A. Clearly, there is path independence when areas A and B are equal, which is not in general the case. To see this we use the Slutsky decomposition to write the changes in demand in (1.6), as:

$$\frac{\partial \hat{x}_i(q)}{\partial q_j} = \frac{\partial x_i(q, I)}{\partial q_j} + x_j \frac{\partial x_i(q, I)}{\partial I}. \quad ^{16}$$

From Young's Theorem cross-price substitution effects in demand are equal, with:

$$\frac{\partial^2 E}{\partial q_1 \partial q_2} = \frac{\partial \hat{x}_1(q)}{\partial q_2} = \frac{\partial \hat{x}_2(q)}{\partial q_1} = \frac{\partial^2 E}{\partial q_2 \partial q_1},$$

where the difference in the changes in surplus in (1.6) becomes:

$$\Delta S_{12} - \Delta S_{21} = \left\{ x_1 \frac{\partial x_2(q, I)}{\partial I} - x_2 \frac{\partial x_1(q, I)}{\partial I} \right\} dq_1 \, dq_2. \quad (1.7)$$

Clearly, there is path independence when the income effects for the two goods are identical, which is the case for homothetic and quasi-linear preferences. Before examining these preferences it should be noted that the welfare change in (1.7) is path independent for infinitesimally small price changes, with $dq_1 dq_2 = 0$. This will make dollar changes in utility for the marginal policy changes examined in later chapters path independent.[17]

Homothetic Preferences

When $x_i(\partial x_j/\partial I) = x_j(\partial x_i/\partial I) \ \forall_{i,j}$, consumer demands have the same income elasticities, with: $\eta_{iI} = \eta_{jI} = \eta_I$, where $\eta_{iI} = (I/x_i)(\partial x_i/\partial I)$. From the budget constraint,
we have $\sum_i k_i\eta_{iI} = \eta_I \sum_i k_i = \eta_I = 1 \ \forall_i$, with $k_i = p_ix_i/I$ being the budget share for
each good i, and: $\sum_i k_i = 1$. It is the constancy of the marginal utility of income along
the linear income expansion paths that makes the welfare measures for homothetic
preferences path independent. Thus, each dollar change in ordinary surplus converts
into the same utility. This is confirmed as:

Proposition 1. *If the marginal utility of income is independent of the relative prices, with*
$\lambda = \lambda(I)$, *then preferences must be homothetic.*

Proof. From the first-order conditions to the consumer problem in (1.1) and (1.2),
we have:

$$\lambda = \frac{\partial u/\partial x_i}{q_i} = \frac{\sum_i(\partial u/\partial x_i)x_i}{\sum_i q_ix_i} = \frac{\sum_i(\partial u/\partial x_i)x_i}{I}. \tag{1.8}$$

All homothetic functions are monotonic transformations of a homogeneous function
of degree 1.[18] Thus, when u is linearly homogenous, by Euler's Theorem:

$$\sum_i \frac{\partial u}{\partial x_i}x_i = u,$$

so that $\lambda = u/I$ is independent of the relative prices and depends solely on income.
This is confirmed by using Roy's Identity to obtain the demand for each good i, as:

$$x_i = -\frac{\partial V}{\partial q_i}\frac{1}{\lambda},^{[19]} \tag{1.9}$$

with $V = V(q, I)$ being the indirect utility function. After differentiating (1.9) with
respect to income, we have:

$$\frac{\partial x_i}{\partial I} = -\frac{1}{\lambda}\left\{\frac{\partial\lambda}{\partial q_i} + x_i\frac{\partial\lambda}{\partial I}\right\} \qquad \forall_i.^{[20]} \tag{1.10}$$

With λ being independent of the relative prices by assumption, we have: $\partial\lambda/\partial q_i = 0 \ \forall_i$,
and since it is homogenous of degree -1, Euler's Theorem can be used to write (1.10)
as: $\partial x_i/\partial I = x_i/I$, which implies homothetic preferences, with:[21]

$$\frac{\partial x_i}{\partial I}\frac{I}{x_i} = 1 \qquad \forall_i. \qquad \square$$

Corollary. *Income (I) should be chosen as numeraire when preferences are homothetic to
make the welfare measures under ordinary demand schedules path independent.*[22]

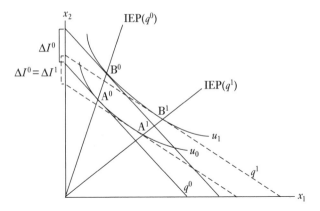

Figure 1.16 *Homothetic preferences and constant λ*

The constancy of λ for homothetic preferences is illustrated in Figure 1.16 where the change in utility is the same when income is raised by a dollar at the relative price q^0, as it is when income is raised by a dollar at the relative price q^1. With linear income expansion paths, the indifference curves are radial expansions from the origin that cut every income expansion path the same distance from the origin. Furthermore, if the utility function is homogeneous of degree 1, then the marginal utility of income will be constant along the income expansion paths, that is, it will be independent of money income as well as the relative prices.

Quasi-linear Preferences
This provides path independent welfare measures by excluding goods from income effects. They are frequently adopted in public economics applications to make the ordinary and compensated demand schedules for goods coincide with each other. If goods 1 and 2 are free of income effects, with $\partial x_1/\partial I = \partial x_2/\partial I = 0$, there is no difference in the changes in surplus for the two price paths in (1.7). But income effects must affect at least one good in the consumption bundle, and it will be good n in the following analysis. Once again, path independence results from the constancy of the marginal utility of income, which is confirmed by:

Proposition 2. *If the marginal utility of income depends only on the relative price q_n, with $\lambda = \lambda(q_n)$, then preferences must be quasi linear for all goods $i \neq n$.*

Proof. By Euler's Theorem, $(\partial\lambda/\partial q_n)q_n = -\lambda$, and with $\partial\lambda/\partial q_i = 0 \ \forall_{i\neq n}$ and $\partial\lambda/\partial I = 0$ by assumption, the change in demand in (1.10) becomes:

$$\frac{\partial x_i}{\partial I} = -\frac{1}{\lambda}\left\{\frac{\partial\lambda}{\partial q_i} + x_i\frac{\partial\lambda}{\partial I}\right\} = 0 \qquad \forall i \neq n. \qquad \square$$

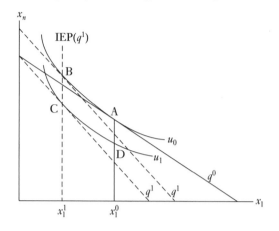

Figure 1.17 *Quasi-linear preferences and constant* λ

Corollary. *The price of good n should be chosen as numeraire when preferences are quasi-linear to make the welfare measures under ordinary demand schedules path independent.*

The intuition is illustrated in Figure 1.17 where the price of good 1 rises. Since the income effect falls on good n in the move from B to C, the change in demand for good 1 is due solely to the substitution effect from A to B. By making the indifference curves vertically parallel over good 1, the marginal utility of income is the same at each relative price, that is, distance BC is the same as distance AD. (Point D is the tangency point on the new indifference curve u_1 for the initial relative price q^0.)

In summary, changes in consumer surplus under ordinary demand schedules are unreliable when the marginal utility of income changes with real income, and the problem arises because ordinary surplus is not derived directly from preferences. The next section does this by measuring surplus underneath compensated demand schedules.

Willingness-to-Pay Measures of Consumer Surplus are based solely on substitution effects, where the benefits a consumer derives from a good is the bundle of other goods that will just replace it. The substitution effects are isolated by compensating transfers from the government budget, where a potential gain is the surplus revenue a policy change will generate after funding the transfers to hold utility constant; it is revenue the government could pay as foreign aid at no cost to private utility by undertaking the policy change. Conversely, a potential loss is the amount the policy change drives the government budget into deficit after consumers have been compensated for its effects; it is foreign aid the government would need to balance its budget without reducing the consumer's utility. These welfare changes are path independent because compensated demands have identical cross-price effects.

Governments rarely make compensating transfers to offset the effects of their policy changes on consumers, so analysts respond to this by using hypothetical transfers to isolate potential welfare changes. These are welfare changes that could be realized as actual outcomes by making the compensating transfers. However, it creates a dilemma for analysts wanting to report actual welfare changes based on observable equilibrium outcomes. If potential welfare changes are not going to be realized as actual outcomes then it is difficult to explain their meaning to non-economists. One response is to separate the efficiency and equity effects for actual dollar changes in utility so that people can make their own assessments about the final welfare changes. Potential welfare changes are frequently referred to as efficiency effects because they isolate changes in real income from using resources more efficiently, while equity effects identify how these potential welfare effects are distributed across consumers.

Hatta (1977) proves an important relationship between the efficiency and equity effects for marginal policy changes, and does so in a single (aggregated) consumer economy with constant producer prices. It finds dollar changes in utility are compensated welfare effects scaled by a coefficient for the income effects. Since this coefficient is independent of the policy changes, income effects will play no role in finding optimal outcomes. In later chapters this decomposition is generalized to economies with variable producer prices and heterogeneous consumers, and is used to establish welfare tests for Pareto improvements. At this point the intuition for the Hatta decomposition is demonstrated using a very simple example.

Consider a single price-taking consumer who purchases two goods, x_1 and x_2, to maximize utility, $u = u(x_1, x_2)$, when good 1 is subject to a specific dollar tax t per unit purchased.[23] The dollar change in utility from marginally raising this tax is computed using (1.3), as:

$$\frac{du}{dt}\frac{1}{\lambda} = (p_1 + t)\frac{\partial x_1}{\partial t} + q_2\frac{\partial x_2}{\partial t}, \qquad (1.11)$$

where p_1 is the producer price of good 1, and $q_1 = p_1 + t$ its consumer price. When expenditure is constrained by fixed money income (M), with:

$$M = (p_1 + t)x_1 + q_2 x_2, \qquad (1.12)$$

the change in welfare in (1.10) can be solved, as:

$$\frac{du}{dt}\frac{1}{\lambda} = -x_1. \qquad (1.13)$$

This is the dollar change in ordinary consumer surplus to the left of the Marshallian demand curve, but it does not account for the consumer surplus collected as tax revenue (with $R = tx_1$). In a cost–benefit analysis transfers of surplus are included in the welfare measures, and a conventional Harberger analysis does this by returning tax revenue to the consumer as a lump-sum transfer ($L = R$), where income (I) becomes:

$$I = M + L = (p_1 + t)x_1 + q_2 x_2. \qquad (1.14)$$

The standard Harberger measure of the welfare loss is obtained by using this constraint to write (1.11) as:

$$\frac{du}{dt}\frac{1}{\lambda} = \frac{\partial R}{\partial t} - x_1 = t\frac{\partial x_1}{\partial t}. \qquad (1.15)$$

Since demand for good 1 is a function of prices and money income, this loss can be decomposed as:

$$t\frac{\partial x_1}{\partial t} = t\frac{\partial x_1(q, I)}{\partial q_1}\frac{\partial q_1}{\partial t} + t\frac{\partial x_1(q, I)}{\partial I}\frac{\partial I}{\partial t} \cdot{}^{24} \tag{1.16}$$

With constant producer prices we have $\partial q_1/\partial t = 1$, while the change in income is solved using (1.14), as $\partial I/\partial t = \partial R/\partial t = t(\partial x_1/\partial t) + x_1$. After substituting these changes into (1.16), and using the Slutsky decomposition, the welfare loss in (1.15) is decomposed as:

$$\frac{du}{dt}\frac{1}{\lambda} = \frac{t(\partial\hat{x}_1(q)/\partial q_1)}{1-\theta},{}^{25} \tag{1.17}$$

with: $\theta = t(\partial x_1(q, I)/\partial I)$. Hatta isolates the income effect in the coefficient AIM $= (1-\theta)$, and writes the marginal excess burden for the tax, as:

$$\frac{du}{dt}\frac{1}{\lambda} = \frac{t(\partial\hat{x}_1(q)/\partial t)}{\text{AIM}}.{}^{26}$$

There is good economic intuition for this decomposition. The compensated welfare loss from increasing the tax $(t\partial\hat{x}_1(q)/\partial t)$ is the amount it raises the government budget deficit at constant utility. It is the outside compensation the government would need to balance its budget after compensating the consumer for the loss in utility. When this deficit is financed by a lump-sum transfer from the consumer, each dollar will reduce utility by one over the Hatta coefficient AIM. This means the dollar loss in utility originates from the substitution effect, and the smaller the substitution effect, the smaller the loss in utility. To see why, consider the tax change illustrated in Figure 1.18 where the two goods are perfect complements.

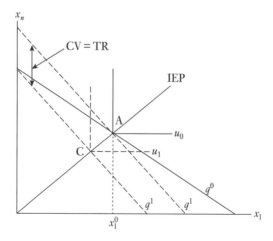

Figure 1.18 *Tax inefficiency with perfect complements*

After the tax rises, and before the revenue is returned to the consumer, demand moves from A to C. When the revenue is returned as a lump-sum transfer, demand moves back along the income expansion path (IEP) to A due to the absence of any substitution effect. Thus, once the revenue is returned there is no welfare change. If the consumer was willing to substitute between the two goods the new consumption bundle after returning the tax revenue would lie to the left of bundle A along the old budget line on an indifference curve below u_0. Then there would be a welfare loss due to the substitution effect.

In later chapters the Hatta decomposition arises naturally in a general equilibrium setting where surplus transfers are included through the private and public sector budget constraints. If the Hatta coefficient is positive, then there must be efficiency gains for policy changes to generate dollar gains in utility. Before demonstrating this proposition the familiar partial equilibrium measures of compensated changes in consumer surplus will be summarized.

The Compensating Variation (CV). It is the lump-sum compensation that will offset the effects of a policy change on the consumer by holding utility constant at the initial level (u_0). By totally differentiating the minimum expenditure function $E(q, u_0)$, we have:

$$dE = \sum_i \frac{\partial E(q, u_0)}{\partial q_i} dq_i + \frac{\partial E(q, u_0)}{\partial u} du,$$

where the CV solves $(du/\lambda) = dE - \sum_i \hat{x}_i(q, u_0)\, dq_i - \text{CV} = 0$.[27] For small changes in prices and income, we have:

$$\text{CV} = dE - \sum_i \hat{x}_i(q, u_0)\, dq_i, \qquad (1.18)$$

and for discrete changes:

$$\text{CV} = E^1 - E^0 - \int_g \sum_i \left(\frac{\partial E(q, u_0)}{\partial q_i} \right) dq_i,$$

with

$$\text{CV} = E^1 - E(q^1, u_0). \qquad (1.19)$$

It is illustrated in Figure 1.19 for a combined increase in the price of good 1 and decrease in money income.

The Equivalent Variation (EV). It is the lump-sum compensation made before the policy change takes place to replicate the change in utility. It is the lump-sum transfer that holds utility constant at its new level (u_1). By totally differentiating the minimum expenditure function $E(q, u_1)$, we have:

$$dE = \sum_i \frac{\partial E(q, u_1)}{\partial q_i} dq_i + \frac{\partial E(q, u_1)}{\partial u} du,$$

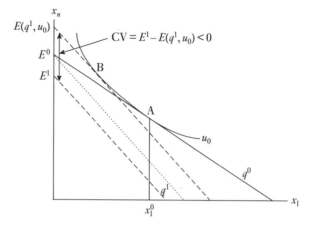

Figure 1.19 *The compensating variation*

where the EV solves $du/\lambda = dE - \sum_i \hat{x}_i(q, u_1)\, dq_i - EV = 0$. For small changes in prices and money income, it is:

$$EV = dE - \sum_i \hat{x}_i(q, u_1)\, dq_i, \tag{1.20}$$

and for discrete changes:

$$EV = E(q^0, u_1) - E^0. \tag{1.21}$$

The EV for a simultaneous rise in the price of good 1 and fall in money income is illustrated in Figure 1.20. The derivation follows the convention adopted above for the CV, so it too will be negative when prices rise and money income falls.

1.2.2 Welfare Changes for Many Consumers

For most policy changes there are winners and losers, but the gains and losses cannot be aggregated in any meaningful way when consumers have ordinal non-comparable utility functions. Indeed, the well known Arrow (1950, 1951) impossibility theorem proves a social welfare function (SWF), that measures aggregate welfare from individual preferences, cannot exist for ordinal non-comparable utility functions when it has unrestricted domain (to rank all the possible states that determine consumer utilities), is Paretian and non-dictatorial, and makes choices independently of irrelevant alternatives.[28]

Since most people regard these restrictions as being reasonable, subsequent work has looked at proving the existence of an SWF by abandoning ordinal noncomparability. In the non-existence proof the SWF must be unaffected by monotone transformations

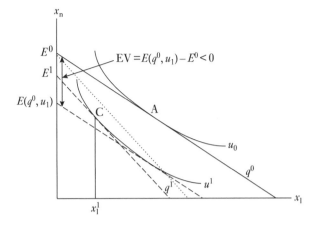

Figure 1.20 *The equivalent variation*

of the consumer utility functions. Unfortunately this rules out most of the potentially useful information about individual preferences that could be used to make social welfare rankings. The social choice literature considers differing degrees of comparability. Sen (1977), for example, examines *cardinal unit comparability* to allow comparisons of welfare changes across consumers, but not comparisons of their utility levels, while others allow full comparability of both levels and changes in welfare. The SWF of Bergson (1938) and Samuelson (1954), which is widely used in applied welfare applications, is a function of the individual consumer utility functions, with:

$$W(u(x)),^{29} \qquad (1.22)$$

where $u(x)$ is now defined as the vector of consumer utilities $u(x) = [u^1(x^1), \ldots, u^H(x^H)]$. Since the utility function for each consumer is defined solely over their consumption vector it rules out the possibility of them being affected by comparing consumption levels with other consumers. For this reason (1.22) is referred to as an *individualistic* SWF, and with social welfare mapping from individual utility levels it assumes full comparability. Thus, utility is measured in units that can be meaningfully compared across consumers. The individualistic SWF can take different functional forms to reflect variations in social attitudes to inequality, and this is demonstrated by Atkinson (1973) and Feldstein (1973) who define it as:

$$W(u(x)) = \left(\sum_{h=1}^{H} (u^h)^\gamma \right)^{1/\gamma} \qquad \gamma \leq 1,$$

where γ is a constant reflecting society's aversion to inequality. If $\gamma = 1$ it is utilitarian and society is completely indifferent to inequality. At the other extreme as γ approaches $-\infty$ it is Rawlsian where society maximizes utility for the individual who is worst off.[30]

Even when no specific functional form is chosen for the Bergson–Samuelson function in (1.22) it is normally assumed that social welfare rises with Pareto improvements. This assumption is made in following chapters where interpersonal utility comparisons are obtained for marginal policy changes by totally differentiating (1.22), as:

$$dW = \sum_h \frac{\partial W}{\partial u^h} \sum_i \frac{\partial u^h}{\partial x_i^h} \, dx_i^h.$$

At an interior solution, price-taking consumers have $(\partial u^h / \partial x_i^h) = \lambda^h q_i \; \forall_i$, with λ^h being the marginal utility of income for individual h and q_i the consumer price of good i, where the change in social welfare becomes:[31]

$$dW = \sum_h \beta^h \sum_i q_i \, dx_i^h, \tag{1.23}$$

with $\beta^h = (\partial W / \partial u^h) \lambda^h$ being the marginal social utility of a dollar of income for consumer h, which is commonly referred to as the *distributional weight*. Clearly, income redistribution matters if consumers have different weights, and whenever analysts assign values to them they are making interpersonal utility comparisons. But there is no universal agreement about the weights to use so that distributional effects must involve subjective assessments that can impact on the evaluation process.

There are range of different views about the way to deal with distributional effects, and they include:

(1) Dréze and Stern (1990) and Dréze (1998) argue policy analysts should accept responsibility for making subjective judgements about the welfare weights and report final welfare changes based on them;

(2) Boadway (1976) proposes the widely accepted practice of reporting efficiency and distributional effects separately to let policy-makers see what role the distributional weights play in the evaluation process. This also allows them to determine the efficiency costs of income redistribution policies;

(3) Bruce and Harris (1982) and Diewert (1983) identify Pareto improvements by combining transfer and other policy changes. They use transfer policies to convert potential welfare gains into higher utility for every consumer; and,

(4) Harberger (1971) and Parish (1976) assign the same weight of unity to every consumer and then sum their dollar changes in utility. Thus, they assume *a dollar is a dollar* for consumers where aggregate dollar gains can be converted into Pareto improvements by lump-sum redistributions of income.

The formal analysis begins by using the Harberger approach in Chapter 2, and distributional effects are isolated using the other approaches in Chapter 3. When consumers have the same distributional weights in a conventional Harberger analysis the welfare change in (1.23), becomes:

$$\frac{dW}{\beta} = q \, dx.[32] \tag{1.24}$$

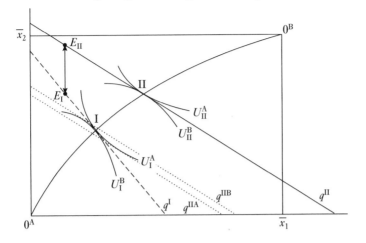

Figure 1.21 *The Boadway paradox*

It is a dollar measure of the change in social welfare, which is solved in following chapters by using the economy's private and public budget constraints.

Summing Compensated Welfare Changes over Consumers. This is less complicated due to the absence of distributional effects. When measuring CVs and EVs, most textbooks adopt a partial equilibrium analysis by holding commodity prices fixed. However, in a general equilibrium setting relative commodity prices can change endogenously with compensating transfers. When they do, Boadway (1974) demonstrates a paradox that can undermine the ability of CVs to isolate potential welfare gains. In a 2 good-2 person endowment economy Boadway finds the sum of the CVs for a lump-sum redistribution of income is not zero along a non-linear contract curve.

The paradox is illustrated in Figure 1.21 where the initial competitive equilibrium outcome at I is supported by endowment E_I. Consider a redistribution of income (measured in units of good 2) from consumer B to consumer A which moves the endowment point vertically to E_{II} on price line q^{II}. This endowment will support the new competitive equilibrium at point II on the contract curve. In fact, any reallocation that moves the new endowment point onto price line q^{II} will achieve this outcome; it is therefore independent of the choice of numeraire.[33] The paradox is isolated by computing the CVs that move each consumer from point II back onto their initial indifference curve at the unchanged relative price q^{II}. Since there is an excess demand for good x_1 and an excess supply of good x_2, we must have $CV^A + CV^B > 0$ (with $CV^A > 0$ and $CV^B < 0$).

Now consider what happens when the relative price is allowed to change endogenously with the compensating transfers. As income is transferred from A to B the relative price rises to eliminate the excess demand for good 1 and the excess supply of good 2. The equilibrium moves from point II back along the contract curve to point I, where the market clearing price returns to q_I. Thus, in the compensated equilibrium

$d\hat{q} = 0$, and the CVs sum to zero, with:

$$CV^A = \int (\bar{x}^A - \hat{x}^A) \, d\hat{q} + \Delta\hat{L} = \Delta\hat{L},$$

and

$$CV^B = \int (\bar{x}^B - \hat{x}^B) \, d\hat{q} - \Delta\hat{L} = -\Delta\hat{L}.$$

The lump-sum transfer from A to B ($\Delta\hat{L}$) is the vertical distance between the two endowment points in Figure 1.21, which completely reverses the initial income redistribution. Alternatively, it is the horizontal distance between the price lines q^{I} and q^{II} from point II when x_1 is numeraire.

It may be argued that consumers, when asked to reveal their CVs, would do so at the new relative price q^{II}.[34] But since they observe the relative price change in the move to point II, they will anticipate an opposite price change when the CVs return them to point I. In general equilibrium agents anticipate market clearing prices, even if they are price takers themselves, because as traders they operate inside the institutions that set these prices. By this logic, they will compute their CVs for the redistribution of income using the initial relative price q^{I} that clears both markets. In any case, the CVs measured at the unchanged price q^{II} cannot support a competitive equilibrium because the goods markets do not clear at this price.[35] In following chapters the Boadway paradox is avoided by allowing prices to change endogenously with the compensating transfers.

Compensated Changes in Consumer Surplus with Multiple Price Changes. These are path independent, not because the marginal utility of income is constant, but because the cross-price compensated demand elasticities are equal.[36] This is confirmed by computing the CV for multiple price changes, as:

$$CV = -\int_g \sum_i x_i(q, u_0) \, dq_i,$$

where g is a specified path for the price changes. If the prices of goods 1 and 2 are raised, with all other prices held constant, then:

(a) path g_{12} : $CV_{12} = -\int_{q_1^0}^{q_1^1} x_1(q_1, q_2^0, \ldots, u_0) \, dq_1 - \int_{q_2^0}^{q_2^1} x_2(q_1^1, q_2, \ldots, u_0) \, dq_2,$

which solves to be:

$$CV_{12} = E(q_1^0, q_2^0, u_0) - E(q_1^1, q_2^1, u_0),^{37}$$

and

(b) path g_{21} : $CV_{21} = -\int_{q_2^0}^{q_2^1} x_1(q_1^0, q_2, \ldots, u_0) \, dq_2 - \int_{q_1^0}^{q_1^1} x_2(q_1, q_2^1, \ldots, u_0) \, dq_1,$

which solves to be: $CV_{21} = E(q_1^0, q_2^0, u_0) - E(q_1^1, q_2^1, u_0) = CV_{12}.$

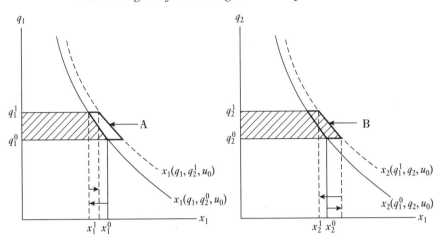

Figure 1.22 *CVs for multiple price changes*

Both these changes in surplus are illustrated in Figure 1.22 where the two goods are net substitutes. When q_1 rises first, the summed CVs are the shaded regions, but if the price changes are reversed, the CV is larger in the market for good 1 by area A and smaller in the market for good 2 by area B. These differences are determined by the cross-price changes in the compensated demands, where for small price changes, we have:

$$CV_{12} - CV_{21} = \frac{\partial x_1(q^0, u_0)}{\partial q_2} \, dq_1 \, dq_2 - \frac{\partial x_2(q^0, u_0)}{\partial q_1} \, dq_2 \, dq_1.$$

By Shephard's Lemma and Young's Theorem the CVs must be equal, with:

$$CV_{12} - CV_{21} = \frac{\partial^2 E(q^0, u_0)}{\partial q_1 \partial q_2} \, dq_1 \, dq_2 - \frac{\partial^2 E(q^0, u_0)}{\partial q_2 \partial q_1} \, dq_2 \, dq_1 = 0.$$

Thus, since areas A and B are equal by the symmetry of the cross-price changes in demand the compensated welfare changes are path independent.

1.3 APPLICATION: MEASURING THE SOCIAL DEADWEIGHT LOSSES FROM DISTORTING TAXATION

This section computes the excess burden for a single commodity tax on a consumer facing constant producer prices. It is an application that provides a number of very useful insights into welfare measures obtained in later chapters. The conventional measure of the social deadweight loss (DWL) for a commodity tax, with utility held

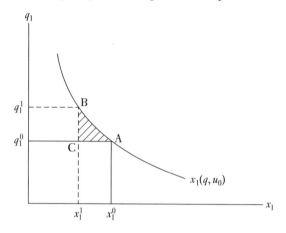

Figure 1.23 *The welfare cost of taxation*

constant at its initial level u_0, is:

$$\text{DWL} = -\text{CV} - T(q^1, u_0).^{38} \tag{1.25}$$

It is the net reduction in government revenue illustrated in Figure 1.23 for the consumption tax on good 1. To hold utility constant the government makes a lump-sum transfer to the consumer of $-\text{CV} = q_1^0 \text{AB} q_1^1$, which is partially funded from the tax revenue in $T = q_1^0 \text{CB} q_1^1$. The net fall in government revenue in ABC is a potential welfare loss; it is foreign aid the government would need to receive to balance its budget.

There are a number of different ways this excess burden is measured in the literature, but basically one of two welfare concepts can be used.[39] Uncompensated demand schedules provide dollar measures of the loss in utility, while compensated demand schedules isolate potential reductions in net government revenue. Four possible demand schedules are illustrated in Figure 1.24 for good 1 normal, where each differs by the size of the income effect. The ordinary demand curve $x_1(q, I)$ is derived for constant money income (i.e. the tax revenue is not returned to the consumer). When tax revenue is returned to the consumer money income rises, but not sufficiently to hold utility constant. This puts the consumer on the Bailey (1954) demand schedule $x_1(q, I + T)$, and since it allows income to change endogenously with the tax revenue it is steeper than the ordinary demand curve. There are two compensated demand schedules—$x_1(q, u_0)$ holds utility constant at the pre-tax level u_0, while $x_1(q, u_1)$ holds it constant at the post-tax level u_1.

This provides four different measures of the welfare cost, and they are summarized in Table 1.1. For good 1 normal, tax revenue increases with the size of the income transfer to the consumer. It is therefore smallest for the ordinary demand schedule where no revenue transfer is made, and largest for the compensated demand schedule with utility constant at u_0. If utility is held constant at its post-tax level (u_1) tax revenue is the same as it is along the ordinary demand schedule.[40]

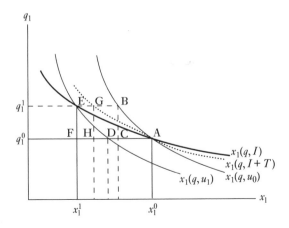

Figure 1.24 *The welfare cost of taxation*

The difference between actual tax revenue and compensated tax revenue creates a dilemma for policy analysts wanting to simultaneously report actual outcomes and measure the efficiency effects of taxes. Indeed, it is evident in measures of tax inefficiency that combine actual and compensated welfare changes. For example, Boadway and Bruce (1984) measure the DWL as ABGH—it is the CV less the actual tax revenue along the Bailey demand schedule.[41] Ballard (1988) use this to compute the marginal social cost of funds for taxes in the United States. The DWL is difficult to interpret when it is measured by combining actual and hypothetical welfare changes that cannot be realized as an actual equilibrium outcome. Even though the compensated welfare changes are often based on hypothetical compensation, they can at least be realized as actual equilibrium outcomes, which is why they are referred to as potential welfare changes.

Willig (1976) approximates changes in consumer surplus by noting the CV and the EV for a price change are upper and lower bounds on the change in consumer surplus under the ordinary demand schedule. However, Auerbach (1985) observes that this approximation does not apply to the welfare loss which is smaller for both the EV and the CV than it is using the DWL under the ordinary demand schedule.

Table 1.1 *Different measures of the welfare cost*

Demand	ΔCS	T	DWL
$x_1(q, I)$	$q_1^0 AEq_1^1$	$q_1^0 FEq_1^1$	AEF
$x_1(q, I + T)$	$q_1^0 AGq_1^1$	$q_1^0 HGq_1^1$	AGH
$x_1(q, u_0)$	$q_1^0 ABq_1^1$	$q_1^0 CBq_1^1$	ABC
$x_1(q, u_1)$	$q_1^0 DEq_1^1$	$q_1^0 FEq_1^1$	DEF

1.3.1 Measuring the Welfare Costs from Multiple Commodity Taxes

In a general equilibrium setting there are frequently resource reallocations across tax-distorted markets where the welfare effects are included as changes in tax revenue. This can be demonstrated by computing the excess burden from imposing a number of commodity taxes on a consumer facing constant producer prices. For $n - 1$ taxes and n consumption goods, the compensated welfare loss (with utility held constant at u_0), is:

$$\text{DWL} = -\Delta E + \int_g \sum_{i=1}^{n-1} x_i(q, u_0) \, dq_i - \sum_{i=1}^{n-1} t_i x_i(q^1, u_0). \tag{1.26}$$

Consider an example where taxes are introduced sequentially along path g starting with t_1 first, then $t_2 \ldots t_{n-1}$. With constant money income ($\Delta E = 0$), the excess burden becomes:

$$\text{DWL} = \int_{q_1^0}^{q_1^1} x_1(q_1, q_2^0, u_0) \, dq_1 + \int_{q_2^0}^{q_2^1} x_2(q_1^1, q_2, u_0) \, dq_2 + \cdots$$
$$- t_1 x_1(q^1, u_0) - t_2 x_2(q^1, u_0) + \cdots. \tag{1.27}$$

It is illustrated in Figure 1.25 for taxes on two goods 1 and 2, which are assumed to be net substitutes, with t_1 introduced first. The initial equilibrium is denoted by ● in each market, while the final equilibrium in the presence of the two taxes is denoted by ■. Tax revenue in the compensated equilibrium is the sum of the two heavily lined rectangles. A measure of the compensated DWL is obtained by deducting this

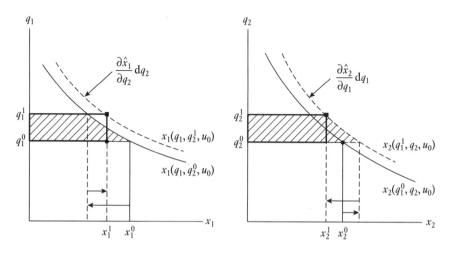

Figure 1.25 *Measuring the DWLs for multiple taxes*

tax revenue from the CVs in the cross-lined areas in each market. By path independence, this is the same measure of the deadweight loss when t_2 is introduced first.

Harberger (1964) computes this DWL by summing the marginal excess burden from incrementally increasing each tax sequentially along a defined path. For $n - 1$ taxes and n goods the aggregate welfare loss is:

$$\text{DWL} = E(q^1, u_0) - E^1 - \sum_{i=1}^{n-1} t_i x_i(q^1, u_0),$$

where the marginal deadweight loss for individual tax k, is:

$$\text{MDWL}_k = \frac{\partial \text{DWL}}{\partial t_k} = -\sum_{i=1}^{n-1} t_i \frac{\partial x_i(q^1, u_0)}{\partial t_k}. {}^{42}$$

It can be greater or less than zero in the presence of existing taxes on other goods. When they are net substitutes for good k the tax change generates extra revenue in these markets, and it is the welfare gain from partially undoing the marginal excess burden of their taxes. Conversely, if other taxed goods are net complements for good k the fall in tax revenue in these markets is the welfare loss from increasing the excess burden of their taxes. These welfare effects in related markets are measured as changes in tax revenue because the taxes are the difference between marginal benefits and costs in each market. As taxed activities expand the government collects the net consumption gain as tax revenue.

Harberger then computes the aggregate DWL by integrating the MDWLs over all the taxes, as:

$$\text{DWL} = -\int_g \sum_{k=1}^{n-1} \sum_{i=1}^{n-1} t_i \frac{\partial x_i(q, u_0)}{\partial q_k} \, dt_k, \tag{1.28}$$

where g is a path that determines the order in which the taxes are introduced. The welfare change from introducing the first tax (t_1) is illustrated in Figure 1.26.

Each shaded rectangle represents the marginal deadweight loss from small increases in the tax, and are equal to $t_1(\partial \hat{x}_1 / \partial q_1)$. Tax t_2 is then introduced in small increments in the presence of tax t_1. The additional welfare effects are illustrated in Figure 1.27 where the two goods are net complements. As t_2 rises the triangular deadweight loss in the market for good 2 grows larger, and it is supplemented by a rectangular deadweight loss in the market for good 1 as tax revenue falls with demand. Since tax t_1 is the amount marginal value exceeds marginal cost in this market the welfare loss is equal to the fall in tax revenue. Thus, the tax on good 2 exacerbates the welfare loss from the existing tax on good 1 by driving demand even lower.

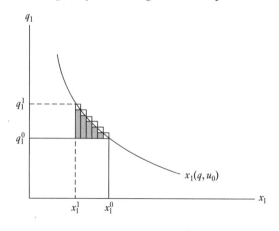

Figure 1.26 *Summing MDWLs*

The welfare cost from this sequence of incremental tax changes is:

$$\text{DWL} = -\int_{t_1^0}^{t_1^1} t_1 \frac{\partial x_1(q_1, q_2^0, u_0)}{\partial q_1} \, dt_1$$

$$-\int_{t_2^0}^{t_2^1} \left\{ t_2 \frac{\partial x_2(q_1^1, q_2, u_0)}{\partial q_2} + t_1 \frac{\partial x_1(q_1^1, q_2, u_0)}{\partial q_2} \right\} \, dt_2. \tag{1.29}$$

The first two terms are the respective triangular deadweight losses across the markets for good 1 and 2, while the third term is the rectangular deadweight loss in the market

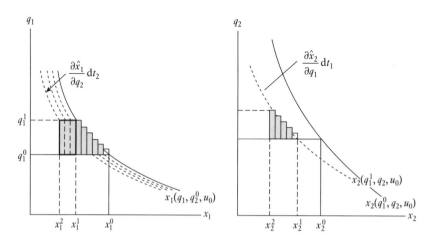

Figure 1.27 *Summing MDWLs in the presence of an existing tax*

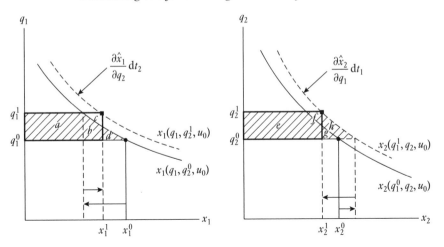

Figure 1.28 *Comparing the DWL measures*

for good 1. Both approaches will yield the same measure of the deadweight loss, as is confirmed in Figure 1.28 for the two taxes when goods 1 and 2 are net substitutes. When the DWL is computed using (1.27) by deducting the compensated tax revenue from the sum of the CVs, we have:

$$DWL = -\, CV - R = (a + b + d + e + f + g + h) - (a + b + c + e + f)$$
$$= d + g + h - c.$$

It is the same as the DWL obtained using the Harberger approach in (1.29) which integrates the marginal deadweight losses from introducing each tax sequentially, as:

$$DWL = (b + d + g + h) - (b + c) = d + g + h - c.$$

A number of approximations are used to measure the DWLs for multiple taxes. One is the *Hotelling formula* that assumes the own and cross-price changes in demand are constant, with:

$$DWL_{Hotelling} = -\frac{1}{2}\sum_{i=1}^{n-1}\sum_{k=1}^{n-1} t_i t_k \frac{\partial x_i(q, u_0)}{\partial q_k}.$$

Terms with $i = k$ are familiar triangular losses in surplus, while terms with $i \neq k$ are the rectangular changes in tax revenue. This is similar to the approximation used by Harberger who applies a Taylor series expansion to linearize the triangular DWL areas.

1.4 SUMMARY AND CONCLUSIONS

A number of important issues are raised by this overview. First, due to the absence of cardinal utility functions welfare changes for individual consumers are measured as dollar changes in utility. However, income (or the good chosen as numeraire) is unreliable as a proxy for utility whenever the marginal utility of income changes with real income because it makes dollar changes in utility path dependent. But, as the Hatta decomposition demonstrates, this problem does not arise for marginal policy changes. For marginal policy changes income effects are an independent scaling coefficient on the efficiency effects, so that they play no role in the welfare analysis in single (aggregated) consumer economies.[43] This result is important for the conventional Harberger analysis used in following chapters to derive shadow prices of goods. Since they are path independent, the welfare effects of projects with multiple inputs and outputs are not affected by the order in which the shadow prices are computed. Clearly, not all policy changes are marginal, but governments will often make large changes in a sequence of incrementally small steps. For example, taxes are adjusted gradually, and spending on roads, health, and defence is allocated to individually small projects. Indeed, this practice is much more likely if there is uncertainty about the political and budgetary implications of large policy changes. Also, most of the major international aid agencies lack the information needed to properly measure the welfare effects of large scale policy reforms in developing countries. That is one of the main reasons why welfare effects are computed for small increases in each activity in the economy to see how current policies distort the allocation of resources. This conveniently identifies areas where policy reform is most urgently needed, even though it does not indicate how large the final changes have to be to reach a social optimum.

One of the most contentious areas in applied welfare analysis is the aggregation of welfare changes over multiple consumers, especially when there are winners and losers. A Harberger analysis simply adds unweighted dollar changes in consumer utilities, while the alternative approach assigns welfare weights to them before they are aggregated. But these weights are subjectively chosen and there is considerable scope for disagreement about the role distributional effects should play in the evaluation process, particularly when there are trade-offs between the efficiency and equity effects. The compensation principle establishes a middle ground between these two approaches. It relies on hypothetical revenue transfers between consumers to test for preferred policy choices. The Kaldor test looks to see whether winners can compensate losers after the change, while the Hicks test looks to see that losers cannot pay winners to block the policy change beforehand. Bruce and Harris, and Diewert combine transfer policy choices with other policy changes to test for Pareto improvements.[44] They choose patterns of revenue transfers to convert potential gains into higher utility for every consumer. This approach rules out policy choices that rely solely on distributional effects to be socially profitable.[45]

A conventional Harberger analysis is used in Chapter 2 to obtain shadow prices for goods. They are measured as aggregate dollar changes in utility, which by the

Hatta decomposition, are path independent. Distributional concerns are examined in Chapter 3 where the approach recommended by Dréze and Stern is compared to the approach recommended by Bruce and Harris, and Diewert.

NOTES

1. Formal derivations of the first and second fundamental theorems of welfare economics are provided in Myles (1995). There are three requirements for them to hold—non-satiation, the existence of competitive equilibrium, and finiteness of the number of goods and consumers in the economy.
2. Strictly speaking, all the allocations on that part of the indifference curves that constitute the trading lens, except where they intersect, are Pareto improvements.
3. Slutsky compensation is illustrated for an individual who consumes two goods from fixed money income. When the price of good 1 rises the consumer receives compensation to rotate the budget constraint around the initial bundle x^0. This allows the consumer to choose a new bundle x^1 in the preferred set on the higher indifference curve u^1. Most courts determine compensation payments on this basis because they are based on observed prices and consumption. In contrast, exact Hicksian compensation cannot be determined without knowing what the initial indifference curve u^0 looks like.
4. Strictly speaking this is a welfare loss for the consumer but not society as a whole. Most of this loss is surplus transferred by the price change to other consumers, and the transfers are taken into account when welfare changes are aggregated across consumers. In the following discussion we show how the value of the change in final consumption demand is equal to the dollar change in consumer surplus for a marginal price change when money income is held constant.
5. One can easily show how the Laspeyres quantity index overstates the gain for a price fall.
6. It should be noted that when point E lies below point D the Paasche measure understates the true welfare loss.
7. When the price change is differentially small the Laspeyres and Paasche quantity index measures are identical and are equal to the area underneath the demand schedule. Also, the Laspeyres and Paasche price index measures are identical and equal to changes in consumer surplus to the left of the demand schedules.
8. This is confirmed by totally differentiating the budget constraint, where $q\,dx = dI - x\,dq$.
9. Green (1976) succinctly illustrates the problems that arise using aggregate price–quantity data in a simple 2 person–2 good economy.
10. In economies with production there is a grand UPF derived from the full set of point (or situation) UPFs. The point UPF maps the combinations of utilities from redistributing a given production between consumers (for a given policy setting). Boadway and Bruce (1984) derive the point and grand UPFs in Edgeworth box diagrams.
11. This was demonstrated earlier in footnote 3.
12. It is sometimes referred to as the Kaldor–Hicks criterion following the support from Hicks (1939) for the Kaldor test.
13. Recall that the endowments are non-traded internationally.
14. In this section, superscript h is omitted from the consumption vector and the utility function. It is an ordinal utility function which provides rankings over consumption bundles, and is unaffected by monotone transformations. Thus, indifference schedules can be re-scaled without affecting the rankings. But it means the utility measures are non-comparable across consumers, which makes it difficult to aggregate welfare changes. This problem is examined in Section 1.2.2. For an ordinal utility function to exist consumer preferences must be complete, transitive, reflexive and continuous, and unless otherwise stated, they are also assumed to be strictly quasi-concave to make the indifference schedules strictly convex to the origin in the commodity space.
15. The exposition here closely follows Auerbach (1985).
16. By writing the compensated demand for any good i as: $x_i(q, u_0) = x_i(q, I(q, u_0))$, we have:

$$\frac{\partial \hat{x}_i(q)}{\partial q_j} = \frac{\partial x_i(q, I)}{\partial q_j} + \frac{\partial x_i(q, I)}{\partial I}\frac{\partial I(q, u_0)}{\partial q_j},$$

where the hat denotes a compensated welfare change, with: $(\partial \hat{x}_i(q)/\partial q_j) = (\partial x_i(q, u_0)/\partial q_j)$. The income effect is solved using the minimum expenditure function, as:

$$\frac{\partial I(q, u_0)}{\partial q_j} = \frac{\partial E(q, u_0)}{\partial q_j} = x_j.$$

17. This is why the conventional Harberger shadow prices derived in Chapter 2, which are measured as dollar changes in utility, are path independent. It is also confirmed by the generalized Hatta decomposition which finds income effects are independent of marginal policy changes.

18. This is demonstrated in Silberberg and Suen (2001) on pages 347–353. The utility function $u = x_1 x_2 + x_1^2 x_2^2$ is an example of a homothetic function that is not homogenous. But it is straightforward to show that it is a monotonic transformation of the linearly homogeneous utility function $u = \sqrt{x_1}\sqrt{x_2}$.

19. From Roy's Identity we have: $\partial V / q_i = -\lambda x_i$.

20. By differentiating demand in (1.9) we have: $\partial x_i / \partial I = -(\partial^2 V / \partial q_i \partial I)(1/\lambda) + (\partial V / \partial q_i)(1/\lambda^2)(\partial \lambda / \partial I)$ (1.10) is obtained by using Young's Theorem, where: $\partial^2 V / \partial q_i \partial I = \partial^2 V / \partial I \partial q_i = \partial \lambda / \partial q_i$, and Roy's Identity.

21. There is good intuition for the marginal utility of income being homogeneous of degree -1. The real value of each dollar of income will be halved when all prices and money income are doubled. In other words, the consumer will have to spend twice as many dollars to buy the same real bundle of goods (at unchanged relative prices). Thus, by Euler's Theorem: $(\partial \lambda / \partial I) I = -\lambda$.

22. Since the marginal utility of income is affected by monotone transformations of the utility function it will in general be a function of money income for homothetic preferences. Thus, for path independent welfare measures in general equilibrium, where income is endogenously determined, the marginal utility of income will have to be independent of money income as well. This is the case when consumers have utility functions that are homogenous of degree 1, so that $\lambda = V/I$, with V being the indirect utility function, where:

$$\frac{d\lambda}{dI} = \frac{dV}{dI}\frac{1}{I} - \frac{V}{I^2} = 0.$$

23. Assume the tax change has no affect on the market price of the good, which is the case in Hatta where goods are produced at constant aggregate marginal cost.

24. Diamond and Mirrlees (1971) and Atkinson and Stern (1974) use a similar model to Hatta but obtain a different welfare decomposition. They compute the effect of the tax change for a single (aggregated) consumer in an economy with a linear production frontier that holds producer prices constant. Diamond and Mirrlees, and Atkinson and Stern rule out lump-sum transfers and use distorting taxes to make revenue transfers, whereas Hatta uses notional lump-sum transfers to isolate the welfare effects of the tax change. Thus, Diamond and Mirrlees, and Atkinson and Stern decompose (1.15) by applying the Slutsky decomposition to the change in demand in (1.16) where they get additive income and substitution effects. In effect, they hold money income constant by not returning the change in tax revenue to the consumer. In contrast, Hatta allows money income to change by returning the tax revenue in a conventional Harberger manner and obtains a different decomposition. The two approaches will be reconciled in Chapter 7.

25. In later chapters the compensated welfare changes are isolated as net changes in government revenue. For this example, the efficiency loss from marginally raising the tax, solves:

$$\frac{d\hat{R}}{dt} = t\frac{\partial \hat{x}_1(q)}{\partial q_1} + x_1 - CV_t,$$

where the compensating variation to hold utility constant is $CV_t = x_1$.

26. Analysis in later chapters will prove $1/\text{AIM}$ is the shadow value of government revenue, which measures the amount utility changes when a dollar of revenue is endowed on the government who balances its budget by making lump-sum transfers.

27. This is obtained using Shephard's Lemma, with $\partial E / \partial q_i = \hat{x}_i$ for all i, and the fact that $\partial E / \partial u = 1/\lambda$.

28. For a clear explanation of the Arrow impossibility theorem see Chapter 9 in Deaton and Muellbauer (1980). A proof is provided in Myles (1995). Strictly speaking Arrow examines a social welfare functional because it is a mapping over individual preference functions, that is, it is a function of functions.

29. Bergson (1938) initially described the individualistic SWF, while Samuelson (1954) was the first to use it in formal analysis.
30. This is the Rawls (1971) *maximin* criterion.
31. For an interior solution consumers choose positive quantities of each good. Corner solutions are examined in Chapter 4.
32. The variable x is now defined as the vector of summed consumption demands for goods over consumers, with $x_i = \sum_h x_i^h$ for each good i.
33. Brekke (1997) demonstrates the choice of numeraire will matter when consumers have different marginal rates of substitutions for goods. And this is generally the case for public goods where consumers have different marginal valuations.
34. This is somewhat misleading. The CVs are not computed by asking consumers about them. Rather, they are transfers that would have to be made in equilibrium to return consumers to their initial indifference curves.
35. The analysis is extended to economies with commodity taxes and production in Jones (2001). Blackorby and Donaldson (1990), Johansson (1998) and Peck (1998) all identify problems using the compensation principle when prices do not change endogenously with the compensating transfers to clear markets.
36. Silberberg (1972) demonstrates this by presenting a unifying treatment of the welfare measures underneath the ordinary (Marshallian) and compensated (Hicksian) demand schedules.
37. This is obtained from:

$$\Delta S_{12} = E(q_1^0, q_2^0, u_0) - E(q_1^1, q_2^0, u_0) + E(q_1^1, q_2^0, u_0) - E(q_1^1, q_2^1, u_0).$$

38. If utility is held constant at the new level, then: $\text{DWL} = -\text{EV} - T(q^1, u_1)$.
39. Fullerton (1991) provides a clear exposition of the different measures of the excess burden used in applied work.
40. If x_1 is inferior the tax revenue declines with the income transfers.
41. The Bailey demand schedule is the uncompensated demand schedule derived in general equilibrium. Any surplus transfers, like those collected as tax revenue, are returned to consumers, where this makes their income endogenous.
42. This assumes constant money income, with $E^1 = E^0$, and uses Shephard's Lemma.
43. Any cross-price income effects offset each other when price changes are differentially small, as is confirmed by (1.6) which isolates the source of path dependence.
44. Bruce and Harris (1981) show that, for incrementally small policy changes, there are no contradictions using the Kaldor and Hicks compensation tests for welfare improvements.
45. Foster and Sonnenschein (1970) identify another problem with the compensation principle. They find circumstances where extra income can make consumers worse off (even when producer prices are constant) in tax distorted economies with multiple equilibria. Once this happens it is possible for a pure lump–sum redistribution of income to have efficiency gains. This will be examined in Chapters 2 and 3.

2

Conventional Shadow Prices

For a variety of reasons there are distortions in markets that drive economic activity away from a social optimum. Governments raise revenue with distorting taxes to provide goods and services and to redistribute income. There are also externalities when private property rights are not assigned to resources because it is too costly to do so, or for social reasons they are held as communal assets. Private markets often under-provide public goods when they are non-excludable. Other distortions arise from non-competitive behaviour on both the demand and supply sides of the market.[1] In the presence of distortions like this market prices will not in general be measures of the marginal social valuations of goods and services. Thus, while market prices guide private outcomes, they cannot be used to guide public policy in these circumstances. Consider a project that produces an extra unit of good 1 using inputs 2 and 3. At market prices it has private profit of:

$$\pi^p = p_1 - p_2 a_{2,1} - p_3 a_{3,1},$$

with a_{i1} being the input–output coefficient for each $i \in 2, 3$. In a competitive market $\pi^P = 0$, but when market prices are distorted it is unlikely that the marginal social profit is zero. If, for example, output is taxed its market price will understate the social value of the project revenue, while taxes on inputs will cause their prices to overstate the social cost of production. To identify welfare improving policy changes, including tax reform, competition policy, or public sector provision of goods and services, analysts need prices that measure the marginal social valuations of goods.

They can be obtained using:

(1) *The Utopian Approach* which uses market prices in a non-distorted economy. This is appropriate when policy changes eliminate price distortions all together, which is rarely, if ever, the case; or,

(2) *The Incremental Approach* that computes shadow (or social) prices in the presence of existing distortions. It views policy reform as an incremental process that moves the economy towards a social optimum.

Harberger (1968) and Parish (1972, 1973) use the incremental approach to derive shadow pricing rules in a partial equilibrium (PE) setting. The *shadow price* (S) of any good is the welfare gain from endowing a unit of it on the economy, and it is isolated using lump-sum transfers to balance the government budget.[2] In other words, it is a welfare change computed for a balanced equilibrium. In project evaluation, outputs and inputs are valued using their shadow prices, where the shadow profit for the project

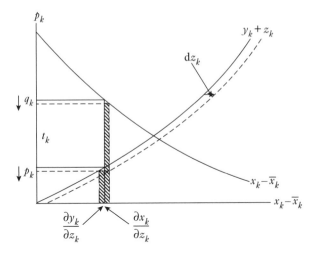

Figure 2.1 *The shadow price of a non-traded good*

that marginally increases output of good 1, is:

$$\pi^S = S_1 - S_2 a_{2,1} - S_3 a_{3,1}.$$

It is the change in social welfare from undertaking the project. The Harberger–Parish shadow pricing rules were extended in the OECD manual by Little and Mirrlees (1969), and the UNIDO guidelines by Dasgupta, Marglin, and Sen (1972). At that time the agencies used shadow prices to isolate socially profitable projects they could fund in developing countries. In recent times, however, more of their funds are allocated as subsidized loans when governments commit to undertake mutually agreed policy reforms. These policies can be isolated by shadow pricing the marginal profits for each good and service produced in the economy to determine how current policies distort economic activity. They are normally reported as domestic resource cost ratios, where activities with marginal social losses benefit from current policies, while those with marginal social profits are hurt by them. Policy reforms seek to exploit these differences by moving resources towards activities with social profits and away from those with social losses.[3]

The Harberger–Parish shadow price of a non-traded good k is illustrated in Figure 2.1 when it is subject to a specific production tax t_k. Consumers purchase $x_k - \bar{x}_k$ of the good, with x_k being what they consume and $\bar{x}_k$ their initial endowment, and output is produced by private (y_k) and public (z_k) firms. When the government sells another unit of the good (dz_k) its market price falls to displace private production and increase private demand. The welfare change is the sum of the additional consumption benefits and the resource cost saving, with:

$$S_k = q_k \frac{\partial x_k}{\partial z_k} - p_k \frac{\partial y_k}{\partial z_k},$$

where the consumer price (q_k) measures the marginal consumption benefit, and the producer price (p_k) the marginal resource cost saving. The relationship between the shadow and producer prices is obtained by using the market clearing condition ($x_k - \bar{x}_k = y_k + z_k$) and the price–tax relationship ($q_k = p_k + t_k$) to write the shadow price, as:

$$S_k = p_k + t_k \frac{\partial x_k}{\partial z_k} > p_k.^4$$

By selling a unit of good k the government collects sales revenue p_k and extra tax revenue $t_k(\partial x_k / \partial z_k)$. Since consumers receive this revenue as a lump-sum transfer when the government balances its budget, the shadow price is higher than the producer price by the fall in tax inefficiency. Clearly, the relationship between the shadow and producer prices depends on the price elasticities of demand and supply; the more elastic the supply, and the less elastic the demand, the closer they are to each other.

The relationship between the shadow and consumer price is obtained by using the market clearing condition to re-write the shadow price, as:

$$S_k = q_k + t_k \frac{\partial y_k}{\partial z_k} < q_k.$$

The tax wedge between the marginal consumption benefits and the resource cost saving causes the consumer price to overstate the social cost of the good. Thus, in markets with increasing marginal costs, the shadow price lies between the consumer and producer prices, with:

$$q_k > S_k > p_k.$$

It is unlikely that the shadow price of the good will be equal to its free-trade price, that is, its market price in the absence of tax.[5] Ultimately, its value will depend on the point elasticities of the demand and supply schedules. As the tax wedge approaches zero, however, all three prices converge to the free-trade price.

As derived above, the Harberger–Parish shadow price of good k is a *reduced form* expression which summarizes the demand–supply responses as functions of the policy change dz_k. In applied work numerical values for the shadow prices are computed using empirical estimates of the price elasticities of demand and supply. To express the shadow price of good k in these terms we decompose the changes in demand and supply over the variables that consumers and producers take as given, namely, prices and money income, with $x_k = x_k(q, I)$ and $y_k = y_k(p)$. Then the price and income changes are solved as functions of the exogenous policy choices, in this case, dz_k. The price of good k is the only one to change in a partial equilibrium analysis, where a *structural form* expression for the Harberger–Parish shadow price, is:

$$S_k = q_k \frac{\partial x_k(q, I)}{\partial q_k} \frac{\partial q_k}{\partial z_k} - p_k \frac{\partial y_k(p)}{\partial p_k} \frac{\partial p_k}{\partial z_k}.$$

By defining the tax in specific terms, the price changes are equal, with: $\partial q_k/\partial x_k = \partial p_k/\partial x_k$, and are solved using the market clearing condition, as:

$$\frac{\partial p_k}{\partial z_k} = \frac{\partial q_k}{\partial z_k} = \frac{1}{(\partial x_k(q,I)/\partial q_k) - (\partial y_k(p)/\partial p_k)}.$$

This allows us to write the shadow price, as:

$$S_k = \alpha q_k + (1 - \alpha)p_k,$$

with

$$\alpha = \frac{\partial x_k(q,I)/\partial q_k}{\{(\partial x_k(q,I)/\partial q_k) - (\partial y_k(p)/\partial p_k)\}}.$$

There are obvious ways to extend this partial equilibrium analysis. One is to use Bailey (1954) demands to account for changes in consumer income when the government makes revenue transfers to balance its budget.[6] They are the general equilibrium demands with endogenous income. By selling another unit of good k the government collects sales revenue (p_k) and extra tax revenue ($t_k(\partial x_k/\partial z_k)$). Once this additional revenue is transferred to consumers the extra income affects their demands and, as a consequence, the level of private activity. Another extension would account for welfare effects when resources flow into other distorted markets. Stiglitz and Dasgupta (1971), Diamond and Mirrlees (1971, 1976), Diewert (1983), Dréze and Stern (1985, 1990), Little and Mirrlees (1969, 1972), Sieper (1981), Squire (1989) and Warr (1982) extend the analysis in the following important ways:

1. They use *general equilibrium (GE) analysis* to include welfare effects when resources are reallocated across distorted markets. For example, some inputs used in the production of good k may themselves be subject to price distortions. In these circumstances, the producer price will not (in general) measure the social value of the resource cost saving. Little and Mirrlees (1969) find, however, that the ratio of the shadow prices of fully traded goods are equal to the ratio of their border prices in small open economies, while Diamond and Mirrlees, and Stiglitz and Dasgupta find that, with Ramsey optimal taxes, the ratios of the shadow prices of non-traded goods are equal to the ratios of their producer prices in the absence of private profit. Both these results simplify the computational task in project evaluation considerably.

2. Each study formalizes *the government's role* in the economy. In most, the government is treated as a passive agent to avoid the difficult task of solving its objective function. This approach is general enough to account for endogenous policy responses by analysing them separately. In some studies, for example, Warr, the government maximizes social welfare, so that shadow prices are obtained as the outcome of a second best optimization problem in the presence of fixed distortions. Typically, however, governments are influenced by a much broader set of considerations when making policy choices. For example, tariffs are levied on imports when domestic producers who benefit have greater political influence than those in society who bear the costs. In other words, the public interest can be compromised by private interest concerns.

3. *Compensated welfare measures* are used to isolate potential gains. Sieper derives a relationship between the uncompensated and compensated shadow prices by generalizing the Hatta (1977) decomposition. This relationship, which proves the income effects are irrelevant in project evaluation, provides economic intuition for the Little–Mirrlees result above.

4. *Lump-sum transfers are replaced by trade and income taxes* when governments fund their projects with distorting taxes. Diamond and Mirrlees, and Stiglitz and Dasgupta obtain shadow prices in this setting. Sieper computes them as *implementation-problem corrected* shadow prices to account for changes in tax inefficiency, and compares them to the conventional Harberger (lump-sum) shadow prices. These *revised* shadow prices are used in Chapter 6 to formalize the role played by the marginal social cost of public funds in policy evaluation work.

These and a number of other extensions will be made in the remainder of the book. A simple GE model with non-traded goods is used in the rest of this chapter to obtain *conventional* Harberger shadow prices in a single (aggregated) consumer economy.[7] That is, shadow prices that are isolated by lump-sum transfers when consumers have the same distributional weights. A generalized Hatta decomposition is then used to compute the compensated shadow prices which isolate the potential welfare gains.

2.1 A GENERAL EQUILIBRIUM MODEL OF A TAX-DISTORTED ECONOMY

The following model and notation is taken from Diamond and Mirrlees (1971), and Sieper with slight modifications. There are $h = 1, \ldots, H$ consumers in the economy who each maximize utility $u^h(x^h)$ by choosing a consumption vector x^h with $i = 0, 1, \ldots, N$ non-traded goods.[8] Aggregate welfare changes are measured using the *individualistic* social welfare function in (1.22). Initially, they are obtained in a single (aggregated) consumer economy (with $\beta^h = \beta$ for all h) as dollar changes in social welfare, which solve:

$$\frac{dW}{\beta} = \sum_h \sum_i q_i \, dx_i^h = q \, dx^h.\text{[9]} \tag{2.1}$$

The value of the changes in final consumption demand in (2.1) are constrained by the private sector budget constraints, where for each consumer h:

$$E^h \equiv qx^h = q\bar{x}^h + \rho^h py + g^h L \equiv I^h,$$

where E^h is expenditure; I^h income; q the vector of consumer prices; p the vector of producer prices; y the vector of private net-outputs with $y_i > 0$ for each output i and $y_i < 0$ for each input i; ρ^h the share of profits from private production (py), with $\sum_h \rho^h = 1$; $\bar{x}^h$ the vector of primary factor endowments; and $g^h L$ the share (g^h) of the lump-sum transfers (L) received from the government, with $\sum_h g^h = 1$.

When the budget constraints are aggregated across consumers, we have:

$$E \equiv qx = q\bar{x} + py + L \equiv I. \tag{2.2}$$

Initially, the only distortions are specific production taxes (or subsidies) that drive wedges between consumer and producer prices, with:

$$q_i = p_i + t_i, \tag{2.3}$$

where

$$t_i > 0 \begin{cases} \text{is a tax when } y_i > 0, \\ \text{a susbidy when } y_i < 0, \end{cases} \qquad t_i < 0 \begin{cases} \text{is a subsidy when } y_i > 0, \\ \text{a tax when } y_i < 0. \end{cases}$$

All the goods can be taxed except good 0 which is chosen as numeraire, and specific taxes are used because it conveniently makes $dq_i = dp_i \; \forall_{i \in N}$ when prices change endogenously. In a competitive equilibrium the price changes will clear the goods markets, with: $x_i = \bar{x}_i + y_i + z_i \; \forall_{i \in N}$.[10] In following chapters welfare changes are examined in the presence of other price distortions, including price controls, non-competitive behaviour and externalities. Initially, however, the only distortions are taxes to make the analysis less complicated.[11]

The lump–sum transfers in (2.2) are solved using the government budget constraint, with:

$$L = T + pz - R, \tag{2.4}$$

where R represents an exogenous foreign aid payment, $T = t(y + z)$ tax revenue, and z the vector of public sector net outputs; pz is therefore profit on public production.

Two equilibrium concepts are used to separate the income and substitution effects in project evaluation:

1. In *full equilibrium* the government makes revenue transfers to balance its budget (with $dR = 0$) and welfare gains are measured as dollar changes in social welfare (dW/β).[12]
2. In a *compensated equilibrium* the government makes revenue transfers to hold consumer utilities constant (with $dW/\beta = 0$) and efficiency gains are measured as surplus government revenue $(d\hat{R})$.

Welfare measures in full equilibrium are based on actual outcomes and can be estimated using observed data. This makes them attractive in applied welfare applications. However, as demonstrated previously in Chapter 2, they are difficult to interpret when there are winners and losers. In contrast, compensated welfare measures are free of distributional effects, but are much more difficult to estimate because the changes in activity are not normally observable.

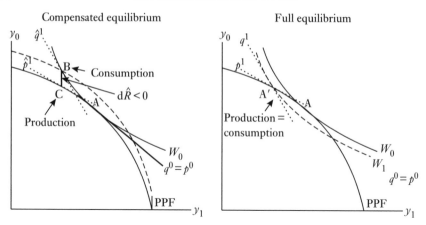

Figure 2.2 *The welfare loss from introducing a commodity tax on good 1*

Both these equilibrium concepts can be illustrated in a competitive economy that produces non-traded goods y_0 and y_1. Two welfare changes are considered, one by introducing a tax on good 1, and the other by computing the shadow price of good 1. To simplify the analysis assume that there are a large number of identical consumers, no initial public production of either good and no initial taxes or other market distortions. Since the tax will affect activity, outside compensation is required to hold consumer utilities constant. The compensated welfare loss is illustrated in the left panel of Figure 2.2 as BC units of good 0. Starting from the initial equilibrium at point A, the tax drives a wedge between the relative consumer and producer prices of good 1 so that demand and supply fall by the same amount. BC is the outside compensation (in units of the numeraire good 0) that would hold social welfare constant at W_0; it is the size of the government budget deficit ($d\hat{R} < 0$) after funding the CVs for the tax.

When the DWL is funded by foreign aid revenue, it supplements production at point C to satisfy consumption demand at point B. If, as is normally the case, there is no foreign aid payment, then the government will impose lump-sum taxes on domestic consumers to fund the budget deficit BC, where utility falls in full equilibrium to W_1. This is illustrated in the right diagram of Figure 2.2 where the tax drives demand and supply around the efficient production frontier (PPF) from A to A'.[13] At A' the higher consumer price is tangent to indifference curve W_1 and the lower producer price to the production frontier PPF. The move from the compensated equilibrium at B in the left diagram to the full equilibrium at A' in the right diagram is due solely to income effects. Notice how the relative price will change endogenously to equate demand and supply in both markets when the welfare loss BC is transferred from the domestic economy to balance the government budget at A' on PPF.

The shadow price of good 1 is illustrated in Figure 2.3. After a unit of the good is endowed on the economy (dz_1) its relative price falls to crowd out private supply and increase private demand. In the compensated equilibrium the government uses

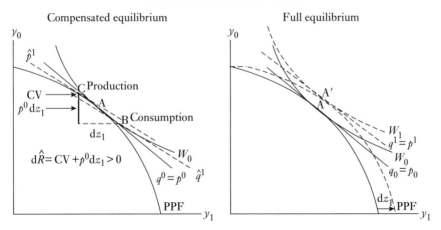

Figure 2.3 *The welfare gain from endowing another unit of good 1 on the economy*

lump-sum transfers to withdraw units of the numeraire good 0 from the economy to hold consumer utilities constant at point B on W_0. This moves production to point C and demand to point B at the market clearing price $\hat{p}^1 = \hat{q}^1$. The government ends up collecting surplus revenue from the compensating variation (CV) and the sales revenue ($p^0 \, dz_1$); it is the vertical line segment below point C. (Note that the CV is zero for the small change dz_1, where the gain in consumer surplus exactly offsets the loss in producer surplus when the relative price of good 1 falls. Thus, in the absence of distortions, the shadow price of good 1 is equal to its market price.) Once the government transfers this surplus revenue to domestic consumers the PPF moves to the right by one unit of good k where, in the full equilibrium illustrated in Figure 2.3, utility rises to W_1. The increase in real income moves the equilibrium outcome from A to A' where the new market clearing price is $p^1 = q^1$. Whether it rises or falls from p^0 depends on the way surplus revenue is distributed to consumers and their marginal propensities to consume. (Once again, in the absence of distortions, the shadow price of good 1 is equal to its market price.)

Most studies obtain welfare changes in full equilibrium models as dollar changes in utility. For examples see Bruce and Harris (1981, 1982), Diewert, Stiglitz and Dasgupta, Diamond and Mirrlees, Dréze and Stern, and Harberger. They normally isolate efficiency effects by holding producer prices constant, which is appropriate when the economy has a linear production possibility frontier. There are examples of this in Diamond and Mirrlees (1971), and Atkinson and Stern (1974). Sieper generalizes the Hatta decomposition to economies with variable producer prices and finds the income effects will play no role in the evaluation of incrementally small policy changes. This result, which is demonstrated in Section 2.2.3, justifies Harberger's claim that income effects for most policy changes are small enough to ignore. In fact, there are no aggregate income effects from marginal changes in optimally chosen policy variables.

2.1.1 A Conventional Welfare Equation

Harberger (1971) argues persuasively for using lump–sum transfers to separate the welfare effects of policy changes in a cost–benefit analysis. Indeed, they isolate the shadow prices of individual outputs and inputs so that policy evaluation can be divided across specialist agencies. For example, finance and treasury departments can special-ize in computing the social cost of raising government revenue, while social security, defence, and other spending agencies can specialize in measuring the social value of their respective public services. Each government agency can work in isolation when welfare effects are separated in this way. Welfare changes for projects that com-bine these policy changes are determined by computing the shadow value of their profits.

For incrementally small policy changes aggregate welfare effects are computed by solving the value of the change in final consumption demand in (2.1) using the aggregated private sector budget constraint in (2.2), where:

$$\frac{\mathrm{d}W}{\beta} = -z \, \mathrm{d}p - (y + z) \, \mathrm{d}t + \mathrm{d}L. \tag{2.5}$$

These are familiar changes in private surplus to the left of demand and supply sched-ules plus revenue transfers from the government budget. With specific taxes $-z \, \mathrm{d}p$ measures the fall in private surplus when producer prices rise endogenously. This is confirmed by using the market clearing conditions for each commodity to write it as $-z \, \mathrm{d}p = y \, \mathrm{d}p - (x - \bar{x}) \, \mathrm{d}q$, where $y \, \mathrm{d}p$ is the gain in producer surplus and $-(x - \bar{x}) \, \mathrm{d}q$ the loss in consumer surplus due to endogenous price rises.[14] The second term in (2.5) is a loss in private surplus due to higher taxes, while the last term is the increase in private consumption expenditure financed by lump–sum transfers from the govern-ment budget. These transfers are solved by using the government budget constraint in (2.4), as:

$$\mathrm{d}L = \mathrm{d}T + z \, \mathrm{d}p + p \, \mathrm{d}z - \mathrm{d}R, \tag{2.6}$$

with $\mathrm{d}T = t(\mathrm{d}y + \mathrm{d}z) + (y + z) \, \mathrm{d}t$ being the change in tax revenue.

Notice how changes in private surplus in (2.5) are transfers to the government budget in (2.6). Once the government balances its budget they do not appear in the final welfare change. A *conventional welfare equation* is obtained by substituting (2.6) into (2.5), where:

$$\frac{\mathrm{d}W}{\beta} = p \, \mathrm{d}z + t(\mathrm{d}y + \mathrm{d}z) - \mathrm{d}R.^{15} \tag{2.7}$$

In the absence of distributional effects, welfare changes in (2.7) are ultimately deter-mined by changes in economic activity, that is, by changes in final consumption demand. There are gains from extra public production ($p \, \mathrm{d}z$) and increases in demand for goods valued above their social cost due to taxes (where the net welfare gain is

Table 2.1 *The exogenous policy variables*

Full equilibrium	Compensated equilibrium (^)
z, t, g, R	z, t, g, W

$t(\mathrm{d}y + \mathrm{d}z))$. And consumers are worse off when the government makes foreign aid payments (with $\mathrm{d}R > 0$).[16]

A competitive equilibrium solves here as a function of the exogenously chosen primary factor endowments, production technologies, preferences, and policy variables. Since policy variables are the only changes considered in the following analysis, the welfare measures will be computed as reduced form functions of these variables. We use the full and compensated equilibrium closures of the economy to separate the efficiency and equity effects for policy changes; revenue transfers balance the government budget in full equilibrium, but they hold consumer utilities constant in the compensated equilibrium. The exogenous variables for these equilibrium closures are summarized in Table 2.1.

Unless otherwise stated, all the partial derivatives are functions of these variables, and to simplify the notation unmarked derivatives will be used for the conventional Harberger terms isolated by lump-sum transfers (e.g. $\partial T / \partial z_k = \partial T(z, t, g, R) / \partial z_k$), while capped derivatives represent compensated changes in activity (e.g. $\partial \hat{T} / \partial z_k = \partial T(z, t, g, W) / \partial z_k$). Whenever consumers have different marginal propensities to consume income the equilibrium outcomes are a function of the vector of transfer shares $g = (g^1, \ldots, g^H)$; they determine how much consumer incomes change when the government balances its budget.[17]

Harberger (1964) identifies two types of problems in applied welfare economics; *substitution effect only* problems, that redistribute given resources within the economy, and combined *income and substitution effect* problems, that result from exogenous changes in real income.[18] Tax changes, price controls, and production quota are all examples of substitution effect only problems, while foreign aid payments and shadow prices are examples of income and substitution effect problems.[19] When shadow prices are used to evaluate projects the welfare changes are for *substitution effect only* problems because the income effects from endowing outputs on the economy are offset by income effects from using inputs to produce them.[20] That is the reason why Harberger's fundamental welfare equation applies to *substitution effect only* problems. In the current setting it is obtained from (2.8) by setting $\mathrm{d}R = \mathrm{d}z = 0$. Any welfare effects must result from moving resources between distorted activities. Indeed, most public policy is about reallocating resources in the economy, including taxes to fund government spending and regulations to impose constraints on private activity. Thus, when a conventional welfare analysis separates the welfare effects of these policy changes using lump-sum transfers it makes them *income and substitution effect* problems. But once they are combined inside projects they revert to *substitution effect only* problems. This distinction makes it much easier for people to understand how shadow prices are used in project evaluation. Most initially find the concept of endowing goods on the economy quite confusing, but once it is clear how the endowments for the outputs and inputs will offset each other inside projects the shadow prices make much more sense.

2.2 CONVENTIONAL (HARBERGER) SHADOW PRICES

The shadow price of any good k is obtained from the conventional welfare equation in (2.7) by endowing a unit of it on the government, where:[21]

$$S_k = \frac{dW}{dz_k}\frac{1}{\beta} = p_k + \frac{\partial T}{\partial z_k}. \tag{2.8}$$

It is the familiar Harberger–Parish weighted average formula with additional welfare effects from changes in other taxed activities.[22] Each component of the shadow price in (2.8) is revenue transferred from the government budget. By selling another unit of good k the government collects sales revenue (p_k) and additional tax revenue ($\partial T/\partial z_k$) when taxed activities expand. This would suggest that the shadow price can be isolated by its impact on the government budget.[23] But that is not the case because price changes transfer private surplus to the government budget when the public sector trades in markets (z). And these transfers are reversed once the government balances its budget with lump-sum transfers. This can be confirmed by isolating the lump-sum transfers in the shadow price in (2.8) using (2.5), where:

$$S_k = -z\frac{\partial p}{\partial z_k} + \frac{\partial L}{\partial z_k}.$$

To simplify the analysis the welfare effects in related markets are removed by assuming good k is the only good the public sector produces, and the only good subject to tax. The first term $(-z_k(\partial p_k/\partial z_k))$ is the direct change in private surplus from a lower producer price, while the second term $(\partial L/\partial z_k)$ is the lump-sum transfer to balance the government budget. They are illustrated in Figure 2.4 where the public sector initially produces half the output of good k.

A marginal increase in output by the public sector drives down the market price to simultaneously increase private demand and crowd out private supply. Consumer surplus rises by (d) and private profit falls by (f). With a specific tax this net gain in private surplus is equal in value to the fall in profit on public production, where:

$$-z_k\frac{\partial p_k}{\partial z_k} = (e) = (d) - (f).$$

At the same time, the extra output generates a government budget surplus equal to the sales revenue in $(a) + (b)$, plus the tax revenue in $(c) - (d) + (e) + (f) = (c)$, less the fall in profit on public production in (e), where from (2.6), we have:

$$\frac{dL}{dz_k} = p_k + \frac{dT}{dz_k} + z_k\frac{dp_k}{dz_k} = (a) + (b) + (c) - (e).$$

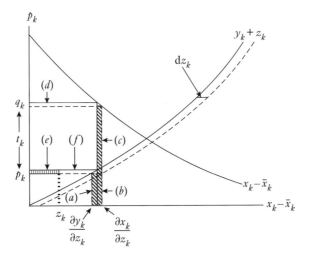

Figure 2.4 *The shadow price of good k*

When this surplus revenue is transferred to consumers the shadow price becomes:

$$S_k = (a) + (b) + (c).$$

Notice how the increase in private surplus in (d)–(f) is a transfer from the government budget as lost profit in (e). It is reversed when the government makes lump-sum transfers to balance its budget.[24] Due to the absence of distortions in other markets this is the Harberger–Parish shadow price derived earlier. A general equilibrium analysis makes it clear where welfare gains come from, and what role the lump-sum transfers play. It also includes welfare effects from changes in other taxed activities. In particular, the taxes on inputs used to produce good k. Consider its shadow price in the presence a tax on labour ($y_n < 0$) when it is used as an input to private production, where:

$$S_k = p_k + t_k \frac{\partial x_k}{\partial z_k} + t_n \frac{\partial y_n}{\partial z_k}.$$

As private output of good k contracts there is a fall in employment that reduces tax revenue and lowers the shadow price. This exacerbates the welfare effects of the tax on employment. In fact, Goulder and Williams III (2003) find these general equilibrium effects important for estimates of the excess burden of taxation. They argue that the welfare effects from taxes on inputs are usually more significant than the taxes on their outputs. In particular, they identify the income taxes on capital and labour. Their findings suggest input taxes may significantly reduce the shadow prices of goods. In effect, these taxes cause input prices to overstate the value of the resource cost saving when private production contracts.

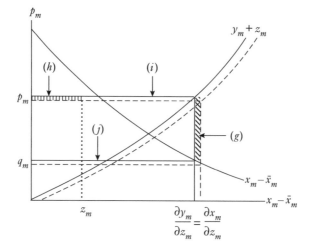

Figure 2.5 *Related market effects*

2.2.1 Welfare Effects in Related Markets

There are additional welfare effects in the shadow price of good k if resource flows affect activity in other distorted markets. An example is provided in Figure 2.5 where resources flow from private production of good k to the production of good m. Approximately one third of this good is produced by the government, and it is subject to a specific production subsidy. As resources flow into this activity the welfare loss in (g) reduces the shadow price of good k. If good m was subject instead to a tax the reverse would apply. The subsidy also affects the lump-sum transfers for good k because government revenue falls by $(g) + (h)$; it is the additional subsidy cost in $(g) - (h) - (i) + (j) = (g)$, plus the fall in profit on public production in (h).[25]

There are other welfare effects when private demand for good m changes. If goods k and m are gross substitutes the extra output of good k will reduce demand for good m, thereby lowering the welfare loss from the subsidy by contracting activity. The reverse applies when the two goods are gross complements. Different welfare effects arise in the presence of non-tax distortions, and they are examined later in Chapter 4.

2.2.2 Efficiency Effects

Once the government compensates consumers for the effects of its policy changes the welfare effects are isolated as changes in net government revenue. They are potential welfare changes that could actually be realized by making the compensating transfers. For example, a potential gain is the surplus revenue the government could raise from a policy change at no cost to utility. And since it is measured at constant utility it is free of any distributional effects.

Compensated welfare changes are derived using the conventional welfare equation in (2.7), with $dW/\beta = 0$, as:

$$d\hat{R} = p\,d\hat{z} + t(d\hat{y} + d\hat{z}). \tag{2.9}$$

This provides conventional Harberger terms isolated by compensating transfers which are solved using (2.5), with $dW/\beta = 0$, as:

$$d\hat{L} = z\,d\hat{p} + (y + z)\,d\hat{t}. \tag{2.10}$$

They are the compensating variation (CV) for changes in prices and taxes, and are familiar areas to the left of the compensated demand curves. What makes them different to the standard textbook presentation is the way prices change endogenously to clear the goods markets. This makes the sum of the CVs for consumers reliable measures of potential welfare gains.[26]

The *compensated shadow price* of any good k is derived from (2.9) by endowing a unit on the government, where the potential gain, is:

$$\hat{S}_k = \frac{d\hat{R}}{dz_k} = p_k + \frac{\partial\hat{T}}{\partial z_k}. \tag{2.11}$$

It has the same structure as the uncompensated shadow price in (2.8), but differs by measuring the compensated change in tax revenue, which is determined solely by substitution effects. The role of the compensating transfers can be isolated using (2.6), where:

$$\hat{S}_k = p_k + z_k\frac{\partial\hat{p}_k}{\partial z_k} + \frac{\partial\hat{T}}{\partial z_k} - \frac{\partial\hat{L}}{\partial z_k}.$$

The first three terms are direct changes in government revenue, while the last term is the cost to government revenue of making the compensating transfers. This decomposition is illustrated in Figure 2.6 where effects in related markets are ignored and the public sector initially produces half the output of good k.

Government revenue rises by the sales revenue in $(a) + (b)$ and the additional tax revenue in $(c) = (c) - (d) + (e) + (f)$, but falls by the lower profit in (e), where:

$$p_k + z_k\frac{\partial\hat{p}_k}{\partial z_k} + t_k\frac{\partial\hat{x}_k}{\partial z_k} = [(a) + (b)] - (e) + (c).$$

Compensating transfers must offset the increase in consumer surplus in (d) and repay the lost private profit in (f), where from (2.10), we have:

$$\frac{d\hat{L}}{dz_k} = z_k\frac{\partial\hat{p}_k}{\partial z_k} = -(d) + (f) = -(e).$$

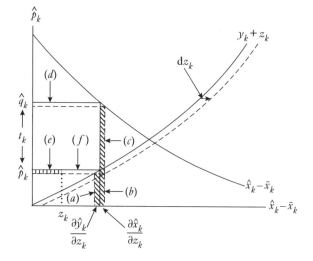

Figure 2.6 *The compensated shadow price*

The compensated measure of the Harberger–Parish shadow price is obtained by adding this transfer to the direct change in government revenue, where:

$$\hat{S}_k = (a) + (b) + (c).$$

Once again, this confirms the partial equilibrium analysis of Harberger and Parish where the shadow price is the weighted sum of the additional consumption benefits and resource cost saving. Perhaps the most significant difference is the role the transfers play in the compensated equilibrium. They balance the government budget in full equilibrium, whereas in the compensated equilibrium they offset changes in private surplus. As a consequence they flow in the opposite direction to augment direct changes in net government revenue. This difference is important because the size and direction of the revenue transfers will determine the change in tax inefficiency when compensating transfers are made with distorting taxes in Chapter 6.

2.2.3 Income Effects and the Shadow Value of Government Revenue

As noted earlier, the compensated shadow price in (2.11) is a potential gain. It can be likened to the amount of foreign aid a unit of good k would finance at no cost to domestic utility. In making this analogy it must be assumed that the change in utility of foreign recipients has no impact on domestic welfare, which is why these gains are sometimes referred to as the domestic income that can be thrown into the sea. Another way to view a potential gain is to regard it as foreign aid revenue that the economy would need to replicate the welfare effect of selling another unit of good k. Ultimately, potential gains are distributed to domestic consumers when the government balances its budget, and this raises their utility. Sieper proves the uncompensated shadow price in (2.8) is the change in social welfare from transferring the compensated shadow price in (2.11) as a lump-sum revenue transfer to consumers. The relationship is obtained by writing social welfare as a function of the vector of public policy variables z, t, g, and R, where the change in foreign aid payments that would offset the welfare effect of endowing another unit of good k on the economy solves:

$$dW(z, t, g, R) = \frac{\partial W}{\partial z_k} d\hat{z}_k + \frac{\partial W}{\partial R} d\hat{R} = 0.$$

After multiplying this expression by $1/\beta$ and rearranging terms, we have:

$$\frac{d\hat{R}}{dz_k} = \hat{S}_k = -\frac{(\partial W(z, t, g, R)/\partial z_k)/\beta}{(\partial W(z, t, g, R)/\partial R)/\beta} = \frac{S_k}{S_R},$$

where $S_R = -(\partial W(z, t, g, R)/\partial R)/\beta$ is the *shadow value of government revenue*. It provides the welfare decomposition by Sieper, where:

$$S_k = S_R \hat{S}_k.^{27} \tag{2.12}$$

This generalizes the Hatta (1977) decomposition to variable producer prices, where the shadow value of government revenue is the inverse of the Hatta coefficient (AIM); it is the change in social welfare from endowing a unit of revenue on the public sector when its budget is balanced using lump–sum transfers in policy evaluation. It converts potential welfare gains into dollar changes utility, and by doing so, isolates income effects.

Note that there are two sets of revenue transfers in (2.12); the first is compensating transfers to isolate efficiency effects ($\hat{S}_k$), while the second is revenue transfers when the government balances its budget (S_R).[28] The compensating transfers in $\hat{S}_k$ are a function of the policy change k due to the different substitution effects for heterogeneous consumers, while the revenue transfers in S_R are not, that is, they are independent of the policy change. When the government uses the same pattern of revenue transfers in S_R, the income effects will play no role in isolating optimal policy choices. To see this, reconsider the *public project* that produces a unit of good 1 using inputs 2 and 3, where its *shadow profit* is:

$$\pi^S = S_1 - S_2 a_{2,1} - S_3 a_{3,1}$$

with $a_{i1} = -\partial z_i/\partial z_1$ being the input–output coefficients for $i \in 2, 3$. Using the welfare decomposition in (2.12) it becomes:

$$\pi^S = S_R(\hat{S}_1 - \hat{S}_2 a_{2,1} - \hat{S}_3 a_{3,1}) = S_R \hat{\pi}^S,$$

where the welfare change inside the parentheses is the compensated shadow profit for the project. At a social optimum there is no potential gain to distribute to consumers (where $\hat{\pi}^S = 0$), so their utilities do not change (with $\pi^S = 0$).[29] Moreover, away from this optimum actual profits ($\pi^S > 0$) are a signal of potential welfare gains ($\hat{\pi}^S > 0$) whenever the shadow value of government revenue is positive ($S_R > 0$). On this basis, there is no need to compute compensated profit to identify potential gains. Instead, analysts can isolate them using dollar changes in utility.

Something should be said at this point about the size and sign of the shadow value of government revenue. If extra income makes consumers worse off it is negative, and projects with potential gains will reduce consumer utilities. When the government balances its budget using lump-sum transfers, the shadow value of government revenue is obtained from (2.7) by endowing a dollar of surplus revenue on the economy, where:

$$S_R = -\frac{dW}{dR}\frac{1}{\beta} = 1 - \frac{\partial T}{\partial R}.^{30} \tag{2.13}$$

Welfare rises by more or less than the initial dollar of revenue due to income effects that change tax revenue. After receiving a dollar of surplus revenue the government transfers it to consumers. If they spend extra income on taxed activities the additional tax revenue will generate further surplus revenue for the government to return to them. Consequently, social welfare rises by more than the initial dollar of surplus revenue when taxed goods are normal. Clearly, tax revenue falls when taxed goods are inferior, where this can make the shadow value of government revenue negative. Hatta examines the size and sign of these income effects in the so-called *C-economy* (with a linear production possibility frontier) for changes in commodity taxes.

Recall from (1.17) that the Hatta coefficient $(1 - \theta)$ isolates income effects from policy changes, and is therefore related to the shadow value of government revenue. In fact, it is clear from (2.12) that the Hatta coefficient is the inverse of the shadow value of government revenue. This is confirmed by the structural form decomposition of the welfare change in (2.13), where:

$$S_R = \frac{1}{1 - \theta} \tag{2.14}$$

with:

$$\theta = \sum_i t_i \sum_j \frac{\partial y_i(p)}{\partial p_j}\alpha_j$$

and

$$\alpha_j = -\sum_i \delta_{ji}\frac{\partial x_i(q, I)}{\partial I}.^{31}$$

Proof. Decompose the change in tax revenue in (2.13), as:

$$\frac{\partial T}{\partial R} = \sum_i t_i \sum_j \frac{\partial y_i(p)}{\partial p_j}\frac{\partial p_j}{\partial R},^{32} \tag{2.15}$$

where N prices change to clear all $N+1$ commodity markets.[33] The price changes are solved using the goods market clearing conditions, which provide the following system of equations stacked over the N goods, where:

$$\left| \frac{\partial x_i(q, I)}{\partial q_j} - \frac{\partial y_i(p)}{\partial p_j} \right| \left| \frac{\partial p_j}{\partial R} \right| + \left| \frac{\partial x_i(q, I)}{\partial I} \right| \frac{\partial I}{\partial R} = |0|.[34]$$

By substituting the change in consumer income: $\partial I/\partial R = \sum_j x_j(\partial p_j/\partial R) + (\partial T/\partial R) - 1$, and using a Slutsky decomposition, the price changes for each good j, are:

$$\frac{\partial p_j}{\partial R} = \alpha_j \left(\frac{\partial T}{\partial R} - 1 \right) \tag{2.16}$$

with

$$\alpha_j = -\sum_i \delta_{ji} \frac{\partial x_i(q, I)}{\partial I}, \quad \text{and} \quad |\delta_{ji}| = \left| \frac{\partial \hat{x}_i(q)}{\partial q_j} - \frac{\partial y_i(p)}{\partial p_j} \right|^{-1}.[35]$$

Once the price changes in (2.16) are substituted into (2.15), the change in tax revenue becomes: $\partial T/\partial R = -\theta/(1-\theta)$ and (2.13) solves as (2.14). □

Sieper provides economic intuition for the welfare change in (2.14). When a dollar of surplus revenue is endowed on the government it will be transferred as higher real income to consumers whose spending generates extra tax revenue of θ. In turn, this revenue is transferred to consumers and it generates additional tax revenue of θ^2 which is also returned to consumers. The process continues until welfare rises by $1/(1-\theta)$. As an aside, note how this multiplier is determined by changes in tax inefficiency and not by changes in total government revenue. Recall from (2.4) that the government collects revenue from both taxes and profit on its production. Since public profit is matched by an equal and opposite change in private surplus it does not affect the real income of consumers when it is transferred back to them. The same thing does not apply, however, to changes in tax revenue due to the excess burden of taxation, which is why the shadow value of government revenue differs from unity through the changes in tax inefficiency that do impact on the real income of consumers. This is illustrated in Figure 2.7 for a taxed good k which is assumed normal.

To eliminate welfare changes in related markets assume that there are no other taxes and this is the only market where the government trades. The welfare changes in the shadow value of government revenue can be identified by using (2.5) to separate the direct change in private surplus from the lump-sum revenue transfers, as:

$$S_R = -z_k \frac{\partial p_k}{\partial R} - \frac{\partial L}{\partial R}.$$

When a dollar of revenue is transferred to consumers they demand more good k and drive up its price. Private surplus falls by $(b) - (d)$, where:

$$-z \frac{\partial p_k}{\partial R} = (d) - (b) = -(c).$$

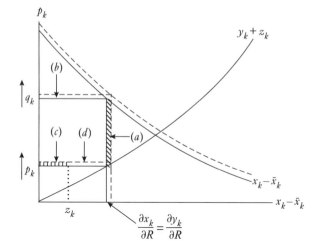

Figure 2.7 *The shadow value of government revenue*

There is also additional tax revenue in (a) and additional public profit in (c), where the surplus government revenue is solved using (2.6), as:

$$-\frac{\partial L}{\partial R} = -\frac{\partial T}{\partial R} - z_k \frac{\partial p_k}{\partial R} + 1 = (a) + (c) + 1.$$

Once this surplus revenue is transferred to consumers to balance the government budget, it offsets the direct fall in private surplus in (c), and raises utility (measured in dollars) by:

$$S_R = 1 + (a).$$

The reduction in tax inefficiency makes the shadow value of government revenue positive and larger than unity. However, when extra income makes consumers worse off the shadow value of government revenue will be negative. Foster and Sonnenschein (1970) identify circumstances where this happens for *marginal tax changes*. They show that multiple equilibrium outcomes are possible in single-consumer economies with commodity tax distortions, and consider two cases:

1. *Linear Production Possibility Frontiers—Constant Producer Prices.* When firms produce outputs with a single input using constant returns to scale technologies aggregate marginal costs are constant. It is referred to as a C-economy where producer prices do not change endogenously. In these circumstances, the consumer budget constraints can be used to write the Hatta coefficient, as:

$$\text{AIM} = 1 - \theta = \sum_i p_i \frac{\partial x_i(q, I)}{\partial I}. \text{[36]}$$

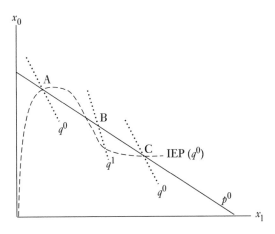

Figure 2.8 *Constant producer prices*

Clearly, there must be inferior goods for it to be negative. An example is illustrated in Figure 2.8 in a single consumer economy with two goods where the income expansion path for the initial tax distortion $q^0 - p^0$ cuts the consumption frontier more than once due to good 0 being inferior. With non-satiation the income expansion path must cut an odd number of times.

The equilibrium outcomes at A and C are for the same tax $(q^0 - p^0)$, while B is associated with a higher tax $(q^1 - p^0)$. Utility rises as consumption moves along the frontier from A to C. Starting at B and reducing the tax to $(q^0 - p^0)$ could move the economy to A where utility is lower. If this happens extra real income drives down utility, with $S_R < 0$. Clearly, this is ruled out by adopting homothetic preferences where the equilibrium allocations are unique in the presence of tax distortions since both goods are normal. However, as Foster and Sonnenschein show, this will not rule out multiple equilibria along non-linear production frontiers when there are more than two goods.

2. *Non-Linear Production Possibility Frontiers—Variable Producer Prices.* If goods are produced with increasing (aggregate) marginal costs, producer prices change endo-genously as resources move between markets. By using the market clearing conditions and the private sector budget constraints the Hatta coefficient becomes:

$$1 - \theta = \sum_i p_i \frac{\partial x_i(q, I)}{\partial I} - \sum_i t_i \sum_s \frac{\partial \hat{x}_i(q)}{\partial q_s} \alpha_{sI},$$

where α_{sI} is the producer price change for each good s due to income effects.[37]

The first term is positive when goods are normal, but that will not stop the second term being larger and negative when there are more than two goods. The two good case is illustrated in Figure 2.9 for a single consumer economy with homothetic preferences.

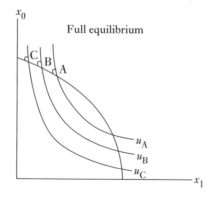

Figure 2.9 *Variable producer prices*

There are three tax-distorted equilibrium outcomes at A, B, and C. In the move from A to C the tax wedge increases, thereby raising the consumer's marginal valuation for good 1 and lowering its marginal cost. Thus, utility falls as the tax rises, with $S_R > 0$. This is confirmed by decomposing the Hatta coefficient for the two good case, as:

$$1 - \theta = \sum_i p_i \frac{\partial x_i(q_1, I)}{\partial I} - t_1 \frac{\partial \hat{x}_1(q_1)}{\partial q_1} \alpha_{1I}$$

with

$$\alpha_{1I} = \frac{-\partial x_1(q_1, I)/\partial I}{(\partial \hat{x}_1(q_1)/\partial q_1) - (\partial y_1(p_1)/\partial p_1)}.$$

With both goods normal the income effect raises the relative price of good 1, so that $\alpha_{1I} > 0$ and $1 - \theta > 0$. When there are three or more goods, however, the sign of the Hatta coefficient can be negative due to cross-price effects.

Perhaps stable equilibrium adjustment mechanisms provide the most satisfactory way of ruling out Foster–Sonnenschein effects. Foster and Sonnenschein consider a number of these mechanisms, one uses Slutsky compensation to overcompensate consumers for a policy change and then withdraws income until full equilibrium is achieved at the highest possible utility. For the example illustrated in Figure 2.8, a reduction in the tax at B would move the economy to equilibrium C where utility is higher than it would be at A.[38] In applied work Foster–Sonnenschein effects can be tested empirically by estimating the shadow value of government revenue. A computable expression is obtained in Chapter 3 to facilitate this task.

Finally, the generalized Hatta decomposition in (2.12) can be confirmed by deriving structural form expressions for the shadow prices in (2.8) and (2.11), where:

$$S_k = \frac{p_k + t_k + \sum_i t_i \sum_j (\partial y_i(p)/\partial p_j)\delta_{jk}}{1 - \theta} \,{}^{39}$$

with: $p_k + t_k + \sum_i t_i \sum_j (\partial y_i(p)/\partial p_j)\delta_{jk} = \hat{S}_k$, and from (2.14): $S_R = 1/(1 - \theta)$.

In following chapters, a conventional Harberger cost–benefit analysis is used to measure the welfare effects for a range of incrementally small policy changes. Local Foster–Sonnenschein effects (LFSE) will be ruled out by assumption to make the shadow value of government revenue positive. However, that does not guarantee every consumer is made better off by efficiency gains due to distributional effects in the shadow value of government revenue. Whenever the government balances its budget it must choose how to distribute revenue across consumers, where different transfer shares have different welfare effects. These transfer policy choices are rarely made explicit in conventional cost–benefit studies because they are non-distorting. As such, they are usually pushed to the background of the analysis. If transfer shares are chosen to make every consumer better off, then efficiency gains will convert into Pareto improvements. This is examined in detail in Chapter 3.

2.3 PROJECT EVALUATION

Now the shadow profit for the project that produces a unit of good 1 can be computed using the shadow pricing rules in the previous section, where from (2.8), we have:

$$\pi^S = p_1 - p_2 a_{21} - p_3 a_{31} + \frac{dT}{dz_1}$$

with $a_{i1} = -\partial y_i / \partial y_1$ being the input–output coefficient for each $i \in 2, 3$, and

$$\frac{dT}{dz_1} = \frac{\partial T}{\partial z_1} - \frac{\partial T}{\partial z_2} a_{21} - \frac{\partial T}{\partial z_3} a_{39}$$

the total change in tax revenue from the project.

If the public sector uses the same technology as competitive private firms, their first-order condition ($p_1 - p_2 a_{21} - p_3 a_{31} = 0$) can be used to write the shadow profit, as:

$$\pi^S = \frac{dT}{dz_1}.$$

By moving resources between producers with the same production costs the project is a *substitution effect only* problem. Any welfare gains must therefore come from expanding taxed activities, otherwise there is no shadow profit from the project. There is a result in Diamond and Mirrlees (1976), which is examined in Chapter 9, where shadow prices are equal to producer prices in economies with linear production frontiers. In this situation, the public project has no impact on final consumption because it crowds out the same private output.

However, when the public sector is a less efficient producer than private firms due to soft budget constraints and principle–agent problems, the project becomes an *income and substitution effect* problem. This is confirmed by writing the shadow profit for the project, as:

$$\pi^S = p_2(a_{2,1}^y - a_{2,1}^z) + p_3(a_{3,1}^y - a_{3,1}^z) + \frac{dT}{dz_1},$$

where a_{i1}^y and a_{i1}^z for $i \in (2, 3)$ are the input–output coefficients for private and public producers, respectively. The sum of the first two terms is negative when the public sector is less efficient. It represents an exogenous reduction in real income from producing goods less efficiently. One of the reasons governments undertake privatization programmes is to reverse these efficiency losses. There can be efficiency gains from extra public output of goods produced by a single-price monopolist (which are identified later in Chapter 4). These gains may offset, at least partially, some of the public sector production inefficiency, and are the reason why there is often voter opposition to privatization programs.

If the shadow profit for the project is positive (with $\pi^S > 0$) there will be efficiency gains (by the Hatta decomposition in (2.12)) when Foster–Sonnenschein effects are ruled out locally (to make $S_R > 0$). It will also be a strict Pareto improvement when the government distributes its surplus revenue to make the personal shadow value of government revenue positive for every consumer. The distributional effects of the transfer policy choices are examined in Chapter 3.

2.4 CONCLUDING REMARKS

A Harberger cost–benefit analysis was used in this chapter to derive conventional shadow prices that look through market distortions to measure the marginal social valuations of goods. They are the prices used in project evaluation to measure changes in social welfare. Goods with shadow prices above their producer prices are under-consumed from a social point of view, while the reverse applies when shadow prices are lower than their producer prices. A number of important insights are provided by a general equilibrium analysis. First, welfare changes are ultimately determined by changes in economic activity, that is, by changes in final consumption demand. All the surplus transfers wash out through the private and public sector budget constraints. That leaves the final dollar change in utility equal to the efficiency effect multiplied by the shadow value of government revenue, which is the (generalized) Hatta coefficient. Since the shadow value of government revenue is independent of the policy change, income effects will play no role in a conventional welfare analysis.

Dréze and Stern derive the shadow value of government revenue but do not examine its role in project evaluation, while Bruce and Harris and Diewert use it implicitly in their welfare tests for Pareto improvements. Distributional effects are isolated in Chapter 3 by decomposing the shadow value of government revenue. This provides a convenient way of measuring the welfare effects of revenue transfers made by the government to balance its budget. The difference between the shadow value of government revenue and the conventional marginal cost of public funds (MCF) is examined later in Chapter 7. Both play different, but related roles in policy evaluation.

The second important insight from a general equilibrium analysis is the role played by lump-sum revenue transfers in a conventional Harberger analysis. Since they are non-distorting they conveniently separate the welfare effects of each component of a project. This is particularly useful in practice because it allows policy evaluation to be performed by separate agencies without them knowing how their activities will be combined inside projects. For example, the social cost of raising public funds can be separated from the welfare gains for the spending programmes they will finance. If the government balances its budget with distorting taxes rather than lump-sum transfers, then changes in tax inefficiency must be included in the welfare analysis. This is done by computing revised shadow prices in Chapter 6 using a conventional analysis with notional (hypothetical) lump-sum transfers that are offset through changes in distorting taxes. By using this approach it will be possible to once again separate policy evaluation across specialist agencies even though actual lump-sum transfers are ruled out.

NOTES

1. There can also be quantitative restrictions, like production quota, which drive wedges between consumer and producer prices.
2. The role played by lump-sum transfers in a conventional (Harberger) cost–benefit analysis is carefully examined in later sections of this chapter. They are replaced by transfers with distorting taxes in Chapter 6.
3. When the shadow price of a good is used to evaluate a public sector project it is computed by endowing a unit of it on the government, since that is where the activity originates. To evaluate private activity, the good is endowed on the private sector of the economy. This difference will matter when the government balances its budget with distorting taxes rather than lump-sum transfers. The welfare effects of revenue transfers with distorting taxes are examined in Chapters 6 and 7.
4. Market clearing requires: $x_k - \bar{x}_k = y_k + z_k$, so that: $(\partial x_k / \partial z_k) - (\partial y_k / \partial z_k) = 1$.
5. If the demand and supply schedules are linear the shadow price is the same as the free trade price in this setting.
6. Bailey (1954) demands are general equilibrium demands where prices and money income change endogenously in full equilibrium. A Bailey demand schedule was used in Figure 1.24 to compute the marginal excess burden for a commodity tax when tax revenue is returned to consumers as lump-sum transfers in the conventional Harberger manner.
7. In a single (aggregated) consumer economy the same distributional weights are assigned to consumers. It is often referred to as the 'dollar is a dollar' assumption, but consumers do not have to be identical in any other respect. Equity effects will be included in the analysis in Chapter 3 by assigning different distributional weights to consumers.
8. Internationally traded goods are included in Chapter 5.
9. This is derived as (1.23) in Chapter 1. Recall that aggregate demand for good i is $x_i = \sum_h x_i^h$, and variables without subscript i are vectors of the consumption goods, with x being the $N + 1$ vector of summed consumption demands for goods over consumers.
10. By Walras' Law all $N + 1$ markets must clear when prices are set to clear N of them.
11. When this economy is solved as a computable general equilibrium by specifying functional forms for utility and production, there can be problems if endowed goods are taxed. It is possible for the taxes to drive consumption to the endowment point where small relative price changes have no real effects. Conversely, subsidies create non-convexities in consumer budget constraints at the endowment point that can lead to multiple equilibrium outcomes. Shoven (1974) avoids this problems by assuming that there are no subsidies, while another solution is to make all the endowments non-taxed goods. The following analysis assumes consumption is not driven to the endowment point for any consumer, and there are no multiple equilibria when subsidies are included. For the most part, taxes are the main distortions in the analysis.
12. This is also referred to as a 'balanced equilibrium'.
13. Foster and Sonnenschein (1970) show that multiple equilibrium outcomes are possible in tax distorted economies, and they cannot be ruled out by adopting homogeneous utility functions when there are more than two goods. This is examined in Section 2.2.3.
14. Recall that with specific taxes (and subsidies) $dp_i = dq_i \ \forall_i$.

15. Equation (2.7) can be obtained by solving the lump-sum transfers using (2.4) and then substituting them into the private sector budget constraint which becomes:

$$(p + t)x = (p + t)\bar{x} + py + pz + t(y + z) - R.$$

After totally differentiating this constraint (holding $\bar{x}$ constant), we have:

$$(p + t)\,dx + x(dp + dt) = \bar{x}(dp + dt) + p\,dy + y\,dp$$
$$+ p\,dz + z\,dp + (y + z)\,dt + t(dy + dz) - dR.$$

Then the dollar change in utility in (2.1) and the first-order conditions for price-taking firms (with $p\,dy = 0$) are used to write the welfare change, as:

$$\frac{dW}{\beta} = (\bar{x} - x + y + z)(dp + dt) + p\,dz + t(dy + dz) - dR.$$

Equation (2.7) is obtained by using the market clearing conditions $\bar{x}_i + y_i + z_i = x_i \; \forall_i$.

16. We assume domestic consumers receive no utility from foreign aid payments. This allows us to compute surplus revenue in the compensated equilibrium before it is returned to the private economy. It is a hypothetical exercise that separates the efficiency and equity effects of policy changes. If surplus revenue is paid as foreign aid then changes in domestic utility would have to be reversed when the surplus is redirected back to the private economy.

17. If the government wants to convert efficiency gains from policy changes into Pareto improvements it will choose the transfer shares to raise the real income of every consumer.

18. Harberger also includes changes in foreign prices to account for terms of trade effects when there are internationally traded goods.

19. It is clear from Figure 2.2 that the commodity tax change is a 'substitution effect only' problem because it moves the full equilibrium outcome around the PPF from A to A′, while in Figure 2.3 it is clear how the shadow price of good 1 is an 'income and substitution effect' problem because it shifts the PPF up in full equilibrium.

20. This is the case when the government uses the same production technologies as private firms. But if the government uses different technologies, which is likely due to the different incentives faced by public firms, public sector projects become 'income and substitution effect' problems.

21. If shadow prices are used to evaluate public sector projects the goods are endowed on the government, but if they are used to evaluate private sector projects, the goods are endowed on consumers since they collect the sales revenue. This distinction matters when the government balances its budget with distorting taxes because the revenue transfers determine the change in tax inefficiency. Revenue transfers with distorting taxes are examined in Chapter 6.

22. The shadow price in (2.8) can be written as:

$$S_k = p_k + t_k + t_k \frac{\partial y_k}{\partial z_k} + \sum_{i \neq k} t_i \frac{\partial x_i}{\partial z_k}.$$

From the market clearing condition, we have: $\partial x_k / \partial z_k = 1 + \partial y_k / \partial z_k$, where this makes the shadow price: $S_k = q_k(\partial x_k / \partial z_k) - p_k(\partial y_k / \partial z_k) + \sum_{i \neq k} t_i(\partial x_i / \partial z_k)$. A PE analysis ignores effects in related markets in the last term.

23. Dréze and Stern (1990) point out that it is misleading to evaluate the welfare effects of government policy by measuring its impact on the government budget. This is a valid criticism when welfare effects are measured as dollar changes in utility. But, as demonstrated below in Section 2.2.2, it is entirely appropriate to measure the welfare effects of government policy by its impact on the budget surplus in the compensated equilibrium. Once the government makes compensating transfers to offset the effects of its policy changes on the private sector, potential gains will be isolated as surplus government revenue, and potential losses as budget deficits.

24. In Chapter 6, the revenue transfers will be used to determine the change in tax inefficiency when the government balances it budget with distorting taxes.

25. Once again, $(h) + (i) = -(j)$ with a specific subsidy.

26. When prices change endogenously to clear markets the CVs will sum to zero for lump-sum redistributions of income between consumers. This avoids the problem isolated in the 'Boadway (1974) paradox' illustrated in Figure 1.21.

27. Bruce and Harris, Diewert, Dixit (1975), and Kawamata (1974) use a similar welfare decomposition. They do not refer to the coefficient that isolates the income effects as the shadow value of government revenue. Dréze and Stern (1990) derive the shadow value of government revenue without considering its role in applied welfare analysis. In Chapter 3 the distributional effects will be isolated by decomposing the shadow value of goverment revenue over consumers.

28. These revenue transfers are examined in detail in Chapter 3 where distributional effects are examined.

29. In distorted markets there may be multiple equilibria where $\hat{\pi}^S = \pi^S = 0$. To find the social optimum we use second-order conditions to confirm the necessary condition is satisfied globally, rather than locally. For incremental policy changes, however, we can identify potential gains with $\hat{\pi}^S > 0$ by using $\pi^S > 0$ when $S_R > 0$.

30. When reference is made to a unit of revenue as a dollar it is in fact a unit of good 0 the numeraire good. They are synonymous if units of good 0 are normalized to make its market price a dollar.

31. This is derived as proposition 8 in Sieper.

32. Recall from Table 2.1 that the unmarked derivatives here are functions of the exogenous variables (z, t, g, R).

33. Since good 0 is numeraire its price is fixed at unity, and by Walras Law all $N + 1$ markets clear when N of them clear.

34. These are obtained using the market clearing condition for each good i.

35. When the lump-sum transfers are solved using the government budget constraint, consumer income is: $I = q\bar{x} + py + T + pz = px + tx$, and the Slutsky decomposition for each good i, is:

$$\frac{\partial \hat{x}_i(q)}{\partial q_j} = \frac{\partial x_i(q, I)}{\partial q_j} + x_j \frac{\partial x_i(q, I)}{\partial I}.$$

36. Changes in output are determined by changes in consumer demand when producer prices are fixed. By using the market clearing conditions with constant producer prices, the change in tax inefficiency becomes:

$$\theta = \sum_i t_i \frac{\partial y_i}{\partial I} = \sum_i t_i \frac{\partial x_i(q, I)}{\partial I}.$$

When consumers exhaust their income, we have: $\sum_i q_i(\partial x_i(q, I)/\partial I) = 1$, where this makes AIM:

$$1 - \theta = \sum_i (q_i - t_i) \frac{\partial x_i(q, I)}{\partial I} = \sum_i p_i \frac{\partial x_i(q, I)}{\partial I}.$$

37. By solving the endogenous price changes we have $\alpha_{sI} = -\sum_i \delta_{si}(\partial x_i(q, I)/\partial I)$, with δ_{si} being an element of the matrix:

$$|\delta_{si}| = \left| \frac{\partial \hat{x}_i(q)}{\partial q_s} - \frac{\partial y_i(p)}{\partial p_s} \right|^{-1}.$$

38. Hatta uses a Marshallian adjustment process to show the points A and C in Figure 2.8 are stable equilibria since both goods are normal. It is a process, where:

   (1) consumer prices are determined by a bidding process to clear any excess demand for output which cannot change instantaneously; and,
   (2) producers adjust output in the next period if there are differences between the relative producer prices and relative marginal production costs.

39. Detailed workings are provided in Appendix 1.

3

Distributional Effects

The welfare changes in Chapter 2 were obtained using a conventional Harberger analysis, which assumes *a-dollar-is-a-dollar* for consumers and sums their dollar changes in utility. In effect, there is a single (aggregated) consumer in the economy and distributional effects play no role in the analysis. Support for this approach is not based on consumers having the same marginal utility of income, but rather, on the view that aggregate dollar gains represent potential Pareto improvements. While this seems reasonable enough when lump-sum redistribution is possible, it is less satisfactory, however, when income is transferred with distorting taxes. Indeed, there may not be sufficient tax instruments to make the necessary income redistribution for a Pareto improvement. Recall from earlier discussion in Section 1.2.2 that there are essentially two ways of accommodating distributional effects in a cost–benefit analysis. Dréze and Stern (1990) multiply dollar changes in utility for consumers by their subjectively chosen distributional weights and sum them, while Bruce and Harris (1982) and Diewert (1983) invoke the compensation principle to test for Pareto improvements.

When different distributional weights are assigned to consumers it is possible for policy changes with efficiency losses to raise social welfare by *improving* the distribution of income. However, as noted in Chapter 1, there is no objective way to determine these weights, thereby creating potential disagreements between analysts evaluating the same policy change. Since income constrains final consumption demand most analysts use the distribution of measured income as a surrogate for the distribution of utilities over consumers. Even if questions about the validity of using the value of final consumption demand as a proxy for measuring utility are set to one side, it is economic and not measured income that best measures the value of the change in final consumption demand. But economic income is difficult to measure because it includes changes in the values of assets held by consumers and a significant portion of home-produced consumption. Normally they are not included in measured income. Also, there are life-cycle variations in income which consumers smooth by borrowing and saving. They can lead to large differences between consumption and income at any point in time.

Essentially, there is no objective way of choosing the distributional weights for consumers.[1] The approach of Bruce and Harris (1982) and Diewert (1983), which invokes the compensation principle, assumes social welfare increases with Pareto improvements, and explicitly recognizes the transfer policy choices governments must make when they distribute surplus revenue to consumers.[2] This makes choosing the

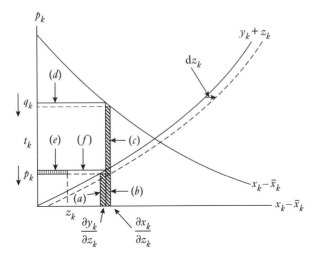

Figure 3.1 *The shadow price of good k*

welfare weights less important. Both approaches will be used in this chapter to compute the shadow prices of goods. The tests for Pareto improvements are extended to allow revenue transfers with distorting taxes in Chapter 6 to make the shadow pricing rules with distributional effects much more useful for applied work.

Before proceeding to a formal analysis the distributional effects are illustrated using a partial equilibrium analysis to derive the shadow price of good k when it is subject to a specific tax. The welfare changes are illustrated in Figure 3.1 where, for simplicity, there is a single (aggregated) consumer (C) and another single (aggregated) shareholder (S) who receives the profit from private production.

Price falls when the public sector (G), which initially produces half the output, sells another unit. Consumer surplus rises by (d) and private profit falls by (f). There is also surplus government revenue of $(a) + (b) + (c) - (e)$ that is transferred to the private economy when the government balances its budget; it is the sales revenue in $(a) + (b)$ and the extra tax revenue in (c), less the fall in public sector profit in (e).[3] If none of this surplus revenue is transferred back to the consumer or the shareholder, the welfare change based on the Dréze and Stern approach, is:

$$dW = \beta^C(d) - \beta^S(f) + \beta^G((a) + (b) + (c) - (e)),$$

where β^h is the distributional weight for $h \in$ C, S, and G. Social welfare may actually fall, despite the aggregate increase in private surplus, if the shareholder weight is relatively large. The increase in aggregate surplus is confirmed by a conventional analysis where the shadow price collapses to $(a) + (b) + (c)$ when agents have the same distributional weights (with $\beta^C = \beta^S = \beta^G = \beta$).[4]

Now consider the approach of Bruce–Harris–Diewert where a transfer policy is chosen to divide the surplus government revenue between the consumer and shareholder to make both of them better off. For example, there is a Pareto improvement from transferring all the surplus revenue to the shareholder if it is larger than the fall in private profit, with $(a) + (b) + (c) - (e) > (f)$, where the change in aggregate welfare becomes:

$$dW = \beta^C(d) + \beta^S((a) + (b) + (c) - (e) - (f)) > 0.$$

However, if there is insufficient surplus revenue to offset the fall in private profit, with $(a)+(b)+(c)-(e) < (f)$, then some of the gain in consumers surplus in (d) will have to be transferred to the shareholder for a Pareto improvement. In most conventional cost–benefit studies the pattern of revenue transfers used to balance the government budget is rarely made explicit. Analysts typically assume that winners can compensate losers if there are positive aggregate dollar gains in utility. But this cannot be guaranteed when prices change endogenously with the revenue transfers in general equilibrium, which is why Bruce and Harris and Diewert combine transfer policy choices with other policy changes to test for Pareto improvements. Moreover, it cannot be guaranteed when revenue transfers are made with distorting taxes due to the changes in tax inefficiency and additional distributional effects. Both these approaches will now be formalized.

3.1 A CONVENTIONAL WELFARE EQUATION WITH DISTRIBUTIONAL EFFECTS

Recall that when changes in social welfare are computed using the individualistic function in (1.22), we have:

$$dW = \sum_h \beta^h \sum_i q_i \, dx_i^h, \qquad (3.1)$$

where $\beta^h = (\partial W / \partial u^h) \lambda^h$ is the distributional weight for each consumer h.[5] As noted earlier, the values assigned to these weights are usually negatively correlated with consumer incomes (where differences in income are used as a proxy for differences in wealth and therefore utility). Each consumer faces the budget constraint:

$$E^h \equiv qx^h = q\bar{x}^h + \rho^h py + L^h \equiv I^h \qquad \forall_h, \qquad (3.2)$$

where ρ_i^h i's h's share of firm i's profits $(p_i y_i)$, with $\sum_h \rho_i^h = 1$. By using these constraints the change in social welfare in (3.1), becomes:

$$dW = \sum_h \beta^h \{DE_p^h \, dp + DE_t^h \, dt + g^h \, dL\}, \qquad (3.3)$$

with $DE_{p_i}^h = \bar{x}_i^h - x_i^h + \rho_i^h y_i$ and $DE_{t_i}^h = \bar{x}_i^h - x_i^h$ being, respectively, the distributional effects on consumer h from changes in the prices and taxes on each good i. Higher prices increase net seller surplus by $DE_{p_i}^h \, dp_i$, while higher taxes reduce net consumer surplus by $DE_{t_i}^h \, dt_i$. The last term in (3.3) is each consumer's share (g^h) of the revenue transfer when the government balances its budget, with $\sum_h g^h = 1$. It is convenient to summarize the distributional effects by defining vectors of *distributional characteristics* similar to those used by Boadway (1976) and Slemrod and Yitzhaki (2001), where the welfare change in (3.3), becomes:

$$\frac{dW}{\bar{\beta}} = dL - DC_p z \, dp + DC_t(\bar{x} - x) \, dt, \tag{3.4}$$

with

$$\bar{\beta} = \sum_h \beta^h g^h \qquad \text{for the transfer shares;}$$

$$DC_{p_i} = \frac{\sum_h \beta^h DE_{p_i}^h}{\bar{\beta}(\bar{x}_i - x_i + y_i)} \qquad \text{for marginal increases in the producer price of good } i;[6]$$

and,

$$DC_{t_i} = \frac{\sum_h \beta^h DE_{t_i}^h}{\bar{\beta}(\bar{x}_i - x_i)} \qquad \text{for marginal increases in the production tax on good } i.[7]$$

Public policy impacts directly on private surplus through changes in producer prices and taxes in the last two terms of (3.4), respectively. There are also indirect effects through the revenue transfers (dL) when the government balances its budget. The revenue transfer shares can affect the change in social welfare in two ways. One is through the vector of transfer shares (g), which distributes the initial change in real income across consumers, while the other is through their impact on prices. When the government distributes surplus revenue to the private economy the extra real income impacts endogenously on prices and transfers private surplus between consumers and the government budget. The distributional effects from choosing the transfer shares are isolated in $\bar{\beta}$, while the distributional effects from the endogenous price changes are captured in the second term of (3.4). If consumers have the same weights, with $\beta^h = \beta \; \forall_h$, the welfare change in (3.4) collapses to the conventional welfare change in (2.5), since $\bar{\beta} = \beta$ and $DC_{p_i} = DC_{t_i} = 1 \; \forall_i$.

The lump-sum transfers in (3.4) are solved using the government budget constraint in (2.4), as:

$$dL = dT + p \, dz + z \, dp - dR. \tag{3.5}$$

After they are substituted into (3.4) the conventional welfare equation with distributional effects, is:

$$\frac{dW}{\bar{\beta}} = \frac{dW}{\beta} + (1 - DC_p)z \, dp - (1 - DC_t)(\bar{x} - x) \, dt. \tag{3.6}$$

It is the conventional welfare equation in (2.7) plus welfare effects from income redistribution in the last two terms. If lump-sum transfers are ruled out, distorting taxes must be used to balance the government budget, and the tax changes are solved using (3.5) with $dL = 0$. This will be examined later in Chapter 6 where revised shadow prices are computed to account for changes in tax inefficiency.

3.2 MEASURING DISTRIBUTIONAL EFFECTS—THE DRÉZE–STERN APPROACH

If the distributional effects for a policy change are deemed socially *desirable* they may, in some circumstances, be used to justify efficiency losses. Alternatively, if they are deemed *undesirable*, the policy change may be rejected when it has efficiency gains. Clearly, the final decision whether to accept or reject policies on these grounds will depend crucially on the distributional weights assigned to consumers. This can be demonstrated by deriving shadow prices of goods with distributional effects and comparing them to the conventional Harberger shadow prices in Chapter 2.

3.2.1 Shadow Prices

When a unit of good k is endowed on the public sector the change in social welfare is obtained from the conventional welfare equation in (3.6), as:

$$\bar{S}_k = \frac{dW}{dz_k}\frac{1}{\bar{\beta}} = S_k + (1 - DC_p)z\frac{\partial p}{\partial z_k}, \tag{3.7}$$

where distributional effects from the revenue transfers $(\partial L/\partial z_k = S_k + z(\partial p/\partial z_k))$ are included in $\bar{\beta}$, and for the price changes $(-z(\partial p/\partial z_k) = (\bar{x} - x + y)(\partial p/\partial z_k))$ in the vector of distributional characteristics DC_p. Consider the partial equilibrium example illustrated in Figure 3.1 with many consumers and firms in the market for good k. When the revenue transfer, $(a) + (b) + (c) - (e)$, and the net increase in private surplus, $(e) = (d) - (f)$, are weighted by distributional characteristics, we have:

$$\frac{dW}{dz_k} = \bar{\beta}((a) + (b) + (c) - (e)) + \bar{\beta}\,DC_{P_k}(e).$$

This collapses to the conventional Harberger shadow price in (2.8) when consumers have the same welfare weights (since $DC_{P_k} = 1$ and $\bar{\beta} = \beta$). There are a number of reasons why analysts are reluctant to estimate the shadow prices in (3.7). First, the informational requirements are considerable, and for most studies are too costly to obtain since data is required for individual consumer demands and shareholdings in every market. Also, the subjectively chosen weights can be manipulated for political reasons to justify policies that may not be in the best interest of society at large. Indeed, aid agencies are reluctant to finance projects in developing countries that can only be justified by distributional effects. Many of these countries do not have sufficient national income to sacrifice to income redistribution. Instead, they are encouraged to undertake policy changes that will expand national income. If policies with efficiency gains have significant *adverse* distributional effects they may not be undertaken. In any case, it may be more appropriate to deal with income redistribution separately through social security and other transfer payments than through individual projects. This has the advantage of reducing rent-seeking activities that seek to influence individual policy reforms on distributional grounds. Before proceeding to look at the welfare tests for Pareto improvements we first isolate the efficiency effects from policy changes. In the final analysis they will generate the changes in real income that ultimately impact on the welfare of consumers.

3.2.2 Efficiency Effects

In the compensated equilibrium the government makes revenue transfers to offset any distributional effects from its policy changes (so that $du^h = 0 \; \forall_h$). Thus, compensated shadow prices are the same as those derived previously in Chapter 2. Recall how they measure surplus revenue the government can generate after compensating consumers for the effects of a policy change. The compensating transfers for extra output of good k are solved using (3.3), with $dW = 0$, as:

$$g^h \frac{d\hat{L}}{dz_k} = -DE_p^h \frac{\partial \hat{p}}{\partial z_k} \qquad \forall_h. \tag{3.8}$$

Since these transfers hold the real income of every consumer constant the distributional effects must be captured in the shadow value of government revenue which, by the generalized Hatta decomposition, isolates income effects. The impact of transfer policy choices on the shadow value of government revenue is examined next as a way to identify Pareto improvements.

3.3 IDENTIFYING PARETO IMPROVEMENTS—THE BRUCE–HARRIS–DIEWERT APPROACH

While revenue transfers in a conventional Harberger analysis change endogenously to balance the government budget, the vector of transfer shares is an exogenous policy decision. The choice, however, is rarely made explicit on the grounds that aggregate welfare gains are a signal that winners can compensate losers. There are two reasons why this view may be misplaced. First, governments rarely make lump-sum transfers, and their ability to choose the pattern of revenue transfers across consumers may be restricted when they use distorting taxes. Second, aggregate dollar gains may not provide sufficient revenue for winners to compensate losers when producer prices change endogenously with the revenue transfers. That is why the Bruce–Harris–Diewert welfare tests for strict Pareto improvements make the transfer policy choices explicit. Their approach will be implemented here by using a generalized Hatta decomposition to separate the income effects in the shadow price of good k in (3.7).

3.3.1 Income Effects and the Shadow Value of Government Revenue

Since equilibrium outcomes are functions of the exogenous policy variables z, t, g, and R, we can write the indirect utility function for each consumer, as $v^h(z, t, g, R)$, where the individualistic social welfare function in (1.22) becomes:

$$W = W(v^1(z, t, g, R), \ldots, v^H(z, t, g, R)). \tag{3.9}$$

There are an infinite number of ways the government can distribute surplus revenue to consumers in g, and these choices affect the equilibrium outcomes when consumers have different marginal propensities to consume income. The change in foreign aid payments that would offset the welfare effects of endowing another unit of good k on the economy can be solved using the social welfare function in (3.9), as:

$$dW = \sum_h \beta^h (S_k^h \, d\hat{z}_k - S_R^h \, d\hat{R}) = 0, \tag{3.10}$$

where for each consumer h, $S_k^h = (\partial v^h / \partial z_k) / \lambda^h$ is the personal shadow price of good k, and $S_R^h = -(\partial v^h / \partial R) / \lambda^h$ their personal shadow value of government revenue.[8] Since the compensating transfers hold the utility of every consumer constant, we must have $S_k^h \, d\hat{z}_k - S_R^h \, d\hat{R} = 0 \; \forall_h$, where this provides a personalized Hatta decomposition, of:

$$S_k^h = S_R^h \hat{S}_k \qquad \forall_h, \tag{3.11}$$

with $\hat{S}_k = d\hat{R} / dz_k$ being the aggregate efficiency gain. When the government distributes the surplus revenue ($\hat{S}_k$) to consumers their personal shadow value of government revenue (S_R^h) converts it into utility. The final change in utility for each consumer (S_k^h) is determined by (a) their share (g^h) of the aggregate efficiency gain, and (b) the distributional effects from the endogenous price changes. This is confirmed by decomposing the personal shadow value of government revenue for each consumer h, as:

$$S_R^h = S_R \left\{ g^h + \sum_s (DE_s^h + g^h z_s) \alpha_{sI} \right\}, \qquad [9] \tag{3.12}$$

where α_{sI} is the change in producer price s due to income effects.[10] The first term inside the brackets is h's share of the revenue transfers, while the second term is the distributional effects from the endogenous price changes that accompany these transfers. Since the price changes transfer surplus between consumers they are purely distributional, with $\sum_h (DE_s^h + g^h z_s) \alpha_{sI} = 0 \; \forall_s$.[11] Thus, giving consumers an equal share of the surplus revenue (with $g^h = \bar{g} \; \forall_h$) will not guarantee $S_R^h > 0$. Indeed, if the price changes reduce surplus for some consumers by more than their share of the revenue transfer (with $\sum_s (DE_s^h + g^h z_s) \alpha_{sI} < \bar{g}$) then $S_R^h < 0$. These consumers are made worse off by efficiency gains unless the transfers are personalized to make $S_R^h > 0$.

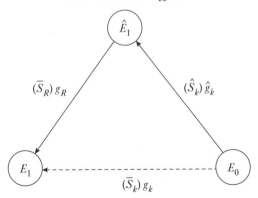

Figure 3.2 *Lump-sum transfers for* dz_k

At this point it is important to note that there are three sets of personalized lump-sum transfers in the welfare decomposition in (3.10), and they are summarized in the flow chart in Figure 3.2. The policy change (dz_k) moves the economy from the initial equilibrium at E_0 to the final equilibrium at E_1, where the actual welfare change ($\bar{S}_k = \sum_h \beta^h S_k^h / \bar{\beta}$) will depend on the vector of (actual) transfer shares (g_k) the government uses to balance its budget. Two further sets of revenue transfers are used to separate the income and substitution effects in the actual welfare change ($\bar{S}_k$). Compensating transfers ($\hat{g}_k$) isolate the efficiency gain ($\hat{S}_k$) in the compensated equilibrium at $\hat{E}_1$, and they are a function of the policy change (dz_k) since consumers have different substitution effects. Once this surplus revenue ($\hat{S}_k$) is transferred to consumers it takes them to the final equilibrium at E_1, where the transfer shares (g_R) determine the distributional effects from the policy change. Thus, the actual transfer shares (g_k) are a combination of the compensating transfer shares ($\hat{g}_k$), which are project specific, and the surplus revenue transfer shares (g_R) that determine the shadow value of government revenue ($\bar{S}_R = \sum_h \beta^h S_R^h / \bar{\beta}$).

If the transfer shares (g_R) are chosen to make the personal shadow value of government revenue in (3.12) positive for every consumer (with $S_R^h > 0\ \forall_h$), then there are strict Pareto improvements (in the absence of Foster–Sonnenschein effects) whenever policy changes have efficiency gains ($\hat{S}_k > 0$).[12] This is the basis for the following welfare test in Bruce and Harris:

Theorem. *In the absence of local Foster–Sonnenschein effects (LFSE), the necessary and sufficient condition for a welfare gain from any marginal policy change k in an economy with heterogeneous consumers and a government who balances its budget using lump-sum transfers is* $\hat{S}_R > 0$.

Proof. By ruling out LFSE we have $S_R > 0$, and by choosing personalized lump-sum transfers to make $g^h + \sum_s (DE_s^h + g^h z_s) \alpha_{sI} > 0\ \forall_h$, the shadow value of government revenue in (3.12) is positive for every consumer. Thus, from (3.11), there are strict Pareto improvements (with $S_k^h > 0\ \forall_h$) whenever $\hat{S}_k > 0$. □

It is clear from the decompositions in (3.11) and (3.12) how the transfer and other policy changes are combined in this test. The welfare test for strict Pareto improvements in Diewert is slightly more general because it does not rule out local Foster–Sonnenschein effects. Indeed, by allowing consumers to have a negative shadow value of government revenue, it is possible for policy changes with efficiency losses to have strict Pareto improvements. An example might be a radial tax increase that moves consumers from low to high utility outcomes in the presence of multiple equilibria.[13] However, once Foster–Sonnenschein effects are ruled out the welfare test in Diewert also requires efficiency gains. When using a conventional Harberger analysis in following chapters these effects will be ruled out by assumption. Thus, when policy changes have efficiency gains the positive aggregate dollar gains in utility will also be Pareto improvements.

3.3.2 The Welfare Effects from a Lump-sum Redistribution of Income

There are no efficiency gains from a lump-sum redistribution of income (in the absence of Foster–Sonnenschein effects). Any welfare effects must be due solely to differences in the distributional weights assigned to consumers. This can be demonstrated by marginally adjusting the pattern of revenue transfers, with $\sum_h dg^h L = 0$, where the change in social welfare can be decomposed using the SWF in (3.9), as:

$$dW = \sum_h \beta^h (S_g^h \, dg^h - S_R^h \, d\hat{R}^h) = 0,$$

with $S_g^h = S_R^h \hat{S}_g^h$ being the dollar change in utility for each consumer h, and $\hat{S}_g^h = d\hat{R}^h/dg^h$ the compensating variation (CV) that offsets the changes in private surplus. In the absence of LFSE, the CVs must sum to zero, with $\sum_h \hat{S}_g^h = 0$.[14] There are three cases where social welfare is unaffected by a redistribution of income:

1. If consumers have the same distributional weights (with $\beta^h = \beta \; \forall_h$) the welfare change is obtained from (3.3) and (3.5), as:

$$dW = \beta \sum_h (\bar{x}^h - x^h + \rho^h y + g^h z) \frac{\partial p}{\partial g^h} \, dg^h = 0.$$

   Even though endogenous price changes transfer surplus between consumers, there is no welfare change because they sum to zero. The same result also applies for a large (discrete) redistribution of income.
2. When the initial distribution of income is socially optimal (i.e. β optimal) consumers will have the same distributional weights. Thus, social welfare is unaffected by a marginal redistribution of income, with $dW = 0$.

   But this is unlikely to hold for a large (discrete) redistribution due to endogenous changes in the welfare weights.
3. Finally, a marginal redistribution of income will not affect social welfare if the transfers of private surplus due to endogenous price changes are exactly offset by

the income transfer for each consumer. This is confirmed by using (3.3) and (3.4), where:

$$dW = \sum_h \beta^h (\bar{x}^h - x^h + \rho^h y + g^h z) \frac{\partial p}{\partial g^h} dg + \sum_h \beta^h L \, dg^h.$$

The first term isolates the transfers of private surplus due to endogenous price changes, while the second term isolates the income transfers. There is no welfare change when:

$$(\bar{x}^h - x^h + \rho^h y + g^h z) \frac{\partial p}{\partial g^h} dg^h = -L \, dg^h \qquad \forall_h.$$

While this special case is fairly unlikely it does provide insight into the way income redistribution affects social welfare when consumers have different distributional weights. In particular, it highlights the indirect effects of endogenous price changes which can, in some circumstances, undermine or even overturn the increase in income from redistribution for some consumers.

3.4 PROJECT EVALUATION

The role of distributional effects in project evaluation can be demonstrated by using the shadow prices in (3.4) to compute the shadow profit for a project that produces a unit of good 1 using inputs 2 and 3. In the presence of distributional effects, it is:

$$\bar{\pi}^S = \sum_h \beta^h (S_1^h - S_2^h a_{21} - S_1^h a_{31}), \tag{3.13}$$

where a_{i1} is the input–output coefficient for $i \in 2, 3$. If the same pattern of revenue transfers (g_R) is used for each component of the project, the Hatta decomposition in (3.11) allows us to decompose this profit, as:

$$\bar{\pi}^S = \sum_h \beta^h S_R^h (\hat{S}_1 - \hat{S}_2 a_{21} - \hat{S}_3 a_{31}). \tag{3.14}$$

Thus, the income effects will play no role in finding the optimal supply of good 1 in these circumstances. Furthermore, if the revenue transfers are chosen to make $S_R^h > 0 \ \forall_h$, there is a strict Pareto improvement whenever the project is socially profitable, with $\bar{\pi}^S > 0$.

3.5 CONCLUDING REMARKS

It is clear from the analysis in this chapter that distributional effects can significantly increase the computational task in project evaluation. Data is required for the market trades of individual consumers, their shareholdings and their initial wealth. This task is often simplified by amalgamating consumers into groups within prescribed income ranges. But these additional requirements, by themselves, do not justify ignoring distributional effects.

Perhaps a more controversial aspect of measuring them is the need to assign values to the distributional weights in the first place. Dréze and Stern express the view that policy analysts should accept this responsibility and present their findings based on the weights they choose. Boadway argues that the efficiency and equity effects should be reported separately to indicate how the welfare changes are affected by subjectively chosen weights. This latter view is fairly widely supported in applied work and it is common practice to report the welfare measures for different sets of distributional weights.

As noted in earlier discussion there are good practical reasons for separating efficiency and equity effects. In developing countries, international aid agencies are reluctant to accept projects if they are not socially profitable in the absence of distributional effects. In other words, projects that reduce aggregate income but *improve* the distribution of income. When countries have low per-capita income and high unemployment, it is difficult to accept policy reforms or projects with efficiency losses. After all, potential gains can be redistributed through social security transfers if there are adverse distributional effects. In some circumstances though, policy changes that raise aggregate income may not be adopted if distributional effects are deemed sufficiently bad to result in civil unrest, or cannot be undone using social security transfers.

Other analysts argue that the distributional effects should be addressed directly through social security transfers, rather than on a project by project basis. This is especially the case for incremental projects or policy changes. However, in the absence of lump-sum transfers, potential gains cannot be costlessly redistributed to undo equity effects. That is to say, income redistribution is costly and it may, in some circumstances, be more efficient to account for them in project evaluation than to deal with them separately. In any case, if lump-sum transfers are possible, income would be redistributed to equate the distributional weights across consumers in the first place. But this raises the more fundamental issue addressed in Chapter 1 when looking at the second fundamental theorem of welfare economics. In economies that rely on private markets to determine production and consumption choices, secure private property rights to resources are crucial. Gains from trading these rights drives resource allocation, and when the income from resources is redistributed it undermines ownership claims. This applies to redistributions that are the by-product of projects and other policy changes, as well as to direct redistribution policies. Indeed, agents seek compensation for policies that erode their property rights through regulatory takings. These costs are additional to the familiar efficiency costs from using distorting instruments to redistribute income. Some argue property rights emanate from governments and the laws they write, so that they can decide how they should be used. But most societies with democratically elected governments have constitutions that establish the right to life, liberty, and property for each citizen. All other rights emanate from these fundamental rights, and governments are established to protect them. In other words, governments are institutions established by citizens to protect their fundamental rights and not the reverse.

Ultimately, those responsible for making public policy choices will base their final decisions only partially on the way these choices affect social welfare. Private interest also plays an important role. For example, politicians are influenced by votes, particularly in marginal electorates, and by campaign contributions from those who benefit from their policies. This is more likely when beneficiaries are a concentrated political group, while those who bear the costs are a large group with little private incentive to resist the policy choice. Despite these practical realities, the economic assessments made by policy analysts will provide important information to decision-makers and the public at large. It can be used as an important discipline on policy-makers, especially in societies with a free and competitive press.

In following chapters a conventional Harberger analysis is used to evaluate a range of marginal policy changes. When doing so the Bruce–Harris–Diewert approach is adopted by choosing patterns of revenue transfers to make the shadow value of government revenue positive for every consumer. This will make aggregate dollar gains strict Pareto improvements. Occasionally policy changes will be examined using the approach recommended by Dréze–Stern to show how distributional effects are measured. Transfer policy choices are normally pushed into the background of a Harberger analysis because they are lump-sum and can easily be personalized. But in practice, governments balance their budgets with distorting taxes which are likely to restrict the patterns of transfers they can choose. The welfare test for strict Pareto improvements in Bruce and Harris is extended to allow revenue transfers with distorting taxes in Chapter 6.

NOTES

1. Harberger (1968) compares the distributional weights approach to a basic needs approach for including equity effects in a social cost–benefit analysis. The basic needs approach recognizes the external benefits individuals get when others consume more of particular goods and services. For example, most get satisfaction when the hungry consume additional food, the sick are made well, and the illiterate get educated. Indeed, they are willing to pay something to see these things happen. Under a basic needs approach it is not the utility of the recipient that enters the donor's utility function, which is the case for distributional weights. Instead, it is the consumption of particular goods and services by recipients. Harberger provides simple examples where the distributional weights approach leads to, what most people would deem, unacceptable compression in the degree of income inequality. In contrast, the basic needs approach appears to better reflect the issues people talk about when they express concern for those who are less well off than themselves. Also, by isolating equity concerns as social externalities it is a straightforward extension of the conventional welfare analysis. However, social externalities, like distributional weights, are based on subjective estimates that analysts are unlikely to agree on.

2. Coates (2000) recommends a welfare test that ranks policy changes by their ability to achieve a given distributional outcome at lowest social cost. In particular, an efficient policy change by this test is one that Pareto dominates all other feasible policy changes capable of achieving similar distributional effects. It does not have to be efficient in the conventional sense that it generates a potential (compensated) gain. In contrast, the approach of Bruce and Harris, and Diewert makes efficiency gains a necessary condition for welfare improving policy changes, while the ability to undo any distributional effects and convert these gains into Pareto improvements is the sufficient condition. The approach adopted by Coates acknowledges the fact that policy changes with efficiency losses are chosen by governments for their distributional characteristics, so it looks for the most efficiency policy change to achieve these distributional effects. Such policy changes would not pass the welfare test of Bruce and Harris, and Diewert. However, in many circumstances distributional outcomes are not the driving motivation for

the policy changes governments make. Instead, they make reforms to raise national income, and then look for ways to distribute these gains separately through tax policy and social security payments. Indeed, this is what the major international aid agencies do in developing countries that typically do not have the national income to sacrifice to redistribution policies.

3. With a specific tax the loss in tax revenue is (d) is offset by the increase in tax revenue in $(e) + (f)$. Thus, the net change in tax revenue is:

$$(c) + (e) + (f) - (d) = (c).$$

4. For the specific tax $(d) = (e) + (f)$.

5. The distributional weights are assumed positive here, with $\beta^h > 0 \, \forall_h$, but it is feasible that the weights could be negative for some consumers. This is likely when the rich getting richer is deemed socially inequitable. Policy-makers may be concerned that greater inequality erodes social cohesion and should therefore be taken into account in the social welfare function. Indeed, if the rich are getting richer through corruption in public and other institutions, social welfare may be eroded by the fact that people do not have an equal opportunity to create private wealth under the existing rules.

6. The aggregate net supply of good i by consumers and firms is:

$$\sum_h (\bar{x}_i^h - x_i^h + \rho_i^h y_i) \equiv \bar{x}_i - x_i + y_i.$$

7. The aggregate net demand for each good i by consumers is defined as:

$$\sum_h (\bar{x}_i^h - x_i^h) \equiv \bar{x}_i - x_i.$$

8. This change in social welfare can also be written as:

$$dW = \bar{S}_k \, d\hat{z}_k - \bar{S}_R \, d\hat{R} = 0,$$

where $\bar{S}_k = \sum_h \beta^h S_k^h / \bar{\beta}$ and $\bar{S}_R = \sum_h \beta^h S_R^h / \bar{\beta}$ are the conventional shadow prices with distributional effects. They measure, respectively, the change in social welfare from endowing a unit of good k and a unit of surplus revenue R on the economy.

9. The welfare decomposition in (3.11) is confirmed by writing the personal shadow price of good k, as:

$$S_k^h = \hat{S}_k S_R \left\{ g^h + \sum_s (DE_{p_s}^h + g^h z_s) \alpha_{sI} \right\} + \sum_s (DE_{p_s}^h + g^h z_s) \delta_{sk},$$

where $\delta_{sk} = \partial \hat{p}_s / \partial z_k$ is the compensated change in the producer price of each good s due to extra output of good k. Since the compensating transfers offset the changes in private surplus, with $\sum_s (DE_{p_s}^h + g^h z_s) \delta_{sk} = 0 \, \forall_h$, we have from (3.12), that:

$$S_k^h = \hat{S}_k S_R \left\{ g^h + \sum_s (DE_{p_s}^h + g^h z_s) \alpha_{sI} \right\} = \hat{S}_k S_R^h.$$

The conventional (lump-sum) shadow value of government revenue (S_R) defined in (2.14) is derived without distributional effects. It can be obtained here by assigning the same welfare weights to consumers, and noting $\sum_h DE_{p_s}^h = -z_s \, \forall_s$. Thus, the sum of the personal shadow values of government revenue in (3.12) will collapse to S_R.

10. By using the structural decomposition demonstrated in Chapter 2, we have $\alpha_{sI} = -\sum_i \delta_{si} (\partial x_i(q, I) / \partial I)$, with δ_{si} being an element of the matrix:

$$|\delta_{si}| = \left| \frac{\delta \hat{x}_i(q)}{\partial q_s} - \frac{\partial y_i(p)}{\partial p_s} \right|^{-1}.$$

11. By using the market clearing condition for each good s, we have:

$$\sum_h DE_{p_s}^h = -z_s \ \forall_s.$$

12. Foster–Sonnenschein effects are examined in Section 2.2.3.
13. Foster and Sonnenschein (1970) consider stable market clearing mechanisms which rule this case out.
14. The Boadway (1974) paradox is avoided by allowing prices to change endogenously with the compensating transfers. This was examined in Section 1.2.2. If Foster–Sonnenschein effects are not ruled out there can be efficiency effects from a lump-sum redistribution of income.

4

Non-tax Distortions in Markets

It is rare for taxes (and subsidies) to be the only distortions in markets. Governments use price controls, both ceilings and floors, and restrict production with quota. There are also inefficiencies from non-competitive behaviour by sellers and buyers. Sometimes, this is due to government policies that restrict entry into markets, while on other occasions, the barriers to entry arise naturally from fixed and sunk costs. Costs and benefits are external to price in some markets when private property rights to resources are too costly to assign and trade. There may be political constraints, where for example, governments are reluctant to assign private rights to resources they prefer to keep as communal assets. The air space is a resource that everyone uses, but is difficult, if not impossible, to partition between users. Also, non-excludable public goods are underprovided by private producers when they cannot raise sufficient revenue from consumers to cover their costs.

In this chapter, shadow prices of goods are derived in the presence of non-tax distortions. Public goods are examined separately in Chapter 10. A market distortion drives activity away from its socially efficient level. In a single (aggregated) consumer economy there are no distributional effects to consider, so that the efficient allocation of resources will maximize the potential welfare gains. For simplicity, these gains are defined for outcomes free of transaction costs. In some circumstances, however, they are necessary costs of trade that need to be taken into account. For example, externalities arise when it is too costly to assign and trade private property rights over resources like the air and waterways. An efficient outcome will maximize the net consumption benefits by choosing the least costly property right allocations, and this crucially depends on the form these costs take, that is, whether they are one-off fixed costs, or costs that vary with property right trades.

In project evaluation, labour is a major input to public activity, and there are a range of tax and non-tax distortions that impact on labour markets, including minimum wage laws and barriers that restrict the flow of labour between regions. The *shadow wage* is derived in this chapter to identify the welfare effects of these non-tax distortions, and they are compared to the welfare effects of wage taxes. It is also derived in the presence of unemployment using the two-sector model of the labour market in Harris and Todaro (1970). In this model, workers can freely migrate between the two sectors, and unemployed workers get no benefits from leisure or social security payments. The analysis will be extended to include these benefits, and to compare the effects of differential employed costs and wage taxes across geographic regions. If employment costs are the minimum necessary costs of attracting labour to a region, the shadow wage is the market wage in each region (where they differ by the employment costs). In contrast, the shadow wage is a weighted average of the market wages when there are different taxes in each region.

It will be apparent from the analysis in this chapter that welfare effects in the presence of non-tax distortions can be quite different from those arising in the presence of taxes. If distortions restrict resource flows, for example, in the way production quota do, then additional public sector demand or supply may not raise activity in these markets. Instead, it can completely crowd out private trade. Once this happens, the shadow prices of goods as outputs will differ from their shadow prices as inputs, which is not the case when taxes restrict trade.

4.1 PRICE CONTROLS

Many governments intervene in markets to hold relative prices above or below their free-trade levels. While this practice is more common in developing countries, it also occurs elsewhere for a variety of reasons. Price ceilings place caps on consumer prices with the intention of benefiting consumers, particularly those with relatively low incomes. These caps are frequently used to hold down the prices of basic items like sugar, rice, bread, rental rates, electricity, etc. In other markets, price floors are intended to benefit producers and expand domestic production. They are used in agricultural commodity markets like wool, coffee, cocoa, and wheat and in labour markets to set minimum wages. On some occasions, prices are stabilized in markets to reduce the income variability for traders who do not have access to private insurance markets.[1] For example, trade taxes and subsidies were used to remove world price variability from domestic rice prices in Indonesia, while a publicly funded storage scheme was used to stabilize wool prices in Australia. Political considerations are an interesting aspect of price controls, as are comparisons of actual outcomes with the stated political objectives.[2] In fact, many stabilization schemes collapse because producer groups use their political influence to turn them into price support schemes. This was indeed the case for the rice price stabilization scheme in Indonesia and the wool price scheme in Australia. These issues will not be examined here, at least explicitly. Instead, the following analysis will measure the welfare effects of price controls taking the political reasons for them as given.

Price controls are implemented in many different ways, and it is important to capture this in the welfare analysis. In some circumstances, they are set by government decree. For example, rent controls in New York city define upper limits on rents for particular types of rental accommodation. On other occasions, governments produce commodities themselves and set prices below the market-clearing level. This is how sugar and bread were traded in much of the former Soviet Union and Africa. Alternatively, some prices are set by a combination of taxes and subsidies. For example, home-price consumption schemes impose taxes on domestic consumers of exportable goods and use the revenue to pay production subsidies to domestic producers. These schemes were once quite common in agricultural commodity markets in Australia, for example, dairy products and dried fruit.[3] In this chapter, price controls are set by decree, and the analysis of home-price consumption schemes is taken up in Chapter 5 where internationally traded goods are included.

4.1.1 Price Ceilings

For a price cap to be effective, at least one other price in the economy has to be pegged. If not, all other N prices will change endogenously to clear their markets, and by Walras Law, that will clear the remaining market. The price cap binds if it holds the price of some good k below its market clearing level relative to good 0 (the numeraire good). By doing so, it creates an excess demand which must be rationed in some way other than through a higher price. In the final analysis, the welfare effects of the price cap will crucially depend on the rationing mechanisms used, and additional rationing costs will reduce welfare by wasting what otherwise would have been private surplus.

Black market trades are frequently observed in markets with price caps, as are rent-seeking activities where consumers outlay time and other resources trying to procure some of the limited supply. On other occasions, excess demand is rationed by consumption vouchers. If they are non-tradeable, surplus is wasted when the goods are consumed by those with the lowest valuations. Rent-seeking costs are not included in the following analysis, and black market trade is ruled out by assuming that there are large penalties and no policing costs. Clearly, a more realistic treatment would have non-identical consumers, and would model the rationing mechanisms explicitly. The following analysis will provide a starting point for these extensions.

Based on these assumptions, the price cap is like a tax when the revenue is returned as a lump-sum transfer to consumers. This is illustrated for good k in Figure 4.1, where the welfare loss is the cross-lined area. It measures the foregone surplus on trade where

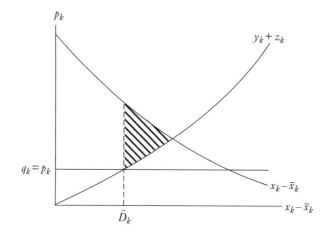

Figure 4.1 *A price cap*

marginal consumption benefits exceed marginal cost. The loss rises when additional rationing costs waste some of the remaining private surplus.

As noted in earlier discussion, the welfare effects of extra public production of this good, and the cross-effects from changes in other markets, will be different under the price cap than under a tax that restricts activity to the same initial level ($\bar{D}_k$). Since the price cap creates excess demand, it places a side constraint on each consumer which is captured in their first-order condition for the good, where:

$$\frac{\partial u^h}{\partial x_k^h}\frac{1}{\lambda^h} = q_k + \frac{\delta_k^h}{\lambda^h} = \bar{q}_k \qquad \forall_h,^4 \tag{4.1}$$

with δ_k^h/λ^h being the extra benefit (measured in units of the numeraire good 0) from marginally relaxing the constraint on the demand for good k. When this cap binds, with $\delta_k^h > 0 \; \forall_h$, the conventional welfare equation in (2.7) becomes:

$$\frac{dW}{\beta} = p\,dz + t(dy + dz) + \frac{\delta_k}{\lambda}\,dx_k, \tag{4.2}$$

with δ_k/λ and dx_k being, respectively, the vector of normalized constraint multipliers and the vector of changes in demands, for consumers. The conventional shadow price of good k is obtained from (4.2), as:

$$S_k = \bar{p}_k + \frac{\partial T}{\partial z_k} + \frac{\delta_k}{\lambda}\frac{\partial x_k}{\partial z_k}, \tag{4.3}$$

where $\bar{p}_k$ is the capped producer price.

It is illustrated in Figure 4.2 in the presence of a production tax by assuming consumers have the same marginal valuation for good k. Since extra public output relaxes

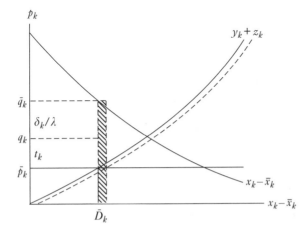

Figure 4.2 *The shadow price with a price cap*

the constraint on consumer demand without changing the producer price, social welfare rises by the extra consumption benefits ($\bar{q}_k$); they are equal to the sales revenue ($\bar{p}_k$) plus the tax (t_k) and the gain from relaxing the constraint on demand (δ_k/λ), with $\bar{q}_k = \bar{p}_k + t_k + \delta_k/\lambda$. Private supply cannot change unless price changes in other markets affect the input costs. In the absence of these cross-price effects, extra public output is matched by a rise in private demand (with $\partial x_k/\partial z_k = 1$), where the shadow price becomes:

$$S_k = q_k + \frac{\delta_k}{\lambda} = \bar{q}_k > \bar{p}_k.$$

The consumer price $\bar{q}_k$ is a dollar measure of the marginal consumption benefits for the good when supply is constrained by a cap on the producer price.

Whenever policy changes in other markets impact on good k the welfare effects are determined solely by changes in private production. Small changes in private demand for good k will have no welfare effects because they do nothing to alleviate the constraint on supply. Hines (1999) considers these cross-effects in the presence of a price cap by raising the tax on a substitute good. To replicate the analysis let goods d and k be gross substitutes (and assume $t_k = 0$). The welfare effect from marginally raising a tax on good d is obtained from (4.2), as:

$$\frac{dW}{dt_d}\frac{1}{\beta} = \frac{\partial T}{\partial t_d} + \frac{\delta_k}{\lambda}\frac{\partial x_k}{\partial t_d}. \tag{4.4}$$

The welfare change in the market for good k is illustrated in Figure 4.3. Cross-effects raise supply in Figure 4.3(a), while they raise demand in Figure 4.3(b). To simplify the analysis we once again assume consumers have the same marginal valuation for the good (with $\bar{q}_k^h = \bar{q}_k \; \forall_h$).

When resources flow from good d to good k the extra output relaxes the constraint on consumer demand (with $\partial y_k/\partial z_k = \partial x_k/\partial z_k$). Social welfare rises by the net consumption gain in the cross-lined area of Figure 4.3(a) (δ_k/λ); it is the welfare gain from satisfying some of the excess demand for good k under the price cap. However, there are no welfare effects from small changes in demand for good k. Consider the increase in demand in Figure 4.3(b) where it is tempting to add area (a) to the welfare loss from the price cap. But it should not be because there is no change in activity.

Indeed, demand can only change in the market for good k when supply changes, and area (a) is already captured as a welfare change in markets where activity is affected by the higher tax on good d.

4.1.2 Price Floors and the Shadow Wage

Market prices are occasionally held above their market clearing levels in an attempt to benefit suppliers. As noted earlier, price floors can be implemented by a combination of policy instruments, but the analysis here will be restricted to floors that are

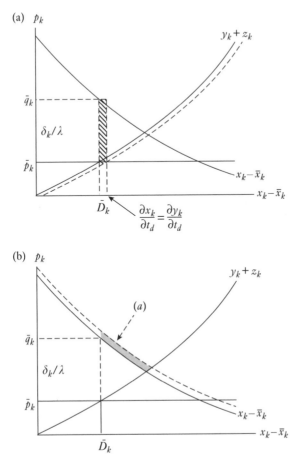

Figure 4.3 *Cross-effects from raising the tax on another good (d)*

established by government decree. Perhaps the most widely recognized example is a minimum wage law that sets the lower bound on wages and salaries paid to workers in a specified segment of the labour market. Minimum wages are set across a large number of industries in Australia, and it has important consequences for the social cost of employment. The shadow wage, which plays an important role in policy evaluation, depends crucially on the institutional arrangements that apply in the labour market, and they include:

1. segmentation across regions where workers with the same skills receive different wages. These may be due to differences in non-pecuniary and pecuniary costs, or different minimum wages;
2. the ability of workers to migrate between segments of the labour market; and,
3. the level of unemployment benefits.

The analysis begins by assuming there is a single labour market in the economy with identical workers. Households divide a fixed endowment of time ($\bar{x}_n$) between leisure (x_n) and labour supply ($\bar{x}_n - x_n$), while firms—both private and public—employ labour, with $y_n < 0$ and $z_n < 0$, respectively. In the presence of a minimum wage and no unemployment benefits, there is an excess supply of labour which restricts the labour–leisure choice. When consumers optimally choose a consumption bundle in the presence of the minimum wage, their marginal valuation for leisure is:

$$\frac{\partial u^h}{\partial x_n^h} \frac{1}{\lambda_h} = q_n - \frac{\delta_n^h}{\lambda^h} = \bar{q}_n,^5 \tag{4.5}$$

where δ_n^h / λ^h is the normalized Kuhn–Tucker multiplier on the labour supply constraint ($\bar{n}^h$). If it binds (with $\delta_n^h / \lambda^h > 0 \ \forall_h$) the conventional welfare equation becomes:

$$\frac{dW}{\beta} = p \, dz + t \, dx - \frac{\delta_n}{\lambda} \, dx_n, \tag{4.6}$$

with δ_n / λ and dx_n being, respectively, the vector of normalized constraint multipliers and the vector of changes in leisure, for consumers. The shadow wage is obtained from (4.6) by marginally reducing the public sector demand for labour, where:

$$S_n = \bar{p}_n + \left(t_n - \frac{\delta_n}{\lambda}\right) \frac{\partial x_n}{\partial z_n} + \sum_{i \neq n} t_i \frac{\partial x_i}{\partial z_n}. \tag{4.7}$$

Welfare effects in the labour market are illustrated in Figure 4.4, where private demand for labour is unaffected by the reduction in public demand (with $\partial y_n / \partial z_n = 0$) and consumers have the same marginal valuation for leisure (with $\bar{q}_k^h = \bar{q}_k \ \forall_h$).[6]

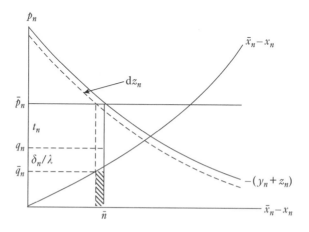

Figure 4.4 *The shadow wage*

As public demand contracts there is an increase in the consumption of leisure (with $\partial x_n/\partial z_n = 1$), where in the absence of cross-effects in related markets, the shadow wage in (4.7) becomes:

$$S_n = q_n - \frac{\delta_n}{\lambda} = \bar{q}_n < \bar{p}_n. \tag{4.8}$$

It measures the dollar value of the benefits consumers get from extra leisure ($\bar{q}_n$). Once private demand for labour is fixed by the minimum wage, public demand impacts solely on the labour–leisure choice. Thus, the marginal social cost of employing labour in the public sector is the opportunity cost of time as leisure ($\bar{q}_n$), which is lower than the minimum wage ($\bar{p}_n$).

However, in a general equilibrium setting, the change in leisure can impact on prices in other markets, where this can in turn impact on private employment. Most derivations of the shadow wage ignore these cross-effects. For example, see the recommendations in the OECD manual of Little and Mirrlees (1969) and the UNIDO guidelines of Dasgupta, Marglin, and Sen (1972), and the derivations in Boadway and Wildasin (1984). If cross-effects change private demand for labour (with $\partial y_n/\partial z_n \neq 0$) the shadow wage becomes:

$$S_n = \bar{q}_n \frac{\partial x_n}{\partial z_n} - \bar{p}_n \frac{\partial y_n}{\partial z_n}.^7 \tag{4.9}$$

Now it exceeds the opportunity cost of supplying labour ($\bar{q}_n$) due to the higher marginal product of labour ($\bar{p}_n$). The welfare changes are illustrated in Figure 4.5 where the shadow wage is the familiar weighted sum of the values of the changes in private activity.

The portion of the extra labour supply absorbed in private employment generates output valued at $\bar{p}_n$ in the shaded rectangle, while the remaining portion consumed as

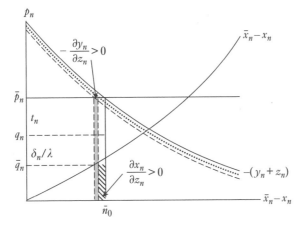

Figure 4.5 *The shadow wage*

leisure generates consumption benefits valued at $\bar{q}_n$ in the smaller cross-lined rectangle. When private employment rises (with $-\partial y_n/\partial z_n > 0$), the shadow wage in (4.9) exceeds the shadow wage in (4.8) by the value of the net marginal product of labour, that is, $-(\bar{p}_n - \bar{q}_n)\partial y_n/\partial z_n > 0$.

Any welfare effects in the labour market that are due to policy changes elsewhere can be demonstrated by computing the shadow price of a good k in the presence of the minimum wage, where:

$$S_k = p_k + \sum_{i \neq n} t_i \frac{\partial x_i}{\partial z_k} + \left(t_n - \frac{\delta_n}{\lambda}\right)\frac{\partial x_n}{\partial z_k}. \tag{4.10}$$

The last term is the welfare loss from reducing employment and increasing leisure (with $-\partial y_n/\partial z_k = \partial x_n/\partial z_k > 0$); it is illustrated in Figure 4.6 as the cross-lined area. The fall in employment exacerbates the welfare loss from the minimum wage.

A number of studies extend the analysis by including involuntary unemployment, migration costs, and differential non-pecuniary benefits (or costs) across geographic regions. Srinivasan and Bhagwati (1978) use the Harris and Todaro model to determine the shadow wage in the presence of unemployment. In this model, a fixed supply of homogeneous labour ($\bar{x}_n$) can migrate freely between a protected sector where workers are paid a minimum wage ($\bar{p}_{nP}$), and an unprotected sector that pays a market clearing wage (p_{nU}), with $\bar{p}_{nP} > p_{nU}$. Each worker in the protected sector has the same probability (π) of being employed at the minimum wage, of

$$\pi = \frac{y_{nP} + z_{nP}}{y_{nP} + z_{nP} - U_E},$$

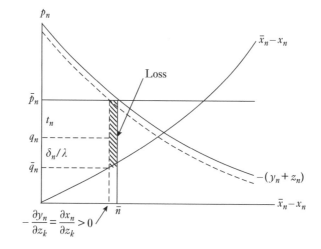

Figure 4.6 *Cross-market effects in the labour market*

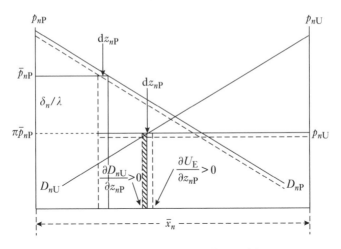

Figure 4.7 *The Harris–Todaro model*

where U_E is unemployment. If workers are risk neutral they migrate to the protected sector (as unemployed workers) until the wage in the unprotected sector rises to the expected minimum wage (with $\pi \bar{p}_{nP} = p_{nU}$). Unemployed workers receive no marginal consumption benefits from leisure here so that the opportunity cost of drawing workers from the pool of unemployment is zero. On this basis, the shadow wage is determined solely by changes in employment in each sector.

The shadow wage in the protected sector is illustrated in Figure 4.7 in the absence of taxes. After the government marginally reduces its demand for protected sector labour, there is an increase in labour supply to the private market. None of this labour is employed in the protected sector because the minimum wage holds private demand for labour constant. Instead, there is a lower probability of employment in the protected sector so workers move to the unprotected sector and the pool of unemployment. The shadow wage is the cross-lined rectangle in Figure 4.7; it is the value of the extra output in the unprotected sector. There is no welfare gain from extra unemployment due to the absence of unemployment benefits and leisure. The shadow wage in the unprotected sector is exactly the same because labour is always drawn from unemployment and leisure when private demand for protected labour is fixed by the minimum wage.

These results can be formalized by writing the market clearing condition in the labour market, as:

$$\bar{x}_n = U_E + D_{nP} + D_{nU},$$

where $D_{nP} = -y_{nP} - z_{nP}$ is the summed private and public demand for labour in the protected sector, and $D_{nU} = -y_{nU} - z_{nU}$ the summed private and public demand for labour in the unprotected sector. There is no leisure in this model (with $x_n^h = 0 \ \forall_h$). With a binding minimum wage in the protected sector, the conventional welfare equation becomes:

$$\frac{dW}{\beta} = p \, dz + t \, dx - p_{nU} \, dU_E + \frac{\delta_{nP}}{\lambda} \, dD_{nP},^8 \tag{4.11}$$

where δ_{nP}/λ and dD_{nP} are, respectively, vectors of normalized constraint multipliers and changes in employment in the protected sector for consumers. The shadow wage for protected sector labour is obtained from (4.11) by marginally reducing public demand, where in the absence of taxes, we have:

$$S_{nP} = \bar{p}_{nP} - \frac{\delta_{nP}}{\lambda} \frac{\partial D_{nP}}{\partial z_{nP}} - p_{nU} \frac{\partial U_E}{\partial z_{nP}}. \tag{4.12}$$

Since the normalized constraint multiplier is the marginal social gain from moving labour into the protected sector it measures the wage premium, with $\delta_{nP}/\lambda = \bar{p}_{nP} - p_{nU}$. Thus, in the absence of changes in private demand for labour in the protected sector ($\partial D_{nP}/\partial z_{nP} = 1$), the shadow wage in (4.12) simplifies to:

$$S_{nP} = p_{nU} \left(1 - \frac{\partial U_E}{\partial z_{nP}} \right) < p_{nU}.^9$$

It is the cross-lined rectangle in Figure 4.7. The shadow wage in the unprotected sector is exactly the same, and is obtained from (4.11) in a similar fashion, as:

$$S_{nU} = p_{nU} - \frac{\delta_{nP}}{\lambda} \frac{\partial D_{nP}}{\partial z_{nU}} - p_{nU} \frac{\partial U_E}{\partial z_{nU}}. \tag{4.13}$$

In the absence of changes in private demand for protected labour, we have $S_{nU} = S_{nP}$. When a public project employs labour it comes from unemployment and the unprotected sector which have the same expected wage.

Boadway and Bruce (1984) extend the analysis of Srinivasan and Bhagwati by including leisure for the unemployed. These benefits encourage more labour to migrate from the unprotected sector into unemployment. And this reduces the welfare gain from relaxing the constraint on labour supply to the protected sector (δ_{nP}/λ) by driving up the unprotected sector wage. It is higher than the expected wage in the protected sector by the marginal consumption benefits from leisure, with $p_{nU} > \pi \bar{p}_{nP}.^{10}$ Unemployed workers are willing to accept a lower expected wage in the protected sector, where the shadow wage becomes:

$$S_{nP} = p_{nU} - \pi \bar{p}_{nP} \frac{\partial U_E}{\partial z_{nP}} < p_{nU}.$$

These derivations of the shadow wage confirm recommendations made in the OECD manual by Little and Mirrlees (1969). In labour markets segmented by minimum wage laws the shadow wage is the market wage for unprotected labour; that is, the sector that provides all the labour for public projects in these circumstances. This important and useful result is extended in a number of ways. First, by allowing private demand

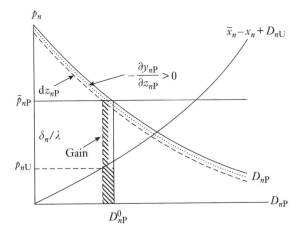

Figure 4.8 *The shadow wage in a two sector model*

for protected sector labour to change endogenously with producer prices, and then by introducing differential employment costs and taxes.

1. *Endogenous Changes in Protected Sector Labour Demand.* While a minimum wage fixes the price of labour in the protected sector, it cannot stop other prices changing. Indeed, a public sector project that employs labour will drive up the wage in the unprotected sector, and by moving resources between markets, will cause product prices to change endogenously. If these price changes affect the private demand for protected sector labour the shadow wage is no longer the market wage in the unprotected sector. This proposition is confirmed by using the market clearing condition for the labour market to write the shadow wage in (4.12), in the absence taxes, as:

$$S_{nP} = p_{nU} - (\bar{p}_{nP} - P_{nU})\frac{\partial y_{nP}}{\partial z_{nP}},^{11}$$

with $p_{nU} = \bar{p}_{nP} - \delta_{nP}/\lambda$. The welfare effects are illustrated in Figure 4.8 where private demand for protected labour rises endogenously (with $-\partial y_{nP}/\partial z_{nP} > 0$). Now the shadow wage exceeds the unprotected wage by the extra marginal product of labour employed in the protected sector. Thus, when the government undertakes a project the social cost of employing labour is bounded between the market wages in each sector. However, if private demand for protected labour falls endogenously, the shadow wage is less than the market wage in the unprotected sector. In effect, extra public employment increases private employment, and this reduces the social cost of labour by partially undoing the welfare loss from the minimum wage.

2. *Differential Employment Costs.* A constant marginal cost (m_{nP}) of employing labour in sector P will be introduced in the absence of a minimum wage. It is quite common to observe wage differences across geographic regions due to non-pecuniary costs

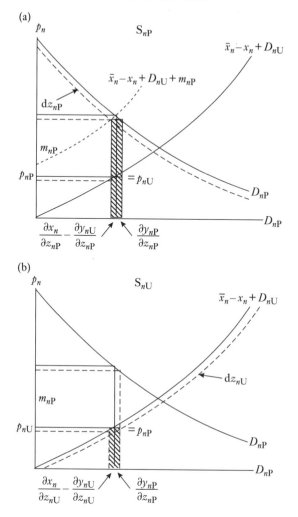

Figure 4.9 *The shadow wage rate with differential employment costs*

(or benefits). For example, farm labourers and mine workers in outback Australia face hotter and harsher conditions than the same labourers in coastal regions. If this cost, whether borne by workers or firms, is a necessary cost of employment in these regions the shadow wage will depend on the sector where a public project employs labour. This is illustrated in Figure 4.9 when private demand for labour is unaffected by endogenous price changes in other markets. In the absence of taxes, the shadow wage rate in sector P is illustrated in panel (a), as:

$$S_{nP} = p_{nP} + m_{nP}.^{12}$$

There is no inefficiency in the labour market when the employment cost is a necessary cost of attracting labour to sector P, so the market wage ($p_{nP} + m_{nP}$) is the shadow wage. By this same reasoning, the shadow wage in sector U, where no employment cost is incurred, is the market wage, with:

$$S_{nU} = p_{nU}.$$

One might be tempted to conclude from this example that shadow wages are market wages when the differential employment costs are replaced by taxes. However, that is not the case because taxes are non-necessary costs of trade.

3. *Differential Wage Taxation.* It is not uncommon for different wage taxes to apply to the same labour. For example, taxes can be lower in rural areas when governments, for political reasons, want to promote activity in these regions. In the absence of price controls the wage tax raises the cost of labour in each sector; it rises most where the tax is highest. This is demonstrated by levying a tax on labour employed in sector P and none on labour in sector U. Labour migration will equate the after-tax wage in each sector, where the gross-of-tax wage in sector P is higher by the tax.

The shadow wage in sector P is illustrated in Figure 4.10. It is a weighted average of the wages paid by firms to labour in each sector, where the wage differential reflects the higher marginal product of labour in sector P which is subject to the tax. When the public sector marginally reduces its demand for labour the wages in both sectors will fall to increase private employment. Social welfare rises by the value of the additional output produced in each sector; it is area (*a*) in sector U plus area (*b*) in sector P. The shadow wage in sector U is identical because additional labour is absorbed in exactly the same way. This is confirmed using the welfare equation in (4.11) where, in the absence of minimum wages and taxes in related markets, the shadow wage in

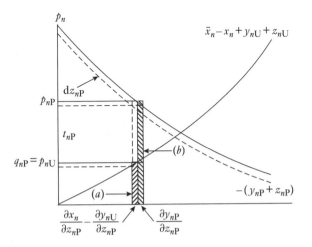

Figure 4.10 *The shadow wage and tax differentials*

sector P is:

$$S_{nP} = p_{nP} + t_{nP}\left(1 + \frac{\partial y_{nP}}{\partial z_{nP}}\right),$$

with $t_{nP} < 0$ for an input tax. The shadow wage in sector U is:

$$S_{nU} = p_{nU} + t_{nP}\frac{\partial y_{nP}}{\partial z_{nU}}.$$

Since the after tax wage in each sector is equated by labour migration, with $p_{nU} = p_{nP} + t_{nP}$, we have $S_{nP} = S_{nU}$. Thus, it makes no difference in project evaluation where the public sector employs labour because it is ultimately drawn from the two sectors in the same way.

The three cases just considered provide good examples of the way shadow wages are computed under different institutional arrangements. They demonstrate the importance of knowing how markets function in project evaluation, where seemingly similar conditions can lead to quite different outcomes. With migration costs the shadow wage differs across the two sectors, but with a differential wage tax the shadow wage is the same in each sector.

4.2 PRODUCTION QUOTA

It is quite common for governments to constrain activity in markets by issuing licences to restrict the number of producers, or by using production quota to restrict the quantity (or value) of output supplied. Taxi-cab licence plates are one of the most common examples of a licencing scheme. But entry into most professions, like the medical and building industries, are also subject to licence restrictions. Until recently, there were egg and milk quota in Australia to restrict the quantity of each product supplied by producers.

A variety of reasons are used to justify these schemes, and they include a desire to limit entry to *suitably qualified* suppliers as a quality guarantee for consumers, barriers to avoid *destructive competition*, and price support for producers. Once again, the welfare effects will crucially depend on the type of scheme used. Volume quota place upper bounds on output that do not change with producer prices, while licencing schemes restrict entry and allow output to change endogenously with producer prices. In some situations the licences themselves are endogenous. For example, additional taxi-cab plates may be issued in the face of sustained increases in demand due to consumer frustration with higher prices and longer delays, or because the government can collect extra revenue from selling the plates.

In the presence of volume quota on a good k that restricts supply to $\bar{Q}_k$, the conventional welfare equation is:

$$\frac{dW}{\beta} = p\,dz + t(dy + dz) + \delta_k\,dy_k, \tag{4.14}$$

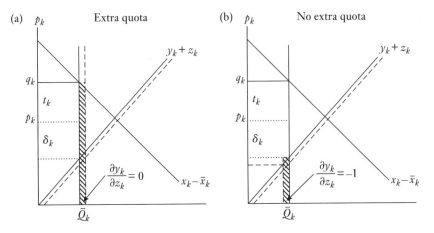

Figure 4.11 *The shadow price with volume quota on production*

where δ_k and dD_nP are, respectively, the vectors of constraint multipliers and endogenous changes in private output. For each firm, the constraint multiplier measures the dollar gain in profit from marginally increasing their quota.[13] Using (4.14), the conventional shadow price of good k, is:

$$S_k = p_k + t_k + (t_k + \delta_k)\frac{\partial y_k}{\partial z_k} + \sum_{i\neq k} t_i \frac{\partial y_i}{\partial z_k}, \tag{4.15}$$

where the final welfare change depends on whether or not additional quota is issued with the extra public output.

The two possibilities are illustrated in Figure 4.11 by ignoring effects in related markets in the last term of (4.15). Private demand rises when additional quota are issued with the extra public output. On this basis, the shadow price is the consumer price (q_k), and is illustrated in Figure 4.11(a). However, without additional quota the extra public output must crowd out private supply, where the shadow price is the resource cost saving ($p_k - \delta_k$) illustrated in Figure 4.11(b).

Whenever policy changes in other markets impact on demand and supply in the market for good k the production quota will rule out additional welfare effects by holding activity constant. Any changes in consumer valuations and production costs will impact solely on quota rent, but unless the quota is increased, no additional resources can flow into this market.

The welfare effects are slightly different when value quota or other licencing schemes are used to restrict activity. The difference between volume and value quota on imports is illustrated in Chapter 5. Most licencing schemes place restrictions on who can enter a market, but that does not stop output changing endogenously with producer prices. Quite often these entry restrictions increase marginal production costs, and as non-necessary costs of trade, are a welfare loss. Sometimes, the licences change endogenously with private activity, where in the absence of a model of government regulation, this can best be analysed as a separate exogenous policy change.

4.3 NON-COMPETITIVE BEHAVIOUR

There are circumstances where entry barriers give traders power to set prices (at least within a transactions cost band). These barriers may be fixed costs that are sunk or regulatory barriers, and can apply to both buyers and sellers. The extent of market power will depend on the number of other traders in the market and the cost of entry and exit. For illustrative purposes consider a monopolist facing no threat of entry due to large fixed and sunk costs. In the extreme, it could extract all private surplus by setting access fees equal to the surplus of each consumer and a product price equal to marginal cost.

While this outcome may be efficient, it is unlikely to be deemed equitable. This section examines non-competitive behaviour by a single-price monopolist and rules out access fees and multi-part pricing. Indeed, leakage in demand can often make these pricing policies ineffective.

When a single-price monopolist supplies good k the conventional welfare equation becomes:

$$\frac{\mathrm{d}W}{\beta} = p\,\mathrm{d}z + t(\mathrm{d}y + \mathrm{d}z) - y_k\frac{\partial p_k}{\partial y_k}\mathrm{d}y_k, \tag{4.16}$$

where the conventional shadow price of good k, is:

$$S_k = p_k - y_k\frac{\partial p_k}{\partial z_k} + \frac{\partial T}{\partial z_k}. \tag{4.17}$$

It is much easier to interpret the welfare changes by using the first-order condition for the monopolist to rewrite this shadow price, in the absence of taxes, as:

$$S_k = p_k\frac{\partial x_k}{\partial z_k} - \mathrm{MC}\frac{\partial y_k}{\partial z_k}.^{14} \tag{4.18}$$

It is illustrated in Figure 4.12 where the demand schedule for the monopolist is market demand net of public production. A marginal increase in public output shifts this demand schedule to the left. (And the marginal revenue schedule (MR_k) shifts by half this distance when demand is linear.) The monopolist responds by reducing output to lessen the fall in the market price. Social welfare rises by the resource cost saving in $\mathrm{MC}_k(\partial y_k/\partial z_k)$, and the value of the extra consumption benefits in $p_k(\partial x_k/\partial z_k)$. It can also be illustrated using the shadow price derived in (4.17) as $S_k = p_k - (a) < p_k$, since $(a) = (b)$ by profit maximization. In effect, there is a welfare gain from extra public output because it undermines the market power of the monopolist by making its demand schedule more own-price elastic. Normally, the shadow price will exceed the producer price when distortions drive activity below the efficient level, but that is not the case here because the monopolist sets the producer price above marginal cost (MC_k).

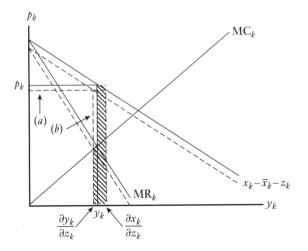

Figure 4.12 *A single-price monopolist*

It is still the case, however, that the shadow price lies between the marginal consumption benefits and production costs as a signal there are welfare gains from expanding activity.[15]

If policy changes in other markets impact on demand and supply in the market for good k, the welfare effects are similar to those arising in the presence of a tax. By way of illustration, suppose a unit of some good $j \neq k$ is endowed on the economy. Its shadow price is obtained using the conventional welfare equation in (4.16), as:

$$S_j = p_j + \frac{\partial T}{\partial z_j} + (p_k - MC_k)\frac{\partial y_k}{\partial z_j}. \tag{4.19}$$

Cross-effects in the monopoly market are captured in the last term of (4.19) and are illustrated in Figure 4.13 when extra output of good j drives up demand for good k. Welfare rises by the shaded rectangle, which is the excess of the consumption benefit over MC on each extra unit of good k produced and consumed. This is equivalent to the gain in a competitive market with a production tax that is set to maximize tax revenue. A similar gain arises from cross-effects that lower the MC of producing good k.

Now let us suppose that there is a *single-price monopsonist* who is the sole buyer of good k when it is produced by a large number of price-taking firms. The conventional shadow price is illustrated in Figure 4.14 in the absence of a production tax.

Extra output moves the supply schedule $(y_k + z_k)$ to the right. This moves the marginal cost schedule (MFC_k) for the monopsonist to the right by half that distance for the linear case illustrated. Since demand rises less than the increase in output, the market price falls and crowds out private production. The shadow price is the additional consumption benefits and resource cost saving illustrated in the cross-lined areas in Figure 4.14. When a specific tax restricts output to the same level in a competitive

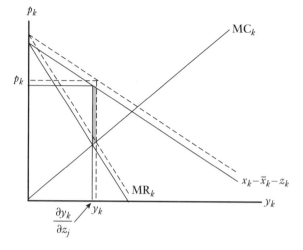

Figure 4.13 *Cross-effects in a monopoly market*

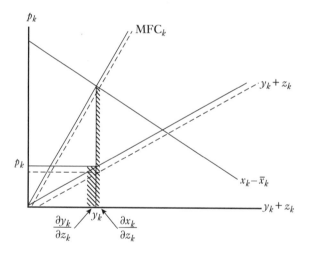

Figure 4.14 *A single-price monopsonist*

market, private demand would rise more and private supply would fall less. That means the shadow price is lower under the monopsony outcome.

4.4 EXTERNALITIES

Whenever private property rights are too costly to assign or trade there is scope for private costs and benefits to diverge from social costs and benefits, where this can lead to lost potential gains from trade. In project evaluation, it is important to recognize this source of inefficiency. Once private property rights break down, marginal production and consumption choices have welfare effects that are external to the market prices. For example, consumers who listen to loud music can impose external costs (or benefits) on neighbours, while producers using water in a lake or stream can impose external costs (or benefits) on other users.

Externalities do not always arise in the absence of formal property right allocations. Sometimes, they are traded informally between the affected parties. For example, the producer who pollutes the water in a lake may negotiate with harmed parties to internalize the externality. It may involve compensating payments by the producer to avoid more restrictive intervention, or compensating payments by the harmed parties to have the pollution in the lake reduced. The latter outcome is more likely when the producer can clean the water before returning it to the lake or can substitute out of water into other inputs at relatively low cost. The solution will largely depend on the nature of the externality and the alternatives available to the affected parties. Informal property-right trades are efficient, in a second-best sense, if they are the least costly way to solve the externality among all the feasible alternatives.

When the demand–supply decisions of individual agents have external effects on others there is scope for them to behave strategically. Bergstrom, Blume, and Varian (1986) and Cornes and Sandler (1985) recognize this when they model the private supply of public goods. They incorporate the strategic interactions between private contributors by using their first-order conditions. The analysis in this section will assume the affected parties are price takers who do not negotiate with each other. It can be extended to allow strategic interactions by amending the first-order conditions for the optimizing choices of agents.

If there is a constant production externality of c_k dollars in the market for good k the conventional welfare equation becomes:

$$\frac{\mathrm{d}W}{\beta} = p\,\mathrm{d}z + t(\mathrm{d}y + \mathrm{d}z) - c_k(\mathrm{d}y_k + \varepsilon_k\,\mathrm{d}z_k),^{[16]} \qquad (4.20)$$

where $c_k > 0$ is a constant external cost; $c_k < 0$ a constant external benefit; $\varepsilon_k = 1$ if the externality arises on public output; and, $\varepsilon_k = 0$ if there is no externality on public output.

The conventional shadow price of good k in the presence of this externality is obtained from (4.20), as:

$$S_k = p_k - c_k\left(\frac{\partial y_k}{\partial z_k} + \varepsilon_k\right) + \frac{\partial T}{\partial z_k}. \qquad (4.21)$$

Welfare effects in the market for good k are illustrated in Figure 4.15. MC_k^S is the social marginal cost schedule, which is higher than the private marginal cost schedule

Non-tax Distortions

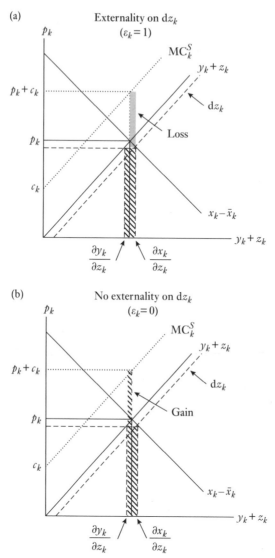

Figure 4.15 *A negative production externality*

by the externality. If the externality is not internalized, the market outcome will be determined by the intersection of the private cost and demand schedules.

In the absence of tax distortions, the shadow price of good k is:

$$S_k = p_k - c_k \frac{\partial x_k}{\partial z_k} < p_k \qquad \text{for } \varepsilon_k = 1;[17]$$

and

$$S_k = p_k - c_k \frac{\partial y_k}{\partial z_k} > p_k \qquad \text{for } \varepsilon_k = 0.$$

When the externality arises on public production (with $\varepsilon_k = 1$) the shadow price is less than the market price. Public output exacerbates the existing welfare loss by expanding the distorted activity even further. Indeed, too many resources are already allocated to this activity when private producers do not face the full costs of their actions. The shadow price is illustrated in Figure 4.15(a) as the sales revenue (p_k) minus the welfare loss from the externality on the increase in private activity $(-c_k(\partial x_k/\partial z_k) < 0)$. However, with no externality on public production (with $\varepsilon_k = 0$) the shadow price will exceed the market price as a signal that the public sector is a more efficient producer. It is illustrated in Figure 4.15(b) as the sales revenue (p_k) plus the welfare gain from reducing the externality by crowding out private production $(-c_k(\partial y_k/\partial z_k) > 0)$.[18]

Many governments impose taxes (or other levies) on producers to internalize the external costs when they are relatively large. A Pigouvian tax eliminates the welfare loss by internalizing the externality (with $t_k = c_k$) where, in the absence of any other taxes, the shadow price in (4.21) becomes:[19]

$$S_k = p_k \qquad \text{for } \varepsilon_k = 1;$$

and

$$S_k = p_k + t_k \qquad \text{for } \varepsilon_k = 0.$$

Now the shadow price is the producer price when the externality arises on public output (with $\varepsilon_k = 1$) because it measures the net gain from selling another unit of the good. There is a gross gain of $p_k + t_k$ less the externality (which is equal to the tax).[20] Once the externality is internalized the market price is a true measure of the marginal social value of the good (in the absence of other distortions). However, the shadow price will exceed the producer price by the tax (t_k) when the externality does not arise on public production (with $\varepsilon_k = 0$). This is a signal the public sector is a more efficient producer, where the resource cost saving from crowding out private supply is now higher by the externality, while the consumption benefit from increasing private demand is higher by the tax (which is equal here to the externality). In effect, the tax measures the efficiency gain from replacing private with public production.

There are analogous welfare effects for a positive consumption externality. In the presence of a constant external benefit ($c_k < 0$) the shadow price of good k, in the absence of any other taxes, is:

$$S_k = p_k - c_k \frac{\partial x_k}{\partial z_k} > p_k \qquad \text{for } \varepsilon_k = 1;$$

and

$$S_k = p_k - c_k \frac{\partial y_k}{\partial z_k} < p_k \qquad \text{for } \varepsilon_k = 0.$$

Both cases are illustrated in Figure 4.16 where the MB_k^S is the schedule of marginal social consumption benefits. When the externality is not internalized, the equilibrium outcome is determined by the schedule of private marginal consumption benefits $(x_k - \bar{x}_k)$, where too few resources are allocated to the market. Thus, the shadow

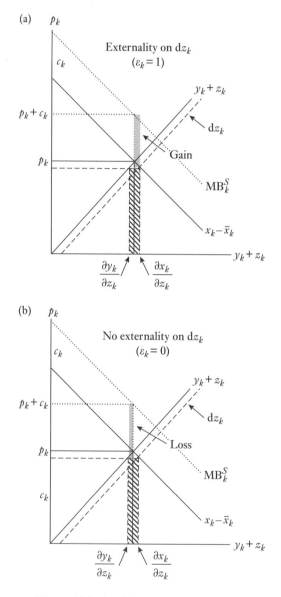

Figure 4.16 *A positive consumption externality*

price will exceed the market price if there are external benefits from public production because it expands private consumption. However, the reverse applies when there are no external benefits from public production since it crowds out private supply which does generate the externality. If a Pigouvian subsidy is used to internalize the external benefit (with $t_k = c_k < 0$) then the shadow price will be equal to the producer price when $\varepsilon_k = 1$. But it will fall below the producer price when $\varepsilon_k = 0$.

Thus, in the absence of taxes and subsidies, the shadow price exceeds the producer price as a signal that public output is preferable whenever public production generates positive externalities and avoids negative externalities. However, the reverse applies if public production causes negative externalities and has no external benefits.

Cross-effects from policy changes in other markets can be illustrated by computing the shadow price of some good j in the presence of the externality on good k, where:

$$S_j = p_j + \sum_{i \neq k} t_i \frac{\partial y_i}{\partial z_j} + t_j + (t_k - c_k) \frac{\partial y_k}{\partial z_j}. \tag{4.22}$$

The last term is a welfare gain from expanding private supply of good k when it is subject to a net positive externality (with $t_k - c_k > 0$). The reverse applies if output of good k contracts or it is subject to a net negative externality (with $t_k - c_k < 0$). There are no cross-effects when the externality is internalized by a Pigouvian tax (with $t_k = c_k$) because the social benefits and costs of trading good k are equalized at the margin.

4.5 CONCLUDING REMARKS

Taxes are not the only distortions in markets. Governments set price ceilings and floors, and issue production quota and licences. At times, they use combinations of these policies to achieve particular outcomes. Some distortions arise from the absence of private property right allocations to resources that can lead to external costs and benefits. On other occasions, there are distortions from non-competitive behaviour by buyers and sellers. While many of these distortions can be compared to taxes and subsidies, at least in a static sense, they typically do not have the same welfare effects. For example, the impact of a binding price cap on trade can be replicated by a tax if goods are allocated to the highest valued users at no additional cost to private surplus under the cap. However, there are quite different welfare effects from changes in demand and supply under each policy. An increase in demand cannot raise activity in the presence of the price cap that fixes supply, whereas supply does increase in the presence of tax. Moreover, there are likely to be different trading (or rationing) costs under each of these policies that will also lead to differences in their welfare effects.

Another insight from the analysis in this chapter is the important difference between marginal trading costs and taxes. If trading costs are necessary costs of trade they do not distort market prices. And when they are included in the market prices the shadow and market prices coincide, which is not the case with trade taxes. This was demonstrated by comparing the effects of differential employment costs and taxes on the shadow wage. There are many examples of wage differences for the same type of labour located in different geographical regions. When market wages adjust to compensate labour for differential employment costs they are the shadow wages in each region. However, when market wages adjust to differential taxes they are not the shadow wages in each region because taxes are non-necessary costs of trade from a social point of view.

The analysis in this chapter has reinforced the important insight that welfare changes originate from changes in final consumption. Unless policy or other exogenous changes impact on final consumption, which determines consumer utilities, there can be no welfare effects. At a practical level, it means that there are no welfare changes in markets where activity is unaffected by policy changes. While this seems an obvious point to make, it is nevertheless tempting to alter measures of inefficiency to account for endogenous changes in private surplus when demand and supply schedules move over unchanged output. For example, the deadweight loss from production quota that fixes the supply of a good is unaffected by endogenous changes in demand. The same observation applies in markets subject to price controls when they stop activity changing.

The welfare effects of a much richer array of market distortions can be modelled using the approach examined in this chapter. Non-competitive behaviour with strategic interactions between agents can be included by using the marginal conditions for their optimizing choices when solving the conventional welfare equation for marginal policy changes. This was illustrated for a single-price monopolist but can readily be extended to accommodate other equilibrium outcomes. The analysis becomes more complicated, however, when there is asymmetric information between agents. Indeed, analysts will need to know what information agents have and what technologies they use to collect information, before the welfare measures can be properly assessed.

NOTES

1. It is usually argued that traders are excluded from private insurance by moral hazard and adverse selection problems when there is asymmetric information.
2. Cox (1980) examines the political economy of setting and enforcing price controls and finds differences are explained by the weights on controlled prices in the official price index, elasticities of supply and demand, and the structural characteristics of industries. Papps (1993) obtains shadow prices of goods that are subject to price controls.
3. For an excellent summary of these schemes see Sieper (1982).
4. Each consumer faces an upper bound on the amount of good k they can consume $(\bar{D}_k^h)$, where their optimization problem, solves:

$$\mathcal{L}^h = u^h(x^h) + \lambda^h(I^h - qx^h) + \delta_k^h(\bar{D}_k^h - x_k^h).$$

The last term is the non-negativity constraint on demand for good k.
5. Each consumer faces a constraint on their labour supply $(\bar{n}^h)$, where their optimization problem solves:

$$\mathcal{L}^h = u^h(x^h) + \lambda^h(I^h - qx^h) + \delta_n^h(\bar{n}^h - (\bar{x}_n^h - x_n^h)).$$

6. Since labour is a net input (with $y_n < 0$), the tax $(t_n < 0)$ drives its consumer price below the price paid by firms.

7. This is obtained from (4.7) by using the market clearing condition, where:

$$\frac{\partial x_n}{\partial z_k} = \frac{\partial y_n}{\partial z_k} + 1.$$

8. The optimization problem for the representative consumer who faces a binding constraint on labour supplied to the protected sector ($\bar{n}_P^h$), is:

$$\mathcal{L}^h = u^h(x^h) + \lambda^h(I^h - qx^h) + \delta_{nP}^h(\bar{n}_P^h - (\bar{x}_n^h - U_E^h - D_{nU}^h)),$$

where $D_{nP}^h = \bar{x}_n^h - U_E^h + D_{nU}^h > 0$ is labour supplied to the public and private firms in the protected sector, $U_E^h > 0$ unemployment in the protected sector, and $D_{nU}^h > 0$ labour supplied to public and private firms in the unprotected sector. When each consumer chooses unemployment optimally (in the absence of taxes on labour income), we have:

$$\frac{d\mathcal{L}^h}{dU_E^h}\frac{1}{\lambda^h} = \frac{\partial I^h}{\partial U_E^h} + \frac{\delta_{nP}^h}{\lambda^h} = 0.$$

Since the value of labour income for each consumer h, is:

$$\bar{p}_{nP}(\bar{x}_{nP}^h - U_E^h - D_{nU}^h) + p_{nU}(U_E^h + D_{nU}^h),$$

the change in income from raising unemployment is: $\partial I^h/\partial U_E^h = -(\bar{p}_{nP} - p_{nU})$. From the first-order condition for optimally chosen unemployment, we have:

$$\frac{\delta_{nP}^h}{\lambda^h} = \bar{p}_{nP} - p_{nU}.$$

In words, consumers allocate time to unemployment until the marginal value of relaxing the constraint on supplying labour to the protected sector is equal to the difference between the protected and unprotected wage rates.

9. By using the market clearing condition for the labour market, we have: $1 - (\partial U_E/\partial z_{nP}) = -\partial y_{nU}/\partial z_{nP} > 0$, where the shadow wage becomes:

$$S_{nP} = -p_{nU}\frac{\partial y_{nU}}{\partial z_{nP}} > 0.$$

This is the cross-lined rectangle illustrated in Figure 4.7.

10. The optimization problem for each consumer h is the same problem summarized in the previous footnote, with the exception being the inclusion of unemployment in the utility function where the first-order condition for optimally chosen unemployment becomes:

$$\frac{d\mathcal{L}^h}{dU_E^h}\frac{1}{\lambda^h} = \frac{\partial u^h}{\partial U_E^h}\frac{1}{\lambda^h} + \frac{\partial I^h}{\partial U_E^h} + \frac{\delta_{nP}^h}{\lambda^h} = 0.$$

Now the value of labour income for each consumer h, is:

$$\bar{p}_{nP}(\bar{x}_{nP}^h - U_E^h - D_{nU}^h) + p_{nU}D_{nU}^h + \pi\bar{p}_{nP}U_E^h,$$

with the change in income from raising unemployment being:

$$\frac{\partial I^h}{\partial U_E^h} = -(\bar{p}_{nP} - \pi\bar{p}_{nP}).$$

Since the marginal value of relaxing the constraint on employment in the protected sector is $\delta_{nP}^h/\lambda^h = \bar{p}_{nP} - p_{nU}$, the first-order condition for optimally chosen unemployment can be used to show the unprotected sector wage is higher than the expected wage in the protected sector by the marginal consumption benefits from leisure, with:

$$\frac{\partial u^h}{\partial U_E^h}\frac{1}{\lambda^h} = p_{nU} - \pi\bar{p}_{nP} > 0.$$

11. Using the market clearing condition for the labour market, we have:

$$\frac{\partial x_{nP}}{\partial z_{nP}} - \frac{\partial y_{nU}}{\partial z_{nP}} = 1 + \frac{\partial y_{nP}}{\partial z_{nP}}.$$

12. This is derived from the conventional welfare equation:

$$\frac{\mathrm{d}W}{\beta} = p\,\mathrm{d}z + m_{nP}\,\mathrm{d}z_{nP} + t(\mathrm{d}y + \mathrm{d}z),$$

using the *virtual* budget constraint: $qx = q\tilde{x} + p(y + z) + m_{nP}(y_{nP} + z_{nP}) + t(y + z)$, with $m_{nP}(y_{nP} + z_{nP}) < 0$ and the first-order condition for private firms: $p\,\mathrm{d}y + m_{nP}\,\mathrm{d}y_{nP} = 0$.

13. In the presence of binding quota, the first-order condition for profit maximizing firms is:

$$p\,\mathrm{d}y - \delta_k\,\mathrm{d}y_k = 0,$$

where δ_k is the economic rent from issuing another unit of quota.

14. The first-order condition for the monopolist, is:

$$\left(y_k\frac{\partial p_k}{\partial y_k} + P_k - MC_k\right)\mathrm{d}y_k,$$

with $MC_k = -\sum_{i\neq k} p_i(\partial y_i/\partial y_k)$. Equation (4.18) is solved using the market clearing condition:

$$1 + \frac{\partial y_k}{\partial z_k} = \frac{\partial x_k}{\partial z_k}.$$

15. One way to eliminate the welfare loss from the single-price monopolist is to pay a production subsidy equal to the gap between the marginal and average revenue schedules at the efficient outcome (where demand cuts the marginal cost schedule). Of course, the efficient subsidy will be smaller if it is financed with distorting taxes.

16. Detailed workings are provided in Appendix 2.

17. This is obtained using the market clearing condition, where:

$$\frac{\partial x_k}{\partial z_k} = \frac{\partial y_k}{\partial z_k} + 1.$$

18. An obvious question arises when the government is able to produce the good without causing the externality. Does it have access to a technology not available to private firms? If there are resource costs from eliminating the externality they will be included in project evaluation as larger input–output coefficients for the public sector. It also assumes that there is a production technology that produces the good without causing the externality.

19. When the marginal external cost varies with activity the Pigouvian tax is set equal to the externality at the social optimum.

20. With a Pigouvian tax and $\varepsilon_k = 1$ the shadow price is:

$$S_k = p_k - c_k\left(\frac{\partial y_k}{\partial z_k} + 1\right) + t_k\left(\frac{\partial y_k}{\partial z_k} + 1\right) = p_k.$$

5

International Trade

Countries buy and sell goods and services from each other, and international trade flows have increased significantly in recent decades due to reductions in trade barriers. Transactions costs have fallen with more efficient transportation services and less costly information flows. At the same time, greater public awareness of the potential benefits from trade have reduced political barriers. Exporters and importers gain by exploiting differences in marginal benefits and costs across countries, but there are still losers within each country from reducing trade barriers. For example, lower import prices make domestic producers of these goods worse off, but by less (in dollar terms) than the gains to consumers. Despite the net gains, tariffs and quota are frequently used to protect domestic producers when they are smaller groups with greater political influence than consumers. Some of their political influence is undermined by increased public awareness of the social costs of protection, but, trade restrictions remain, albeit, at lower levels. In many developing countries a significant proportion of domestic activity is transacted in black (or unofficial) markets where it cannot be taxed. Indeed, most taxes will drive a share of activity into black markets, and some taxes more so than others. International trade flows are sometimes easier to tax because they pass through defined geographical entry points. That provides many governments with a convenient way to raise revenue, especially in developing countries with poorly developed domestic infrastructures to collect taxes on domestic trade.

Trade restrictions can take many different forms. In the former Soviet Union, for example, exports were taxed to discourage flows of goods away from the domestic economy, where this reflected a desire to promote and preserve the supply of goods to the home market. Few direct barriers were placed on imports because they enhanced domestic supply. Many former members of the Soviet Union still have trade barriers that reflect this ethos. But, as is made clear by the Lerner (1936) symmetry theorem, taxes on exports are effectively taxes on imports and vice versa. By reducing domestic prices of exportable goods, they raise the relative prices of importable goods. In other words, export taxes can be replicated by a set of tariffs on imports. After all, exports generate the foreign exchange that funds the flow of imports.

Indeed, domestic demand for foreign exchange is determined, in present value terms, by imports, and domestic supply of foreign exchange by exports. Any taxes (and subsidies) that distort these trade flows are taxes on foreign exchange, and they cause the shadow prices of traded goods and foreign exchange to differ from their respective market prices. There are a number of important relationships between the shadow and market prices of traded goods. Little and Mirrlees (1969) derive the important result that, in small economies, relative shadow prices of fully traded goods are equal to their relative border prices (which are world prices measured in units of domestic currency). This is particularly convenient for applied work because border prices are readily available. The generalized Hatta decomposition will be used to provide intuition for the result under both fixed and flexible exchange rates.

Traditionally, the shadow exchange rate has played a central role in project evaluation in small open economies. Harberger (1978) used it to compute shadow prices of traded goods by converting their foreign prices into domestic utility. The shadow and official exchange rates normally diverge in economies with distorted markets. Fontaine (1969), Harberger (1968) and Schydlowsky (1968) derive a formulae for the shadow exchange rate which is recommended in the UNIDO Guidelines of Dasgupta, Marglin, and Sen (1972). However, Sieper (1981) finds the shadow exchange rate is irrelevant in project evaluation (in single-aggregated consumer economies). By choosing foreign exchange as numeraire, the shadow exchange rate is the shadow value of government revenue, which isolates income effects. And by the Hatta decomposition, they are irrelevant in project evaluation. However, this is no longer the case when some other good is chosen as numeraire. When foreign exchange is converted into the numeraire good there are changes in the official exchange rate that affect the real exchange rate, that is, the relative price of non-traded to traded goods. Once this happens, the shadow exchange rate is not the shadow value of government revenue, and it will play a role in project evaluation.

This chapter derives shadow prices of traded goods in the presence of trade restrictions. The shadow exchange rate is obtained under fixed and floating exchange rate regimes to examine the role of the choice of numeraire in project evaluation, and to reconcile the seemingly contradictory views of Harberger and Sieper about the role the shadow exchange rate plays in policy evaluation. Finally, effective rates of protection and domestic resource cost ratios for traded goods are derived and then compared to examine the economic information they provide. Both are frequently used by major international aid agencies.

A number of adjustments must be made to the basic model used in previous chapters to accommodate international trade flows. We introduce a set of fully traded goods (T) that trade under small country conditions, that is, their world prices are not affected by domestic demands and supplies. Quota restrictions, which are ruled out for fully traded goods, are examined separately in a later section. Thus, there are now $N + 1 + T$ goods in the economy, and the primary factors are included in the set of non-traded goods. All commodities, except the numeraire good, may be subject to specific production taxes, where the relationship between their consumer and producer prices, is:

$$q_i = p_i + t_i \qquad \forall_{i \in T, N} \quad \text{with } t_i > 0 \begin{cases} \text{for a tax when } y_i > 0, \\ \text{a subsidy when } y_i < 0, \end{cases}$$

$$t_i < 0 \begin{cases} \text{for a subsidy when } y_i > 0, \\ \text{a tax when } y_i < 0. \end{cases} \tag{5.1}$$

As noted earlier, most governments levy taxes on international trade flows (referred to here as trade taxes), and they are included by defining the net demand for each traded good i, as: $m_i = x_i - y_i - z_i$, with $m_i > 0$ for imports and $m_i < 0$ for exports. These goods have domestic prices (p_i^w) that are equal to their world prices measured in units of foreign currency (p_i^{w*}) multiplied by the official exchange rate (e). When these trade flows are subject to specific taxes (τ_i) they have producer prices, of:

$$p_i = p_i^w + \tau_i - t_i \qquad \forall_{i \in T} \quad \text{with } \tau_i > 0 \begin{cases} \text{for a tax when } m_i > 0, \\ \text{a subsidy when } m_i < 0, \end{cases}$$

$$\tau_i < 0 \begin{cases} \text{for a subsidy when } m_i > 0, \\ \text{a tax when } m_i < 0. \end{cases} \quad (5.2)$$

This tax structure is general enough to allow different taxes on the domestic demand for and supply of internationally traded goods. Consider the importable good k illustrated in Figure 5.1, which is subject to separate, but equal taxes on domestic consumers and producers. It is achieved by combining a production tax t_k with a tariff τ_k, where the tax is twice the size of the tariff to offset the implicit production subsidy in the tariff. For a consumption tax on this good, there would need to be a tariff and production tax set at the same rate.

With the inclusion of trade taxes, government tax revenue becomes:

$$T = t(y + z) + \tau m.$$

As was previously the case, non-traded goods prices change endogenously to equate demand and supply in these markets, with $x_i = \bar{x}_i + y_i + z_i \ \forall_{i \in N+1}$. However, this is not possible for fully traded goods because their world prices are exogenous. Instead,

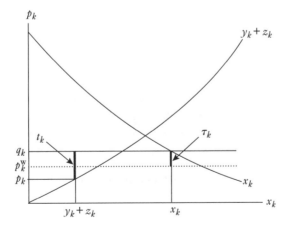

Figure 5.1 *An importable good k*

there is a balance of payments equation:

$$B = eF - p^w m, \tag{5.3}$$

with $B > 0$ a surplus in the balance of payments, $F > 0$ an exogenous gift of foreign exchange (which the government receives), and $p^w m > 0$ the trade deficit. In full equilibrium, the official exchange rate (e) adjusts to achieve balance of payments (with $B = 0$), where the market clearing condition for traded goods is $F = p^w m$.[1] Thus, with trade taxes and exogenous foreign exchange transfers, net government revenue is:

$$R = t(y + z) + \tau m + eF + pz - L. \tag{5.4}$$

After making these adjustments, the conventional welfare equation with international trade flows, becomes:

$$\frac{dW}{\beta} = p\,dz + t(dy + dz) + \tau\,dm + e\,dF - dR.\text{[2]} \tag{5.5}$$

There are now additional welfare effects from changes in trade tax revenue ($\tau\,dm$) and exogenous foreign exchange flows (dF).

5.1 CONVENTIONAL HARBERGER SHADOW PRICES OF FULLY TRADED GOODS

International trade makes very little difference to the basic structure of the shadow prices obtained in earlier chapters, where from (5.5) we have:

$$S_k = \left.\frac{dW}{dz_k}\frac{1}{\beta}\right|_{dR=0} = p_k + \frac{\partial T}{\partial z_k}, \tag{5.6}$$

with

$$\frac{\partial T}{\partial z_k} = \sum_i t_i \frac{\partial y_i}{\partial z_k} + t_k + \sum_i \tau_i \frac{\partial m_i}{\partial z_k}.$$

It is still the producer price plus endogenous changes in tax revenue when resources flow between distorted activities, with additional welfare effects in the presence of trade taxes. There are, however, some important differences between the shadow prices of non-traded goods and fully traded goods in small open economies. This can be demonstrated by separating the welfare effects in related markets (RME) and then using the price–tax relationships in (5.2) to write the shadow price in (5.6) for any fully traded good k, as:

$$S_{k \in T} = p_k^w + \tau_k \frac{\partial x_k}{\partial z_k} + (t_k - \tau_k)\frac{\partial y_k}{\partial z_k} + \text{RME}. \tag{5.7}$$

Endowing one unit of a traded good on the economy is equivalent to a gift of foreign exchange equal to its world price (p_k^{w*}). Once converted into domestic currency it raises domestic real income by the border price of the good (p_k^w), and this has income effects from moving resources across distorted activities in the last three terms of (5.7). The second and third terms are welfare effects from changes in the domestic demand and supply of good k when they are subject to trade and production taxes.

Shadow prices of fully traded goods are normally derived using the *traditional approach* recommended in Fontaine, Harberger, and Schydlowsky. They use the shadow exchange rate to convert the foreign exchange embodied in extra output of traded goods into utility. This approach will be demonstrated in the next section.

5.2 THE SHADOW EXCHANGE RATE

Like all shadow prices, the shadow exchange rate (S_e) looks through the veil of distortions and computes the gain in social welfare from endowing another unit of foreign exchange on the economy. In the presence of distortions, it will normally diverge from the official exchange rate. Fontaine, Harberger, and Schydlowsky derived the shadow price of any fully traded good k, as:

$$S_{k \in T} = S_e p_k^{w*}, \tag{5.8}$$

where the shadow exchange rate is obtained from the welfare equation (5.5), as:

$$S_e = \left. \frac{dW}{dF} \frac{1}{\beta} \right|_{dR=0} = e + \frac{\partial T}{\partial F}. \tag{5.9}$$

Since p_k^{w*} is the amount of foreign exchange endowed on the economy by an extra unit of traded good k, the shadow exchange rate converts it into social welfare. It is exactly the same welfare change as the shadow price derived in (5.6).[3] There is a large literature that examines different derivations of the shadow exchange rate. Most differ by the types of distortions included in the analysis. In applied work, most analysts use the traditional formula recommended in the UNIDO guidelines, but it relies on a number of important simplifying assumptions that may not always be appropriate.

5.2.1 The Traditional Formula for the Shadow Exchange Rate

The traditional formula recommended by Fontaine, Harberger, and Schydlowsky is derived with a fixed official exchange rate. This makes foreign exchange the numeraire good (with $e = 1$), where (5.9) becomes:

$$S_e = 1 + \sum_i t_i \frac{\partial y_i}{\partial F} + \sum_{i \in T} \tau_i \frac{\partial m_i}{\partial F}. \tag{5.10}$$

It can be rewritten using the balance of payments equation in (5.3), as:

$$S_e = \sum_{i \in T}(p_i^w + \tau_i)\frac{\partial m_i}{\partial F} + \sum_i t_i \frac{\partial y_i}{\partial F}. \quad {}^4 \tag{5.11}$$

Two simplifying assumptions convert this into the traditional formula, and they are:

(a) non-traded goods are free of taxes and other distortions (with $\sum_{i \in N} t_i(\partial y_i/\partial F) = 0$); and,

(b) trade taxes are the only distortions in traded goods markets (with $t_i = 0 \; \forall_{i \in T}$).

In effect, this eliminates all the production taxes in (5.11). The first assumption removes welfare effects in related markets, while the second equates the domestic consumer and producer price of each traded good. Finally, the traditional formula is obtained from (5.11) by expressing the specific trade taxes in *ad valorem* terms (with $\tau_i = \bar{\tau}_i p_i^w$), where:

$$S_e = \sum_i (1 + \bar{\tau}_i)\frac{p_i^w \partial m_i}{\partial F}. \quad {}^5 \tag{5.12}$$

Whenever the economy receives foreign exchange it will be absorbed through increases in imports and/or decreases in exports. By focussing on these adjustments, the traditional formula overlooks distortions in non-traded goods markets and rules out combinations of trade and other taxes in tradeable goods markets. In reality, there are income effects from extra foreign exchange that will impact on non-traded goods, and they are frequently subject to tax and other distortions. Also, trade taxes are not the only distortions on tradeable goods. For example, an importable good may well be subject to a tariff and a consumption tax that drives the consumer price above the producer price. These possibilities are captured in the general formula for the shadow exchange rate in (5.11).

The traditional formula is illustrated in Figure 5.2 for an economy with two fully traded goods, one an importable (M) and the other an exportable (X). Imports are subject to a tariff and exports to a tax, and for simplicity there are no distortions in the remaining domestic markets. By using the traditional formula in (5.12), the shadow exchange rate is:

$$S_e = \frac{p_M^w \partial m_M + p_X^w \partial m_X}{\partial F} + \frac{\tau_M \partial m_M + \tau_X \partial m_X}{\partial F}, \tag{5.13}$$

where the first term is the domestic value of the foreign exchange spent on net imports, which must be unity to absorb the extra unit of foreign exchange. The second term is the change in government revenue. In Figure 5.2, the first term in (5.13) is the increase in demand for foreign exchange in $(b) + (d)$ when imports rise plus the fall in the supply of foreign exchange in $(e) + (f) + (g) + (h)$ when exports fall. For balance of payments equilibrium, these changes must absorb the extra unit of foreign exchange, with $(b) + (d) + (e) + (f) + (g) + (h) = 1$.

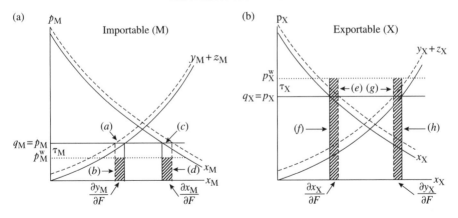

Figure 5.2 *The shadow exchange rate*

The second term in (5.13) is the extra tariff revenue in $(a) + (c)$ less the fall in export tax revenue in $(e) + (g)$. They are, respectively, the welfare gain from expanding imports and the welfare loss from contracting exports when both are subject to taxes. Thus, the shadow exchange rate is:

$$S_e = 1 + [(a) + (c)] - [(e) + (g)].$$

In the absence of any trade taxes, the shadow and official exchange rates must be equal to each other. They are also equal in the special circumstances where the loss in export tax revenue exactly offsets the increase in tariff revenue. If there is a net rise in trade tax revenue, with $(a) + (c) - (e) - (g) < 0$, the official exchange rate rises above the shadow exchange rate, while the reverse applies for a net fall in trade tax revenue.

5.2.2 Fixed versus Flexible Exchange Rates—and the Choice of Numeraire

As noted earlier, traditional derivations of the shadow exchange rate are undertaken with a fixed official exchange rate. At the time, most developing countries pegged their exchange rates against other currencies. This effectively makes foreign exchange the numeraire good (with $e = 1$) because the government must hold surplus revenue as foreign exchange reserves to prevent the official exchange rate from changing. Sieper proves that the shadow exchange rate is irrelevant in project evaluation in these circumstances for a single (aggregated) consumer economy.

Perhaps the easiest way to demonstrate this result is to note that the shadow exchange rate is the shadow value of government revenue when *foreign exchange is chosen as the numeraire good*. When the government receives a unit of foreign exchange and holds it as surplus revenue, the compensated shadow exchange rate will be unity, with $\hat{S}_e = 1$. By holding onto this foreign exchange, there is no change in the official exchange rate or any other relative price. Once this surplus is transferred in a lump-sum to consumers, the change in social welfare is obtained using the generalized Hatta decomposition in (2.12), as $S_e = S_R \hat{S}_e = S_R$, where the shadow exchange rate isolates the income effects from an extra unit of foreign exchange. On this basis, the shadow price of the fully traded good k in (5.8) can be derived as:

$$S_{k \in T} = S_e p_k^{w*} = S_R p_k^{w*}, \tag{5.14}$$

with $e = 1$ and $p_k^{w*} = p_k^{w}$.

Whenever foreign exchange is the numeraire good the shadow exchange rate will isolate income effects, which are irrelevant in project evaluation in the single (aggregated) consumer economy. To see this, take the ratio of the shadow price of any non-traded good n to the shadow price of any traded good k, where:

$$\frac{S_{n \in N}}{S_{k \in T}} = \frac{S_R(p_n + (\partial \hat{T}/\partial z_n))}{S_e p_k^{w*}}. \tag{5.15}$$

With $S_R = S_e$, the shadow exchange rate is eliminated from (5.15), which is not the case, however, when some non-traded *good (0) is chosen as numeraire* because additional foreign exchange appreciates the official exchange rate, where the shadow exchange rate becomes:

$$S_e = S_R \hat{S}_e = S_R \left(e + \frac{\partial \hat{T}}{\partial F} \right). \tag{5.16}$$

Now there are substitution effects in $\hat{S}_e$, and the shadow exchange rate (S_e) is no longer the shadow value of government revenue. When a unit of foreign exchange is endowed on the government it is converted into units of the numeraire good 0. This appreciates the official exchange rate in the compensated equilibrium, where the ratio of the shadow price of any non-traded good n to the shadow price of any traded good k, becomes:

$$\frac{S_{n \in N}}{S_{k \in T}} = \frac{S_R(p_n + (\partial \hat{T}/\partial z_n))}{S_R(e + (\partial \hat{T}/\partial F)) p_k^{w*}}.^6 \tag{5.17}$$

While the income effects (in S_R) cancel, the substitution effects from the endogenous changes in the official exchange rate do not. Fane (1991*b*) makes this point in a partial defence of the traditional approach. But it is only a partial defence since the traditional approach advocates using the shadow exchange rate with a fixed official rate. In these circumstances, Sieper is correct to claim the shadow exchange rate is irrelevant in project evaluation.

Clearly, the shadow exchange rate will not impact on the relative shadow prices of fully traded goods in small open economies, irrespective of the good chosen as numeraire, because traded goods endow foreign exchange on the economy without affecting their world and domestic prices. Ultimately, the welfare effects are due to income effects from additional foreign exchange, which is confirmed by the relationship in (5.8). Even when good 0 is numeraire the substitution effects from changes in the official exchange rate are independent of the traded good that generates the foreign exchange in a small open economy, where for any two fully traded goods j and k, we have:

$$\frac{S_{j \in T}}{S_{k \in T}} = \frac{S_R(e + (\partial \hat{T}/\partial F))p_j^{w*}}{S_R(e + (\partial \hat{T}/\partial F))p_k^{w*}} = \frac{p_j^{w*}}{p_k^{w*}}. \tag{5.18}$$

It makes no difference whether foreign exchange comes from imports falling or exports rising, it affects the official exchange rate in the same way when world prices are exogenous.

Recall from (5.14) that the shadow exchange rate is the shadow value of government revenue when foreign exchange is numeraire. In the compensated equilibrium, the government holds surplus revenue as foreign exchange reserves, with $\hat{S}_e = 1$. When surplus foreign exchange is transferred to the private economy, we have $S_e = S_R \hat{S}_e = S_R$. If good 0 is numeraire then its shadow price becomes the shadow value of government revenue. Now the government holds surplus revenue in the compensated equilibrium as units of good 0, where:

$$\hat{S}_0 = \frac{d\hat{R}}{dz_0} = p_0 = 1. \tag{5.19}$$

When it is transferred to the private economy, we have $S_0 = S_R \hat{S}_0 = S_R$. Thus, the shadow price of good 0 is irrelevant in project evaluation in these circumstances because it isolates income effects. In effect, the choice of numeraire determines the real currency the government uses. When it makes compensating transfers in general equilibrium the choice of numeraire matters because consumers have different valuations for different goods. This is confirmed in the next section by shadow pricing fully traded goods using different numeraire goods.

5.3 COMPENSATED SHADOW PRICES AND THE CHOICE OF NUMERAIRE

By comparing the derivations of the shadow price of the fully traded good k in (5.15) and (5.17) it is apparent that the choice of numeraire matters for the compensated welfare changes. This is confirmed by deriving compensated shadow prices of fully traded goods using different numeraire goods.

Foreign Exchange is Chosen as Numeraire (with $e = 1$). Domestic prices of traded goods do not change endogenously when foreign exchange is chosen as numeraire. Since these goods are supplied to domestic consumers at constant marginal cost, they have *compensated* shadow prices equal to their border prices.[7] This is confirmed using

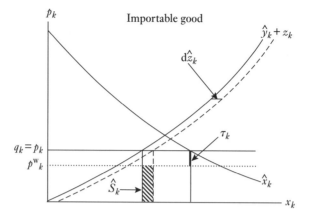

Figure 5.3 *Foreign exchange as numeraire*

the welfare equation in (5.5), with $dW/\beta = 0$, where:[8]

$$\hat{S}_{k \in T} = \left. \frac{d\hat{R}}{dz_k} \right|_{dW/\beta=0} = p_k^w = p_k^{w*}.^{[9]} \tag{5.20}$$

The intuition for this result is explained for an importable good subject to a tariff using Figure 5.3. When the government sells a unit of good k it receives net revenue of $p_k - \tau_k = p_k^w$ units of the numeraire good—foreign exchange. In effect, the good exactly replaces a unit of imports, thereby releasing foreign exchange (p_k^{w*}) which the government holds as surplus revenue in the compensated equilibrium. It represents a potential welfare gain that can be distributed to the private economy. No relative prices change, and the budget surplus rises by the border price, with $\hat{S}_k = p_k^w = p_k^{w*}$. Once the government transfers this surplus foreign exchange to the private sector to balance its budget private surplus will rise by even more when the income effect expands taxed activities. It is captured as the change in tax revenue in the uncompensated shadow price in (5.6), and is confirmed using the welfare decomposition in (2.12), where:

$$S_{k \in T} = S_R \hat{S}_k = S_R p_k^w,^{[10]}$$

with $S_R = S_e = 1 + \partial T/\partial R$.

When Good 0 is Chosen as Numeraire (with $p_0 = 1$). Now the official exchange rate changes endogenously, where the *compensated* shadow price of any fully traded good k, becomes:

$$\hat{S}_{k \in T} = \left. \frac{d\hat{R}}{dz_k} \right|_{dW/\beta=0} = p_k + \frac{\partial \hat{T}}{\partial z_k}.^{[11]} \tag{5.21}$$

After the government sells a unit of traded good k it collects revenue in units of good 0, and this releases foreign exchange that will appreciate the official exchange rate.

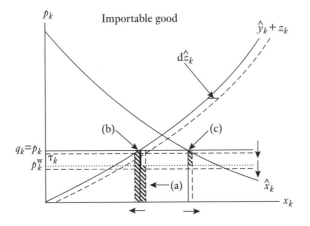

Figure 5.4 *Good 0 as numeraire*

There are consequent changes in domestic prices that impact on taxed activities. The welfare changes in the market for importable good k are illustrated in Figure 5.4. As domestic supply of good k increases marginally it reduces imports and the demand for foreign exchange. This appreciates the official exchange rate in the compensated equilibrium and lowers the domestic prices of traded goods, thereby moving resources between distorted markets. The welfare effects in the market for good k are equal to the net change in government revenue which rises by the sales revenue in (a) plus the additional tariff revenue in $(b) + (c)$ from the lower domestic price. In the absence of distortions in other markets, the compensated shadow price is:

$$\hat{S}_{k \in T} = p_k^w + \tau_k \left(\frac{\partial \hat{x}_k}{\partial z_k} - \frac{\partial \hat{y}_k}{\partial z_k} \right) = (a) + \{(b) + (c)\}.$$

Once the government transfers this surplus good 0 in (5.21) to the private economy, welfare rises by the uncompensated shadow price in (5.7).

In summary, the choice of numeraire determines how the government holds surplus revenue in the compensated equilibrium. It is of no consequence in a partial equilibrium setting, where relative prices are exogenous, whether the government converts surplus revenue into foreign exchange or units of some other good 0. But the same is not true in a general equilibrium setting because the choice of numeraire leads to different relative price changes. Since the compensated equilibrium has to be a potential equilibrium, it must isolate the amount of the numeraire good the government needs to buy or sell to hold welfare constant in the face of a policy change. If foreign exchange is chosen as numeraire, compensated welfare gains are isolated by changes in foreign exchange reserves. Alternatively, when good 0 is chosen as numeraire, the government holds surplus revenue in units of that good. In effect, the choice of numeraire makes its shadow price the shadow value of government revenue, and by isolating income effects,

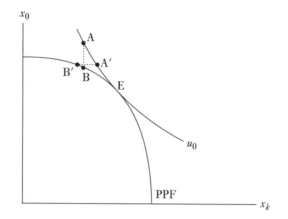

Figure 5.5 *Compensated welfare changes with different numeraire goods*

it is irrelevant in project evaluation in single (aggregated) consumer economies. Indeed, that is why Sieper finds the shadow exchange rate irrelevant when the official exchange rate is fixed.

The role of the numeraire is illustrated in Figure 5.5 by measuring the excess burden for a commodity tax in a single (aggregated) consumer economy that produces two non-traded goods k and 0.[12]

In the absence of tax distortions, the initial equilibrium is at E with utility u_0. After the tax on good k is introduced it drives a wedge between the relative consumer and producer prices. If good 0 is numeraire the new equilibrium outcome will be at point A on the initial indifference curve where production occurs at point B on the production possibility frontier (PPF). The excess burden is AB units of good 0 since that is the outside compensation required as foreign aid to hold utility constant. However, when good k is numeraire the compensated equilibrium changes with consumption at A' on u_0 and production at point B' on PPF. Now the excess burden is A'B' units of good k.

Note how, in each case, there are different relative prices and different consumption and production bundles. Once the government funds the excess burden by transferring units of the numeraire good from consumers, the final full equilibrium outcome converges to a point between B and B' on the PPF on a lower indifference curve. Clearly, this outcome is independent of the numeraire good chosen, but the numeraire matters for measuring the efficiency losses because it defines how the outside compensation is paid to consumers. If compensation is paid in monetary terms in this setting it has no real effects. Instead, there are equal proportional changes in all nominal prices. Compensation must be paid in real terms to be effective.

5.4 THE LITTLE–MIRRLEES (1969) RESULT

Little and Mirrlees (1969) prove the relative shadow prices of fully traded goods (in small open economies) are the ratio of their border prices. The result is extremely useful in project evaluation because border prices are relatively easy to obtain, and it can be formally stated for any two fully traded goods j and k, as:

$$\frac{S_{j\in T}}{S_{k\in T}} = \frac{p_j^w + \tau_j + \sum_i t_i(\partial y_i/\partial z_j) + \sum_{i\in T} \tau_i(\partial m_i/\partial z_j)}{p_k^w + \tau_k + \sum_i t_i(\partial y_i/\partial z_k) + \sum_{i\in T} \tau_i(\partial m_i/\partial z_k)} = \frac{p_j^w}{p_k^w}. \tag{5.22}$$

It is not immediately obvious why the endogenous changes in tax revenue cancel from this price ratio. However, it follows directly from the traditional approach used for computing the shadow prices of fully traded goods in (5.8) which allows us to write the relative shadow price, as:

$$\frac{S_{j\in T}}{S_{k\in T}} = \frac{S_e p_j^{w*}}{S_e p_k^{w*}} = \frac{p_j^w}{p_k^w}. \tag{5.23}$$

Note from (5.18) that this result is independent of the choice of numeraire. Basically, it is due to the small country assumption that makes world prices exogenous. When good 0 is numeraire extra output of fully traded goods will generate additional foreign exchange and appreciate the official exchange rate. However, the appreciation is not determined by the physical characteristics of the traded good, but rather by the foreign exchange it generates, that is, its world price.

5.5 THE TWIN DEFICITS

Dréze and Stern (1990) make the observation that it is incorrect to cost a policy change by measuring its impact on the government budget deficit in full equilibrium.[13] This was confirmed in Chapter 2 by separating welfare changes into direct changes in private surplus and revenue transfers when the government balances its budget. Clearly, changes in net government revenue do not account for direct changes in private surplus because they do not affect the government budget. But, as noted previously in Chapter 2, a policy change can be costed by its impact on the government budget in the compensated equilibrium since direct changes in private surplus are offset by compensating transfers. In these circumstances, all the welfare effects are determined solely by their impact on net government revenue. Moreover, when foreign exchange is chosen as the numeraire good these changes in net government revenue will be matched by corresponding changes in the balance of payments. Indeed, it is quite common for welfare effects to be measured as changes in the balance of payments. For example, a compensated change in tax inefficiency is the increase in the budget deficit from marginally raising a distorting tax when taxpayers are compensated for any lost surplus. When foreign exchange is numeraire the budget deficit is matched by a corresponding balance of payments deficit; it is foreign aid the government would need to receive to balance its budget.

This can be illustrated using the price–tax relationships in (5.1) and (5.2) to write the government budget surplus in units of foreign exchange, as:

$$R = B = F - p^{w*}m,^{14} \tag{5.24}$$

where the compensated shadow price of any good k becomes:

$$\hat{S}_k = -\sum_i p_i^{w*} \frac{\partial \hat{m}_i}{\partial z_k}. \tag{5.25}$$

If good k is fully traded its shadow price is the world price p_k^{w*} since $\partial \hat{m}_k / \partial z_k = -1$ and $\partial \hat{m}_i / \partial z_i = 0$ for all $i \neq k$. An extra unit of the good releases foreign exchange equal to its world price which the government holds as surplus revenue. Thus, there are no relative price changes to affect private activity in a small economy.

When good 0 is chosen as numeraire the compensated welfare effects are isolated by changes in the quantity of good 0 the government holds. This is confirmed by using the price–tax relationships to rewrite net government revenue in (5.4), as:

$$R = \bar{x}_0 + y_0 + z_0 - x_0, \tag{5.26}$$

where the shadow price of any good k is now:

$$\hat{S}_k = \frac{d\hat{R}}{dz_k} = \frac{\partial \hat{y}_0}{\partial z_k} - \frac{\partial \hat{x}_0}{\partial z_k}. \tag{5.27}$$

When the government sells a unit of good k it collects sales and tax revenue and makes compensating transfers in units of good 0. Thus, the shadow price is the net amount of good 0 the government collects in (5.27).

5.6 QUOTA PROTECTION

While tariffs are widely used in practice to raise revenue and protect import competing producers quota restrictions on imports are also important. By holding imports below their free trade level, they drive up domestic prices and create rent. In a static sense, quota and tariff restrictions are fully equivalent, but they have different welfare effects when domestic demand, domestic supply, or world prices change. As a requirement for accession to the WTO countries must replace quota and other quantitative restrictions on international trade flows with tariffs. Quota restrictions are a less visible form of protection than tariffs, and are more restrictive when domestic demand increases, or when world prices or domestic marginal production costs fall.

There are two types of quota–volume and value. Volume quota set an upper limit on the quantity of imports $(\bar{m}_i)$ with $m_i \leq \bar{m}_i$ for importable good i. In contrast, value quota set upper limits on the value of a good imported $(\bar{v}_i)$, where value is normally determined at free-on-board (f.o.b.) prices, with $p_i^w m_i \leq \bar{v}_i$ for importable good i. Binding quota create rent by driving domestic prices above their border prices. Governments normally collect some or all of this rent by selling the quota. They collect all of it if the quota are sold in a competitive market with no transactions costs. Typically, traders are invited to make sealed bids and the quota are allocated to the highest bidder (who pays their bid or the next highest bid). The larger the number of bidders, the larger the proportion of rent collected by the government in the absence of collusion or corruption.

To illustrate the welfare effects of quota restrictions assume imports of a good Q are subject to quota, and the quota rent accrues (at no transactions cost) to the government budget. For both types of quota, net government revenue in (5.4), is:

$$R = T + pz + eF + (\bar{p}_Q - p_Q^w)\bar{m}_Q - L \qquad \text{for volume quota,} \qquad (5.28)$$

and,

$$R = T + pz + eF + (\bar{p}_Q m_Q - \bar{v}_Q) - L \qquad \text{for value quota.} \qquad (5.29)$$

When quota holders sell imports on the domestic market they collect revenue (net of taxes) of $\bar{p}_Q$ on each unit. To allow for the possibility of a tariff on quota imports, and taxes on domestic demand and supply, write the price–tax relationship for the quota traded good, as:

$$q_Q = p_Q + t_Q \qquad \text{and} \qquad p_Q = \bar{p}_Q + \tau_Q - t_Q. \qquad (5.30)$$

5.6.1 The Shadow Value of Import Quota

A marginal increase in import quota will raise social welfare, by:

$$\frac{dW}{d\bar{m}_Q}\frac{1}{\beta} = (\bar{p}_Q - p_Q^w) + \frac{\partial T}{\partial \bar{m}_Q}.^{15} \qquad (5.31)$$

There is quota rent $(\bar{p}_Q - p_Q^w)$ and additional tax revenue when resources flow into other taxed activities (with $\partial T/\partial \bar{m}_Q > 0$). The welfare changes in the market for good Q are illustrated in Figure 5.6 when imports are also subject to a tariff.

As quota imports expand the domestic price falls to crowd out domestic supply and increase domestic demand. The lower price is not illustrated to avoid putting too much information in the figure. When traders use the quota, they receive revenue of $\bar{p}_Q$ from selling the good to domestic consumers and outlay p_Q^w (in domestic currency) on imports. This generates quota rent of $\bar{p}_Q - p_Q^w$ and extra tariff revenue τ_Q. In the absence of distortions in other markets, the price–tax relationship in (5.30) can be used to write the shadow value of the quota in (5.31), as:

$$\frac{dW}{d\bar{m}_Q}\frac{1}{\beta} = \bar{p}_Q - p_Q^w + \tau_Q = p_Q - p_Q^w, \qquad (5.32)$$

which is the cross-lined area in Figure 5.6. The tariff plays no allocative role here, it simply transfers some of the quota rent to the government budget.[16] In practice, however, the tariff may be the most effective way for the government to collect this rent when there are problems doing so by selling the quota. For example, corruption and collusion between bidders can reduce the revenue collected at quota auctions.

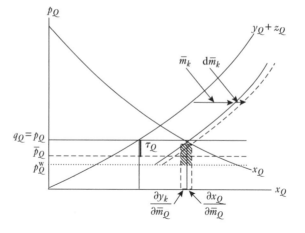

Figure 5.6 *The shadow value of volume quota*

If quota are defined in value terms the level of imports will change endogenously with the border price (p_Q^w). A marginal increase in value quota imports will raise social welfare by:

$$\frac{\mathrm{d}W}{\mathrm{d}\bar{v}_Q}\frac{1}{\beta} = (\bar{p}_Q - p_Q^w)\frac{\partial m_Q}{\partial \bar{v}_Q} + \frac{\partial T}{\partial \bar{v}_Q}.[17] \tag{5.33}$$

Once again, quota rent is collected on the additional imports, which rise less now because the exchange rate depreciation raises the border price of the good. These changes are illustrated in Figure 5.7 when good Q is subject to a tariff.

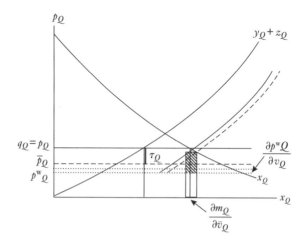

Figure 5.7 *The shadow value of value quota*

Increasing the value quota by \$1 raises imports by $1/p_Q^w$ at the initial exchange rate. This is equivalent to an increase in the volume quota by $1/p_Q^w$ under a fixed exchange rate. When the extra imports depreciate the exchange rate, the border price rises and reduces the quantity of imports below $1/p_Q^w$. Thus, the welfare gain is the quota rent on these imports plus the extra tariff revenue in the cross-lined area in Figure 5.7.

With a flexible exchange rate, imports under the value quota are endogenous, but they are fixed under volume quota. If policy changes in other markets appreciate the exchange rate, the border price of good Q falls and imports rise under value quota while they do not change under volume quota. Extra imports make domestic producers worse off and domestic consumers better off by driving down the domestic price of the good.

5.6.2 The Shadow Prices of Quota Protected Goods

In the presence of quota restrictions, the domestic prices of imported goods are determined by domestic demands and supplies. Once quota imports are exhausted, demand is satisfied from higher priced domestic production (when marginal cost increases). If the public sector produces another unit of importable good Q when imports are restricted by *volume quota*, its shadow price is:

$$S_Q = p_Q + \frac{\partial T}{\partial z_Q}.{}^{18}$$ (5.34)

It has the same structure as the shadow price of a non-traded good. The welfare effects in the market for good Q are illustrated in Figure 5.8 in the absence of taxes and tariffs. Extra public output reduces the domestic price ($\bar{p}_Q$) and this drives down private

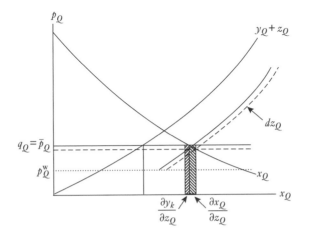

Figure 5.8 *The shadow price of an importable good protected by volume quota*

production and increases demand. The shadow price is the resource cost saving plus the additional consumption benefits illustrated in the cross-lined area in the figure. In the absence of distortions in other markets, the shadow price is equal to the producer price (p_Q), which is higher than the border price.

Additional welfare effects arise when importable good Q is restricted by *value quota*, where its shadow price becomes:

$$S_Q = p_Q + \frac{\partial T}{\partial z_Q} + (\bar{p}_Q - p_Q^w) \frac{\partial m_Q}{\partial z_Q}. \tag{5.35}$$

The last term is the extra rent when the exchange rate appreciates and increases quota imports.[19] This term does not appear when imports are restricted by volume quota because endogenous changes in the exchange rate do not alter the quantity of imports. Instead, it changes the quota rent which is a transfer of surplus from domestic consumers to the government budget.

5.7 HOME-PRICE CONSUMPTION SCHEMES

It is quite common for governments to subsidize exports, which they justify doing on political grounds as a way to promote domestic employment and to increase foreign exchange earnings. Sometimes, they subsidize new exports when domestic producers are not competitive on world markets, and most governments prefer implicit subsidies to stop the costs appearing in their budget statements. For example, Australian dairy and dried fruit producers were paid subsidies funded directly from taxes on their domestic consumers to promote exports. This is called a *home-price consumption scheme* because it ties the production subsidy to a consumption tax, and since domestic production exceeds domestic demand the consumption tax must be larger (in specific terms) than the subsidy paid to producers.[20] Once the two instruments are linked in this way the subsidy changes endogenously with domestic demand. The scheme is illustrated in Figure 5.9 for exportable good k.

A combined consumption tax and production subsidy can be replicated using the price–tax relationships in (5.1) and (5.2) with an export subsidy τ_k and production tax t_k. The export subsidy taxes domestic consumers and subsidizes domestic producers, while the production tax reduces the subsidy to the level that makes the scheme self-financing, with: $s_k = \tau_k - t_k$. Tax revenue is the vertical cross-lined rectangle plus area (a), and it is equal to the subsidy cost in the horizontal cross-lined rectangle plus area (a). The dashed curve is a rectangular hyperbola that determines the subsidy payable from consumption tax revenue at each level of production. Ignoring any administrative costs, we have:

$$\tau_k x_k = (\tau_k - t_k)(y_k + z_k).^{21} \tag{5.36}$$

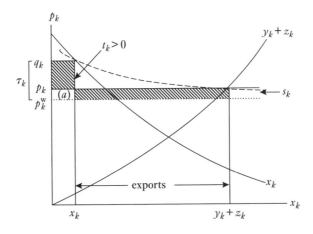

Figure 5.9 *A home-price consumption scheme*

In the presence of a home-price consumption scheme the conventional shadow price of good k is obtained from the welfare equation in (5.5), as:

$$S_k = p_k^w + \frac{\partial T}{\partial z_k} + \frac{\partial T}{\partial t_k} \frac{dt_k}{dz_k}.^{22}$$ (5.37)

Since extra output generates foreign exchange of p_k^{w*} which is transferred to consumers, it impacts on taxed activities. Two separate effects can change the production subsidy. One is through changes in domestic demand and the resulting tax revenue, while the other is through changes in domestic production and the resulting subsidy cost. These changes must offset each other because the scheme is self-financing. When domestic demand is unaffected by extra public output of the good, and there are no related markets effects, the shadow price will be:

$$S_k = p_k^w - s_k \frac{\partial y_k}{\partial s_k} \frac{ds_k}{dz_k},$$ (5.38)

where from (5.36), we have $ds_k/dz_k < 0$.[23] The welfare changes are illustrated in Figure 5.10 when the subsidy is paid on public output.

An increase in public output will drive down the per unit subsidy, thereby reducing private production (with $\partial y_k/\partial s_k > 0$) and expanding exports. Thus, social welfare rises by the additional foreign exchange earnings (p_k^w) and the resource cost saving on the fall in private production. Since domestic marginal cost exceeds the border price of the good by the subsidy, the shadow price is the border price (p_k^w) plus the fall in production inefficiency ($s(\partial y_k/\partial z_k) > 0$). If no subsidy is paid on extra public output, it will be exported without crowding out private production, and the shadow price will just be the border price of the good (in the absence of cross-effects on demand and distortions in other markets).

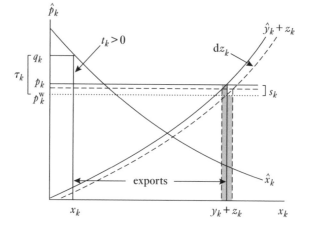

Figure 5.10 *The shadow price of output with a home-price consumption scheme*

Once cross-effects impact on private demand the welfare effects are ambiguous. When it rises, the increase in tax revenue will fund a larger subsidy, thereby mitigating some of the subsidy cost on the extra public output. The reverse applies when domestic demand falls.

If the public sector uses good k as an input to production it has a different shadow price. It is illustrated in Figure 5.11 as a marginal increase in demand which raises extra tax revenue to fund a larger production subsidy.

Social welfare falls by the reduction in foreign exchange earnings on exports absorbed by the increase in domestic demand plus the subsidy cost on the extra private production. This subsidy cost measures the amount domestic marginal resource cost

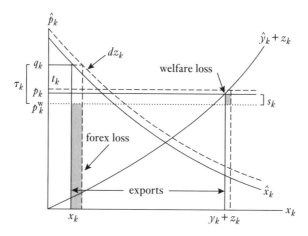

Figure 5.11 *The shadow price of project input with a home-price consumption scheme*

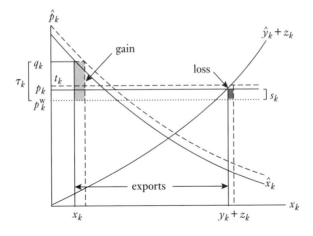

Figure 5.12 *Cross-market effects and home-price consumption schemes*

exceeds the border price. If the tax is not levied on extra public demand, there is no change in the unit subsidy or private production. In these circumstances, the shadow price is confined to the lost foreign exchange on the unit reduction in exports.

Any cross-market effects in project evaluation impact on the shadow price of good k by changing domestic demand and/or supply. For example, a marginal increase in domestic demand will raise consumption tax revenue and increase the production subsidy. This is illustrated in Figure 5.12 where the extra tax revenue is a welfare gain, and the subsidy paid on extra domestic production a welfare loss. There is a net gain because the tax is larger than the subsidy.

If cross-market effects raise domestic production (and leave domestic demand unchanged), there is an unambiguous welfare loss equal to the initial subsidy times the change in exports. When domestic demand and supply both change, welfare may rise or fall in the market subject to the home-price consumption scheme. This scheme provides a good illustration of the welfare changes that arise when policy instruments are endogenously related to each other, and it is important to identify these relationships in a cost–benefit analysis.

5.8 THE EFFECTIVE RATE OF PROTECTION

In policy evaluation work, particularly in developing countries, effective rates of protection are used to determine the net effect of trade policies on value added in the production of traded goods.[24] Measures of protection that focus solely on the way trade policies affect output prices can be quite misleading. Many input prices are also affected by traded policies, and in some circumstances, they can overturn the implicit subsidies or taxes on output. The effective rate of protection (ERP) recognizes this problem by measuring the net protection for domestic producers of tradeable goods. It computes the combined effect of trade policies on input and output prices.

The *nominal rate of protection* (NRP) for any tradeable good k measures the proportionate change in its domestic price due to existing trade policies, with $\text{NRP}_k = (p_k - p_k^w)/p_k^w$, where p_k is the domestic price under existing trade policies and p_k^w the border price. By using the price–tax relationships in (5.2) it becomes $\text{NRP}_k = (\tau_k - t_k^w)/p_k^w$. When good k is importable its domestic producer price will rise by the tariff less the production tax. But a positive NRP does not mean domestic producers are better off under existing trade policies relative to free trade. Indeed, the NRPs on their tradeable inputs can make them worse off. Not all taxes and subsidies are explicit. For example, exporters are sometimes forced by law to sell through export marketing boards that take a share of the sales revenue.[25] There are also implicit taxes on imports when customs agencies raise the cost of landing imported goods. Any taxes and subsidies that affect the domestic prices of tradeable goods should be included in NRP calculations.

When trade policies affect domestic prices of tradeable goods they change value added on domestic production, where value added measures the payments made to domestic factors of production, labour (n) and capital (k). Trade policies that raise output prices will increase value added, while those that raise input prices will reduce it. The ERP captures these effects by measuring the proportionate change in value added due to existing trade policies on the marginal production of any tradeable good j, as:

$$\text{ERP}_j = \frac{\text{VA}_j - \text{VA}_j^w}{\text{VA}_j^w}, \tag{5.39}$$

with:

$\text{VA} = p_j - a_{mj}p_m$—being actual value added on the last unit of the good produced in the presence of the existing policies when firms use a single tradeable input m, with $a_{mj} = -\partial y_m/\partial y_j$ being the input–output (i–o) coefficient under existing policies;[26]

$\text{VA}_j^w = p_j^w - a_{mj}^w p_m^w$—is free-trade (w) value added on the last unit of the good produced, with $a_{mj}^* = -\partial y_m^*/\partial y_j$ being the i–o coefficient in free trade.[27]

ERPs are normally estimated using average i–o coefficients because they are less costly to compute, but the marginal coefficients provide the correct measure of marginal production costs under existing policies and free trade. By using the price–tax relationships in (5.2), the ERP in (5.39) becomes:

$$\text{ERP}_j = \frac{(\tau_j - a_{mj}\tau_m) - (t_j - a_{mj}t_m) - p_m^w(a_{mj} - a_{mj}^w)}{p_j^w - a_{mj}^w p_m^w}.\text{[28]} \tag{5.40}$$

The first two terms in the numerator measure the way taxes affect value added, while the third term accounts for changes in the i–o coefficients. If there are no changes in these coefficients, with $(a_{mj} - a_{mj}^w) = 0$, the ERP collapses to the difference between the output-NRP and the weighted input-NRP as a proportion of free-trade value added.[29] A simple example of this calculation is provided in Table 5.1 for a firm that produces an importable good.

Table 5.1 *The ERP for an importable good*

	Actual	NRP (%)	Free trade (^{W})
Output (p_j)	1	15	0.870
Traded inputs ($a_{mj}p_m$)			
Aluminium	0.314	5	0.299
Zinc	0.272	5	0.259
Chemicals	0.070	5	0.067
Packaging	0.044	15	0.038
	0.700	6	0.663
Non-traded inputs ($a_{sj}p_s$)			
Utilities	0.064	0	0.064
Value added (VA$_j$)	0.236		0.143
ERP (%)			65

Output has been normalized so that each unit has a domestic producer price of $1 under existing policies. It has been decomposed for the last unit produced as 70 cents for tradeable inputs, 6.4 cents for non-traded utilities, and 23.6 cents value added. Free trade prices for tradeable goods are obtained using the NRPs, where for the output j, $p_j^W = p_j/(1 + NRP_j) = 1/1.15 = 0.870$, and for each traded input m, $a_{mj}^W p_m^W = a_{mj}p_m/(1 + NRP_m)$. The non-traded input utilities, which is a composite good for electricity, water, and telecommunications, is treated as a good produced solely from untaxed tradeable inputs. Value added in free trade (14.3 cents) is computed by deducting the input costs (72.7 cents) from the price of output (87 cents). On this basis, the ERP for good j, is:

$$ERP_j = \frac{0.236 - 0.143}{0.143} \times 100 = 65.$$

This means domestic producers benefit from current trade policies which raises their value added by 65%. It would be even larger were it not for taxes on traded inputs that raise production costs by 5.6%.

In practice, a number of factors complicate this calculation. One is how to treat non-traded inputs when they are produced using both traded inputs and domestic factors of production. There are two ways of dealing with non-traded inputs:

(1) *The Corden (1974) Approach*—divides the cost of non-traded inputs between traded input costs and value added. When half the cost of utilities in Table 5.1 is for traded inputs, the ERP will be 53%; and,
(2) *The Balassa and Schydlowsky (1972) Approach*—includes non-traded inputs in value added, where the ERP in Table 5.1 falls to 44%.

The difference between the approaches is explained using Figure 5.13 where non-traded input s is subject to a production tax.

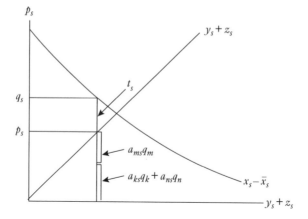

Figure 5.13 *Non-traded input (s)*

Firms that buy this good as an intermediate input pay the consumers price (q_s), which is equal to the sum of the marginal input costs ($\sum_i a_{is}q_i$) and the production tax (t_s). Balassa and Schydlowsky (1972) include the entire cost of input s ($a_{sj}q_s$) in value added for good j, while Corden (1974) adds the traded input cost for good s ($a_{ms}q_m$) to the direct traded input costs for good j, and the production tax (t_s) and payments to capital (k) and labour (l) for good s ($t_s + a_{ks}q_k + a_{ls}q_l$) to good j's value added.

It is important to recognize the peculiar attributes and limitations of the ERP measures. First, the ERP rises as value added (at free-trade prices) falls, all other things constant. Thus, goods that are produced with relatively low value added can have much larger ERPs than goods using larger quantities of these factors, even if they face the same NRPs on their traded inputs and outputs. Second, the ERP can be negative when trade policies raise input prices proportionately more than the price of output. In many developing countries traditional activities, like agricultural production, are disadvantaged relative to new manufacturing and service activities. They often receive little, if any, direct protection from positive output NRPs, but pay inflated input prices due to trade policies used to protect input producers. Third, the ERP is not a reliable way to identify comparative advantage when there are taxes and other distortions in domestic factor markets. For example, minimum wages and income taxes are not accounted for in the ERP calculation. Indeed, there are circumstances where the ERP provides a misleading measure of the effects of government policies on resource allocation. Despite these shortcomings, however, it is very useful in exposing the incidence effects of existing trade policies.

5.9 THE DOMESTIC RESOURCE COST RATIO

A reliable way of identifying the marginal effects of current government policies on resource allocation is to measure the marginal shadow profit for each activity in the economy, where for any good j, we have:

$$\pi_j^S = S_j - a_{mj}S_m - a_{kj}S_k - a_{nj}S_n. \tag{5.41}$$

Activities with positive marginal social profit are harmed by current policies, while the reverse applies to activities with negative marginal social profit. The domestic resource cost ratio (DRCR) rearranges this shadow profit in (5.41) to measure the value of the domestic resources (capital and labour) used to produce a unit of foreign exchange, where for any tradeable good j, we have:

$$\mathrm{DRCR}_j = \frac{a_{kj}S_k + a_{nj}S_n}{S_j - a_{mj}S_m}.^{30} \tag{5.42}$$

Traded goods with DRCRs less than unity are socially profitable and are therefore under-produced from a social point of view. The reverse applies to goods with DRCRs above unity. In applied work, analysts compute these ratios using different valuations for the domestic resources and foreign exchange, some at actual market prices, others at free-trade (or first-best) prices, and others at shadow prices. While shadow prices provide the correct measure of the DRCR, they are more costly to compute. That is why market and free-trade prices are used as alternatives. Srinivasan and Bhagwati (1978) provide an excellent summary of the consequences of using these different prices.

Whenever non-traded inputs are used to produce a good the costs are divided between the factors of production in the numerator of (5.42) and the traded input costs in the denominator. The income effects can be eliminated from the DRCR by using the generalized Hatta decomposition in (2.12) to decompose the shadow prices, where:

$$\mathrm{DRCR}_j = \frac{(a_{kj}\hat{S}_k + a_{nj}\hat{S}_n)S_R}{(\hat{S}_j - a_{mj}\hat{S}_m)S_R}.$$

Thus, there is a potential welfare gain from marginally increasing output of good j whenever $\mathrm{DRCR}_j < 1$.[31] It is quite common for analysts to estimate the DRCRs by using the shadow exchange rate to compute the shadow prices of the traded goods, where:

$$\mathrm{DRCR}_j = \frac{a_{kj}S_k + a_{nj}S_n}{S_e(p_j^{w*} - a_{mj}p_m^{w*})}. \tag{5.43}$$

If foreign exchange is chosen as the numeraire good the shadow exchange rate will play no role in determining the value of the DRCR because it is the shadow value of government revenue which isolates income effects (with $S_e = S_R$). This was demonstrated in equation (5.16), where this allows us to use the Hatta decomposition in (2.12) to write the DRCR in (5.43), as:

$$\mathrm{DRCR}_j = \frac{(a_{kj}\hat{S}_k + a_{nj}\hat{S}_n)S_R}{(p_j^{w*} - a_{mj}p_m^{w*})S_R}.$$

Finally, there is a relationship between ERP_j and $DRCR_j$, and it is obtained by using the price–tax relationships in (5.1) and (5.2), and the shadow prices for traded goods in (5.8), to write the shadow profit in (5.41) for activity j, as:

$$\pi_j^S = (p_j^{w*} - a_{mj}p_m^{w*})\left(1 + ERP_j - DRCR_j\frac{S_e}{e}\right) + \frac{\partial T}{\partial z_j} - a_{mj}\frac{\partial T}{\partial z_m}.^{32} \quad (5.44)$$

The ERP_j is computed using the Corden approach to divide the costs of non-traded inputs between traded inputs and value added. In the absence of any distortions, $\pi_j^S = 0$ because $S_e = e$, $ERP_j = 0$ and $DRCR_j = 1$. However, when there are distortions it is quite possible for ERP_j to be less than zero if $DRCR_j$ is less than unity. In other words, good j can be disadvantaged by trade policies but be socially profitable at the margin due to welfare improving distortions in the factor and related markets.[33]

5.10 CONCLUDING REMARKS

Most countries trade goods and services in international markets, and given the size of these trade flows it is important in applied welfare analysis to understand the different characteristics of the taxes and other policies that apply to them. While lower trade barriers can increase the aggregate value of domestic consumption, there are winners and losers. Unless transfer policies are used to convert the welfare gains into Pareto improvements, there will be political pressure to protect losers using trade barriers. This protection is sometimes explicit, taking the form of taxes and quota restrictions on imports or subsidies on exports. It can also be self financing as was demonstrated by the home-price consumption schemes that were so popular in rural industries in Australia a number of years ago.

Another important aspect of international trade is the different currencies that can be traded in foreign exchange markets. It is quite common for governments to peg their currencies against one, or a basket of other currencies. The shadow exchange rate has played an important, but controversial role in project evaluation. When traded goods are subject to taxes and/or subsidies in small open economies they have shadow prices equal to their world prices (in units of foreign currency) multiplied by the shadow exchange rate. Thus, once the shadow exchange rate is computed it is a straightforward exercise obtaining the shadow prices of traded goods. Little and Mirrlees (1969) exploit this approach by proving the relative shadow prices of fully traded goods are equal to their relative border prices. However, when traded goods are subject to quota or other quantitative restrictions the shadow exchange rate cannot be used in the same way to compute their shadow prices. In these circumstances, their market prices are determined domestically, and they have similar shadow prices to non-traded goods, which are not in general equal to their domestic producer prices.

Many policy analysts use the traditional formula for the shadow exchange rate to compute the shadow prices of fully traded goods. While it has the advantage of being reasonably easy to compute, it nevertheless is based on two simplifying assumptions: (a) additional foreign exchange has no impact on non-traded goods subject to taxes or other distortions, and (b) traded goods are subject only to tariffs or export taxes. A general expression for the shadow exchange rate was derived in this chapter to include welfare effects in related markets and to allow more general tax structures on fully traded goods. Also, the choice of numeraire was examined to reconcile seemingly contradictory views about the role of the shadow exchange rate in project evaluation. Sieper argues that the shadow exchange rate is irrelevant in project evaluation, while Harberger and others hold the opposite view. The difference is resolved by changing the numeraire good. When governments peg their currencies against other currencies it makes foreign exchange the numeraire good. In these circumstances, the shadow exchange rate is the shadow value of government revenue, which isolates income effects. And, by the generalized Hatta decomposition, they are irrelevant in project evaluation. However, if the official exchange rate is flexible some other good must be chosen as numeraire and the shadow exchange rate is no longer the shadow value of government revenue. In these circumstances, the shadow exchange rate will play a role in project evaluation. Indeed, the choice of numeraire matters whenever output changes endogenously with relative prices. If consumers are compensated for a policy change in units of foreign exchange the equilibrium outcome is not the same as the outcome when they are compensated in units of some other numeraire good. This subtle but important difference is easily overlooked because most familiar textbook presentations measure compensating transfers with exogenous prices, where the choice of numeraire is irrelevant. It makes no difference whether consumers are compensated with goods or money when prices are constant. However, there is a difference when prices change endogenously with the compensation.

NOTES

1. In an intertemporal setting where countries can borrow and lend from each other, $F > 0$ would be the increase in foreign borrowing to offset a trade deficit when $p^W m > 0$. In a competitive equilibrium, this extra foreign debt would be matched in present value terms by a stream of expected trade surpluses in the future.

2. With traded goods the dollar change in social welfare in (2.5) is:

$$\frac{dW}{\beta} = \underset{(N)}{-z\,dp} \underset{(T)}{-(m+z)\,(dp^W + d\tau)} \underset{(N)}{-(y+z)\,dt} \underset{(T)}{-y\,dt} + dL,$$

where the change in net government revenue is obtained from (5.4), as:

$$dR = dT + \underset{(N\&T)}{p\,dz} + \underset{(N)}{z\,dp} + \underset{(T)}{z\,(dp^W + d\tau - dt)} + e\,dF + F\,de - dL,$$

with

$$dT = \underset{(N\&T)}{t\,(dy + dz)} + \underset{(N\&T)}{(y+z)\,dt} + \underset{(T)}{m\,d\tau} + \underset{(T)}{\tau\,dm}.$$

The conventional welfare equation in (5.5) is obtained by solving dL using the net change in government revenue, and applying the market clearing conditions:

$(F - p^{w*}m)\, de = 0$—for the balance of payments;

$x_i = \bar{x}_i + y_i + z_i$—for $i \in N + 1$; and,

$m_i = x_i - y_i - z_i$—for $i \in T$. Also, note that in a small open economy: $dp_i^w = p_i^{w*}\, de\ \forall_i$.

3. Endowing a unit of good k on the economy is equivalent to a gift of foreign exchange of $p_k^{w*}\, dz_k = dF$, where this makes the change in tax revenue:

$$\frac{\partial T}{\partial F}p_k^{w*} = \frac{\partial T}{\partial z_k} - t_k + \tau_k,$$

with $p_k^{w*} = \partial F/\partial z_k$. The shadow price in (5.6) is obtained by using (5.8), and the price–tax relationship in (5.2), where:

$$S_k = S_e\frac{dF}{dz_k} = ep_k^{w*} + \frac{\partial T}{\partial z_k} - t_k + \tau_k = p_k + \frac{\partial T}{\partial z_k}.$$

4. By differentiating the balance of payments equation (with $e = 1$) for a marginal increase in foreign exchange, and using the market clearing condition with $B = 0$, we have:

$$1 - \sum_{i \in T} p_i^w \frac{\partial m_i}{\partial F} = 0.$$

5. Normally, analysts compute this traditional formula using average rather than marginal propensities to consume foreign exchange. The correct welfare changes are based on marginal propensities but they are not usually available.

6. This uses the generalized Hatta decomposition in (2.12) to write $S_n = S_R\hat{S}_n$, and obtains the compensated shadow price of the traded good, as: $\hat{S}_k = \hat{S}_e p_k^{w*}$.

7. It is assumed throughout the analysis that changes in domestic demand and supply do not eliminate imports and exports or switch importable goods to exportable goods and vice versa.

8. Using (5.4) the conventional welfare equation in the compensated equilibrium is:

$$d\hat{R} = p\, d\hat{z} + t(d\hat{y} + d\hat{z}) + \tau\, d\hat{m} + e\, d\hat{F}.$$

Once again, the hat (^) over a variable indicates a compensated change with utility held constant for each consumer at its initial level. The compensating transfers are solved using (2.5), with $dW/\beta = 0$, where:

$$d\hat{L} = z\, d\hat{p} + (m + z)(d\hat{p}^w + d\hat{\tau}) + (y + z)\, d\hat{i} + y\, d\hat{i}.$$
$$\quad\ (N) \qquad\qquad (T) \qquad\qquad\quad (N) \qquad (T)$$

9. The compensated shadow price is derived, as:

$$\hat{S}_{k \in T} = p_k^w + \tau_k\frac{\partial \hat{x}_k}{\partial z_k} + (t_k - \tau_k)\frac{\partial \hat{y}_k}{\partial z_k} + \sum_{i \neq k} t_i\frac{\partial \hat{y}_i}{\partial z_k} + \sum_{i \neq k} \tau_i\frac{\partial \hat{m}_i}{\partial z_k},$$

where (5.20) is obtained by noting there are no relative price changes, and as a consequence, no changes in private activity.

10. If the government intervenes in the foreign exchange market to peg the official exchange rate (at unity say), then it must hold onto surplus foreign exchange in the compensated equilibrium to stop it appreciating. When the official exchange rate is pegged at unity, non-traded goods prices adjust to clear all the goods markets, and by Walra's Law there is also balance of payments equilibrium.

11. This is obtained using (5.5), with $dW/\beta = 0$.

12. Three goods would be required to demonstrate the different effects of choosing foreign exchange and a non-traded good 0 as numeraire goods. For balance of payments equilibrium, there would need to be an exportable good and an importable good.
13. See Drèze and Stern (1990: 24, last paragraph).
14. The private sector budget constraint in (2.2) is rewritten using the price–tax relationships in (5.1) and (5.2), as:

$$L = \underset{(N)}{pz} + \underset{(N)}{t(y+z)} + \underset{(T)}{(p^{W} + \tau)(m+z)} + \underset{(T)}{ty} .$$

The public sector budget constraint in (5.4) is revised in a similar way, as:

$$R = T - eF + \underset{(N)}{pz} + \underset{(T)}{(p^{W} + \tau - t)z} - L.$$

The relationship $R = B$ is obtained by using the public sector budget constraint to solve L, and to substitute it into the private sector budget constraint.

15. The conventional welfare equation with volume quota, is:

$$\frac{dW}{\beta} = p\,dz + t(dy + dz) + \tau\,dm + (\bar{p}_Q - p^{W}_Q)d\bar{m}_Q + e\,dF - dR.$$

16. If the tariff is larger than $p_Q - p^{W}_Q$ it will restrict imports below the quota level. In this situation, the quota is non-binding and the tariff determines the level of imports.
17. The conventional welfare equation with value quota, is:

$$\frac{dW}{\beta} = p\,dz + t(dy + dz) + \tau\,dm + (\bar{p}_Q - p^{W}_Q)dm_Q + e\,dF - dR,$$

where $d\bar{v}_Q = p^{W}_Q\,dm_Q + m_Q\,dp^{W}_Q$.

18. Changes in domestic demand and supply are assumed small enough not to drive imports below their quota restricted levels.
19. With value quota restrictions, we have:

$$\frac{\partial \bar{v}_Q}{\partial z_Q} = p^{W}_Q \frac{\partial m_Q}{\partial z_Q} + m_Q \frac{\partial p^{W}_Q}{\partial z_Q} = 0.$$

20. Sieper (1982) provides an excellent summary of the economic effects of the home-price consumption schemes in Australia.
21. Since endowments are non-traded the consumer demand for traded goods must be satisfied entirely from market purchases.
22. The welfare change from marginally increasing public supply of good k, is:

$$S_k = \frac{\partial W}{\partial z_k}\frac{1}{\beta} + \frac{\partial W}{\partial s_k}\frac{1}{\beta}\frac{\partial s_k}{\partial z_k}.$$

It is the conventional shadow price in the absence of the scheme, plus the welfare effect from the change in the subsidy.

23. By using (5.36) we have

$$\frac{ds_k}{dz_k} = -\frac{dt_k}{dz_k} = -\frac{t_k + \tau_k(\partial m_k/\partial z_k) + t_k(\partial y_k/\partial z_k)}{(y_k + z_k) + \tau_k(\partial m_k/\partial z_k) + t_k(\partial y_k/\partial z_k)},$$

and with unchanged demand this simplifies to:

$$\frac{ds_k}{dz_k} = -\frac{dt_k}{dz_k} = -\frac{(\tau_k - t_k)(\partial y_k/\partial z_k + 1)}{(y_k + z_k) - (\tau_k - t_k)\partial y_k/\partial t_k} < 0,$$

$$\text{with } \frac{\partial y_k}{\partial z_k} + 1 > 0 \quad \text{and} \quad \frac{\partial y_k}{\partial t_k} < 0.$$

24. Value added measures the returns paid to domestic factors of production–capital, and labour.
25. Export marketing boards are usually established for goods when countries are large in their world markets. Thus, by restricting exports they can improve the terms of trade for domestic producers.
26. In competitive markets, marginal private profit from producing good j is zero, so that:

$$p_j = a_{kj}p_k + a_{nj}p_n + a_{mj}p_m,$$

where k and n are, respectively, capital and labour inputs. This makes value added under existing policies:

$$VA_j = p_j - a_{mj}p_m = a_{kj}p_k + a_{nj}p_n.$$

27. The small economy assumption is maintained so that world prices are unaffected by changes in domestic trade policies. Thus, free-trade domestic prices are border prices under existing trade policies.
28. This is obtained from the expression:

$$ERP_j = \frac{[p_j^W + \tau_j - t_j - a_{mj}(p_m^W + \tau_m - t_m)] - [p_j^W - a_{mj}^* p_m^W]}{p_j^W - a_{mj}^* p_m^W}.$$

29. By using the NRPs and setting $(a_{mj} - a_{mj}^*) = 0$, the ERP in (5.40) becomes:

$$ERP_j = \frac{NRP_j p_j^W - a_{mj} NRP_m p_m^W}{p_j^W - a_{mj}^W p_m^W}.$$

30. This is obtained by writing (5.41), as:

$$DRCR_j = \frac{\pi_j^S}{S_j - a_{mj}S_m} = 1 - \frac{a_{kj}S_k - a_{nj}S_n}{S_j - a_{mj}S_m}.$$

31. Srinivasan and Bhagwati obtain measures of the DRCR that separate the shadow value of domestic factors used to produce traded input m.
32. Detailed workings are provided in Appendix 3.
33. Findlay and Wellisz (1976) identify circumstances where ERP measures provide the correct rankings for projects.

6

Revised Shadow Prices

Governments raise most of their revenue with distorting taxes, and very little, if any, with lump-sum taxes. This would appear to rule out a conventional cost–benefit analysis which relies on lump-sum transfers to separate the welfare effects of each component of a project. Indeed, Harberger computes shadow prices for individual goods using lump-sum transfers because, as pure income effects, they do not impact on potential welfare gains.[1] Once governments make revenue transfers with distorting taxes, however, there are additional welfare effects from changes in tax inefficiency. Ballard and Fullerton (1992) argue the Pigou (1947), Harberger (1971), and Browning (1976) approach that 'measures the efficiency effects of taxes, given the level of government spending . . . seems poorly suited to the cost–benefit problem of whether the level of government spending should increase, given that the spending must be financed with additional distortionary taxes' (Ballard and Fullerton 1992: 119). Clearly, this statement recognizes the important role of lump-sum transfers in a conventional cost–benefit analysis.

Project appraisal is much more complicated when welfare effects cannot be separated in a conventional manner. For example, Snow and Warren (1996) and Mayshar (1990) obtain a measure of the marginal social cost of public funds that combines the welfare effects of a tax change and the public spending it will fund. In contrast, the conventional measure of the marginal social cost of funds is determined solely by the tax change, and is independent of the way the government spends the revenue.[2] Conventional welfare analysis will be used here to compute the shadow prices of goods when governments make revenue transfers with distorting taxes. They are conventional (lump–sum) shadow prices plus changes in tax inefficiency on the notional lump-sum transfers made to isolate them. This means a conventional welfare analysis can be used even when actual lump-sum transfers are ruled out. And the necessary adjustment to account for changes in tax inefficiency are included in a relatively straightforward manner.

Two sets of revenue transfers were identified in Chapter 3 to separate the efficiency and equity effects of marginal policy changes. One set makes compensating transfers to isolate efficiency gains, while the other set distributes this surplus revenue to consumers. The compensating transfers are determined solely by substitution effects and are therefore policy specific. They will need to be personalized to hold consumer utilities constant, where this may require changes to a potentially large number of tax instruments. However, the same flexibility is not required to make the revenue transfers that balance the government budget unless strict Pareto improvements are required for

Table 6.1 *The exogenous policy variables*

Revenue transfers	Equilibrium closure	
	Full	Compensated ($\wedge$)
Lump-sum	z, t, g, R	z, t, g, W
Distorting taxes (D)	z, L, R	z, L, W

socially profitable projects.[3] And that may also require changes to a potentially large number of taxes. The following analysis assumes that there are sufficient taxes to make the compensating transfers and to realize Pareto improvements.

Once distorting taxes can be used to make revenue transfers there are four possible equilibrium outcomes for the economy, where the exogenous policy variables in each are summarized in Table 6.1.

In the full and compensated equilibrium outcomes, revenue transfers can be made endogenously with lump-sum transfers or distorting taxes. Whenever welfare changes are isolated using distorting taxes they are identified in the following analysis by a subscript D, where for example, the change in tax revenue from extra output of good k, is:

$$\left(\frac{\partial T}{\partial z_k}\right)_D = \frac{\partial T(z, L, R)}{\partial z_k} \qquad \text{in full equilibrium,}$$

$$\left(\frac{\partial \hat{T}}{\partial z_k}\right)_D = \frac{\partial T(z, L, W)}{\partial z_k} \qquad \text{in the compensated equilibrium.}$$

Corden (1974) recognized the need to adjust shadow prices for the effects of distorting taxes and referred to it as the implementation-problem. Sieper (1994) made the appropriate adjustment by deriving *implementation-problem corrected* shadow prices in the compensated equilibrium. They are conventional (lump-sum) shadow prices plus changes in tax inefficiency on compensating revenue transfers when they are made with distorting taxes. A similar correction is made in this chapter to the conventional shadow prices in full equilibrium. We adopt the terminology of Pigou and refer to them as *revised* shadow prices, where for any good k, we have:

$$(S_k)_D = S_k - \sum_i \text{meb}_i \frac{\partial L}{\partial t_i} \left(\frac{dt_i}{dz_k}\right)_D,^4 \tag{6.1}$$

where:

$$\text{meb}_i = -\frac{(\partial W/\partial t_i)(1/\beta)}{\partial L/\partial t_i} \tag{6.2}$$

is the conventional measure of the *marginal excess burden* of tax i; it is the tax inefficiency per dollar change in government revenue.[5] Since these tax changes are made to balance the government budget, they will solve:

$$\left(\frac{\mathrm{d}L}{\mathrm{d}z_k}\right)_{\mathrm{D}} = 0 = \frac{\partial L}{\partial z_k} + \sum_i \frac{\partial L}{\partial t_i}\left(\frac{\mathrm{d}t_i}{\mathrm{d}z_k}\right)_{\mathrm{D}}. \tag{6.3}$$

Recall from Chapter 2 that the conventional shadow price for any good k (S_k) is computed using lump-sum transfers $(\partial L/\partial z_k)$ to balance the government budget. Whenever these revenue transfers are made with distorting taxes, each dollar must be scaled up by the marginal excess burden of taxation to account for changes in tax inefficiency. If extra output of good k drives the budget into surplus then distorting taxes will have to be lowered. The consequent fall in tax inefficiency makes the revised shadow price larger than the conventional shadow price as a signal that selling good k is a more efficient way for the government to raise additional revenue.[6]

The analysis is simplified considerably when the government uses a single tax d to balance its budget, or taxes have the same marginal excess burden (with $\mathrm{meb}_i = \mathrm{meb}_d\ \forall_i$), where the shadow price in (6.1) becomes:

$$(S_k)_{\mathrm{D}} = S_k + \mathrm{meb}_d\,\frac{\partial L}{\partial z_k}.^7 \tag{6.4}$$

It is illustrated in Figure 6.1 where, for simplicity, the analysis assumes no cross-effects between the markets for goods k and d, and no distortions in other markets. (To demonstrate the role of government production in the welfare analysis it is initially set at half the output of good k, a third of the output of good d, with none in other goods markets.) The conventional shadow price, which was previously illustrated

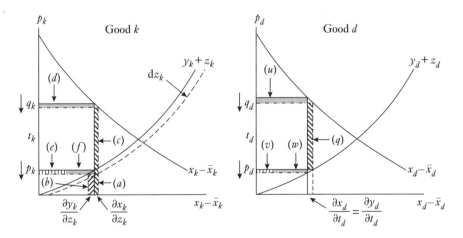

Figure 6.1 *The revised shadow price of good k—in full equilibrium*

in Figure 2.4 (p. 53), is:

$$S_k = p_k + \frac{\partial T}{\partial z_k} = (a) + (b) + (c).$$

In Chapter 2, this was decomposed as the direct increase in private surplus in $(d) - (f) = (e)$ plus a lump-sum transfer when the government balances its budget, which was solved using (2.6), as:

$$\frac{\partial L}{\partial z_k} = p_k + \frac{\partial T}{\partial z_k} + z_k \frac{\partial p_k}{\partial z_k} = (a) + (b) + (c) - (e).$$

Selling another unit of good k generates sales revenue in $(a) + (b)$ and extra tax revenue in (c), but there is a loss on public production in (e). Once this surplus revenue is transferred as a lump-sum payment to consumers the loss in profit in (e) undoes the rise in private surplus in $(d) - (f)$, and the conventional shadow price is the sales revenue in $(a) + (b)$ and the tax revenue in (c). However, when this surplus revenue is transferred to consumers by lowering tax d there is a welfare gain from the reducing the tax inefficiency by (q). The size of this gain is determined by the marginal excess burden of taxation in (6.2), which is solved using equations (2.7) and (2.6), as:

$$\text{meb}_d = \frac{-t_d(\partial y_d/\partial t_d)}{y_d + z_d + t_d(\partial y_d/\partial t_d) + z_d(\partial p_d/\partial t_d)} = \frac{(q)}{(u) + (w) - (q)}. \qquad 8$$

It measures the welfare loss from using tax d to transfer a dollar of revenue to the government budget. The welfare gain in (q) is obtained by multiplying each dollar of the surplus revenue by this marginal excess burden, where the revised shadow price in (6.4), becomes:

$$(S_k)_D = \underbrace{[(a) + (b) + (c)]}_{S_k} + \underbrace{\left(\frac{(q)}{(u) + (w) - (q)}\right)}_{\text{meb}_d} \underbrace{[(a) + (b) + (c) - (e)]}_{\dfrac{\partial L}{\partial z_k}}$$

$$= (a) + (b) + (c) + (q).$$

Tax d must fall until the revenue it transfers to consumers in $(u) + (w) - (q)$ is equal to the budget surplus from an extra unit of good k in $(a) + (b) + (c) - (e)$.[9] The resulting welfare gain in (q) makes the revised shadow price larger in value than the conventional shadow price, with $(S_k)_D = S_k + (q)$.

There are a number of ways to extend this analysis. For example, with taxes in other markets, extra output of good k could drive the budget into deficit by reducing these activities (with $\partial L/\partial z_k < 0$). Tax d would then need to rise, where the increase in tax inefficiency would make the revised shadow price less in value than the conventional shadow price (with $(S_k)_D < S_k$). Clearly, there is no change in tax inefficiency if the government budget is unaffected by extra output of good k (with $\partial L/\partial z_k = 0$), where the revised shadow price will be equal to the conventional shadow price, with $(S_k)_D = S_k$.

6.1 DETERMINANTS OF THE CHANGES IN TAX INEFFICIENCY

The graphical derivation of the revised shadow price in the previous section makes it clear what determines changes in tax inefficiency in policy evaluation. There are two separate components; the marginal excess burden of taxation (meb$_d$), and the size and sign of the revenue transfers to balance the government budget ($\partial L/\partial z_k$). The factors that determine the size of the marginal excess burden for each tax are reasonably straightforward to identify. They include the initial values of the taxes, and how responsive activity is to marginal changes in them. A number of factors determine the size and sign of the revenue transfers for good k, and they are its market price, endogenous change in tax revenue, and the share of output produced by the public sector. By assumption, the only revenue transfers from extra output of good k in Figure 6.1 are confined to those originating in its own market, but they can also arise in related markets, and are affected by other factors. A number of these extensions are now examined.

(i) *Government Trade in Related Private Markets.* When governments buy and sell goods and services in private markets their budgets are affected by endogenous price changes. This was illustrated in Figure 6.1 when the government sold both goods k and d. Public profit was reduced by the lower price of good k and increased by the higher price of good d. If the government also purchases a net input m, then endogenous changes in its price will impact on the government budget. The effects are illustrated in Figure 6.2 by assuming the marginal increase in output of good k raises private demand for input m when two-thirds of it is initially purchased by the government.

A higher consumer price reduces public sector profit by (l) and increases tax revenue by area (j), where the net increase in government revenue is (j) − (l). Now the

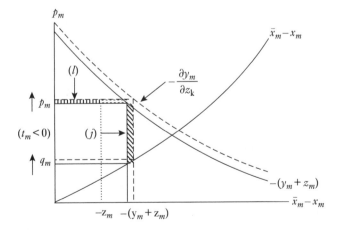

Figure 6.2 *An endogenous fall in public sector profit*

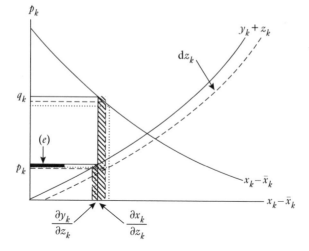

Figure 6.3 *The shadow price with an ad valorem tax*

combined impact of good k on net government revenue, is:

$$\frac{\partial L}{\partial z_k} = (a) + (b) + (c) - (e) - (l) + (j).$$

If $(j) - (l)$ is negative and larger than $(a) + (b) + (c) - (e)$ the budget will move into deficit and tax d will have to rise, where the resulting increase in tax inefficiency makes the revised shadow price of good k smaller in value than its conventional shadow price.

(ii) *Ad Valorem Taxes.* Most taxes are defined as a fixed percentage of the producer prices. Thus, tax wedges change whenever prices change, and their impact on private surplus is no longer matched by offsetting changes in public profit. This is illustrated in Figure 6.3 by deriving the conventional shadow price of good k when it is subject to an *ad valorem* tax.

Extra public output drives down the producer price and reduces the tax wedge. There is now a smaller reduction in the consumer and producer prices, and activity rises more, than was previously the case with a specific tax. The dashed lines illustrate the changes for a specific tax, while the dotted lines are the changes for the *ad valorem* tax. Since private demand rises more and private production falls less, there is a smaller reduction in public sector profit in (e). Also, the change in tax revenue is ambiguous; there is less revenue collected on the initial trade, but a larger tax base.

(iii) *Private Sector Projects.* Private sector projects are evaluated by endowing goods on the private sector of the economy because that is where the sales revenue flows. The impact on the revised shadow price can be illustrated using Figure 6.1. There is now a smaller net increase in government revenue of $(c) - (e)$, when previously it was $(a) + (b) + (c) - (e)$. The sales revenue in $(a) + (b)$ flows directly to the private sector. While this has no impact on the conventional (lump–sum) shadow price, since consumers receive the sales revenue as a lump-sum transfer anyway, it does affect the revised shadow price in (6.4) by reducing the welfare gain in (q). With less surplus revenue to transfer to the private sector there is a smaller fall in tax d, where the revised shadow price in (6.4), becomes:

$$(S_k)_D = \underbrace{[(a) + (b) + (c)]}_{S_k} + \underbrace{\left(\frac{(q)}{(u) + (w) - (q)}\right)}_{\text{meb}_d} \underbrace{[(c) - (e)]}_{\dfrac{\partial L}{\partial z_k}}.$$

Now the revenue transferred to consumers by lowering tax d in $(u) + (w) - (q)$ is equal to the smaller surplus revenue generated by an extra unit of good k in $(c) - (e)$. As a consequence, there is also a smaller reduction in tax inefficiency in (q).

6.2 EFFICIENCY EFFECTS

Efficiency effects determine how much surplus government revenue a policy change will generate at constant utility. If lump-sum transfers are ruled out then compensating transfers will have to be made with distorting taxes. That is why, in the compensated equilibrium, Sieper computes revised shadow prices as conventional shadow prices plus changes in tax inefficiency on the compensating transfers. However, when making this adjustment Sieper is content to use a single tax to make the compensating transfers, which is unlikely in heterogeneous consumer economies. On that basis, we compute the revised shadow price using the welfare equation in (2.9), as:

$$(\hat{S}_k)_D = \hat{S}_k - \sum_i \text{mêb}_i \frac{\partial \hat{L}}{\partial t_i} \left(\frac{d\hat{t}_i}{dz_k}\right)_D, \tag{6.5}$$

where:

$$\text{mêb}_i = -\frac{\partial \hat{R}/\partial t_i}{\partial \hat{L}/\partial t_i} \tag{6.6}$$

is the compensated *marginal excess burden* for each tax i; it is the tax inefficiency per dollar of compensation.[10] Since the tax changes must make compensating transfers to hold consumer utilities constant, they will solve:

$$\left(\frac{d\hat{L}^h}{dz_k}\right)_D = \frac{\partial \hat{L}^h}{\partial z_k} + \sum_i \frac{\partial \hat{L}^h}{\partial t_i} \left(\frac{d\hat{t}_i}{dz_k}\right)_D = 0 \qquad \forall_h. \tag{6.7}$$

Clearly, a potentially large number of taxes will need to change to make these compensating transfers.[11] Indeed, there must be enough tax instruments available to the government for it to personalize the revenue transfers. At this point, one may be

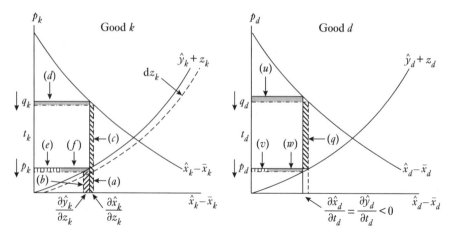

Figure 6.4 *The compensated revised shadow price of good k*

tempted to argue the efficiency gains should be isolated using lump-sum compensation as they are in most cases hypothetical welfare changes. But this overlooks the important point that efficiency gains must be realizable gains for them to be a meaningful measure of a welfare change. In other words, they must be the revenue gains the government could actually realize by making compensating transfers, and if those transfers would in practice be made with distorting taxes then they should be used to isolate the hypothetical efficiency effects. This means that the shadow price in (6.5) is surplus revenue the government could actually collect by making the compensating transfers.

The analysis is simplified considerably when (i) there is a single consumer in the economy with compensating transfers made using a single tax d, or (ii) taxes have the same compensated marginal excess burden, with $\text{mêb}_i = \text{mêb}_d \; \forall_i$. In these circumstances, we can write the shadow price in (6.5), as:

$$(\hat{S}_k)_{\text{D}} = \hat{S}_k + \text{mêb}_d \frac{\partial \hat{L}}{\partial z_k}.^{12} \tag{6.8}$$

It is illustrated in Figure 6.4 where the analysis is again simplified by assuming away distortions in other markets and cross-effects between goods k and d. (Also, the public sector initially produces half of good k, a third of good d, and no other goods.)

The conventional shadow price, which was previously illustrated in Figure 2.6, is:

$$\hat{S}_k = p_k + \frac{\partial \hat{T}}{\partial z_k} = (a) + (b) + (c).$$

This is the amount of surplus revenue the government collects after funding the lump-sum compensation to hold consumer utilities constant. Since another unit of good k

raises private surplus by $(d) - (f) = (e)$, the compensating transfers must take this amount of revenue from consumers, where from (2.10), we have:

$$\frac{\partial \hat{L}}{\partial z_k} = z_k \frac{\partial \hat{p}_k}{\partial z_k} = -(e).$$

However, when this compensation is made by raising tax d the government will collect less revenue than (e) due to the marginal excess burden of taxation in (6.6). It is the efficiency loss on each dollar of compensation and is computed using the conventional welfare equation (2.9) and the transfer equation (2.10), where:

$$\text{mêb}_d = \frac{-t_d(\partial \hat{y}_d / \partial t_d)}{y_d + z_d + t_d(\partial \hat{y}_d / \partial t_d)} = \frac{(q)}{(u) + (w)}.^{13}$$

Notice that this normalization of the tax inefficiency is not the same as the conventional measure in (6.2) which divides the welfare loss by the dollar change in government revenue.[14] This is due to the different role played by the revenue transfers in the compensated equilibrium. Revenue transfers balance the government budget in full equilibrium, whereas they hold consumer utilities constant in the compensated equilibrium. The conventional Harberger measure of the excess burden in (6.2) is the most familiar normalization because cost–benefit studies normally measure actual, rather than compensated, welfare changes.

After combining these welfare effects using the revised shadow price in (6.8), we have:

$$(\hat{S}_k)_D = \underbrace{[(a) + (b) + (c)]}_{S_k} + \underbrace{\left(\frac{q}{(u) + (w)}\right)}_{\text{mêb}_d} \underbrace{[-(e)]}_{\frac{\partial L}{\partial z_k}} = (a) + (b) + (c) - (q).$$

When tax d rises to hold utility constant it must offset the increase in private surplus from extra output of good k in (e) by collecting tax revenue of $(u) + (w) = (e)$. The resulting excess burden in (q) makes the revised shadow price in (6.8) lower in value than the conventional shadow price in (6.4), with $(\hat{S}_k)_D = \hat{S}_k - (q)$. However, this relationship may be reversed by distortions and/or public sector production in other markets. For example, higher prices will reduce private surplus in related markets where the government produces output. If this leads to a net reduction in private surplus from extra output of good k the distorting tax must fall to compensate consumers, where the revised shadow price rises above the conventional shadow price by the reduction in tax inefficiency. Clearly, the revised and conventional shadow prices are equal in the absence of any compensating transfers, which is the case for internationally traded goods under small country conditions.[15]

6.2.1 *Determinants of the Compensated Changes in Tax Inefficiency*

There are two factors that determine the changes in tax inefficiency in the revised shadow prices in (6.5) and (6.8). First, there is the welfare loss from marginally raising the tax $(\partial \hat{R}/\partial t_i)$ which depends on the size of the substitution effects for the tax change. The more responsive activity is to the price change, the larger is the change in tax inefficiency. The second factor is the size of the compensating transfers for both the good being shadow priced $(\partial \hat{L}/\partial z_k)$ and the tax change $(\partial \hat{L}/\partial t_i)$. They are determined by:

(i) *Initial Public Production.* Price changes transfer private surplus to the government budget through changes in public sector profit when the government trades in markets. The more output the public sector produces, the larger is the change in private surplus from endogenous price changes. This is illustrated in Figure 6.5 for good k with no initial public production. With a specific tax extra output reduces the consumer and producer prices of the good by the same amount, where the resulting fall in private profit is exactly offset by the increase in consumer surplus. No compensating transfers are required in these circumstances. However, if the public sector initially produces all the output there is no reduction in private profit to offset the increase in consumer surplus which must instead be offset by compensating transfers. Thus, the size of the compensating transfers will contract with the share of initial public production.

(ii) *Ad Valorem Taxes.* In the presence of specific taxes the changes in consumer surplus from endogenous price changes are offset by the changes in producer profit. This was demonstrated by the analysis in the previous section. However, it is no longer the case for *ad valorem* taxes as the tax wedges will change endogenously with producer prices. Consider the example illustrated in Figure 6.6 where private demand for good m, which the government does not buy or sell, rises with the extra output of good k.

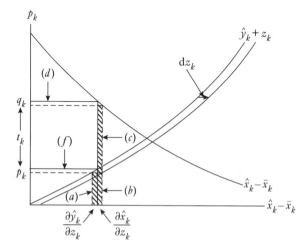

Figure 6.5 *The compensated shadow price with no initial public production*

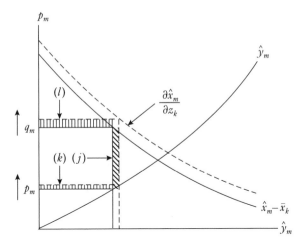

Figure 6.6 *An ad valorem tax*

The higher producer price increases the tax wedge. It reduces consumer surplus by (l), but there is a smaller increase in private profit in (k). Overall, private surplus falls by $(l) - (k)$, which must be offset by compensating transfers. There is no need for any compensation with a specific tax because the consumer and producer prices would rise by the same amount.

(iii) *Externalities.* In some circumstances, market prices do not account for all the marginal costs and benefits of trade. These external costs and benefits can, like taxes and subsidies, lead to allocative inefficiency. But there is an important difference between them because externalities do not transfer revenue between the government and the private economy in the same way as taxes and subsidies, and this difference is important for the shadow prices. Consider the classic example of pollution which raises the marginal social cost of supplying a good above its private cost. In the absence of a Pigouvian tax or private negotiations between affected parties to internalize this externality, too many resources are attracted into a competitive market. This is illustrated in Figure 6.7 for good k when social marginal cost exceeds private marginal cost by a constant per unit external cost of c_k.

When the government sells another unit of the good it collects sales revenue of $(a) + (b)$. Area (d) is a resource cost saving if the externality does not arise from public production, and revenue must be transferred from the private sector to offset this gain. Alternatively, if the externality does arise on public production, there is a welfare loss in (c) which must be offset by compensating transfers.[16]

(iv) *Public Goods.* If consumers cannot be excluded from the benefits provided by a public good, then they have an incentive to free ride off the contributions made by others, and this makes it difficult for suppliers to collect any sales revenue. When public goods endow consumption benefits directly on consumers they must be offset by lump-sum taxes to hold utility constant. Figure 6.8 provides

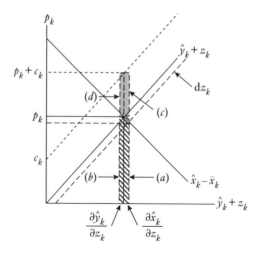

Figure 6.7 *A negative production externality*

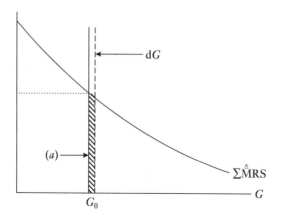

Figure 6.8 *A (non-excludable) public good*

an example of this for a (non-excludable) pure public good G provided solely by the government.

An extra unit of the good confers additional benefits on consumers in (a). None of this surplus is collected as sales revenue so that the shadow price is (a) plus the welfare effects in related markets. It makes no difference whether the good is endowed on the private or public sectors of the economy—the conventional shadow price of the public good is the same.[17] If the surplus in (a) is transferred from consumers with a distorting tax the revised shadow price falls below the conventional shadow price by the change in tax inefficiency.

6.3 INCOME EFFECTS AND THE REVISED SHADOW VALUE OF GOVERNMENT REVENUE

There are many ways to distribute the efficiency gain in (6.5) to consumers using distorting taxes. One is to lower a single tax which would likely make some consumers better off and others worse off. Alternatively, a number of taxes could be changed simultaneously to make every consumer better off. The final choice ultimately determines the distributional effects in the revised shadow value of government revenue, which is the welfare change from endowing a dollar of revenue on the government who balances its budget with distorting taxes. The Hatta decomposition in (2.12) can be generalized to accommodate endogenous revenue transfers with distorting taxes by writing social welfare as a function of the vector of public production z and foreign aid payments R, with $W_D(z, R)$. The foreign aid payment that would offset the welfare effects from endowing a unit of good k on the economy, solves:

$$dW_D = (W_k)_D \, d\hat{z}_k + (W_R)_D \, d\hat{R} = 0.^{18}$$

After rearranging terms, we have:

$$(\hat{S}_k)_D = \left(\frac{d\hat{R}}{dz_k}\right)_D = -\frac{(W_k)_D/\beta}{(W_R)_D/\beta} = \frac{(S_k)_D}{(S_R)_D},$$

where: $(S_R)_D = -(dW/dR)_D(1/\beta)$ is the *revised shadow value of government revenue*. This allows us to decompose the revised shadow price of any good k in (6.1), as:

$$(S_k)_D = (S_R)_D(\hat{S}_k)_D.^{19} \tag{6.9}$$

Once again, there are two sets of revenue transfers in (6.9); the first are tax changes to isolate the efficiency gain in $(\hat{S}_k)_D$, while the second are tax changes to distribute this surplus revenue to consumers in $(S_R)_D$. Since the compensating tax changes are determined by substitution effects that differ over consumers they are a function of the policy choice k. In contrast, the tax changes to distribute surplus revenue to consumers in $(S_R)_D$ can have the same distributional effects for any policy change. Indeed, when surplus revenue is used to raise the utility of every consumer (with $du^h/dz_k > 0 \; \forall_h$), which is likely to require multiple tax changes, there are strict Pareto improvements whenever $(S_k)_D > 0$. These distributional effects will be examined in Chapter 7 using the marginal social cost of public funds (MCF).

A reduced form expression for the revised shadow value of government revenue is obtained from the conventional welfare equation in (2.7), as:

$$(S_R)_D = S_R - \text{meb}_d \frac{\partial L}{\partial R}.^{20} \tag{6.10}$$

Once again, it is the conventional shadow price (S_R) plus the change in tax inefficiency when tax d is used to make the revenue transfers $(\partial L/\partial R)$ to balance the government budget. If the government wants to choose a different pattern of revenue transfers to change the distributional effects it will have to change more than one tax or personalize the tax changes. In such circumstances the change in tax inefficiency in the second term of (6.10) will be the weighted sum of the revenue transfers for each tax where the weights are the marginal excess burdens. Indeed, it will be similar to the second term in the shadow price of good k in (6.1).

6.4 PROJECT EVALUATION

The role of distorting taxes in project evaluation can be demonstrated by computing the shadow profit for a public project that produces a unit of good 1 using inputs 2 and 3 as:

$$(\pi^S)_D = (S_1)_D - (S_2)_D a_{21} - (S_3)_D a_{31}.$$

When tax d is used to balance the government budget, we have from (6.4) that:

$$(\pi^S)_D = (1 + \mathrm{meb}_d)\left(p_1 - p_2 a_{21} - p_3 a_{31} + \frac{\mathrm{d}T}{\mathrm{d}z_1}\right) + \mathrm{meb}_d z \frac{\mathrm{d}p}{\mathrm{d}z_1}, \qquad (6.11)$$

with:

$$\frac{\mathrm{d}T}{\mathrm{d}z_1} = \frac{\partial T}{\partial z_1} - \frac{\partial T}{\partial z_2} a_{21} - \frac{\partial T}{\partial z_3} a_{31},$$

being the aggregate change in tax revenue; and,

$$z\frac{\mathrm{d}p}{\mathrm{d}z_1} = \sum_i z_i \frac{\partial p_i}{\partial z_1} - \sum_i z_i \frac{\partial p_i}{\partial z_2} a_{21} - \sum_i z_i \frac{\partial p_i}{\partial z_3} a_{31},$$

the aggregate change in profit on public production.

The first term in (6.11) is the surplus government revenue transferred to consumers by lowering tax d, and it is scaled up by the marginal excess burden of taxation (meb_d) to account for the reduction in tax inefficiency. The second term is the change in public profit due to endogenous price changes, and since it offsets direct changes in private surplus, the welfare effects are confined to changes in tax inefficiency. If the public sector produces the good as efficiently as competitive private firms (with $p_1 - p_2 a_{21} - p_3 a_{31} = 0$), the shadow profit for the project becomes:

$$(\pi^S)_D = (1 + \mathrm{meb}_d)\frac{\mathrm{d}T}{\mathrm{d}z_1} + \mathrm{meb}_d z \frac{\mathrm{d}p}{\mathrm{d}z_1}.$$

Based on Harberger's characterization of policy changes the project is a *substitution effect only* problem where the welfare changes are confined to resource reallocations across distorted markets. Conversely, if the public sector is less efficient than private firms due to soft budget constraints and/or principal–agent problems, the shadow profit for the project will be:

$$(\pi^S)_D = (1 + \text{meb}_d)\left(p_2(ay_{21} - az_{21}) + p_3(ay_{31} - az_{31}) + \frac{dT}{dz_1}\right) + \text{meb}_d z\frac{dp}{dz_1},$$
(6.12)

where ay_{i1} and az_{i1} for $i \in (2,3)$ are, respectively, the input–output coefficients for private and public producers. This makes the project an *income and substitution effect* problem where the first two terms inside the brackets in (6.12) measure the fall in real income and the remaining terms in (6.12) the welfare effects from resource reallocations across distorted activities.

Any distributional effects must be contained in the revised shadow value of government revenue, $(S_R)_D$, because it isolates all the income effects from the project. If the government uses the same tax d (or a combination of taxes) to distribute surplus revenue to consumers the revised shadow value of government revenue will be independent of the policy change, where the shadow profit for the project can be decomposed using the generalized Hatta decomposition in (6.9), as:

$$(\pi^S)_D = (S_R)_D\{(\hat{S}_1)_D - (\hat{S}_2)_D a_{21} - (\hat{S}_3)_D a_{31}\} = (S_R)_D(\hat{\pi}_1^S)_D.$$

In these circumstances, income effects play no role in finding the optimal supply of good 1, since $(\pi_1^S)_D = 0$ whenever $(\hat{\pi}_1^S)_D = 0$. Moreover, when surplus government revenue is distributed by distorting tax changes that make every consumer better off, then $(\pi_1^S)_D > 0$ is a strict Pareto improvement.[21]

6.5 CONCLUDING REMARKS

Perhaps, the most important implication of the analysis in this chapter is that conventional shadow prices do not have to be abandoned in project evaluation when lump-sum transfers are ruled out. Instead, they can be adjusted in a straightforward manner to accommodate revenue transfers with distorting taxes, where the revised shadow price of any good is its conventional shadow price plus the change in tax inefficiency on the revenue transfers. If a good generates surplus revenue for the government budget then the revised shadow price will exceed the conventional shadow price by the reduction in tax inefficiency from lower distorting taxes. This change in tax inefficiency is determined by the marginal excess burden of taxation and the size of the revenue transfers that must be made to balance the government budget.

In many public economics applications, the marginal social cost of public funds (MCF) is used in project evaluation to account for the welfare effects of distorting taxes. But it does not appear, at least explicitly, in any of the welfare changes in this chapter. Instead, the marginal excess burden of taxation is used to amend the conventional welfare changes. The conventional MCF will be defined in Chapter 7 and used to obtain revised shadow prices for goods. This will allow us to reconcile welfare measures obtained using shadow prices, with welfare changes obtained in many public economics applications using the MCF. It has the useful byproduct of highlighting the difference between the MCF and the shadow value of government revenue, which are quite separate welfare measures that play an important, but separate role in cost–benefit analysis.

NOTES

1. There are no efficiency effects from lump-sum transfers when local Foster and Sonnenschein (1970) effects are ruled out. These effects were examined in Chapter 2. Also, there are no efficiency effects from lump-sum redistributions of income when prices change endogenously with compensating transfers. This avoids the problem identified in the Boadway (1974) paradox which was examined in Chapter 1.
2. The marginal social cost of public funds, and its role in applied welfare analysis, is examined in Chapter 7.
3. There are welfare tests in Diewert (1983) that isolate Pareto improvements for small policy changes when governments use one or a number of distorting taxes.
4. This is formally derived in Appendix 4.
5. Since the tax inefficiency in (6.2) is measured as a dollar change in social welfare, it includes income effects. The standard measure, which is presented in Diamond and McFadden (1974) and Auerbach and Hines (2002), is based purely on substitution effects, where they separate the income and substitution effects by holding producer prices constant. Their analysis is extended in following chapters by separating these effects with variable producer prices.
6. Taxes are assumed to be set at or below their revenue maximizing levels. This rules out the possibility of Laffer curve effects where reductions in marginal tax rates increase government revenue.
7. By using the conventional welfare equation in (2.7) and the transfer equation in (2.6), this revised shadow price becomes:

$$(S_k)_D = p_k + \frac{\partial T}{\partial z_k} - \left(\frac{\sum_i t_i (\partial y_i / \partial t_d)}{(y_d + z_d) + \sum_i t_i (\partial y_i / \partial t_d) + \sum_i z_i (\partial p_i / \partial t_d)} \right)$$
$$\times \left(p_k + \frac{\partial T}{\partial z_k} + \sum_i z_i \frac{\partial p_i}{\partial z_k} \right).$$

8. When taxes are Ramsey (1927) optimal they have the same marginal excess burdens. Optimal tax rules are examined in Chapter 9.
9. Area (v) is a rise in profit that offsets the fall in tax revenue on public production.
10. This welfare change is derived in Appendix 5.
11. The compensating tax changes are solved by stacking the constraints in (6.7) over consumers, where in vector notation, we have $[g_k^h] = -[g_t^h][dt_{ik}]$, where $[g_k^h]$ is the $(H \times 1)$ vector of compensating transfers for the policy change k, $[g_t^h]$ the $(H \times t)$ matrix of compensating transfers for the multiple tax changes and $[dt_{ik}]$ the $(t \times 1)$ vector of tax changes. The tax changes are therefore $[dt_{ik}] = -[g_t^h]^{-1}[g_k^h]$.
12. By using the conventional welfare equation in (2.9), and the revenue transfer equation in (2.10), this shadow price becomes:

$$(\hat{S}_k)_D = p_k + \frac{\partial \hat{T}}{\partial z_k} - \left(\frac{\sum_i t_i (\partial \hat{y}_i / \partial t_d)}{(y_d + z_d) + \sum_j z_j (\partial \hat{p}_j / \partial t_d)} \right) \sum_j z_j \frac{\partial \hat{p}_j}{\partial z_k}.$$

13. When taxes are Ramsey optimal they have the same compensated marginal excess burden. In Chapter 9, we show that this also coincides with them having the same uncompensated marginal excess burden in a single consumer economy where income effects are irrelevant in project evaluation.
14. Notice it is the tax inefficiency per dollar change in government revenue from all sources, not just from taxes. The public sector makes profit on its production, and this revenue also changes with distorting taxes.

15. The compensated shadow prices of fully traded goods are equal to their border prices in small open economies with fixed official exchange rates. This was demonstrated in Chapter 5. In effect, these goods are supplied to the domestic economy at constant border prices. Diamond and Mirrlees (1976) find the compensated shadow prices of goods are equal to their producer prices in economies with linear production frontiers. In the absence of endogenous price changes extra public output in any market will completely crowd out the same private output where the resource cost saving is their respective producer prices.

16. Externalities are examined in Chapter 4.

17. It is quite possible for production costs to differ between the two sectors of the economy. But this is captured separately by shadow pricing the production inputs. The shadow prices of public goods are derived formally in Chapter 10 where they are used to obtain a revised Samuelson condition for the optimal provision of public goods with distorting taxation.

18. The partial welfare changes are $(W_k)_D = (dW/dz_k)_D$ and $(W_R)_D = (dW/dR)_D$.

19. This relationship is confirmed in Appendix 6 where shadow prices are decomposed using structural form expressions when taxes are Ramsey optimal.

20. The notional lump-sum transfers in (6.10) are solved using (2.6), as:

$$\frac{\partial L}{\partial R} = -S_R + z\frac{\partial p}{\partial R},$$

where this allows us to write the revised shadow value of government revenue, as:

$$(S_R)_D = S_R\{1 + \text{meb}_d\} - \text{meb}_d z\frac{\partial p}{\partial R}.$$

21. There is a detailed examination of distributional effects with distorting taxes in Section 7.6.

7

The Marginal Social Cost of Public Funds

Governments raise most of their revenue with taxes that impose excess burdens on taxpayers. By contracting the tax base these taxes reduce private surplus by more than the revenue they collect. Relatively little revenue is raised with non-distorting taxes because few activities are unaffected by relative price changes, especially over time when resources can be reallocated across markets, and lump-sum taxes are not politically attractive. The need to use distorting taxes makes the marginal social cost of public funds (MCF) a central issue in the evaluation of public policy, where socially profitable projects must generate sufficient additional benefits to cover the excess burden of taxation.

A number of factors make the MCF a potentially confusing concept. First, the MCF is not a shadow price.[1] Indeed, it is a very different concept to the shadow value of government revenue, but they each have an important role to play in policy evaluation. The conventional Harberger (1964) measure of the MCF is the cost to private surplus of using a tax to transfer a dollar of revenue from the private to the public sector. In project evaluation it is used to adjust each dollar of revenue for changes in tax inefficiency when the government balances its budget with distorting taxes. It is one plus the marginal excess burden of taxation (MEB), with $MCF = 1 + MEB$, where the marginal excess burden is computed by marginally raising the tax and returning revenue to taxpayers as a lump-sum transfer. Thus, for a non-distorting tax the MCF is unity. Since it is computed by returning tax revenue to taxpayers, the MCF cannot be used to measure welfare gains from endowing surplus revenue on the government. In other words, it cannot be used as the generalized Hatta coefficient to convert efficiency gains into utility. Instead, that role is performed by the shadow value of government revenue. This chapter will demonstrate the role of the conventional MCF in project evaluation by rearranging the revised shadow prices derived in Chapter 6. It conveniently provides a basis for comparing the different but related roles of the MCF and the shadow value of government revenue.

Indeed, no clear distinction is made between these two welfare measures in the applied welfare literature, which is probably because the Hatta (1977) decomposition is not widely used to separate income effects in project evaluation. Some studies examine the shadow value of government revenue but refer to it as the MCF. For example, Dahlby (1998) argues the MCF for a lump-sum tax can differ from unity when income effects from the revenue transfer impact on taxed activities. However, Dahlby is actually measuring the shadow value of government revenue and not the

MCF. There are income effects from endowing surplus revenue on the government, but that is not how the MCF is computed. Instead, the government collects revenue with a tax and then returns it to taxpayers as lump-sum transfers to compute the marginal excess burden of taxation. Thus, the MCF for a lump-sum tax must always be unity.

A second source of confusion arises from the different measures of the MCF used in applied work. Håkonsen (1998), Mayshar (1990), and Snow and Warren (1996) examine a number of them in detail. Some analysts compute changes in tax inefficiency as compensated welfare effects while others measure them as dollar changes in utility. There are similar differences in the way changes in tax revenue are measured. A further complication arises when compensated changes in tax inefficiency are normalized over uncompensated changes in tax revenue.[2] While it is not incorrect to use different measures of the MCF, they should reflect the equilibrium closure of the economy. In full equilibrium, changes in tax inefficiency are dollar changes in utility from marginally raising taxes and should be normalized by the resulting changes in tax revenue to balance the government budget. However, in a compensated equilibrium changes in tax inefficiency are increases in the government budget deficit and should be normalized by the compensating revenue transfers made to offset the tax changes. This provides the correct measure of the MCF for each equilibrium closure of the economy.

There is another potential source of confusion when analysts use a modified measure of the MCF which 'ultimately depends not just on the tax, but also on the nature of the government expenditure under consideration' (Ballard and Fullerton 1992: 125). Ballard and Fullerton (1992), and Wildasin (1984) use it to compute the revised Samuelson condition of Pigou (1947).[3] By including a *spending effect* identified in Diamond and Mirrlees (1971) and Stiglitz and Dasgupta (1971), the modified MCF is a function of the tax change and the extra government spending its funds.[4] In contrast, the conventional MCF is determined solely by the tax change since the revenue is returned to taxpayers as lump-sum transfers. Indeed, a conventional Harberger analysis separates welfare effects for each policy change by using lump-sum transfers to balance the government budget, which is the reason why the *spending effect* is not included in the MCF. Instead, it is included with the welfare effects from changes in government spending.[5] Once the tax and spending changes are brought together inside a project the net change in revenue transfers determines the size and sign of the tax change.

By comparing the modified MCF to the conventional Harberger measure it is possible to explain, at least partially, why there are large differences in the empirical estimates of the MCF for wage taxes in the United States. Some studies measure the modified MCF and others the conventional measure. The comparison also explains why Ballard and Fullerton obtain empirical estimates of the MCF for lump-sum taxes that are less than unity, where they compute the modified MCF with a positive spending effect.

7.1 CONVENTIONAL COST–BENEFIT ANALYSIS AND THE MCF

Before proceeding to demonstrate the role of the MCF in applied welfare analysis, consider what it actually measures.

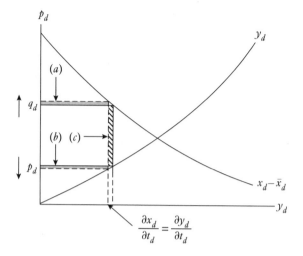

Figure 7.1 *The conventional MCF*

Definition. *The conventional Harberger measure of the marginal social cost of public funds for any tax d is the direct cost to private surplus from using it to transfer a dollar of revenue between the private and public sectors of the economy.*

A partial equilibrium measure is illustrated in Figure 7.1 for a production tax on good d when none of the good is produced by the government.

A marginal increase in the tax reduces private surplus by $(a) + (b)$ and generates additional tax revenue in $(a) + (b) - (c)$, where the conventional MCF is:

$$\mathrm{mcf}_d = 1 + \mathrm{meb}_d = \frac{(a) + (b)}{(a) + (b) - (c)},$$

with $\mathrm{meb}_d = (c)/[(a) + (b) - (c)]$. The change in tax inefficiency in (c) is the welfare change from marginally raising tax d when the revenue is returned to taxpayers as lump–sum transfers. Clearly, the MCF is unity if the tax change has no impact on activity, with $(c) = 0$. In this situation, each dollar of tax revenue will reduce private surplus by a dollar. Once the tax change affects activity it will reduce private surplus by more than a dollar due to the change in tax inefficiency in (c).

In project evaluation the MCF is used to scale up the revenue transfers the government makes to balance its budget when it uses distorting taxes. To demonstrate its role we separate these transfers from other welfare changes. Consider the revised shadow price in (6.4). By subtracting and adding the revenue transfers for good k it can be rearranged, as:

$$(S_k)_{\mathrm{D}} = \left(S_k - \frac{\partial L}{\partial z_k} \right) + \mathrm{mcf}_d \frac{\partial L}{\partial z_k}, \tag{7.1}$$

where:

$$\text{mcf}_d = 1 + \text{meb}_d = -\frac{((\partial W/\partial t_d)(1/\beta) - (\partial L/\partial t_d))}{\partial L/\partial t_d}, \tag{7.2}$$

is the conventional MCF for tax d; it is the direct cost to private surplus of transferring a dollar of revenue to the government budget.

This decomposition of the shadow price in (7.1) identifies the welfare changes as direct changes in private surplus; the first term isolates changes in consumer and producer surplus due to endogenous price changes, while the second term is surplus revenue transferred from the government budget using tax d. Each dollar of the revenue transfers $(\partial L/\partial z_k)$ are converted into private surplus by the MCF. If tax d falls the reduction in tax inefficiency will raise the revised shadow price in (7.1) above the conventional (lump-sum) shadow price in (2.8), with $(S_k)_D > S_k$. The revenue transfers in (7.1) are solved using the government budget constraint in (2.4), as:

$$\frac{\partial L}{\partial z_k} = S_k + z \frac{\partial p}{\partial z_k}. \tag{7.3}$$

To simplify the analysis without compromising the main message, assume there is no initial public production of any good. What this does is protect private surplus from the effects of endogenous price changes (with $z(\partial p/\partial z_k) = 0$), where the shadow price in (7.1), becomes:

$$(S_k)_D = \text{mcf}_d S_k. \tag{7.4}$$

Now all the welfare effects from policy changes are determined solely by their impact on the government budget, where for good k we have $\partial L/\partial z_k = S_k$. The MCF scales them up for changes in tax inefficiency when the government balances its budget using tax d. The shadow price in (7.4) is illustrated in Figure 7.2 by assuming away distortions in other markets and cross effects between the markets for goods k and d. Shaded areas are direct changes in private surplus due to price changes, while cross-lined areas are indirect changes through revenue transfers from the government budget.

After selling another unit of good k the government collects surplus revenue of $S_k = (a) + (b) + (c)$, which is the sales revenue in $p_k = (a) + (b)$ and the tax revenue in $\partial T/\partial z_k = (c) - (d) + (f) = (c)$. With no initial public production the gain in consumer surplus in (d) will offset the loss in private profit in (f), where the first term in (7.1), is:

$$S_k - \frac{\partial L}{\partial z_k} = ((a) + (b) + (c)) - ((a) + (b) + (c)) = 0.$$

Thus, any gain in private surplus must come as a revenue transfer from the government budget, with:

$$\frac{\partial L}{\partial z_k} = (a) + (b) + (c).$$

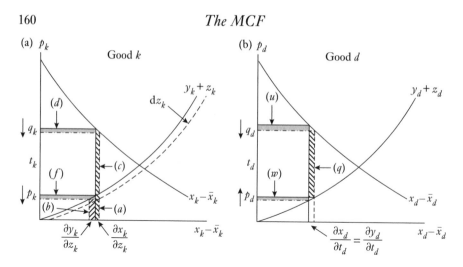

Figure 7.2 *The revised shadow price of good k—without initial public production*

When this transfer is made by lowering tax d each dollar will raise private surplus by mcf_d, which is illustrated in Figure 7.2(b), as:

$$\text{mcf}_d = \frac{(u) + (w)}{(u) + (w) - (q)}.$$

It is the gain in private surplus in $(u) + (w)$ per dollar change in tax revenue in $(u) + (w) - (q)$. Once these changes in private surplus are combined using (7.4), we have:

$$(S_k)_D = \left(\frac{(u) + (w)}{(u) + (w) - (q)} \right) [(a) + (b) + (c)] = (a) + (b) + (c) + (q).$$

$$\underbrace{\qquad\qquad\qquad}_{\text{mcf}_d} \quad \underbrace{\qquad\qquad}_{S_k}$$

Since tax d must fall to balance the government budget the tax revenue in $(u) + (w) - (q)$ has to be equal to the budget surplus generated by extra output of good k in $(a) + (b) + (c)$. The reduction in tax inefficiency in (q) is the amount the revised shadow price exceeds the conventional shadow price. It is the welfare gain from raising government revenue more efficiently through selling good k rather using tax d.[6]

The analysis is slightly more complicated when there is initial public production because endogenous price changes transfer private surplus to the government budget as public profit. When tax d is used to undo these transfers there are additional changes in tax inefficiency. This is confirmed by substituting the revenue transfers in (7.3) into (7.1), where the revised shadow price becomes:

$$(S_k)_D = \text{mcf}_d S_k + \text{meb}_d z \frac{\partial p}{\partial z_k}.[7] \tag{7.5}$$

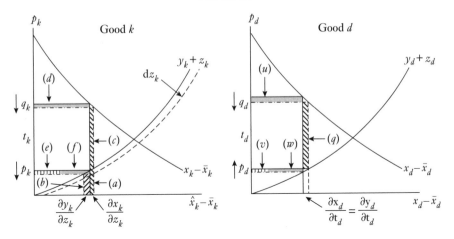

Figure 7.3 *The revised shadow price of good k—with initial public production*

The additional welfare effect in the second term is the change in tax inefficiency when tax d is used to return the change in public profit to the private economy.[8] It is illustrated in Figure 7.3 by assuming away distortions in other markets and cross effects between the markets for goods k and d. (Also, assume the government initially supplies approximately half the output of good k and one-third of the output of good d.) After selling another unit of good k the government collects surplus revenue of:

$$\frac{\partial L}{\partial z_k} = (a) + (b) + (c) - (e),$$

where (e) is the fall in public profit. With a specific tax this fall in public profit is equal to the rise in private surplus, with:

$$S_k - \frac{\partial L}{\partial z_k} = ((a) + (b) + (c)) - ((a) + (b) + (c) - (e)) = (e).$$

Consumer surplus rises by (d) while private profit falls by (f). But this net gain in private surplus is matched by an equal fall in public profit, with $(e) = (d) - (f)$, which reduces the surplus government revenue transferred to consumers. Thus, it makes no direct contribution to the welfare gain. Instead, it has an indirect effect on welfare by reducing the amount tax d falls to balance the government budget.

Once these welfare changes are combined using the shadow price in (7.5), we have:

$$(S_k)_D = (e) + \left(\frac{(u) + (w)}{(u) + (w) - (q)}\right)[(a) + (b) + (c) - (e)] = (a) + (b) + (c) + (q).$$

$$\underbrace{\left(S_k - \frac{\partial L}{\partial z_k}\right)}_{} \quad \underbrace{\text{mcf}_d}_{} \quad \underbrace{S_k}_{}$$

Now when tax d falls to balance the government budget it returns tax revenue of $(u) + (w) - (q)$ to consumers, which is smaller due to the extra public profit in (v). But the surplus revenue generated by good k in $(a) + (b) + (c) - (e)$ is also smaller due to the loss in public profit in (e). If these changes in public profit offset each other, with $(e) = (v)$, then the change in tax inefficiency in (q) is unaffected by including initial public production. When they do not offset each other, however, initial public production will affect the size of the change in tax inefficiency in (q).

Despite these complications, however, the role of the MCF in welfare analysis is clear. Whenever the government balances its budget using distorting taxes each dollar of revenue must be scaled by the MCF to account for changes in tax inefficiency.

7.2 SEPARATING THE INCOME AND SUBSTITUTION EFFECTS IN THE MCF

What determines the value of the MCF? This question has been extensively examined in the applied welfare literature. Most economists familiar with the conventional MCF expect it to exceed unity for a single distorting tax, but there are a number of reasons why this may not be the case.[9] Atkinson and Stern (1974) identify a *revenue effect* that can make the conventional MCF less than unity. It is the income effect from a tax change that can work against the substitution effect. For this to happen in Figure 7.3 good d would need to be inferior with an income effect larger than the substitution effect so that (q) is negative for the lower tax.[10] They argue this revenue effect will impact on the optimal level of government spending relative to the same spending funded from a lump-sum tax. This claim is examined by first isolating the compensated MCF to demonstrate the role played by the distortionary effects of taxation. Then the income effects in the conventional MCF are separated using the Hatta decomposition to show why they play no role in project evaluation even though they impact on the MCF. The reason is that income effects from tax changes must be offset by income effects from other policy changes at a social optimum where the compensated shadow profit for any project is zero.

7.2.1 Efficiency Effects

The efficiency effects for policy changes are isolated by making compensating transfers to offset direct changes in private surplus. When these transfers are made with distorting taxes the compensated MCF will account for any distortionary effects of taxation. To demonstrate the role played by the compensated MCF in project evaluation the compensating transfers for extra output of good k are added to and subtracted from the revised shadow price in (6.8), where:

$$(\hat{S}_k)_D = \left(\hat{S}_k + \frac{\partial \hat{L}}{\partial z_k}\right) - \frac{\partial \hat{L}/\partial z_k}{\text{m}\hat{c}f_d},^{11} \qquad (7.6)$$

with

$$\text{m}\hat{\text{c}}\text{f}_d = -\frac{1}{1 - \text{m}\hat{\text{e}}\text{b}_d} = \frac{\partial\hat{L}/\partial t_d}{(\partial\hat{R}/\partial t_d) + (\partial\hat{L}/\partial t_d)}, \tag{7.7}$$

being the compensated MCF for tax d; it is the compensated change in private surplus on each dollar of revenue collected by the government using tax d.

Now the net change in government revenue is decomposed in (7.6) as a direct change due to extra output of good k in the first term, and an indirect change through the compensating transfers to consumers in the second term. Note how the compensating transfers are discounted by the compensated MCF when they are made with distorting tax d. Government revenue rises by less than each dollar of revenue transferred from consumers with tax d due to the excess burden of taxation. The compensating transfers for good k are solved using (2.10), as:

$$\frac{\partial\hat{L}}{\partial z_k} = z\frac{\partial\hat{p}}{\partial z_k}.$$

Clearly, there are none in the absence of initial public production ($\partial\hat{L}/\partial z_k = 0$) because changes in consumer surplus are offset by changes in private profit. Under these circumstances, the revised and conventional compensated shadow prices are equal to each other, with: $(\hat{S}_k)_D = \hat{S}_k$. But with initial public production the transfers can be substituted into (7.6) to write the revised shadow price, as:

$$(\hat{S}_k)_D = \left(\hat{S}_k + z\frac{\partial\hat{p}}{\partial z_k}\right) - \frac{z(\partial\hat{p}/\partial z_k)}{\text{m}\hat{\text{c}}\text{f}_d}.^{12} \tag{7.8}$$

It is illustrated in Figure 7.4 by assuming away cross-effects between goods k and d. (Also, the government initially produces approximately half the output of good k and one-third of the output of good d.) After the government sells another unit of good k, it must transfer revenue from consumers to offset the effects of the price change on their surplus, with:

$$\frac{\partial\hat{L}}{\partial z_k} = (f) - (d) = -(e).$$

This will offset the gain in consumer surplus in (d) and the loss in private profit in (f), which is equal to the fall in public profit in (e). There is also a direct change in government revenue, of:

$$\hat{S}_k - \frac{\partial\hat{L}}{\partial z_k} = (a) + (b) + (c) - (e).$$

It is the sales revenue in (a) + (b) and the extra tax revenue in (c) less the fall in public profit in (e). When tax d is used to make the compensating transfers in (f) − (d) = (e) each dollar generates additional government revenue, of:

$$\frac{1}{\text{m}\hat{\text{c}}\text{f}_d} = \frac{(u) + (w) - (q)}{(u) + (w)} < 0,$$

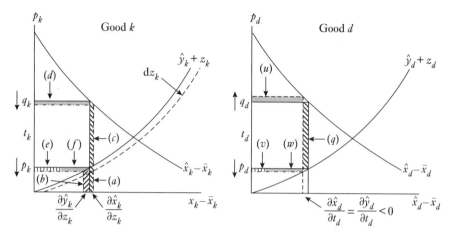

Figure 7.4 *The revised compensated shadow price of good k—and the MCF*

where $(u) + (w) - (q)$ is extra tax revenue and $(u) + (w)$ the compensating variation (CV) for the tax change. Once these changes in government revenue are combined using (7.8) the revised shadow price becomes:

$$(\hat{S}_k)_\mathrm{D} = (a) + (b) + (c) - (e) - \frac{(u) + (w) - (q)}{(u) + (w)}[-(e)] = (a) + (b) + (c) - (q).^{13}$$

Now the revised shadow price is less than the conventional shadow price, with $(\hat{S}_k)_\mathrm{D} < \hat{S}_k$, due to the increase in tax inefficiency when tax d is raised to offset the net gain in private surplus.

7.2.2 Income Effects

Policy analysts understand the way distortionary effects impact on the MCF, but it is less clear what role the income effects play. The task of isolating income effects in the MCF is much more complicated in a general equilibrium setting where producer prices change endogenously. That is why welfare decompositions in the literature usually hold producer prices constant. Hatta, and Atkinson and Stern separate the income effects in the MCF in a single consumer economy with no public production and a linear production frontier. They obtain quite different decompositions which are now demonstrated and then reconciled.

In an economy with constant producer prices and no public production (with $dp_i = z_i = 0 \; \forall_i$) the MCF for any tax d in (7.2), becomes:

$$\mathrm{mcf}_d = \frac{1}{1 + \sum_i (t_i/y_d)(\partial y_i/\partial t_d)}.^{14} \tag{7.9}$$

Any income effects are included in the change in tax revenue. By using the market clearing condition for good d (with $y_d = x_d - \bar{x}_d$), we have:

$$\sum_i \frac{t_i}{y_d} \frac{\partial y_i}{\partial t_d} = \sum_i \frac{t_i}{(x_d - \bar{x}_d)} \frac{\partial x_i(q, I)}{\partial q_d} \frac{\partial q_d}{\partial t_d} + \sum_i \frac{t_i}{(x_d - \bar{x}_d)} \frac{\partial x_i(q, I)}{\partial I} \frac{\partial I}{\partial t_d}. \quad (7.10)$$

Only the consumer price of good d changes, with $\partial q_d / \partial t_d = 1$ and $\partial q_i / \partial t_d = 0$ $\forall i \neq d$, when producer prices are constant. The different decompositions by Hatta, and Atkinson and Stern are due to the way they each compute the change in income $(\partial I / \partial t_d)$ in (7.10).

(i) The Decomposition by Hatta (1977). The consumer budget constraint $E \equiv qx = q\bar{x} + ty - R \equiv I$ is used to solve the income effect for the tax change, as:

$$\frac{\partial I}{\partial t_d} = \sum_i t_i \frac{\partial y_i}{\partial t_d} + x_d.^{15}$$

By substituting this into (7.10) and using a Slutsky decomposition the MCF in (7.9), becomes:

$$\mathrm{mcf}_d^H = \frac{1}{1 - (\mathrm{m\hat{e}b}_d / (1 - \theta))},^{16} \quad (7.11)$$

where $\mathrm{m\hat{e}b}_d \equiv -\sum_i (t_i / (x_d - \bar{x}_d))(\partial \hat{x}_i(q) / \partial q_d)$ is the compensated marginal excess burden of taxation which measures the *distortionary effect* of the tax change, and $\theta = \sum_i t_i (\partial x_i(q, I) / \partial I)$ the income effects that Atkinson and Stern refer to as the *revenue effect*. Consistent with conventional analysis, this measure of the MCF is unity for a non-distorting tax (with $\mathrm{m\hat{e}b}_d = 0$).

(ii) The Decomposition in Atkinson and Stern. This follows Diamond and Mirrlees (1971) by using the consumer budget constraint $qc = 0$, where c_i is net demand for good i, with: $c_i = x_i - \bar{x}_i.^{17}$ With no profits from private production or lump-sum transfers, any change in tax revenue is returned to taxpayers as extra output of other goods. Thus, they do not allow the change in tax d to affect money income, with: $\partial I / \partial t_d = 0$, and therefore use the Slutsky decomposition to write (7.10), as:

$$\sum_i \frac{t_i}{y_d} \frac{\partial y_i}{\partial t_d} = \sum_i \frac{t_i}{(x_d - \bar{x}_d)} \frac{\partial \hat{x}_i(q)}{\partial q_d} - \sum_i t_i \frac{\partial x_i(q, I)}{\partial I},^{18}$$

where this makes the MCF in (7.9):

$$\mathrm{mcf}_d^{AS} = \frac{1}{1 - \mathrm{m\hat{e}b}_d - \theta}.^{19} \quad (7.12)$$

Based on this decomposition the MCF for a non-distorting tax (with $\mathrm{m\hat{e}b}_d = 0$) will differ from unity when there are income effects. The difference between the decompositions in (7.11) and (7.12) may seem irrelevant, but as demonstrated previously, the Hatta decomposition in (7.11) makes income effects irrelevant in project evaluation in single (aggregated) consumer economies, which is not the case for the decomposition in (7.12).

(iii) Reconciling the Decompositions by Hatta (1977), and Atkinson and Stern (1947). The difference between these decompositions is explained by the way extra tax revenue is treated. Atkinson and Stern do not return revenue to taxpayers after marginally raising the tax, while Hatta does. Indeed, Atkinson and Stern, like Diamond and Mirrlees (1971), rule out lump–sum transfers, and they also rule out notional (hypothetical) lump–sum transfers in the conventional manner. Thus, extra revenue from marginally raising a tax must be returned to consumers by lowering another tax or increasing government spending. In contrast, Hatta isolates the welfare effects of the tax change by using notional lump–sum transfers to return the extra revenue to consumers. When these notional transfers are offset by changing another distorting tax or increasing government spending the final welfare change for both approaches is identical. The difference between them is illustrated in Figure 7.5 for a single consumer economy with a taxed good d and a numeraire good 0.

The initial equilibrium is at A on the linear production possibility frontier (Iq^0) with consumer utility of u_0. After the tax on good d increases, consumption shifts to point B along the new budget constraint if the tax revenue is not returned to the consumer. The fall in real income will be $I'' - I$, which is the measure in the decomposition by Atkinson and Stern. When the tax revenue is returned as a lump–sum transfer to consumers the fall in real income is smaller at $I'' - I'$, which is the measure in the decomposition by Hatta.

The two decompositions are compared in Table 7.1 where tax d is assumed to have a positive marginal excess burden (with $mêb_d > 0$).[20] By using the consumer budget

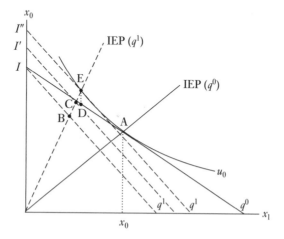

Figure 7.5 *The income effects for* dt_d

Table 7.1 *Comparing the welfare decompositions of the MCF*

	Hatta (1977)	Atkinson and Stern (1974)
	$\dfrac{1-\theta}{1-\text{mêb}_d-\theta}$	$\dfrac{1}{1-\text{mêb}_d-\theta}$
Zero income effects on taxed goods (with $\theta = 0$)	$\text{mcf}_d^H = \text{mĉf}_d > 1$	$\text{mcf}_d^{AS} = \text{mĉf}_d > 1$
Normal taxed goods (with $1-\theta > 0$)	$\text{mcf}_d^H > 1$	$\text{mcf}_d^{AS} > 1$
Inferior taxed goods (with $1-\theta < 0$)	$0 < \text{mcf}_d^H < 1$	$\text{mcf}_d^{AS} < 0$

constraint we can write the Hatta coefficient as:

$$1-\theta = \sum_i -(q_i - t_i)\frac{\partial x(q,I)}{\partial I} = \sum_i p_i \frac{\partial x(q,I)}{\partial I}.^{21}$$

Clearly, it can only be negative with constant producer prices if there are inferior goods. (There is no tax on the numeraire good 0.)

As expected, the two decompositions collapse to the same compensated measure of the MCF (mĉf_d) when there are no income effects (with $\theta = 0$). If taxed goods are normal (with $1 - \theta > 0$) the income effect reinforces the substitution effect and both measures of the MCF exceed unity. If taxed goods are inferior (with $1 - \theta < 0$) the income effects work against the substitution effects to drive both measures of the MCF below unity. Indeed, the measure by Atkinson and Stern is less than zero. Hatta rules this last possibility out by proving $1 - \theta > 0$ in a stable equilibrium.[22]

7.3 THE MCF IN PROJECT EVALUATION

The role of the MCF in a cost–benefit analysis can be demonstrated by evaluating a project that produces one unit of good k with a marginal cost to government revenue of $\text{MRT} = \partial R/\partial z_k$. When this revenue is collected using tax d the social profit for the project, is:

$$(\pi_k^S)_D = (S_k)_D - (S_R)_D\, \text{MRT}. \tag{7.13}$$

In the public economics literature it is common for good k to be a non-excludable public good that endows consumption benefits on private consumers once it is provided. Typically, the government collects no sales revenue from these goods and funds them from general tax revenue. One way to replicate the project that produces the public good is to endow good k directly on the private sector of the economy (free of charge). This gives consumers marginal benefits equal to the price p_k. In the absence of initial public production the shadow price of good k and the shadow value of government revenue, respectively, become:

$$(S_k)_D = p_k + \text{mcf}_d \frac{\partial T}{\partial z_k} \qquad \text{and} \qquad (S_R)_D = \text{mcf}_d \left(1 - \frac{\partial T}{\partial R}\right),^{23}$$

where this allows us to write the revised shadow profit in (7.13), as:

$$(\pi_k^S)_D = p_k - \text{mcf}_d \left(\text{MRT} - \frac{dT}{dz_k}\right),^{24} \tag{7.14}$$

where $dT/dz_k = (\partial T/\partial R)\text{MRT} + (\partial T/\partial z_k)$ is the total change in tax revenue; it is what Snow and Warren refer to as the *spending effect*. The first term in (7.14) is the direct marginal consumption benefit from good k while the second is the cost to private surplus of funding the government budget deficit. Terms inside the brackets measure the project's net cost to government revenue, where MRT is the revenue used to produce another unit of good k and the dT/dz_k the endogenous change in tax revenue. If the government funds the budget deficit using tax d each dollar of revenue will reduce private surplus by mcf_d.

   The income effects for the project can be isolated using the welfare decomposition in (6.9) to write the shadow profit in (7.13), as:

$$(\pi_k^S)_D = (S_R)_D(\hat{\pi}_k^S)_D, \tag{7.15}$$

where $(\hat{\pi}_k^S)_D$ is the revised shadow profit. All the income effects are isolated in the revised shadow value of government revenue $(S_R)_D$, and are therefore irrelevant in finding the optimal supply of the good (where $(\hat{\pi}_k^S)_D = 0$).[25] That is why the revenue effect identified by Atkinson and Stern in the conventional MCF will not alter the optimal provision of the good, even when it makes $\text{mcf}_d < 1$. Any income effect from the change in government spending on good k must be offset by the income effect from the change in tax d at a social optimum, where the potential benefits and costs are equal at the margin.

7.4 A MODIFIED MEASURE OF THE MCF

Håkonsen, Mayshar (1990), and Snow and Warren derive a modified measure of the MCF that contains welfare effects not included in the conventional Harberger measure. It can be derived by writing the shadow profit for the project in (7.13), as:

$$(\pi_k^S)_D = p_k - \text{mcf}_d^* \text{MRT}, \tag{7.16}$$

where:

$$\text{mcf}_d^* = \text{mcf}_d \left(1 - \frac{dT}{dz_k} \frac{1}{\text{MRT}}\right), \tag{7.17}$$

is the modified MCF.[26]

Table 7.2 *Estimates of the MCF for wage taxes*

Country	Study	Estimate
United States	Ballard and Fullerton (1992)	1.047–1.315
	Fullerton (1991)	1–1.25
	Ballard, Shoven, and Whalley (1985)	1.16–1.31
	Browning (1976, 1987)	1.32–1.47
	Stuart (1984)	1.07–1.57
Canada	Campbell (1995)	1.25
	Dahlby (1994)	1.38
New Zealand	Diewert and Lawrence (1996)	1.18
Australia	Campbell and Bond (1997)	1.19–1.24
	Findlay and Jones (1982)	1.275–1.550

All the welfare effects from the project's impact on the government budget are isolated in the second term in (7.16), where MRT is the cost to revenue of producing the good, and mcf_d^* the combined welfare effect from the changes in tax revenue. Notice how the *spending effect* for the project is included in the modified MCF (mcf_d^*). In a conventional Harberger analysis the change in tax revenue from the project output is not included in the MCF (mcf_d), but is instead accounted for separately in the shadow price of good k. When the spending effect is included in the MCF it becomes a function of government spending (dz_k). Thus, there are as many measures of mcf_d^* as ways the government can spend extra tax revenue. Note how a positive spending effect can make $\mathrm{mcf}_d^* < 1$, even when there is a single distorting tax in the economy. Håkonsen, Mayshar, and Snow and Warren derive the modified MCF in (7.17) as a function of prices and income in a model with wage taxes. However, their analysis will not be replicated here as the focus is on the conceptual differences between the modified and conventional measures of the MCF.

Empirical estimates of the MCF for wage taxes are summarized in Table 7.2 for a number of countries. There are likely to be differences across countries, although tax systems do converge when markets are integrated globally, but the large differences within countries, especially the United States, are puzzling. Fullerton (1991) provides an excellent summary of the reasons for the differences in the United States, and they include:

(1) different parameters in their GE models; and,
(2) different measures of the MCF.

Ballard and Fullerton, Ballard, Shoven, and Whalley, and Stuart all estimate the modified MCF in (7.17), while the remaining studies estimate a version of the conventional measure, although they do so by combining compensated and uncompensated welfare changes.[27]

When the *spending effect* is included in the MCF the estimates are of little use without knowing how the government spends the additional revenue. Moreover, they are only useful for evaluating projects that produce these outputs, unless by coincidence other projects have the same *spending effect*. Each of the United States studies, with the exception of Browning, estimate the modified MCF, and they all conveniently make one estimate where the revenue is spent on a pure public good. While this provides a basis for making comparisons, it is difficult to know how important the spending effect is in each of them. All other studies in the table estimate the conventional MCF. It can be used to evaluate any small project because it is independent of the nature of government spending.

7.5 THE MCF FOR A LUMP-SUM TAX

Anyone familiar with the conventional measure of the MCF expects it to be unity for non–distorting taxes. Recall from (7.2) that the conventional MCF for a tax is $1 + \text{meb}$, where meb is computed by marginally increasing a tax and returning the revenue to taxpayers as a lump–sum transfer. This MCF tells us how private surplus changes with each dollar of revenue transferred between the private and public sectors of the economy. It is not a measure of the social value of endowing another dollar of revenue on the government, but is instead the welfare change from transferring revenue within the economy.

The conventional welfare equation in (2.7) can be used to measure the change in tax inefficiency for a lump–sum tax, where:

$$\frac{dW}{dL}\frac{1}{\beta} = \sum_i t_i \frac{\partial y_i}{\partial L} = 0. \tag{7.18}$$

There is no excess burden since each dollar of revenue the government collects reduces private surplus by a dollar, therefore $\text{mcf}_L = 1$. But a number of empirical studies report estimates of the MCF for a lump–sum tax that are not equal to unity, and there are two reasons for this seeming anomaly:

1. Some studies estimate the modified MCF examined in the previous section. By including the *spending effect* in the MCF Ballard and Fullerton estimate mcf^* in (7.17) for a range of labour supply elasticities in the presence of a proportional wage tax (τ). Their results are summarized in columns 3 and 4 of Table 7.3 where a positive *spending effect* lowers mcf_L^* relative to the conventional measure mcf_L.[28]
   For a lump–sum tax the modified MCF in (7.17), is:

$$\text{mcf}_L^* = 1 - \frac{dT}{dR}. \tag{7.19}$$

   The last term is the *spending effect*, and it is positive when the project generates additional tax revenue by expanding taxed activities. That is why $\text{mcf}_L^* < 1$ in Table 7.3.
2. The conventional MCF is sometimes derived as a shadow price. Triest (1990) references the recent literature that '*attempts to measure the marginal cost (shadow price)*

Table 7.3 *Empirical estimates of the MCF*

Labour supply elasticities[a]		MCF*[b]		Conventional MCF	
Uncompensated	Compensated	mcf^*_τ	mcf^*_L	mcf_τ	mcf_L
0.000	0.100	1.000	0.930	>1	1.000
0.000	0.200	1.000	0.870	>1	1.000
0.000	0.300	1.000	0.816	>1	1.000
−0.105	0.284	0.936	0.774	>1	1.000
−0.022	0.090	0.984	0.922	>1	1.000
0.173	0.234	1.147	0.950	?	1.000

[a] The elasticities are taken from Ballard and Fullerton (1992: table 1).
[b] Estimates of the MCF for a proportional wage tax in Ballard and Fullerton (1992).

of public funds' (Triest 1990: 557), while Dahlby (1998) contrasts the compensated MCF for a lump-sum tax with the uncompensated measure, and argues

> *the Stiglitz–Dasgupta–Atkinson–Stern (SDAS) approach, which is based on the uncompensated elasticities, recognizes that the MCF for a lump-sum tax may be different from one because a lump-sum tax has a "revenue effect" if other distortionary taxes are also levied. In other words, if leisure is a normal good and a distortionary tax on labour income is in place, then a one dollar increase in a lump-sum tax will increase total tax revenue by more than a dollar, and its MCF will be less than one. (Dahlby 1998: 106)*

Both quotations implicitly assume the MCF is the shadow value (cost) of government revenue. But this is not the case. As noted previously, the MCF measures the direct change in private surplus on revenue transfers in equilibrium. It is not the welfare change from endowing additional resources (revenue) on the economy.

One way to demonstrate the difference between the conventional MCF and the shadow value of government revenue, is to use the reduced form expression for the revised shadow value of government revenue in (6.10), where in the absence of public production, we have:

$$(S_R)_D = \text{mcf}_d S_R. \tag{7.20}$$

Endowing a dollar of revenue on the government will raise its budget surplus by a dollar. When this surplus is transferred as a lump-sum payment to the private sector social welfare rises by S_R, which differs from unity due to income effects on taxed activities. They are the income effects identified by Dahlby for a lump-sum tax that do not arise in the conventional MCF. Thus, Dahlby is computing the shadow value of government revenue, which can deviate from unity, and not the MCF. Whenever surplus government revenue is transferred by lowering tax d it generates an even larger gain in private surplus due to the reduction in tax inefficiency when $\text{mcf}_d > 1$. However, if tax d is non-distorting (with $\text{mcf}_L = 1$) the revised shadow value of government revenue will be the same as the conventional measure, with $S_R \equiv (S_R)_L$.

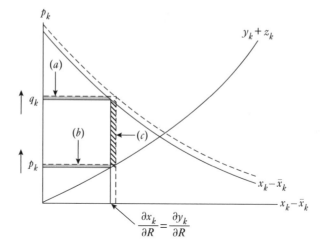

Figure 7.6 *The shadow value of government revenue*

The revised shadow value of government revenue in (7.20) is illustrated in Figure 7.6 by assuming the income effect impacts solely on taxed good k, and there is no initial public production.

When a dollar of revenue is transferred lump sum to consumers they increase their demand for good k, and this raises additional tax revenue in (c), which is also transferred to the consumer to balance the government budget. The final dollar change in social welfare can be decomposed using (2.5), as:

$$S_R = -\frac{dW}{dR}\frac{1}{\beta} = -\frac{\partial L}{\partial R},$$

where the revenue transfers are solved using (2.6), as:

$$S_R = -\frac{\partial L}{\partial R} = 1 + [(a) - (b) + (c)] = 1 + (c).$$

When distorting tax d is used to make these transfers there are additional welfare effects from the change in tax inefficiency, where the revised shadow profit in (7.20), becomes:

$$(S_R)_D = \text{mcf}_d[1 + (c)].$$

Table 7.4 summarizes the shadow value of government revenue and the MCF for a lump–sum tax. If a dollar of revenue is endowed on the government the compensated shadow value of government revenue is a dollar, with $\hat{S}_R = 1$. By holding the dollar as surplus revenue, there is no change in social welfare. Once this surplus is transferred to the private sector, the income effects impact on taxed activities. That is why the uncompensated shadow value of government revenue differs from unity, with $S_R = 1 - \partial T/\partial R$.

Table 7.4 *Lump-sum taxation*

	Compensated (ˆ)	Uncompensated
S_R	1	$1 - \dfrac{\partial T}{\partial R}$
mcf_L	1	1

Contrast this with the conventional MCF. If the government collects a dollar of revenue with a lump-sum tax and compensates taxpayers to hold their utility constant, there is no change in net government revenue. Thus, there is no excess burden from collecting a dollar of tax revenue where the compensated MCF is unity, with $\hat{\text{mcf}}_L = 1$. Equally, when the government collects a dollar of revenue with a lump-sum tax and then balances its budget using lump-sum transfers there is no tax inefficiency. Thus, the cost to private surplus of collecting a dollar of revenue to balance the government budget in project evaluation is a dollar, that is, the uncompensated MCF is unity, with $\text{mcf}_L = 1$.

In summary, the conventional MCF does not measure the welfare effects from endowing extra revenue on the economy, so it cannot be used to convert compensated shadow prices into uncompensated shadow prices.[29] That task is performed by the shadow value of government revenue as is confirmed by the generalized Hatta decomposition in (2.12). Recall how the compensated shadow price is surplus revenue a good will generate for the economy at constant consumer utility. It is equivalent to a gift of revenue from outside the economy, which is converted into utility using the shadow value of government revenue, not the conventional MCF.

7.6 DISTRIBUTIONAL EFFECTS WITH DISTORTING TAXES

Two popular ways of dealing with distributional effects in a conventional cost–benefit analysis were examined in Chapter 3. Dréze and Stern (1990) assign distributional weights to consumers and measure their gains and losses, while Bruce and Harris (1982) and Diewert (1983) choose patterns of revenue transfers to convert efficiency gains into Pareto improvements. When governments use lump-sum taxes they can personalize the revenue transfers, but this may not be possible when they use distorting taxes. These approaches are now re-examined when revenue transfers are made with distorting taxes.

7.6.1 Measuring Distributional Effects—The Dréze–Stern Approach

A policy change may be rejected if the government cannot choose patterns of revenue transfers to make every consumer better off. Alternatively, distributional weights may be assigned to the welfare changes for consumers before summing them. A Harberger

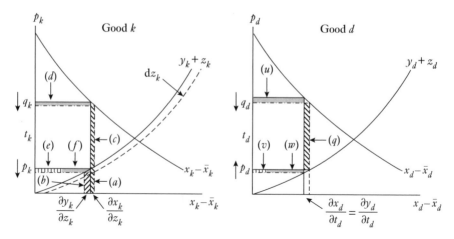

Figure 7.7 *The revised shadow price of good k with distributional effects*

analysis assigns the same weights to consumers, while Dréze and Stern assign different weights. Either way, subjective judgements are being made about the marginal social value of income for each consumer. Once different weights are assigned there are distributional effects in the shadow prices. They were derived in Chapter 3 for the conventional (lump-sum) shadow prices. Whenever revenue transfers are made with distorting taxes the additional welfare effects are included in the revised shadow prices by using the conventional welfare equation in (3.4), with $dL = 0$. If the government uses tax d to balance its budget, the shadow price of good k becomes:

$$(\bar{S}_k)_\mathrm{D} = -\mathrm{DC}_p z \frac{\partial p}{\partial z_k} + \mathrm{m\bar{c}f}_d \frac{\partial L}{\partial z_k}, \qquad (7.21)$$

where

$$\mathrm{m\bar{c}f}_d = \frac{\mathrm{DC}_p\, z(\partial p/\partial t_d) + \mathrm{DC}_{t_d}(x_d - \bar{x}_d)}{\partial L/\partial t_d}, \qquad (7.22)$$

is the MCF with distributional effects.[30]

Once again, the revised shadow price in (7.21) is measured as direct changes in private surplus. The first term is the change in private surplus when producer prices change, and the second is the surplus government revenue distributed to consumers using tax d, where distributional characteristics for the price (DC_p) and tax (DC_{t_d}) changes were defined below the welfare equation with distributional effects in (3.4).

This revised shadow price is illustrated in Figure 7.7 by ignoring price changes in other markets and assuming away cross-effects between the markets for goods k and d. (Also, the public sector initially produces half the output of good k and a third of the output of good d.)

After the government sells another unit of good k consumer surplus rises by (d) and private profit falls by (f) due to the lower market price, with $(d) - (f) = (e)$. It is weighted by the distributional characteristics for the price change, where the first term in (7.21) is:

$$-DC_{p_k} \frac{\partial p_k}{\partial z_k} = DC_{p_k}(e).$$

The extra output of good k generates surplus government revenue of:

$$\frac{\partial L}{\partial z_k} = p_k + \frac{\partial T}{\partial z_k} + z \frac{\partial p}{\partial z_k} = (a) + (b) + (c) - (e).$$

When it is transferred to consumers using tax d the efficiency and distributional effects are isolated in the MCF in (7.22). A fall in tax d, reduces government revenue by $(u) + (w) - (q)$ and raises private surplus by $(u) + (w)$. The rise in public profit in (v) is matched by an equal and offsetting fall in tax revenue. When distributional characteristics are applied to the changes in private surplus the MCF is:

$$\overline{mcf}_d = \frac{DC_{t_d}[(u) + (v) + (w)] - DC_{p_d(v)}}{(u) + (w) - (q)}.$$

After combining these welfare changes using the revised shadow price in (7.21), we have:

$$(\bar{S}_k)_D = [(a) + (b) + (c) - (e)] \left(\frac{DC_{t_d}[(u) + (v) + (w)] - DC_{p_d}(v)}{(u) + (w) - (q)} \right) + DC_{p_k}(e).$$

$$\underbrace{\qquad\qquad}_{S_k + z_k \frac{\partial p_k}{\partial z_k}} \qquad \underbrace{\qquad\qquad}_{\overline{mcf}_d} \qquad \underbrace{\qquad}_{DC_{p_k} z_k \frac{\partial p_k}{\partial z_k}}$$

There are additional distributional effects when prices change in other markets, and they can be illustrated in a similar fashion. If consumers are assigned the same welfare weights (with $DC_{p_k} = DC_{t_d} = 1$) the shadow price in (7.21) collapses to the revised shadow price in (6.4), with $(\bar{S}_k)_D = (S_k)_D$.

Efficiency Effects

Since the compensated welfare changes are, by definition, free of any distributional effects (with $du^h = 0 \ \forall_h$) the revised compensated shadow prices are those derived previously in (6.5). They are net changes in government revenue when distorting taxes are used to make the compensating transfers. The compensating tax changes are solved using (3.4) with $dW = 0$, as:

$$\left(\frac{d\hat{L}^h}{dz_k} \right)_D = -DE^h_p \frac{\partial \hat{p}}{\partial z_k} - \sum_j \left(DE^h_p \frac{\partial \hat{p}}{\partial t_j} + DEt^h_j \right) \left(\frac{d\hat{t}_j}{dz_k} \right)_D = 0 \qquad \forall_h. \tag{7.23}$$

Clearly, this compensation may require changes to a potentially large number of taxes, or in the absence of there being sufficient taxes, personalized tax changes. Since the revenue transfers in (7.23) depend on substitution effects that vary across consumers the compensating tax changes will be a function of the policy change (k), that is, they are project specific. Once the revised efficiency gain in (6.5) is distributed to consumers by changes in distorting taxes each dollar raises social welfare by the shadow value of government revenue. Thus, it isolates any distributional effects in project evaluation.

7.6.2 Identifying Pareto Improvements—The Bruce–Harris–Diewert Approach

Bruce and Harris examine the way governments can influence the distributional effects from policy changes by choosing patterns of revenue transfers when they distribute surplus revenue to consumers. This section extends the Bruce–Harris welfare test for Pareto improvements to allow revenue transfers with distorting taxes.

Income Effects and the Revised Shadow Value of Government Revenue
Efficiency gains can be converted into strict Pareto improvements if there are sufficient tax instruments to personalize the revenue transfers to consumers. When the government uses distorting taxes the foreign aid that would finance the compensating transfers for a marginal increase in the supply of good k are solved using the social welfare function in (3.9), as:

$$(\mathrm{d}W)_\mathrm{D} = \sum_h \beta^h (S_k^h)_\mathrm{D} \, \mathrm{d}\hat{z}_k - \sum_h \beta^h (S_R^h)_\mathrm{D} \, \mathrm{d}\hat{R} = 0, \,^{31} \tag{7.24}$$

with

$$(S_k^h)_\mathrm{D} = (S_R^h)_\mathrm{D} (\hat{S}_k)_\mathrm{D} \qquad \forall_h, \tag{7.25}$$

where $(\hat{S}_k)_\mathrm{D} = (\mathrm{d}\hat{R}/\mathrm{d}z_k)_\mathrm{D}$ is the aggregate efficiency gain, and for each consumer h, $(S_k^h)_\mathrm{D}$ is their personal revised shadow price of good k and $(S_R^h)_\mathrm{D}$ their personal revised shadow value of government revenue. If tax d is used to transfer the efficiency gain to consumers the distributional effects are isolated in the personal revised shadow value of government revenue for each consumer, where:

$$(S_R^h)_\mathrm{D} = S_R \left\{ \mathrm{mcf}_d^h + \sum_s (\mathrm{DE}_s^h + \mathrm{mcf}_d^h z_s) \alpha_{sI} \right\}, \tag{7.26}$$

with mcf_d^h being the personal marginal cost of public funds which replaces the lump-sum transfer share g^h in the conventional shadow value of government revenue in (3.12).[32] If the personal shadow value of government revenue in (7.26) is summed over consumers, we have:

$$\sum_h (S_R^h)_\mathrm{D} = S_R \left\{ \mathrm{mcf}_d + \mathrm{meb}_d \sum_s z_s \alpha_{sI} \right\}.$$

This is the shadow value of government revenue for the single (aggregated) consumer economy in (6.10), with $(S_R)_D = \sum_h (S_R^h)_D$, where all the distributional effects disappear as they should.

Diewert argues that it may be necessary for the government to change a potentially large number of taxes to convert efficiency gains into strict Pareto improvements. These tax changes must make the personal shadow value of government revenue in (7.26) positive for every consumer. The first term in (7.26) is positive (with $\mathrm{mcf}_d^h > 1$) for radial tax increases, and for marginal increases in Ramsey optimal taxes. Thus, reducing a distorting tax to make a revenue transfer will increase private surplus, but it does not guarantee a positive shadow value of government revenue for every consumer when there are endogenous price changes. Indeed, it is possible for some consumers to have $\sum_s (DE_s^h + \mathrm{mcf}_d^h z_s)\alpha_{sI} < 0$. For example, net suppliers of goods can be worse off when the revenue transfers drive down producer prices (with $\sum_s DE_s^h \alpha_{sI} < 0$). Thus, for a strict Pareto improvement it may be necessary to raise some taxes and lower others. If there are not enough commodity taxes to personalize the revenue transfers the government will need to personalize the tax changes on one or a number of commodities, that is, set different personal taxes on the same commodity. This allows us to extend the welfare test in Bruce and Harris.

Theorem. *If, in the absence of local Foster and Sonnenschein (1970) effects (LSFE), when the government balances its budget using distorting taxes to make the personal shadow value of government revenue positive for every consumer, then the necessary and sufficient condition for a welfare gain from any small policy change k in an economy with heterogeneous consumers is $(\hat{S}_k)_D > 0$.*

Proof. By ruling out LFSE we have $S_R > 0$, and by choosing personalized lump-sum transfers to make $\mathrm{mcf}_d^h + \sum_s (DE_s^h + \mathrm{mcf}_d^h z_s)\alpha_{sI} > 0 \ \forall_h$, we have $(S_R^h)_D > 0 \ \forall_h$. Thus, from (7.25), there are strict Pareto improvements (with $(S_k^h)_D > 0 \ \forall_h$) whenever $(\hat{S}_k)_D > 0$. □

Whenever the government uses the same pattern of transfers to distribute surplus revenue to consumers, income effects will play no role in marginal policy evaluation. Moreover, if transfers are chosen to make the shadow value of government revenue positive for every consumer, then aggregate dollar gains in utility will also be strict Pareto improvements.

7.7 PROGRESSIVE TAXATION AND THE MCF

In most countries there are progressive personal taxes on income; a practice which is motivated by equity concerns. Mirrlees (1971) solves optimal income tax schedules for consumers with different skill levels and finds they are not as progressive as one might expect when high-skill, high income consumers have relatively low distributional weights. In fact, the analysis provides qualified support for a linear income tax schedule, and finds the income tax '*a less effective tax for reducing inequalities than has often been thought'* (Mirrlees 1971: 208). Indeed, Harberger (1978) finds support for a regressive income tax rate schedule by noting the distributional benefits from raising the highest marginal tax rate are limited solely to high-tax consumers with relatively low distributional weights, while increases in low marginal tax rates transfer revenue from both low- and high-tax consumers. It does this for high-tax consumers by raising their infra-marginal tax rates.[33]

In this section, a measure of the MCF is derived for a progressive marginal personal tax rate on labour income. Capital income is included in Chapter 8 where social discount rates are obtained in an intertemporal setting. Browning (1987), Dahlby (1998), Mayshar (1991), and Wildasin (1984) each obtain different measures of the MCF for a progressive tax on labour income because they adopt different labour demand–supply elasticities and make different assumptions about the way average tax rates change with income. In Browning and Mayshar, there is a single consumer, while in Dahlby and Wildasin there are heterogeneous consumers. Dahlby clearly explains the differences between their measures of the MCF.

Most countries adopt piecewise linear tax schedules with an initial tax free threshold. Thus, consumers with relatively high incomes pay higher marginal and average tax rates than those with lower incomes. To capture this feature of the tax code an *ad valorem* marginal tax ($t^h < 0$) is levied on labour (n) income for each consumer h. Since infra-marginal labour income is taxed at lower tax rates, the total labour tax revenue collected from each consumer h, will be:

$$T^h = -t^h Y^h + \sum_{j=1}^{h-1} (t^{j+1} - t^j) \bar{Y}^j > 0, \tag{7.27}$$

where $Y^h = p_n(\bar{x}_n^h - x_n^h)$ is pre-tax labour income for consumer h. Also, it is the only taxable income consumers receive, where tax t^j applies to income between the tax bracket $\bar{Y}^{j-1}$ and $\bar{Y}^j$, with $\bar{Y}^0 = 0$. The first term in (7.27) is total tax revenue when all income is subject to tax at the consumer's marginal rate, while the second term refunds tax revenue on income subject to lower infra-marginal tax rates. Clearly, for income in lower tax brackets than the marginal rate for consumer h we have $(t_n^h - t_n^j) \bar{Y}^j < 0$, and in h's tax bracket $(t_n^h - t_n^h) \bar{Y}^h = 0$.

The intuition for this notation is explained using Figure 7.8 where there are three tax brackets and no tax-free threshold. Consumer h is in the third tax bracket and therefore has $t^h = t^3$. When all income is taxed at the marginal rate t_n^3 total tax revenue is $-t^h Y^h = T^h + (a) + (b)$ in the figure, while the second term is the implicit revenue refund which can be decomposed, as:

$$(a) + (b) = -(t^3 - t^1)(\bar{Y}^1 - \bar{Y}^0) - (t^h - t^2)(\bar{Y}^2 - \bar{Y}^1) - (t^3 - t^3)(Y^h - \bar{Y}^2).$$

$$\qquad\qquad (a) \qquad\qquad + \qquad (b) \qquad\qquad + \qquad 0$$

The second term in (7.27) is obtained by rearranging these terms. Since infra-marginal tax revenue is equivalent to a lump-sum transfer from consumer h to the government it has no excess burden, and when it is returned to the taxpayer as a lump-sum transfer it

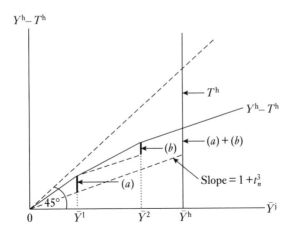

Figure 7.8 *Income with a progressive tax*

has no distributional effects either. However, there are likely to be distributional effects when the revenue is returned through changes in distorting taxes.

There are number of ways the government can raise additional revenue with a progressive income tax. It can increase one or a combination of the tax rates, where the final choice is, at least partially, determined by the desired pattern of changes in average tax rates for consumers. Increasing the top marginal tax rate has no direct affect on average tax rates for consumers in lower brackets, but it is likely to have a relatively large marginal excess burden. In contrast, increasing taxes in lower brackets will raise the average tax rate for all consumers in that and higher brackets, and is likely to have a smaller marginal excess burden. That is one of the main reasons why Harberger and Mirrlees find little support for much progressivity in personal income tax rates.

Dahlby (1998) considers the multiple tax rate changes examined by Musgrave and Thin (1948) to preserve average tax progressivity, liability progression, or residual income progressivity. Another way to raise additional revenue is to decrease one or a number of the income threshold levels for the tax brackets, and Sheshinski (1989) and Slemrod *et al.* (1994) do this to find the optimal tax brackets. As a way to facilitate evaluations of changes in average and marginal tax rates Dahlby defines the average tax on labour income for each consumer h, as:

$$a^h = \sum_{j=1}^{h} t^j \chi^{hj}, \tag{7.28}$$

where $\chi^{hj} = (\bar{Y}^j - \bar{Y}^{j-1})/Y^h$ with $\bar{Y}^j = Y^h$ for $j = h$ and $\bar{Y}^0 = 0$. Thus, changes in average tax rates will solve:

$$da^h = \sum_{j=1}^{h} \left\{ \chi^{hj} + \left(t^h - \frac{a^h}{Y^h} \right) \frac{\partial Y^h}{\partial t^j} \right\} dt^j. \tag{7.29}$$[34]

Once the progressive tax on labour income is included in the consumer budget constraints in (3.2), we have:

$$E^h \equiv q^h x^h = q^h \bar{x}^h - \sum_{j=1}^{h-1}(t^{j+1} - t^j)\bar{Y}^j + \rho^h p y + L^h \equiv I^h \qquad \forall_h, \qquad (7.30)$$

with $q_i^h = p_i + t_i \ \forall_{i \neq n}$ and $q_n^h = p_n(1 + t^h)$. Now the government collects total tax revenue, of:

$$T = (x_{-n} - \bar{x}_{-n})t_{-n} - \sum_h a^h Y^h, \qquad (7.31)$$

where the first term is the commodity tax revenue on goods $i \neq n$.

It is possible to generalize measures of the MCF obtained by Browning, Dahlby, Mayshar, and Wildasin by including government production, commodity taxes, and endogenous producer prices. However, this complicates the analysis without adding much to their findings. A more useful contribution is made here by deriving the MCF under the same circumstances, with constant producer prices, no government production and no commodity taxes, and to then separate the income and substitution effects using the Hatta decomposition.[35] On this basis, the change in social welfare with distributional effects and a progressive income tax, becomes:

$$\frac{dW}{\bar{\beta}} = dL + \sum_h \frac{\beta^h}{\bar{\beta}}\{(Y^h\,da^h + a^h\,dY^h\}.[36] \qquad (7.32)$$

Recall from (7.2) that the MCF for any tax t is defined as the direct cost to private surplus per dollar change in government revenue, with:

$$\bar{mcf}_t = -\frac{(\partial W/\partial t)_D(1/\bar{\beta})}{\partial L/\partial t}. \qquad (7.33)$$

The direct change in private surplus is obtained from (7.32) with $dL = 0$, while the change in government revenue is solved using the government budget constraint with income tax revenue defined in (7.31), as:

$$dL = Y^h\,da^h + a^h\,dY^h - dR, \qquad (7.34)$$

where the MCF in (7.33) for a generic tax change becomes:

$$\bar{mcf} = \frac{\sum_h(\beta^h/\bar{\beta})\,Y^h\,da^h}{\sum_h\left\{Y^h da^h + a^h \sum_{j=1}^h(\partial Y^h/\partial t^j)\,dt^j\right\}}. \qquad (7.35)$$

In the absence of distributional effects (with $\beta^h = \beta \ \forall_h$ and $\bar{\beta} = 1$), the MCF is unity when labour supply is unaffected by taxes changes, and is greater than unity when labour supply falls. Once distributional effects are included the MCF can be greater than, equal to, or less than unity. In a competitive equilibrium each consumer makes consumption choices taking prices and income as given, where the change in labour supply can be decomposed, as:

$$\frac{\partial Y^h}{\partial t^h} = -\frac{\hat{\eta}^h Y^h}{(1-\theta^h)q_n^h} \quad \text{and} \quad \frac{\partial Y^h}{\partial t^j} = 0 \qquad \forall_{j\neq h},\,^{37}$$

with

$$\hat{\eta}^h = -\frac{\partial \hat{Y}^h(q^h, I^h)}{\partial q_n^h} \frac{q_n^h}{Y^h},$$

being the compensated elasticity of labour supply, and, $\theta^h = t^h(\partial Y^h(q^h, I^h)/\partial I^h)$ the Hatta coefficient, which isolates the income effects.

By using this decomposition and the change in the average tax rate in (7.29), the MCF in (7.35), becomes:

$$\text{mcf} = \frac{\sum_h (\beta^h/\bar{\beta}) Y^h \sum_{j=1}^h \{\chi^{hj} - (t^h - (a^h/Y^h))(\hat{\eta}^h Y^h/(1-\theta^h)q_n^h)\}\, dt^j}{\sum_h Y^h \sum_{j=1}^h \{\chi^{hj} - t^h(\hat{\eta}^h Y^h/(1-\theta^h)q_n^h)\}\, dt^j}.$$

$$(7.36)$$

This is entirely consistent with the conventional measure of the MCF which is unity in the absence of distributional effects and non–distorting taxes (with $\hat{\eta}^h = 0$). It also confirms the proposition proved in previous chapters and Section 7.2.2 that income effects will play no role in conventional marginal welfare analysis. The MCF in Browning also has this property because it is the conventional measure, but the expressions in Dahlby, Mayshar, and Wildasin do not because income effects are not solved with tax revenue returned to consumers as lump–sum transfers.[38]

Finally, when Dahlby assumes the change in the average tax rate in (7.29) is unaffected by endogenous changes in income (with $da^h = \sum_j \chi^{hj}\, dt^j$), the MCF in (7.36) collapses to:

$$\text{mcf} = \frac{\sum_h (\beta^h/\bar{\beta}) Y^h \sum_{j=1}^h \chi^{hj}\, dt^j}{\sum_h Y^h \sum_{j=1}^h \{\chi^{hj} - (a^h \hat{\eta}^h Y^h/(1-\theta^h)q_n^h)\}\, dt^j}.$$

It has a similar structure to the MCF in equation 11 of Dahlby except that the income effect here is a scaling coefficient on the change in tax inefficiency whereas it is additive in Dahlby. A range of different tax policy changes can be evaluated using (7.36). For example, multiple tax rates can be changed to achieve specified movements in average tax rates using (7.29). If the government raises a dollar of revenue by increasing the average tax rate for every consumer by the same amount the tax changes solve:

$$da^h = \sum_{j=1}^h \left\{ \chi^{hj} - \left(t^h - \frac{a^h}{Y^h} \right) \frac{\hat{\eta}^h Y^h}{(1-\theta^h)q_n^h} \right\}\, dt^j = 1 \qquad \forall_h,$$

where the MCF is obtained using (7.36), as:

$$\text{mcf} = \frac{\sum_h (\beta^h / \bar{\beta}) Y^h}{\sum_h Y^h \{1 - \hat{\eta}^h / (1 - \theta^h) q_n^h\}}.$$
(7.37)

In a more general setting with endogenous price changes and commodity taxes the MCF is more complicated. There are further distributional effects from the price changes, and additional welfare effects in the marginal excess burden of taxation when income tax changes impact on commodities subject to trade taxes. These effects have been examined in previous chapters and will not be analysed here.

7.8 CONCLUDING REMARKS

One of the more controversial issues in public economics is how to measure the marginal social cost of public funds. It provides important information that governments use to evaluate their spending programmes and to set efficient taxes. Unfortunately, there are large differences in empirical estimates of the MCF for the same taxes, and there are three reasons for this:

(i) different structural parameters are used in the calculations, that is, the demand–supply elasticities for goods;
(ii) some are based on actual welfare changes, others on compensated welfare measures and others on a combination of the two; and
(iii) they estimate different measures of the MCF.

Fullerton provides a very useful summary of the differences due to structural parameters in part (i) and the welfare measures in part (ii). A number of widely cited studies for the United States estimate a modified measure of the MCF that differs from the conventional MCF. Instead of returning tax revenue to consumers as a lump-sum transfer, which is how the conventional measure is obtained, it returns revenue as extra government spending. This introduces additional welfare effects in the modified MCF that will depend on the nature of government expenditure, that is, the *spending effect*. It is therefore a function of government spending, and cannot be used in the same way as the conventional MCF in project evaluation. Dahlby and Mayshar argue the MCF should be measured with government expenditure held constant, which is how a conventional cost–benefit analysis proceeds by using lump-sum transfers to separate the welfare effects of taxation and spending. When they are combined together inside a project the lump-sum transfers are offset by tax changes to balance the government budget. It is not incorrect to include the *spending effect* in the MCF. Rather, it is a less useful measure in project evaluation because it is project specific. Perhaps a greater concern is that the modified MCF will be interpreted as the conventional measure and used with misleading consequences.

The separate but related roles of the MCF and the shadow value of government revenue in project evaluation were also examined in this chapter. No clear distinction is made between these welfare measures in the literature, which is why there are seemingly contradictory statements about the MCF. Indeed, some argue the MCF is a shadow price, but that is not the case. The two measures are related by generalizing the Hatta decomposition to allow revenue transfers with distorting taxes. Since the shadow value of government revenue converts surplus revenue into utility it isolates income effects for marginal policy changes, while the MCF measures the change in private surplus on each dollar of revenue transferred between the private and public sectors of the economy. Perhaps Harberger's distinction between the two types of policy changes in project evaluation provides the easiest way to understand the difference between them. The shadow value of government revenue is an *income and substitution effect* problem while the MCF is a *substitution effect only* problem. The relationship between them was demonstrated by deriving the revised shadow value of government revenue. It is the welfare change when surplus government revenue is transferred to consumers with distorting taxes, where in the absence of initial public production, $(S_R)_D = \text{mcf}_d S_R$. A dollar of surplus revenue will raise the real income of consumers by the conventional shadow value of government revenue (S_R) when it is distributed to them as lump-sum transfers. If the revenue is transferred using distorting tax d each dollar must be scaled up for the change in tax inefficiency by using the conventional MCF, where the final welfare change is the revised shadow value of government revenue, $(S_R)_D$. Finally, the Bruce–Harris welfare test for strict Pareto improvements was extended to economies with distorting taxes by making the personal revised shadow value of government revenue positive for every consumer. While this may require changes to a large number of taxes, it does provide a way of evaluating policy changes without relying on subjectively chosen distributional weights to evaluate the equity effects.

NOTES

1. Triest (1990) refers to the MCF as a shadow price.
2. Examples of this practice can be found in Fullerton (1991) and Boadway and Bruce (1984).
3. A number of empirical studies estimate this modified measure of the MCF for wage taxes in the United States. Their results are summarized in Table 7.2.
4. Atkinson and Stern (1974) illustrate the 'spending effect' using the example of the government raising a tax and using the extra revenue to supply another television channel. If this channel raises the demand for television sets it will generate additional tax revenue when they are subject to tax. This extra revenue is the 'spending effect' included in the modified MCF used by Ballard and Fullerton, and Wildasin.
5. Dahlby and Mayshar both state a preference for including the 'spending effect' in the welfare effects from government spending and not in the MCF.
6. Since the tax change makes $(u) + (w) - (q) = (a) + (b) + (c)$, then $(u) + (w) = (a) + (b) + (c) + (q)$.
7. Sieper (1981) (on page 51) writes this shadow price as:

$$(S_k)_D = -\sum_i z_i \frac{\partial p_i}{\partial z_k} + \text{mcf}_d \left\{ S_k + \sum_i z_i \frac{\partial p_i}{\partial z_k} \right\},$$

and then obtains the compensated shadow price by multiplying it by $1/\text{mcf}_d$. But this is based on the incorrect assumption that the conventional MCF is a shadow price. In fact, the revised shadow value of government revenue $(S_R)_D$ should be used in this way because it converts compensated gains into dollar changes in utility. This correction is explained in Jones (2000).

8. By using the goods market clearing conditions, we have:

$$\sum_i z_i \frac{\partial p_i}{\partial z_k} = \sum_i (x_i - \bar{x}_i - y_i) \frac{\partial p_i}{\partial z_k},$$

where changes in public sector profit are matched by offsetting dollar changes in private surplus. Thus, when the government transfers this extra public profit to consumers it will not raise their utility because it makes good a loss in private surplus due to endogenous price changes.

9. When taxes are Ramsey (1927) optimal the marginal excess burden is the same for each tax, so the MCF is independent of the tax used.

10. A better example where this possibility arises is for a tax on wage income. In this case, the income effects work against the substitution effect when leisure is a normal good. In a more general setting there are also changes in related markets that augment (q).

11. Recall from the derivation of the shadow price in (6.8), where a single tax d is used to make compensating transfers, we need taxes to be Ramsey optimal or a single consumer in the economy. When taxes are Ramsey optimal they have the same marginal excess burden.

12. In the presence of public production the compensating transfers for good $k(\partial \hat{L}/\partial z_k)$ are equal to the fall in profit on public production. The compensating transfers are discounted by the MCF because they are made using tax d.

13. This expression is solved by noting the CV from raising tax d in $(u + w)$ must offset the CV from extra output of good k in (e).

14. Detailed workings are provided in Appendix 7 where the MCF is derived in a more general setting with public production and variable producer prices.

15. In the C-economy with constant marginal production costs, there is zero private profit ($py = 0$), and with no public production net government revenue is: $R = ty - L$. Aggregate income is obtained by solving the lump-sum transfers and substituting them into the consumer budget constraint in (2.2).

16. We use the Slutsky decomposition: $\partial \hat{x}_i(q)/\partial q_d = (\partial x_i(q, I)/\partial q_d) + (x_d \partial x_i(q, I)/\partial I)$ and the market clearing condition with no public production, where: $y_d = x_d - \bar{x}_d$.

17. For c_i negative, consumers are net supplier of good i which firms use as an input to production; an example of this is labour supply.

18. Atkinson and Stern use the Slutsky decomposition:

$$\frac{\partial x_i(q, I)}{\partial q_d} = \frac{\partial \hat{x}_i(q)}{\partial q_d} - (x_d - \bar{x}_d) \frac{\partial x_i(q, I)}{\partial I}.$$

19. Atkinson and Stern decompose the welfare effects of the tax change in (7.10) in the same way as Diamond and Mirrlees who do not explicitly isolate the MCF. Instead, they identify the first-order conditions for Ramsey optimal taxes.

20. With Ramsey optimal taxes $\text{mêb}_d = \text{mêb} \ \forall_d$. Optimal tax rules are examined in Chapter 9.

21. From the consumer budget constraint: $\sum_i q_i (\partial x_i(q, I)/\partial I) = 1$.

22. The sign of the Hatta coefficient is examined in Chapter 2, Section 2.2.3.

23. This is confirmed by using (2.6) to solve the revenue transfers in the shadow prices in (6.4) and (6.10).

24. Shadow profit is computed with initial public production in Appendix 8.

25. In the absence of public production: $(\hat{\pi}_k^S)_D = \hat{\pi}_k^S$.

26. Most studies that derive mcf* do so for a public project that marginally increases the supply of a pure public good (G) when it is funded from a wage tax. For example, the revised Samuelson condition in Snow and Warren, is:

$$\sum \text{MRS} = \text{mcf}_d^* \ \text{MRT},$$

with $\text{mcf}_d^* = \text{mcf}_d(1 - (dT/dR))$ and $dR/dG = (\partial T/\partial R) + (\partial T/\partial G)(1/\text{MRT})$. Their expression for the modified MCF in equation (7.17) is made more complicated by having progressive marginal tax rates above a tax free threshold, but it does nevertheless have the same basic structure by including the change in tax revenue from extra output of the public good. The revised Samuelson condition will be examined as a case study in Chapter 10.

27. Ballard, Shoven and Whalley estimate the marginal excess burden of taxation by deducting *actual* changes in revenue from the cost to surplus measured by equivalent variations. Stuart computes the

MCF by deducting *actual* changes in tax revenue from compensating variations, while Browning estimates the marginal excess burden as the compensated tax inefficiency per dollar change in *actual* tax revenue. Stuart measures the tax inefficiency as the difference between the 'compensating surplus' and the change in actual tax revenue. Hicks (1954) distinguishes between 'compensating surplus' and 'compensating variation'. The former holds utility constant by transferring a numeraire good to consumers, while the latter holds utility constant with lump-sum transfers of revenue. Ballard, Shoven and Whalley, and Stuart include the 'spending effect' in the MCF, while Browning does not. None of these measures coincide with the compensated measures in Auerbach (1985) and Diamond and McFadden (1974) who use compensated (rather than actual) changes in tax revenue. Mayshar argues the '*conceptual problems that underlie the existing excess burden measures may be the source of the dearth of applications*' (Mayshar 1990: 263), while Kay (1980) identifies potential inconsistencies when actual and hypothetical welfare measures are combined in this way. Håkonsen also examines the different measures of the MCF and argues they arise from differences in terminology and in the choice of numeraire.

28. The table also reports estimates of a distorting wage tax (τ), where the compensated labour supply elasticities determine the 'distortionary effect' which raises the conventional MCF (mcf$_\tau$) above unity, while uncompensated labour supply elasticities report net changes in labour supply for the combined effects of marginally increasing government spending on a pure public good and the wage tax, that is, it is the net change in labour supply for a public project. When the uncompensated elasticities are zero the project has no net impact on labour supply. This is where the 'spending effect', which measures the increase in tax revenue when extra output of the public good increases labour supply, is offset by the combined 'distortionary and revenue effects' from the higher wage tax to finance this spending, with mcf$_\tau^* = 1$. With negative uncompensated elasticities the 'spending effect' dominates and drives mcf$_\tau^*$ below unity, while the 'distortionary' and 'revenue effects' dominate with positive uncompensated elasticities to drive mcf$_\tau^*$ above unity.

29. Sieper (1981) uses the conventional MCF to convert revised compensated shadow prices into revised uncompensated shadow prices. Jones (2000) demonstrates why the revised shadow value of government revenue should be used instead. By not recognizing they are two different concepts, Sieper treats $(S_R)_D$ as the MCF.

30. Using (3.4) with $dL = 0$, we have:

$$(\bar{S}_k)_D = DC_p z \frac{\partial p}{\partial z_k} - \left\{ DC_p z \frac{\partial p}{\partial t_d} + DC_{t_a}(y_d + z_d) \right\} \left(\frac{dt_d}{dz_k} \right)_D,$$

where the tax change to balance the government budget, is:

$$\left(\frac{dt_d}{dz_k} \right)_D = \frac{-(S_k + z(\partial p/\partial z_k))}{\partial L/\partial t_d},$$

with: $\partial L/\partial t_d = (x_d - \bar{x}_d) + t(\partial x/\partial t_d) + z(\partial p/\partial t_d)$. In the absence of distributional effects ($DC_p = DC_t = 1$) and with fixed producer prices the MCF in (7.22) collapses to the familiar measure in (7.9), where by the market clearing conditions, we have:

$$\sum_i \frac{t_i}{y_d} \frac{\partial y_i}{\partial t_d} = \sum_i \frac{t_i}{x_d - \bar{x}_d} \frac{\partial x_i}{\partial t_d}.$$

31. By summing the dollar changes in utility over consumers using (3.3) with $dL = 0$, the change in social welfare becomes:

$$(dW)_D = \sum_h \beta^h \{ DE_p^h \, dp + DE_t^h \, dt \}.$$

32. For tax d the personal MCF for consumer h is:

$$\text{mcf}_d^h = -\frac{\{(\bar{x}_d^h - x_d^h) - \sum_s DE_s^h (\partial p_s/\partial t_d)\}}{\partial L/\partial t_d}.$$

The conventional MCF funds is obtained for the single (aggregated) consumer in (7.2) by summing these personal MCF over consumers. When the government use a number of taxes to balance its budget, the revised shadow value of government revenue is:

$$(S_R^h)_D = S_R \sum_s DE_s^h - \sum_i mcf_i^h \frac{\partial L}{\partial t_i} \left(\frac{dt_i}{dR}\right)_D,$$

where the tax changes solve: $(dL/dR)_D = \partial L/\partial R + \sum(\partial L/\partial t_i)(dt_i/dR)_D = 0$.

33. Harberger assumes the governments distributional weight on each dollar of tax revenue received is unity while the distributional weight for each dollar paid by taxpayers is less than unity with weights that vary inversely with income.

34. Dahlby intentionally ignores the impact of endogenous changes in labour income on the average tax rate in (7.29) by setting the second term to zero, where $da^h = \sum_j x^{hj} dt^j$. Mayshar does include the second term in the analysis.

35. This last assumption is perhaps the most controversial because income and commodity taxes both play a significant role in revenue raising, and the interactions between them makes it crucial that they both be included when choosing optimal tax rates, and optimal tax brackets for the progressive personal income tax.

36. Recall from the way the distributional characteristics are defined in equation (3.4) that $\bar{\beta} = \beta$ when consumers have the same distributional weights.

37. This decomposition follows the approach demonstrated in Chapter 2. Notice that changes in the infra-marginal tax rates do not affect income because tax revenue is returned to taxpayers in lump-sum transfers. Only changes in marginal tax rates matter because they distort the labour–leisure choice.

38. In fact, they are computing the shadow value of government revenue. A more detailed discussion of this point is provided in Section 7.5 where it is argued that the conventional MCF for a lump-sum tax is always unity. This is not the case for the decompositions of the MCF in Dahlby, Mayshar, and Wildasin.

8

Time and the Social Discount Rate

A number of important issues arise in an intertemporal setting where policy changes can impact on future consumption flows. The welfare effects are determined by discounting these consumption flows using the social (shadow) discount rate. Whenever consumers carry income into the future by saving, their future consumption grows at the market rate of interest after tax. However, that is unlikely to provide a measure of the change in final consumption demand for the economy as a whole when markets are distorted. Instead, it is computed using the social discount rate. One of the most important distortions in an intertemporal setting are taxes on income, and there are two types of income; atemporal returns to labour and intertemporal returns to capital. In an atemporal setting taxes on income are equivalent to taxes on final consumption demand when taxable income is equal to consumption. But with leisure being a non-marketed good both taxes will distort the labour–leisure choice. Moreover, with multiple time periods not all income is consumed when it is earned as some is saved and carried forward to future consumption. Since interest income on saving is also subject to tax, the income tax will distort the intertemporal consumption choice by raising the relative price of future consumption. It does so by taxing income when it is earned rather than when it is consumed.

A traditional measure of the social discount rate is derived by Harberger (1969), and Sandmo and Dréze (1971) for a linear income tax. It is a weighted average of the market rate of interest (r), which measures the value of the marginal product of capital investment, and the interest rate after tax, which is the return to saving.[1] As such, it is a signal that private investment demand and saving are constrained by taxes on income. Other studies find the social discount deviates from this formula when there are multiple time periods. Marglin (1963a, b) finds it is higher, while Bradford (1975) finds it is approximately equal to the return on saving (i.e. rate of time preference). Sjaastad and Wisecarver (1977) show how these differences are explained by the way private consumers respond to depreciation in public capital. When they increase saving and replace this depreciation the social discount rate becomes the weighted average formula once again.

Income taxation in most countries has two important attributes that should be included in the welfare analysis, and they are non-linear personal taxes and taxes on corporate income. As noted previously in Section 7.7, marginal personal tax rates normally rise with income, and once this feature is included in the analysis there are personal social discount rates that discount future consumption flows for consumers with different after tax returns. One reason why governments levy taxes on the equity income of corporate firms is to discourage shareholders from lowering their effective personal tax liability by holding income inside firms as capital gains. Since they are subject to personal tax on realization and not accrual, shareholders can defer realizing capital gains until future time periods. The corporate tax discourages this activity by collecting revenue on equity income when it accrues, but in a certainty setting without personal taxes, it will lead to an all debt equilibrium where the government collects no corporate tax revenue. There are a number of ways to explain the presence of equity, and the approach of Miller (1977) is adopted here. It exploits two common features of most personal tax codes, and they are progressive personal taxes and lower taxes on capital gains. When high-tax consumers have marginal cash tax rates above the corporate rate they can have a tax preference for equity that pays capital gains, even though it is subject to both corporate and personal tax, if the tax burden is smaller than their marginal cash tax rate. Once debt and equity both trade consumers divide into tax clienteles, but no dividends are paid in this equilibrium because they are subject to greater tax than interest income or capital gains for all consumers. Under this tax structure, bondholders and shareholders have personal social discount rates that reflect the different tax treatment of their tax-preferred securities. Any changes in future consumption flows for equity specialists are discounted using a social discount rate that is determined by their combined personal and corporate tax rates on capital gains, while the social discount rate for debt specialists is determined solely by their marginal tax rate on cash distributions.

Administrative costs and tax evasion are two important features of tax codes that are not included in the welfare analysis in this chapter. Taxes are costly to pay and collect and there are different administrative costs for taxes on income and taxes on consumption. These taxes are normally collected by a central government agency like the Australian Tax Office (ATO) or the Inland Revenue Service (IRS) in the United States who require eligible taxpayers, personal and business, to submit tax returns at prescribed times each year. Most taxpayers, especially business firms, incur costs from complying with these obligations and minimising their tax payments, while tax authorities incur costs to collect the revenue and to minimise tax evasion. In the following analysis there are no compliance costs or tax evasion so as to focus on the familiar distortionary effects of taxation.

In the next section the welfare analysis is extended to a two-period certainty setting where a conventional welfare equation is obtained for a linear income tax to derive the traditional formula for the social discount rate in Harberger, and Sandmo and Dréze. Deviations from this formula in Marglin and Bradford are obtained by extending the analysis to multiple time periods. Personal social discount rates are obtained in Section 8.2 by including non-linear income taxation, and they are extended in Section 8.3 by including a classical corporate tax using the Miller equilibrium. Adjustments for risk are examined in Section 8.4 where the Arrow-Lind theorem is examined to consider whether or not the social discount rate should be lower on public sector projects.

8.1 LINEAR INCOME TAXATION

Consider a two-period certainty setting where each consumer h maximizes utility $u^h(x_0^h, x_1^h)$ with x_t^h being their vector of non-traded consumption goods in each time period $t \in 0, 1$. Changes in social welfare are measured by substituting these utility functions into the individualistic function in (1.22) when private expenditure is constrained in present value terms by the aggregated private and public budget constraint:

$$qx = q\bar{x} + p(y + z) + T - R, \tag{8.1}$$

with present value prices in each period, of:

$$q_{i0} = p_{i0} + t_{i0} \quad \text{and} \quad q_{i1} = \frac{p_{i1}' + t_{i1}'}{1 + r + t_r} = p_{i1} + t_{i1} \qquad \forall i, \tag{8.2}$$

where $q_{i1}' = p_{i1}' + t_{i1}'$ is the consumer spot price for each good i at time 1, r the market rate of interest between time 0 and time 1, and $t_r < 0$ the specific tax on interest income. This notation can be used to expand the present value of private expenditure as $qx = q_0 x_0 + q_1 x_1$. With no second period endowments, we have $q\bar{x} = q_0 \bar{x}_0$. Saving and investment are included by assuming private and public firms produce output in the second period using a capital input (k) purchased in the first period (with $y_{k0} < 0$ and $z_{k0} < 0$), where the present value of private and public profits are, respectively:

$$py = p_{-k0} y_{-k0} + \frac{p_1' y_1 + p_{k0} y_{k0}(1 + r)}{1 + r + t_r},$$

and

$$pz = p_{-k0} z_{-k0} + \frac{p_1' z_1 + p_{k0} z_{k0}(1 + r)}{1 + r + t_r},$$

with y_{-k0} and z_{-k0} being vectors of non–capital net outputs in each sector. Private firms are competitive and have first-order conditions for output in the second period, of:

$$p_1' \, dy_1 + p_{k0} \, dy_{k0}(1 + r) = 0.^2 \tag{8.3}$$

Notice how interest payments increase the cost of capital investment. For capital market equilibrium saving (s_0) must be equal to investment demand, with:

$$s_0 = \bar{x}_{k0} - x_{k0} = -(y_{k0} + z_{k0}). \tag{8.4}$$

The market clearing conditions for all other goods traded in the first period are unchanged, as $\bar{x}_{i0} + y_{i0} + z_{i0} = x_{i0} \; \forall i$, while for goods traded in the second period we have $y_{i1} + z_{i1} = x_{i1}$ $\forall_i$ due to the absence of endowments. These changes make the present value of tax revenue:

$$T = t_0(x_0 - \bar{x}_0) + t_1 x_1 + \frac{t_r p_{k0}}{1 + r + t_r}(y_{k0} + z_{k0}), \tag{8.5}$$

where the last term is tax revenue collected on interest income. By using the price notation in (8.2) we can write the present value of tax revenue on final consumption in the second period as $t_1 x_1 = t_1' x_1/(1 + r + t_r)$.

A conventional welfare equation is obtained by using the aggregate budget constraint for the economy in (8.1) after substituting tax revenue in (8.5), where:

$$\frac{dW}{\beta} = p\,dz + t\,dx + \frac{t_r p_{k0}}{1 + r + t_r}\,dy_{k0}.^3 \tag{8.6}$$

It has the same structure as the conventional welfare equation in (2.7) but differs by including changes in interest tax revenue. This measures the welfare effects from moving resources through time in the presence of a tax on capital income.

8.1.1 The Social Discount Rate—The Weighted Average Formula

Harberger, and Sandmo and Dréze derive the social discount rate in a two-period setting with tax distortions. It is obtained by first computing the shadow price of capital using the conventional welfare equation in (8.6), as:

$$S_{k0} = \frac{dW}{dz_{k0}}\frac{1}{\beta} = \frac{p_{k0}}{1 + r + t_r}\left\{1 + r - t_r\frac{\partial s_0}{\partial z_{k0}}\right\} + t\frac{\partial x}{\partial z_{k0}}, \tag{8.7}$$

where a marginal reduction in public investment (with $dz_{k0} > 0$) increases the supply of capital to the private economy. In the absence of any tax distortions we have $S_{k0} = p_{k0}$. The first term in (8.7) is the welfare gain from expanding private investment in the presence of a tax on interest income, while the last term includes welfare effects when activity changes in related markets subject to tax distortions. The social discount rate (S_r) is obtained by writing the shadow price of capital, as:

$$S_{k0}(1 + r + t_r) = p_{k0}(1 + S_r),^4 \tag{8.8}$$

where in the absence of any distortions we must have $S_r = r$ and $S_{k0} = p_{k0}$. The weighted average formula of Harberger, and Sandmo and Dréze is obtained from (8.8) by using (8.7) when the tax on interest income is the only tax, where:

$$S_r = r - t_r\frac{\partial s_0}{\partial z_{k0}}.^5 \tag{8.9}$$

It is illustrated in Figure 8.1 by a marginal reduction in public investment demand which increases the supply of capital to the private economy. The increase in private investment has a marginal product of r, while the decrease in private saving generates current consumption benefits equal to the interest rate after tax ($r + t_r$).

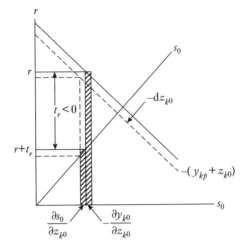

Figure 8.1 *The social discount rate*

Thus, the social discount rate exceeds the private cost of supplying capital, but is less than the value of the marginal product of private investment, with $r > S_r > r+t_r$.[6] There are additional welfare effects when resources flow through other distorted markets. If taxed activities expand the social rate of return rises by the extra tax revenue collected, but the reverse applies if resources are drawn away from taxed activities or moved into subsidized activities. The effects of other distortions like externalities, both positive and negative, price and quantity controls, and non-competitive behaviour can be accommodated in a similar fashion.

8.1.2 The Social Discount Rate with Multiple Time Periods

Introducing multiple time periods can cause the social discount rate to deviate from the weighted average formula of Harberger, and Sandmo and Dréze in (8.9). Marglin identifies circumstances where it is higher, while Bradford finds it lower and approximately equal to the marginal rate of time preference $(r + t_r)$. Sjaastad and Wisecarver show that these differences arise when the private sector does not replace the depreciation in public capital. In the previous section, a marginal increase in public investment would crowd out private investment and increase private saving by pushing up the market rate of interest. The social cost was the foregone current consumption from extra saving and the present value of the foregone future consumption on the lower private investment. These are the terms in the shadow discount rate in (8.9) without commodity taxes, and for convenience will be defined here as:

$$\omega = \psi r + (1 - \psi)\rho, \tag{8.10}$$

where $\psi \equiv -\partial y_{k0}/\partial z_{k0}$ is the fall in private investment, $(1 - \psi) = -\partial s_0/\partial z_{k0}$ the increase in saving, and $\rho = r + t_r$ the marginal rate of time preference. In a two-period setting depreciation plays no role in the analysis because capital produced in period 0 is completely liquidated in period 1 to fund consumption. However, depreciation does play a role if there are multiple time periods. Marglin and Bradford find $S_r \neq \omega$ when the private sector does not replace depreciated public capital. This can be demonstrated by evaluating a public sector project that invests a unit of capital in period 0 with future consumption benefits of $B(\tau)$ in each period τ. For simplicity, units of capital are chosen to make $p_{k0} = 1$, and the only market distortion is the uniform tax on interest income ($t_r < 0$), where the project is socially profitable when:

$$\int_{\tau=0}^{\infty} B(\tau) e^{-\rho \tau} \, d\tau \geq S_{k0}. \qquad (8.11)$$

The role of depreciation can be demonstrated by comparing two different types of projects; one makes capital a perpetuity and the other assumes it generates a consumption benefit in the first period and none thereafter. If capital is a perpetuity it does not depreciate in value over time, whereas capital with a one period benefit depreciates completely at the end of the period. Each case will be examined in turn:

1. The perpetuity has $B(\tau) = \delta \; \forall_\tau$, and is socially profitable when:

$$\int_{\tau=0}^{\infty} \delta \, e^{-\rho \tau} \, d\tau \geq (1 - \psi) + \frac{\psi r}{\rho}.$$

This solves as $\delta/\rho \geq \omega/\rho$, which is the evaluation criterion obtained by Harberger, and Sandmo and Dréze, with $\delta \geq \omega$. On the right-hand side of the relationship, $1 - \psi$ is the fall in current consumption when private saving rises, while $\psi r/\rho$ is the present value of the fall in future consumption when private investment falls.

2. The capital asset with a single period benefit has $B(1) = 1 + \delta$ and $B(\tau) = 0 \; \forall_{\tau > 1}$, and Marglin finds it socially profitable when:

$$\int_{\tau=0}^{\infty} B(\tau) e^{-\rho \tau} \, d\tau \simeq \frac{1 + \delta}{1 + \rho} \geq (1 - \psi) + \frac{\psi r}{\rho}.$$

After rearranging terms the social discount rate is $\delta \geq \omega + \psi(r - \rho)/\rho > \omega$, which is higher than the weighted average formula of Harberger, and Sandmo and Dréze in (8.10).[7] Sjaastad and Wisecarver reconcile this difference by making the observation that consumers do not replace the depreciation in public capital in the analysis by Marglin. They argue consumers do not treat depreciation as income, but instead increase saving to restore public capital and steady-state consumption to their initial values. Once they do, the social cost of marginally increasing public investment at time 0 is $1 - \psi$ in lost current consumption, while the net increase in future consumption in period 1 is $1 + \delta - \psi - \psi r$, where $1 + \delta$ is the consumption flow from the project, $-\psi$ the loss in consumption when saving rises in period 0 to offset the depreciation in public capital, and $-\psi r$ the loss in consumption when private investment falls in period 0. In effect, the public project shifts consumption from period 0 to period 1, and then it returns to its initial steady-state flow when consumers replace the depreciated public capital. In these circumstances, the project is socially profitable when:

$$\frac{1 + \delta - \psi - \psi r}{1 + \rho} \geq (1 - \psi),$$

which provides the evaluation criterion of Harberger, and Sandmo and Dréze using the shadow discount rate in (8.10) with $\delta \geq \omega$.

These examples make it clear why the social discount rate will depend on the amount of reinvestment consumers undertake to offset depreciation in public capital. If they completely offset it the weighted average formula of Harberger, and Sandmo and Dréze is the appropriate discount rate to use, where socially profitable projects satisfy the condition:

$$\int_{\tau=0}^{\infty} B(\tau)e^{-\omega\tau}\, d\tau \geq 1.$$

This is obviously related to the Ricardian equivalence theorem where consumers do not treat public debt as net wealth when they fully anticipate the present value of the tax burden imposed on them or their heirs when it is redeemed in the future. If consumers do not anticipate changes in their net wealth in this way then they may not replace capital depreciation to preserve public capital either, where this causes the social discount rate to deviate from the weighted average formula of Harberger, and Sandmo and Dréze in the manner suggested by Marglin, with $S_r \neq \omega$. While this is not a problem in following sections where the analysis takes place in a two-period setting, it is nonetheless an important consideration for policy evaluation in a multi-period setting.

8.1.3 The Marginal Excess Burden of Taxation

Most governments raise revenue with a combination of income and consumption taxes. Recent tax reforms in Australia and New Zealand have moved to eliminate most of the taxes on production inputs, and have opted instead for a uniform tax on final consumption expenditure combined with a comprehensive income tax. At the same time, consumption taxes were introduced, tax rates on income were lowered, and an imputation tax system was adopted to remove the double taxation of dividends by the corporate tax. Thus, while progressive marginal personal taxes still apply in both countries, attempts have been made to tax income of consumers from all sources at their marginal cash tax rate.[8]

Corporate and non-linear income taxes are examined later in Section 8.2. This section compares the welfare costs of a uniform tax on final consumption demand to a uniform income tax. Each tax has a different base, where the income tax distorts the labour–leisure and intertemporal consumption choices, while the tax on final consumption only distorts the labour–leisure choice. If non-marketed goods like leisure could also be taxed the consumption tax would be equivalent to a lump-sum tax, and it would not distort the labour–leisure choice. Since the consumption tax distorts one rather than two margins of activity it is tempting to conclude it has a smaller marginal excess burden. However, that may not be the case as the income tax base is larger and may generate the same revenue with a lower tax rate.

Frequent reference is made to the income tax as a double tax on saving. This idea is best understood by looking at the way each tax affects future consumption. Consider a given amount of income which is saved for future consumption. The income tax collects revenue at the time the income is earned rather than at the time it is consumed, which reduces saving and the after-tax interest income it would generate. Under a consumption tax, all income saved can grow at interest before it is taxed as future consumption. Basically, an income tax raises more revenue by taxing saving, thereby collecting the tax on future consumption earlier. In effect, the government earns interest on it, whereas this revenue stays with the consumer and is not collected until it is consumed in the future under a consumption tax.

The different excess burdens for these taxes can be illustrated using the conventional welfare equation in (8.6). To simplify the analysis assume there is no government production (with $z_i = 0 \; \forall_i$), and to isolate the labour–leisure and intertemporal choices let private firms employ labour in period 0 as the sole input to production, with $y_0 = y_0(y_{n0})$ and $y_1 = y_1(y_{n1})$ in each period, where they produce until:

$$p_0 \, dy_0 + p_n \, dy_{n0} = 0 \qquad \text{and} \qquad p_1 \, dy_1 + \frac{p_n \, dy_{n1}(1+r)}{1+r+t_r} = 0. \qquad (8.12)$$

Further, let us assume consumers have a single endowment $(\bar{x}_{n0})$, which is the time they allocate to leisure (x_{n0}) and labour supply (with $\bar{x}_{n0} - x_{n0} > 0$) in the first period. By making labour the sole input firms buy in the first period to produce output in the second period we obtain investment and saving from the labour market clearing condition, as $-y_{n1} = \bar{x}_{n0} - x_{n0} + y_{n0} \equiv s_0$. Thus, in the absence of public production and other endowments the market clearing conditions for all the produced goods are $x_{i0} = y_{i0}$ and $x_{i1} = y_{i1} \; \forall_{i \neq n}$.

As a basis for comparing tax rates we define them in *ad valorem* terms, where the uniform tax on final consumption expenditure is $\varphi_C = t_i/p_i > 0 \; \forall_i$, and the income tax $\varphi_Y = t_n/p_{n0} = t_r/r < 0$. This makes the present value of tax revenue:

$$T = \varphi_C p_0 y_0 + \varphi_C p_1 y_1 - \varphi_Y p_{n0}(\bar{x}_{n0} - x_{n0}) + \frac{\varphi_Y r p_{n0} y_{n1}}{1 + r(1 + \varphi_Y)}, \qquad (8.13)$$

where, in the absence of other market distortions, the conventional welfare equation in (8.6) becomes:

$$\frac{dW}{\beta} = \varphi_C p \, dx + \varphi_Y p_{n0} \, dx_{n0} + \frac{\varphi_Y r p_{n0}}{1 + r(1 + \varphi_Y)} dy_{n1}. \qquad (8.14)$$

The welfare changes from distorting the labour–leisure choice are captured in the first two terms, while the third term measures the distortion to the intertemporal consumption choice. A marginal welfare loss for each tax will be computed using

(8.14) when they are levied separately. For a *uniform consumption tax* (with $\varphi_Y = 0$), we obtain:

$$\frac{dW}{d\varphi_C}\frac{1}{\beta} = -\varphi_C p_{n0}\frac{\partial x_{n0}}{\partial\varphi_C}.^{10} \tag{8.15}$$

This is the welfare loss from raising the implicit subsidy to leisure. The marginal welfare loss for the *uniform income tax* (with $\varphi_C = 0$), is:

$$\frac{dW}{d\varphi_Y}\frac{1}{\beta} = \varphi_Y\, p_{n0}\frac{\partial x_{n0}}{\partial\varphi_Y} - \frac{\varphi_Y r p_1}{(1+r)}\frac{\partial x_1}{\partial\varphi_Y}.^{11} \tag{8.16}$$

Notice how the first term in (8.16) is the same as the welfare loss for the consumption tax in (8.15) where $\varphi_C > 0$ and $\varphi_Y < 0$. They are losses from worsening the labour–leisure choice distortion. There is a further loss from the income tax in the second term of (8.16) when it distorts the intertemporal consumption choice. If the income and consumption tax rates are equal (with $\varphi_C = |\varphi_Y|$) the overall welfare loss from the income tax will be larger when future consumption contracts. But, as mentioned earlier, it is unfair to compare the two taxes at the same rate because they have different bases. The appropriate comparison is between the marginal welfare loss per dollar change in tax revenue for each tax, that is, their marginal excess burden, and they are computed by dividing the change in tax inefficiency in (8.15) by:

$$\frac{\partial T}{\partial\varphi_C} = \frac{\partial(\varphi_C p_0 y_0 + \varphi_C p_1 y_1)}{\partial\varphi_C}, \tag{8.17}$$

and the change in tax inefficiency in (8.16) by:

$$\frac{\partial T}{\partial\varphi_Y} = \frac{\partial(\varphi_Y\, p_{n0}(\bar{x}_{n0} - x_{n0}) + \varphi_Y r p_{n0} y_{n1}/(1 + r(1 + \varphi_Y)))}{\partial\varphi_Y}. \tag{8.18}$$

Without empirical data to estimate the equilibrium changes in activity for each tax change it is not possible to determine which one has the lower marginal excess burden.

8.2 NON-LINEAR INCOME TAXATION

In most countries marginal personal tax rates on income are increasing piecewise linear functions after an initial tax-free threshold. Thus, consumers with relatively high incomes have higher marginal and average tax rates than those with lower incomes. Once consumers face different marginal tax rates they will discount future consumption flows using different after-tax returns. To simplify the following analysis assume that there is one step in a piecewise linear marginal personal tax function at income $\bar{Y}^H$ that divides consumers into high (H) and low (L) tax groups (G). Those with income at or below $\bar{Y}^H$ pay the low marginal tax rate $t_r^L < 0$, while those with income above $\bar{Y}^H$ pay the high marginal tax rate $t_r^H < 0$. Thus, within each group consumers have the same marginal tax rate and use the same personal discount factor.

In these circumstances, the aggregate budget constraint for each group in present value terms, is:

$$q^G x^G = q_0 \bar{x}_0^G - \frac{(t_r^H - t_r^L) \bar{Y}^H}{1 + r + t_r^G} + p^G (y^G + z^G) + T^G - R^G$$

$$\text{for } G \in H, L, {}^{12} \tag{8.19}$$

where the present value of the consumer and producer prices in the second period, are:

$$q_{i1}^G = \frac{p_{i1}' + t_{i1}'}{1 + r + t_r^G} = p_{i1}^G + t_{i1}^G \qquad \forall_i \quad \text{and} \quad G \in H, L. \tag{8.20}$$

Note there is an adjustment in the second term of (8.19) to account for the low marginal tax rate (t_r^L) that applies on the initial income ($\bar{Y}^H$) of high-tax consumers; it is an implicit tax refund to lower their average tax rate below their marginal rate. In the following analysis it is assumed consumers do not move between the two tax groups when their income changes endogenously. Thus, endogenous changes in income will not alter the number of consumers in each tax clientele. By using the prices in (8.20), we can write the present value of consumption in (8.19), as:

$$q^G x^G = q_0 x_0^G + \frac{q_1' x_1^G}{1 + r + t_r^G} \qquad \text{for } G \in H, L.$$

Initially the analysis will adopt the production economy used initially in Section 8.1 where firms produce output in the second period using a capital input (k) purchased in the first period. They therefore have profit of:

$$p^G y^G = \rho_0^G p_{-k0} y_{-k0} + \frac{\rho_1^G (p_1' y_1 + p_{k0} y_{k0} (1 + r))}{1 + r + t_r^G} \qquad \text{for } G \in H, L,$$

where ρ_t^G is the profit share for consumers in each group G, with $\rho_t^H + \rho_t^L = 1$ for $t \in 0, 1.{}^{13}$ Similarly, for profit on public production:

$$p^G z^G = g_0^G p_{-k0} z_{-k0} + \frac{g_1^G (p_1' z_1 + p_{k0} z_{k0} (1 + r))}{1 + r + t_r^G},$$

with $g_t^H + g_t^L = 1$ for $t \in 0, 1$. Once again, by following the approach of Harberger who returns tax revenue to taxpayers as lump-sum transfers, the present value of tax revenue collected from each group, is:

$$T^G = t_0 (\bar{x}_0^G - x_0^G) + \frac{(t_r^H - t_r^L) \bar{Y}^H + t_1' x_1^G + t_r^G \rho_1^G p_{k0} y_{k0} + t_r^G g_1^G p_{k0} z_{k0}}{1 + r + t_r^G}, {}^{14}$$

with $(t_r^H - t_r^L)\bar{Y}^H = 0$ for the low tax group. Under these circumstances, the conventional welfare equation becomes:

$$\frac{dW}{\beta} = t_0 \, dx_0 + p_0 \, dz_0 + p_{k0} \, dz_{k0}$$

$$+ \sum_{G \in H,L} \left(\frac{t_1' \, dx_1 + t_r^G \rho_1^G p_{k0} \, dy_{k0} + g_1^G p_1' \, dz_1}{1 + r + t_r^G} \right) - dR. \tag{8.21}$$

While it has the same structure as the previous welfare equations in (8.6) and (8.14) the notable difference is the personalized discount factors on the future consumption flows. They capture the different after-tax returns on saving when consumers face progressive marginal tax rates. We now use this welfare equation in (8.21) to compute the shadow discount rate and the marginal welfare losses for uniform income and consumption taxes.

8.2.1 Personal Social Discount Rates

Once consumers use different discount rates on future consumption flows there are personalized social discount rates in project evaluation. They have the same structure as the traditional Harberger formula in (8.9), and are obtained by first computing the shadow price of capital using (8.21), where in the absence of commodity taxes, we have:

$$S_{k0} = p_{k0} \left\{ 1 - \sum_{G \in H,L} \frac{t_r^G \rho_1^G p_{k0}}{1 + r + t_r^G} \left(1 + \frac{\partial s_0}{\partial z_{k0}} \right) \right\}. \tag{8.22}$$

When a unit of capital is endowed on the economy it raises social welfare by its market price (p_{k0}) plus the extra interest tax revenue when private investment expands (with $\partial y_{k0}/\partial z_{k0} = -(1 + \partial s_0/\partial z_{k0}) < 0$). The relationship between the shadow discount rates and the shadow price of capital, is:

$$S_{k0} = p_{k0} \sum_{G \in H,L} \frac{(1 + S_r^G)\rho_1^G}{1 + r + t_r^G}, \tag{8.23}$$

where the personal social discount rates are solved using (8.22), as:

$$S_r^G = r - t_r^G \frac{\partial s_0}{\partial z_{k0}} \qquad \text{for } G \in H, L. \tag{8.24}$$

In project evaluation these discount rates are used to compute the social value of the changes in future consumption flows for consumers in each tax bracket. In the presence of commodity taxes, the social discount rates in (8.24) will rise by the extra tax revenue collected when these activities expand. The reverse applies when they contract.

8.2.2 The Marginal Excess Burden of Taxation

As noted earlier, the recent tax reforms in both Australia and New Zealand have attempted, where possible, to subject all income for each consumer to the same marginal tax rate, and to tax all final consumption expenditure at the same rate.[15] Thus, even though personal income tax rates are progressive, and different consumers have different marginal tax rates, the reforms have attempted to tax income from all sources at the marginal cash tax rate for each consumer. Ideally, capital gains would also be taxed at this rate on accrual, but due to measurement problems they are taxed on realization. As a consequence, taxpayers can reduce their effective tax rates on accrued capital gains by realizing them in later time periods. For the moment, however, it is assumed that capital gains are taxed on accrual at the same rate as all other cash income.

To analyse the welfare effects of a comprehensive income tax and a uniform consumption tax the amendments made to the model in Section 8.1.2 are adopted where public production is eliminated and labour (n) is the sole input to production in each period, with saving and investment being $s_0 \equiv \sum_G (\bar{x}_{n0}^G - x_{n0}^G) + y_{n0} = -y_{n1}$. A comprehensive *ad valorem* income tax (φ_Y^G) is then applied to the wage and capital income of consumers in each tax group (G). High-tax consumers face the marginal tax rate φ_Y^H on all sources of income and low-tax consumers face the marginal tax rate φ_Y^L, where the conventional welfare equation becomes:

$$\frac{dW}{\beta} = \sum_{G \in H,L} \left(\varphi_C p^G \, dx^G + \varphi_Y^G p_{n0} \, dx_{n0}^G + \frac{\varphi_Y^G r \rho_1^G p_{n0}}{1 + r(1 + \varphi_Y^G)} \, dy_{n1} \right). \tag{8.25}$$

Once again, the marginal tax inefficiency for each tax will be computed when they are levied separately. Since the uniform consumption tax is the same for all consumers its welfare loss is the measure derived previously in (8.15), but the welfare loss for the income tax will change because there are two marginal tax rates. The *marginal welfare loss for the high tax rate* is obtained from (8.25), with $\varphi_C = 0$, as:

$$\frac{dW}{d\varphi_Y^H} \frac{1}{\beta} = \sum_{G \in H,L} \varphi_Y^G p_{n0} \frac{\partial x_{n0}^G}{\partial \varphi_Y^H} + \sum_{G \in H,L} \frac{\varphi_Y^G r \rho_1^G p_{n0}}{1 + r(1 + \varphi_Y^G)} \frac{\partial y_{n1}}{\partial \varphi_Y^H}.^{16} \tag{8.26}$$

It is a more complicated than the welfare loss for the linear tax in (8.16). Notably, there are different distortions to the labour–leisure choices in the first term of (8.26) when consumers face different marginal taxes. Even though the tax rate on low-tax consumers is unchanged they are affected by endogenous price changes as high-tax consumers adjust to their higher tax rate. The *marginal welfare loss for the low income tax rate* looks similar, and is obtained from (8.25), with $\varphi_C = 0$, as:

$$\frac{dW}{d\varphi_Y^L} \frac{1}{\beta} = \sum_{G \in H,L} \varphi_Y^G p_{n0} \frac{\partial x_{n0}^G}{\partial \varphi_Y^L} + \sum_{G \in H,L} \frac{\varphi_Y^G r \rho_1^G p_{n0}}{1 + r(1 + \varphi_Y^G)} \frac{\partial y_{n1}}{\partial \varphi_Y^L}. \tag{8.27}$$

It may be higher or lower than the welfare loss in (8.26) because there are likely to be different endogenous price changes. With a constant interest rate and constant producer prices the welfare losses in (8.26) and (8.27) are determined by the way tax revenue is transferred to consumers. To this point revenue is returned to the consumers who pay it in a lump-sum transfer, where a marginal increase in the high rate has no direct effect on low-tax consumers, and a marginal increase in the low tax rate will have no direct effect on high-tax consumers because it is an infra-marginal tax and they get the revenue back.[17] Consumers with unchanged tax rates are only affected indirectly through their share of the changes in private profit in the second terms of (8.26) and (8.27).

There are different welfare losses, however, when consumers do not get back the revenue they pay. For example, if all the additional tax revenue from either tax change is transferred to low-tax consumers there will be a transfer of private surplus from high-tax consumers. In particular, there is a pure redistribution of income when the infra-marginal tax rate on high-tax consumers is raised. Another way to return the tax revenue from raising one tax is to lower the other one. These tax changes hold government revenue constant and will have a final welfare change equal to the difference in the marginal excess burden for each tax. The marginal excess burden is computed for each tax by dividing the welfare losses in (8.26) and (8.27) by the respective change in tax revenue. For high-tax consumers it is:

$$
\frac{\partial T}{\partial \varphi_Y^H} = \left\{ \partial \left(\sum_{G \in H, L} \varphi_Y^G p_{n0} (\bar{x}_{n0}^G - x_{n0}^G) + (\varphi_Y^H - \varphi_Y^L) p_{n0} \bar{Y}_H \right. \right.
$$
$$
\left. \left. + \frac{\sum_{G \in H, L} \varphi_Y^G \rho_1^G r p_{n0} y_{n1}}{1 + r(1 + \varphi_Y^G)} \right) \right\} \left\{ \partial \varphi_Y^H \right\}^{-1}, \tag{8.28}
$$

and for the low-tax consumers:

$$
\frac{\partial T}{\partial \varphi_Y^L} = \left\{ \partial \left(\sum_{G \in H, L} \varphi_Y^G p_{n0} (\bar{x}_{n0}^G - x_{n0}^G) + (\varphi_Y^H - \varphi_Y^L) p_{n0} \bar{Y}_H \right. \right.
$$
$$
\left. \left. + \frac{\sum_{G \in H, L} \varphi_Y^G \rho_1^G r p_{n0} y_{n1}}{1 + r(1 + \varphi_Y^G)} \right) \right\} \left\{ \partial \varphi_Y^L \right\}^{-1}. \tag{8.29}
$$

As noted previously, any comparison between the marginal excess burden for each tax rate will require empirical estimates of the changes in economic activity.

8.3 CORPORATE TAXATION

Most governments levy a classical corporate tax on the equity income of firms, where interest income is a tax deductible expense. When this tax is combined with progressive marginal personal tax rates equity income is double taxed, once at the corporate

rate then again at the marginal personal tax rate in the hands of shareholders. Since interest income is subject only to personal tax, the taxes discriminate in favour of debt over equity, and this is reflected in the personal discount factors of shareholders which include corporate and personal taxes, while the discount rates for bondholders are determined solely by their personal tax rates.

A number of countries, including Australia, New Zealand, and the United Kingdom, impute all or part of corporate tax collected on dividends as tax credits for shareholders to apply against their personal tax liabilities. The corporate tax is used as a withholding tax on equity income when it accrues inside firms, where the tax credits to shareholders removes the double tax on dividends. If all corporate income is distributed as dividends and interest it is subject only to personal tax, and consumers have no tax preference for debt and equity. In these circumstances, their personal discount factors are the same as those derived in the previous section without a corporate tax. However, the imputation tax system does not completely eliminate consumer tax preferences for income paid to debt and equity. Some consumers have marginal cash tax rates above the corporate tax rate and have an incentive to delay realizing equity income as capital gains to defer their personal tax liabilities. Furthermore, firms pay some of their dividends from income not subject to corporate tax due to differences between taxable and economic income. Once dividends carry no tax credits shareholders have an incentive to delay realizing the income as a capital gain to defer their personal tax liabilities, and this will be reflected in their discount factors.

Due to the large amount of revenue governments raise with a corporate tax it is important to include it in the welfare analysis. A classical corporate tax on its own drives equity out of the economy in a certainty setting. Miller uses progressive marginal personal taxes and the favourable tax treatment of capital gains to explain the presence of equity. When high-tax consumers have marginal cash tax rates above the combined corporate and personal taxes on capital gains they will have a tax preference for equity. In contrast, low-tax consumers will have a tax preference for debt. Most other explanations for the presence of equity are based on uncertainty and leverage related costs which makes the analysis much more complicated. In this section, the corporate tax will be included in a certainty setting in three steps; first as a classical corporate tax without personal taxes, then as a classical corporate tax with progressive personal taxes, and finally as a withholding tax imputed to shareholders. The following analysis adopts the production economy first used in Section 8.1 where firms produce second period output using capital as an input (k) purchased in the first period.

8.3.1 A Classical Corporate Tax without Personal Taxes

In the presence of a corporate tax ($\varphi_F < 0$) on income paid to shareholders the present value of capital invested in private firms, is:

$$-p_{k0}\,y_{k0} = \frac{p_1'y_1(1 + \varphi_F)}{(1 + \varphi_F) + (1 - \rho_1^B)r_E + \rho_1^B r_B(1 + \varphi_F)}, \quad {}^{18} \qquad (8.30)$$

where ρ_1^B is the share of capital funded by selling debt (B) and $\rho_1^E = 1 - \rho_1^B$ the remaining share funded by selling equity (E). In a competitive capital market individual firms take the returns on debt (r_B) and equity (r_E) as given, which must be equal in a certainty setting with no taxes. A more realistic distinction can be made between debt and equity in an uncertainty setting with asymmetric information, but the analysis becomes much more complicated. This section will focus on the role of taxes in a certainty setting and the impact of uncertainty is briefly considered in Section 8.4. The numerator in (8.30) is referred to as the *user cost of capital*, and it discounts the after-tax net cash flows of private firms in the second period ($p'_1 y_1 (1 + \varphi_F)$) to account for the opportunity cost of each dollar of capital. Firms maximize profit by choosing leverage (ρ_1^B) to minimize the user cost of capital and then investment ($y_{k0} < 0$) to maximize their market value ($-p_{k0} y_{k0} > 0$). Thus, in equilibrium they will only supply debt and equity when:

$$r_B(1 + \varphi_F) = r_E.^{19} \tag{8.31}$$

After substituting this relationship between the security returns into (8.30), we have:

$$-p_{k0} y_{k0} = \frac{p'_0 y_1}{1 + r_B}, \tag{8.32}$$

where the market value of the firm is independent of ρ_1^B. This is the Modigliani and Miller (1958) leverage irrelevance theorem, and it holds whenever both securities trade. However, notice from (8.31) that the corporate tax raises the market return on debt above the market return on equity, with $r_B > r_E$. Thus, in the absence of personal taxes and leverage related costs consumers will only purchase debt, which is consistent with the findings in Modigliani and Miller (1963) where private firms in a competitive equilibrium will pay all their income to consumers as interest to avoid paying any corporate tax.[20]

Subsequent studies attempted to explain the presence of equity by including leverage related costs. Initially they focussed on costly default where firms unable to pay their interest commitments are forced to liquidate or reorganize. The associated costs of these activities reduces the net cash flows available to consumers and raises the cost of capital. Since the likelihood of default increases with leverage these expected default costs are increasing functions of leverage. However, uncertainty and asymmetric information are implicit in this explanation. In a common information setting firms must price their debt to compensate bondholders for the risk of default on interest payments. When they do, bondholders have no legal grounds to make claims against firm managers. With asymmetric information, however, bondholders do not have the same information as firm managers about the riskiness of the debt issued, and the law gives them protection in these circumstances. Other studies include lost corporate tax shields, that are leverage-related costs arising from the asymmetric treatment of profits and losses by the corporate tax.[21] Typically, most government do not pay refunds on tax losses or allow them to be traded, neither do they allow them to be carried forward with interest as deductions against future taxable income. As firms increase leverage, they incur additional interest payments that raises the probability of tax losses thereby reducing the real value of their tax deductions. This explanation requires uncertainty but not asymmetric information. More recent studies look at leverage-related costs in the presence of asymmetric information.[22] Unfortunately, there is little empirical support for leverage-related cost arguments. Most estimates of the marginal leverage-related costs find they are too small on their own to offset the corporate tax deductions on interest. Miller responded to these findings by including personal taxes to explain equity in the presence of a classical corporate tax.

8.3.2 A Classical Corporate Tax with Personal Taxes—The Miller Equilibrium

In most countries, income taxes discriminate between consumers and between securities. Personal income taxes are normally progressive and there are lower personal tax rates on capital gains that favour equity over debt. Miller exploits these features of the tax code to find high-tax consumers with a tax preference for equity when it pays capital gains. The analysis will be simplified here by endowing marginal income tax rates on consumers to divide them into two groups—those with high marginal tax rates and those with low marginal tax rates, and within each group they have the same tax rates. In a certainty setting consumers choose between debt and equity by comparing their after-tax returns, and they receive three types of income; interest, dividends, and capital gains. Dividends and interest are taxed as cash distributions (φ_B^h), while capital gains are taxed at a lower rate (φ_E^h), with $|\varphi_E^h| < |\varphi_B^h| \; \forall_h$. The tax rates on corporate income paid to representative consumer h as interest, dividends, and capital gains are summarized in Table 8.1.

Miller provides two reasons for the favourable tax treatment of capital gains:

1. Taxes on capital gains are usually set at lower statutory rates than the taxes on cash distributions. In Australia, for example, capital gains on equity are taxed at half the cash tax rate when shares are held longer than 12 months; and,
2. Capital gains are taxed on realization rather than accrual, where the effective tax rate on accrued capital gains can be reduced by delaying realization.

Table 8.1 highlights the double tax on equity income under a classical corporate tax. In particular it demonstrates why, for all consumers, dividends are subject to higher tax than interest and capital gains. It is the reason why no dividends are paid

Table 8.1 *Marginal taxes rates on corporate income*

Taxes	Debt interest	Equity	
		Dividends	Capital gains
Corporate	—	φ_F	φ_F
Personal	φ_B^h	φ_B^h	φ_E^h

Table 8.2 *Security returns after personal tax*

Debt interest	Equity	
	Dividends	Capital gains
$r_B(1 + \varphi_B^h)$	$r_E(1 + \varphi_B^h)$	$r_E(1 + \varphi_E^h)$

in the Miller equilibrium, which is the infamous dividend puzzle that has attracted so much attention in finance research.[23]

The economic effects of the corporate tax can be demonstrated by combining the equilibrium supply relationship between the debt and equity returns in (8.31) with personal income taxes. Firms will only trade debt and equity when they have the same cost after corporate tax, with $r_B(1 + \varphi_F) = r_E$, where r_E is the return on shares paying dividends and/or capital gains. This drives the market interest rate above the return on equity ($r_B > r_E$). Consumers only pay tax on corporate income when they realize it as a cash distribution, and the after-tax returns on the three different forms of income they receive are summarized for representative consumer h in Table 8.2.

Since dividends are subject to higher tax they do not trade, and this is confirmed by using the supply relationship in (8.31).[24] Thus, consumers will divide into two tax clienteles, when:

$$(1 + \varphi_B^L) > (1 + \varphi_F)(1 + \varphi_E^L) \qquad \text{for low-tax } (L) \text{ consumers who are}$$
debtspecialists; and,

$$(1 + \varphi_B^H) < (1 + \varphi_F)(1 + \varphi_E^H) \qquad \text{for high-tax } (H) \text{ consumers who are}$$
equityspecialists.[25]

Clearly, equity specialists must be high-tax consumers with $|\varphi_B^H| > |\varphi_F|$, and their tax on cash distributions has to be high enough to offset the double tax on capital gains, with $|\varphi_B^H| > |\varphi_F + \varphi_E^H + \varphi_F \varphi_E^H|$. Once consumers divide into tax clienteles they can increase their income through tax arbitrage, and tax arbitrage must be restricted in some way to bound their equilibrium demands for securities. There are three ways of doing this:

(1) Dammon and Green (1987) make tax rates endogenous functions of income and allow tax arbitrage to equate them across consumers;
(2) Jones and Milne (1992) use the government budget constraint to restrict tax arbitrage; and,
(3) Miller (1977) imposes short-selling constraints on consumers to limit tax arbitrage.

If taxes can change endogenously with income, tax arbitrage continues until every consumer has the same marginal tax rate. Similarly, when the government budget constraint is used to bound tax arbitrage the government must equate the marginal tax rates across consumers to stop them from continually driving the budget into deficit. Both these approaches make the analysis more complicated, so we follow Miller by restricting consumer borrowing.[26]

Since consumers in each tax clientele have the same tax rates the security notation is used to refer to each group, where bond specialists discount future consumption flows using $1/[1+r_B(1+\varphi_B)]$ and equity specialists discount theirs using $1/[1+r_E(1+\varphi_E)]$. On that basis, the present value of aggregate expenditure in the second period, is:

$$q_1 x_1 = \frac{q_1' x_1^E}{1 + r_E(1 + \varphi_E)} + \frac{q_1' x_1^B}{1 + r_B(1 + \varphi_B)},$$

and the present value of private profit for each tax clientele (G), using (8.20), becomes:

$$p^G y^G = \rho_0^G p_{-k0} y_{-k0} + \frac{\rho_1^G (p_1' y_1 + p_{k0} y_{k0}(1 + r_B))}{1 + r_G(1 + \varphi_G)} \qquad \text{for } G \in B, E.$$

By assuming the public sector funds all its investment by selling debt (with $g_t^B = 1$ and $g_t^E = 0$ for $t \in 0, 1$), it has present value profit of:

$$p^B z^B = p_{-k0} z_{-k0} + \frac{p_1' z_1 + p_{k0} z_{k0}(1 + r_B)}{1 + r_B(1 + \varphi_B)}.$$

It may seem puzzling that the corporate tax does not feature explicitly in these measures of profit, but it is included through the relationship between the equilibrium security returns in (8.31). Finally, the present value of the tax revenue returned to taxpayers, is:

$$T^G = \varphi_0 p_0(\bar{x}_0^G - x_0^G) + \frac{(\varphi_E r_E - \varphi_B r_B) \bar{Y}^E + \varphi_1 p_1' x_0^G}{1 + r_G(1 + \varphi_G)}$$

$$+ \frac{\varphi_G r_G \rho_1^G p_{k0} y_{k0} + \varphi_G r_G g_1^G p_{k0} z_{k0}}{1 + r_G(1 + \varphi_G)} \qquad \text{for } G \in B, E,$$

where $(\varphi_E r_E - \varphi_B r_B) \bar{Y}^E = 0$ and $g_1^B = 1$ for bondholders, and $g_1^E = 0$ for shareholders.

A conventional welfare equation is obtained by using the aggregate budget constraints in (8.19), where:[27]

$$\frac{dW}{\beta} = p_0 \, dz_0 + p_{k0} \, dz_{k0} + \frac{p_1' \, dz_1}{1 + r_B(1 + \varphi_B)} + \varphi_0 p_0 \, dx_0 + \frac{\varphi_1 p_1' \, dx_1^E}{1 + r_E(1 + \varphi_E)}$$

$$+ \frac{\varphi_1 p_1' \, dx_1^B}{1 + r_B(1 + \varphi_B)} - \left(\frac{(\varphi_F r_B + \varphi_E r_E)\rho_1^E}{1 + r_E(1 + \varphi_E)} + \frac{\varphi_B r_B \rho_1^B}{1 + r_B(1 + \varphi_B)} \right) p_{k0} \, dy_{k0} - dR.$$

$$(8.33)$$

This is similar to the welfare equation in (8.21) with progressive marginal tax rates, but it differs by the inclusion of the corporate tax on equity income. It will be used in Section 8.3.4 to compute the shadow discount rates in the presence of corporate and personal taxes, and to measure the changes in tax inefficiency for income and consumption taxes.

8.3.3 The Corporate Tax as a Withholding Tax

In an attempt to remove the double taxation of equity income the Australian and New Zealand Governments adopted an imputation tax system that uses the corporate tax as a withholding tax. When shareholders receive dividends they are granted tax credits for any corporate tax paid, and they use the credits to offset their personal tax liabilities on these dividends. Since unused credits are refunded, no corporate tax is collected on dividend income. Thus, the imputation system removes the double tax on dividends, where interest and dividends are taxed at the same personal marginal tax rate.

One might be tempted to ask why the corporate tax was not abolished altogether since it is eventually credited back to shareholders in any case. The imputation system is carefully devised to remove the incentive for consumers to delay realizing equity income as capital gains. Without a corporate tax all company income would be subject to tax only in the hands of shareholders, and this would provide them with an incentive to defer realizing capital gains which are taxed on realization rather than accrual. By doing so they can reduce the present value of their tax liabilities, which is why the corporate tax is retained under the imputation tax system. It collects tax revenue on company income as it accrues and is withheld as a credit for shareholders to use against their personal tax liabilities when the income is paid as dividends. This removes the incentive for shareholders to delay realizing income as capital gains when they have personal tax rates below or equal to the corporate rate, which is confirmed by comparing the after-personal-tax returns on dividends and interest in Table 8.3.

Interest income is a cash distribution that is subject only to personal tax, where the return is $r_B(1 + \varphi_B^G)$. Since dividends are paid from income subject to corporate tax which is held as a tax credit, the personal tax liability is assessed on pre-tax income, as $r_E/(1 + \varphi_F)$. Thus, the after-tax dividend return becomes $r_E(1 + \varphi_B^G)/(1 + \varphi_F)$, and there is no personal tax liability whenever $|\varphi_B^G| \leq |\varphi_F|$. Now the after-tax returns on dividends and interest are equal when (8.31) holds.

However, there are two reasons why tax imputation does not completely remove the incentive for consumers to delay realizing income as capital gains:

1. In Australia, high-tax consumers have personal cash tax rates above the corporate rate ($|\varphi_B^H| > |\varphi_F|$), and this leaves them with net personal tax liabilities.

$$-\frac{r_E}{(1 + \varphi_F)}(\varphi_B^G - \varphi_F) > 0,$$

Table 8.3 *Security returns with corporate tax imputation*

Interest	Dividends
$r_B(1 + \varphi_B^G)$	$\dfrac{r_E}{(1 + \varphi_F)}(1 + \varphi_B^G)$

2. Firms pay dividends from income that is not subject to corporate tax when taxable income is less than economic income due to, for example, differences in economic and taxable depreciation allowances. Dividends paid from untaxed income are called unfranked dividends and they do not attract tax credits. Instead, the income is taxed only when it is distributed to shareholders.

Whenever shareholders have net personal tax liabilities they have an incentive to delay realizing the income as capital gains which are subject to a lower effective tax. Indeed, it is the reason why the corporate tax is used as a withholding tax in the first place. In summary, the imputation tax system successfully removes the double tax on dividends, and it also removes consumer tax preferences for debt and equity when marginal personal tax rates are less than or equal to the corporate rate, with $|\varphi_B^G| \leq |\varphi_F|$. There are remaining tax preferences for equity on untaxed corporate income and for high-tax consumers, which is one reason why the Australian and New Zealand governments have lowered income tax rates and introduced a uniform tax on final consumption.

8.3.4 Personal Social Discount Rates and Corporate Tax

Since most countries have corporate and progressive personal taxes it makes sense to compute the shadow discount rate in their presence. Based on the analysis in Section 8.2.1, there are personal shadow discount rates whenever consumers face progressive personal taxes. The main difference made by including a corporate tax is the additional distortion it introduces to the discount rate of shareholders, and this is confirmed by computing the shadow price of capital in the Miller equilibrium, using the conventional welfare equation in (8.33) without commodity taxes, as:

$$S_{k0} = p_{k0} \left\{ 1 - \left(\frac{(\varphi_F r_B + \varphi_E r_E)\rho_1^E}{1 + r_E(1 + \varphi_E)} + \frac{\varphi_B r_B \rho_1^B}{1 + r_B(1 + \varphi_B)} \right) \left(1 + \frac{\partial s_0}{\partial z_{k0}} \right) \right\}.$$

(8.34)

Once again, it is the market price of capital plus the extra tax revenue when private investment expands (with $\partial y_{k0}/\partial z_{k0} = -(1 + \partial s_0/\partial z_{k0}) < 0$). The shadow discount rates are solved using the following relationship:

$$S_{k0} = p_{k0} \sum_{h \in B,E} \frac{(1 + S_r^h)\rho_1^h}{1 + r_h(1 + \varphi_h)},$$

(8.35)

where:

$$S_r^E = r_B - (t_F + t_E)\frac{\partial s_0}{\partial z_{k0}} \qquad \text{and} \qquad S_r^B = r_B - t_B \frac{\partial s_0}{\partial z_{k0}}.^{28}$$

(8.36)

Somewhat surprisingly the discount rates in (8.36) are uncomplicated expressions. They extend the personal discount rates with progressive personal taxes in (8.24) by including the corporate tax and lower effective personal tax on capital gains for shareholders. Since bondholders just pay personal tax their shadow discount rate is the same as the Harberger discount rate in (8.9). The economic intuition for the relationship in (8.35) is relatively straightforward. An extra unit of capital raises social welfare in present value terms by the aggregate dollar gains in utility for shareholders and bondholders, where investment generates extra future consumption flows at the pre-tax rate of return r_B less the fall in tax revenue when private saving contracts. Since consumers face different taxes on income they use different discount factors on their share of the after-tax consumption flows.

8.4 SOCIAL DISCOUNT RATES AND UNCERTAINTY

Once consumers divide into strict tax clienteles the corporate tax will only fall on investors with high enough marginal tax rates to have a tax preference for equity that pays capital gains. This makes the task of computing shadow discount rates much simpler. Strict tax clienteles are much more likely in a certainty setting where consumers demands for securities are determined solely by tax preferences. However, when security demands are also determined by risk preferences consumers may bundle debt and equity together to reduce the variability in their future consumption flows. Once debt and equity are combined to trade-off tax and risk preferences the discount rates are a combination of the after-tax returns on the two securities, where the trade-off will depend on the risky debt and equity instruments firms supply.

A convenient starting point for the uncertainty analysis is to assume common information and no trading costs. This will replicate all the results in previous sections because it provides certainty equivalence. Consider the Miller equilibrium with uncertainty and common information where firms know the risk preferences of consumers. With zero trading costs they create the tax-preferred securities that will satisfy the risk preferences of every consumer. This divides consumer into strict tax clienteles because they can effectively satisfy their risk preferences by holding just tax-preferred securities, that is, the capital market is effectively double complete. Sarig and Scott (1985) and Miller (1988) argue the M–M leverage theorem holds in this setting, even when consumers face short-selling constraints, because firms create their tax-preferred risky securities.

This can be demonstrated by using a state-preference model, and to simplify the analysis assume no public production (with $z_i = 0 \ \forall i$) or foreign aid payments (with $dR = 0$). With a finite number of states ($s = 1, \ldots, S$) in the second period each consumer h will now maximize utility $u^h(x_0^h, x_{11}^h, \ldots, x_{S1}^h)$, where x_{s1}^h is the vector of demands for the $N + 1$ goods in each state s. They each face the budget constraint:

$$p_0 x_0^h - \rho_1^h p_{k0} y_{k0} = p_0 \bar{x}_0^h + p_0 y_0^h,$$

with $-\rho_1^h p_{k0} y_{k0}$ being the amount saved. In the second period, this saving has state-contingent payoffs, of:

$$p_s' x_s^h = -\rho_1^h p_{k0} y_{k0}(1 + r_s) = \rho_1^h p_s' y_s \qquad \forall_s.$$

where p'_s is the vector of producer prices in each state s. Consumers now bundle risky securities together to spread risk, and when the capital market is complete they have access to a full set of linearly independent securities that can be bundled into portfolios to determine their desired pattern of state-contingent consumption. However, when borrowing is constrained to rule out tax arbitrage, they will effectively need access to a full set of primitive securities for the market to be complete. As noted above, this is achieved in a common information setting with no trading costs by firms who create the tax-preferred securities that satisfy the risk preferences of each consumer. In these circumstances, each consumer h uses a personal state contingent discount factor $1/(1+r_s+t_r^h)$, and there are as many different discount factors as steps in the tax function.

Auerbach and King (1983) and Kim (1982) examine firm financial policy with investor leverage clienteles. With costly information firms do not have complete information about the risk preferences of individual consumers, so that they choose capital structures that attract clienteles of investors who can minimize the cost of trading off their risk and tax preferences. In these circumstances, M–M leverage irrelevance fails, and the discount factors are a combination of the after-tax returns on the bundles of securities investors hold, which can differ across consumers due to differences in their risk and tax preferences.

8.4.1 Computing the Risk Premium with the CAPM

In applied work the returns on risky capital assets are frequently computed using mean–variance analysis. Consumers have mean–variance preferences for second period consumption if they maximize expected utility over expenditure when it is funded by portfolios of securities with joint-normally distributed returns. In these circumstances, it is possible to fully describe the distribution of the returns on portfolios by their means and variances. Moreover, when consumers have homogenous expectations and can freely trade a risk-free security they will measure and price risk identically using the capital asset pricing model (CAPM), where the expected return on any risky security j, becomes:

$$\bar{r}_j = r_F + (\bar{r}_M - r_F)b_{jM},^{29} \tag{8.37}$$

with r_F being the risk-free return, $\bar{r}_M$ the expected return on the market portfolio (which is the same bundle of risky securities (M) held by every consumer) and $b_{jM} \equiv \sigma_{jM}/\sigma_M^2$ the beta coefficient for security j; it is the covariance between the returns on security j and the market portfolio M normalized by the variance of the return to M. The beta coefficient measures the amount of market (or non-diversifiable) risk in security j, while $(\bar{r}_M - r_F)$ is the equilibrium premium for a unit of market risk. Thus, $(\bar{r}_M - r_F)b_{jM}$ is the risk premium paid on each dollar of capital invested in security j. In a common information setting, security risk is determined by the market risk in the net cash flows, where (in the absence of taxes) the risk adjusted present value of the capital invested in firms producing any security j, is:

$$V_j \equiv -p_j y_{jk0} = \frac{\bar{X}_j - (\sigma_{XjM}/\sigma_M^2)(\bar{r}_M - r_F)}{1 + r_F}, \tag{8.38}$$

where $\bar{X}_j = p_{j1}' \bar{y}_{j1}$ is the expected net cash flow in period 1, and $(\sigma_{XjM}/\sigma_M^2)/V_j \equiv \sigma_{jM}/\sigma_M^2$ the market risk in security j, which is sometimes referred to as project risk. Since consumers receive the net cash flows as shareholders (ρ_{j1}^h) they ultimately bear the project risk, and are compensated for doing so through the risk premium.

Whether or not this is the proper way to account for risk in project evaluation depends on the validity of the underlying assumptions in the CAPM. If they do not hold in practice the task of computing the risk premium in (8.38) is much more difficult because consumers will, in general, measure and price risk differently. One important implication of the CAPM holding is that public and private sector projects have the same risk premium. But this idea is challenged by the Arrow–Lind Theorem which is examined in the next section.

8.4.2 The Arrow–Lind Theorem

A number of economists advocate using a lower risk premium for public sector projects. Samuelson (1964) and Vickery (1964) argue that the public sector is a large investor that undertakes many projects thereby allowing it to pool risks with uncorrelated returns. This leaves the government facing a lower discount rate on individual projects. However, Bailey and Jensen (1972) claim consumers can eliminate all this diversifiable risk themselves by buying and selling securities traded in the capital market. In a competitive market without trading costs non-diversifiable risk can be eliminated by consumers at no cost, which is the case in the CAPM pricing equation used in the previous section. This means they can achieve the same pooling available to the government and the security returns on both public and private projects will bear the same market (non-diversifiable) risk. If there are costs of diversifying risk, and if the government can do it at lower cost than the private sector, then a lower risk premium on public projects would be appropriate. However, there is evidence this may not be the case due to the absence of any profit motive for public sector employees which can make them less efficient than their (competitive) private counterparts.

Arrow and Lind (1970) take a slightly different approach by arguing a lower discount rate on public projects can be justified by the government's ability to spread risk over a large number of taxpayers when project returns are uncorrelated with income risk. It is an argument based on the law of large numbers where the amount of public project risk each taxpayer ends up bearing is small relative to the economy.[30] Bailey and Jensen contend the majority of government project returns are correlated with national income, which means that they contain market risk that cannot be eliminated by bundling them together. Thus, the Arrow–Lind Theorem implicitly assumes that taxpayers cannot eliminate all the diversifiable risk in these projects by purchasing private insurance contracts and trading marketed securities. In fact, Bailey and Jensen claim it is unlikely that the government can provide the same or better opportunities for consumers, and at lower cost. Moreover, governments normally use distorting taxes to fund their projects, and the efficiency costs make them a more costly way to diversify risk. In contrast, private insurance makes non-distorting income transfers in the absence of trading costs, which are minimized in competitive markets. For example, mutual funds allow consumers to trade risk at lower cost than would be the case from creating their own portfolios of securities for the same purpose.

Frequently, moral hazard and adverse selection problems are used to justify the Arrow–Lind Theorem. With asymmetric information between traders it can be costly for consumers to eliminate diversifiable risk from their income, and it is argued that the government may be able to diversify the risk at lower cost through the tax system or other stabilization policies. But it too is subject to the same asymmetric information problems as private traders, and may not be able to reduce the costs of diversifying risk. Dixit (1987, 1989) cautions that it is important to examine the role of risk spreading by the public sector in the presence of the asymmetric information problems they are trying to overcome. Ultimately, support for using a lower risk premium in the evaluation of public sector projects must rely on some form of failure in the private market for spreading and diversifying risk. Either private risk pooling is more costly than it is for the public sector or the public sector has better information.

8.5 CONCLUDING REMARKS

By including time in a welfare analysis, it is possible to account for the effects of income taxes, both corporate and personal. The social discount rate of Harberger, and Sandmo and Dréze is obtained with a linear income tax. It is a weighted average of the marginal product of capital and the marginal rate of time preference when income from all sources is taxed at the same rate for all consumers. However, these assumptions are violated in two important ways. First, marginal personal tax rates are increasing functions of income, and second, capital gains are taxed on realization rather than accrual.

With progressive marginal tax rates there are personal shadow discount rates on future consumption flows. All consumers in the same tax bracket will have the same discount factor, and there are as many shadow discount rates as steps in the income tax schedule. Clearly, if tax rates are continuous increasing functions of income there could be as many shadow discount rates as consumers. Thankfully, however, most tax functions are piecewise linear and have relatively few steps in them.

When capital gains are taxed on realization rather than accrual, personal income tax rates on cash distributions are higher than the tax rates on accrued capital gains. By delaying realization of capital gains, consumers can lower their effective tax rate on them. Indeed, there are also political reasons why governments choose to set lower statutory tax rates on capital gains. Miller uses this tax treatment of capital gains to explain the presence of equity when firms are subject to a classical corporate tax. With complete capital markets, that is, where double spanning holds, consumers divide into strict tax clienteles and have personal shadow discount rates that are determined by the taxes they face. High-tax consumers with marginal income tax rates above the corporate rate can have a tax-preference for equity if they have sufficiently low personal tax rates on capital gains. When they do, the corporate tax adds an additional distortion to the personal shadow discount rate.

The analysis in this chapter could be extended in a number of important ways, but the most realistic extension would include costly and incomplete information. In such a setting consumers would no longer necessarily divide into strict tax clienteles, where the shadow discount rates would then depend on trade-offs between risk and tax preferences and trading costs. A considerable amount of work has been undertaken to examine the effects of financial policy with incomplete information, but there is some way to go before it can be included in a general equilibrium welfare analysis. The analysis in this chapter has extended previous derivations of the shadow discount rate by including progressive personal and corporate taxes in a certainty (equivalent) setting. This at least makes some progress towards a more general and realistic analysis.

NOTES

1. There are additional welfare effects when marginal changes in capital investment impact on other distorted markets.
2. The first-order conditions for private firms producing output in the first period are $p_0 \, dy_0 = 0$.
3. After substituting (8.5) into (8.1) the aggregate budget constraint for the economy becomes:

$$qx = q\bar{x} + p_0(y_0 + z_0) + \frac{p_1'(y_1 + z_1)}{1 + r + t_r} - R.$$

   The conventional welfare equation is obtained by totally differentiating this constraint using the market clearing conditions and applying the first-order conditions for the optimizing choices of consumers and firms. Since the workings are similar for the derivation of the conventional welfare equation in (2.7) they are not repeated here.
4. We can see from (8.3) that the value at market prices of the marginal product of capital, is:

$$-p_1 \frac{\partial y_1}{\partial y_{k0}} = \frac{p_{k0}}{1 + r + t_r}(1 + r),$$

   with $p_1' = p_1(1 + r + t_r)$. At a social optimum, the value of capital grows by one plus the shadow discount rate in (8.8), where in the presence of commodity taxes, we have:

$$S_r = r - t_r \frac{\partial s_0}{\partial z_{k0}} + \frac{t}{p_{k0}} \frac{\partial x}{\partial z_{k0}}(1 + r + t_r).$$

   This collapses to (8.9) when $t_i = 0 \ \forall_i$.
5. Using the market clearing condition for the capital market in (8.4) we can separate the changes in private saving and investment by writing the social discount rate, as:

$$S_r = -r \frac{\partial y_{k0}}{\partial z_{k0}} - (r + t_r) \frac{\partial s_0}{\partial z_{k0}}.$$

6. This is confirmed by using the market clearing condition for the capital market in (8.4) to rewrite the shadow discount rate in (8.9), as:

$$S_r = r + t_r + t_r \frac{\partial y_{k0}}{\partial z_{k0}},$$

   where $\partial y_{k0} / \partial z_{k0} < 0$.

7. For a one-period project Bradford obtains the evaluation rule $(1 + \delta)/(1 + \rho) \simeq 1$, with $\delta \simeq \rho$, which is lower than ω. Since private saving is a constant fraction of each dollar of benefit from the public project consumers do not fully offset the depreciation in public capital.

8. One of the main reasons for moving from an income to a consumption tax is the difficulty taxing capital gains at the same effective rate as all other sources of income. Normally, they are taxed on realization rather than accrual, where this provides an incentive to delay realization to lower effective tax. There are also problems taxing income paid to foreigners who hold domestic securities.

9. Since the consumption tax applies to final demand there are no taxes on intermediate inputs, with $t_i = 0 \; \forall_{yi<0}$.

10. This is obtained from the conventional welfare equation in (8.14) by using the goods market clearing conditions and the first-order conditions in (8.12).

11. The second term in (8.16) is obtained using the first-order condition for production of output in the second period in (8.12) and the goods market clearing conditions.

12. For each group G, the consumer price vector is the $1 \times (N + 1)$ row vector, with $q^G = (q_1^G, q_2^G, q_3^G, \ldots, q_{N+1}^G)$ for high-tax consumers, while the corresponding vector of demands is the $(N + 1) \times 1$ column vector $x^G = (x_1^G, x_2^G, x_3^G, \ldots, x_{N+1}^G)$, where each element is the aggregate demand for each good by consumers in each tax group, with $x_1^G = \sum_{h \in G} x_1^h$.

13. The profit shares are the portion of capital provided by each group, with:

$$\rho^G = \frac{(\bar{x}_{k0}^G - x_{k0}^G + g^G z_{k0})}{-y_{k0}}.$$

14. Notice the term $-(t_r^H - t_r^L)\bar{Y}^H$ disappears when tax revenue is substituted into the budget constraint. Since tax revenue is returned to taxpayers as lump-sum transfers the infra-marginal tax rate for high tax investors will not appear in the marginal welfare changes. It will, however, appear with changes in tax revenue due to adjustments in the marginal tax rates.

15. For political reasons food and other items were exempted from the consumption tax in Australia, while the same exemptions were not made in New Zealand.

16. The second term was obtained by using the first-order condition for private production in the second period in (8.12) and the market clearing conditions.

17. Consumers do not link their revenue transfers to the taxes they pay. If they did, the taxes would be non-distorting. It is a much more realistic assumption when revenue is raised using a number of different taxes and is returned to taxpayers through a number of different spending programmes. Indeed, few consumers, if any, link the tax revenue they pay to any benefits they get in return.

18. Equation (8.30) is obtained by writing the return to equity after corporate tax, as:

$$(1 - \rho_1^B)r_E \, p_{k0} \, y_{k0} = (1 + \varphi_F)(p_1' y_1 - p_1^B r_B - p_{k0} \, y_{k0}).$$

Note that economic income is measured by deducting the initial value of capital from the firms net cash flows.

19. Firms will maximize their value by selling only equity when $r_B(1 + \varphi_F) > r_E$, and by selling only debt when $r_B(1 + \varphi_F) < r_E$. This arbitrage activity determines the equilibrium relationship in (8.31) when both securities trade.

20. Modigliani and Miller (1963) obtain this outcome with uncertainty, common information, and no transactions costs. In these circumstances, firms will provide sufficient risky debt instruments for consumers to satisfy their risk preferences by holding just debt instruments. In other words, they can create a full set or primitive bonds to trade in every state.

21. For a nice illustration of lost corporate tax shields see DeAngelo and Masulis (1980).

22. For an excellent summary of leverage-related costs with asymmetric information see Harris and Raviv (1991).

23. There is a large literature that looks at explanations for the payment of dividends under a 'classical' corporate tax. They are largely based on one of three factors: (a) Farrar and Selwyn (1967) and Baumol and Malkiel (1967) consider differential transactions cost of paying dividends and capital gains; (b) Auerbach (1979) and Bradford (1981) introduce share repurchase restrictions; and (c) Bhattacharya (1979) and Williams (1988) consider the information signal provided by dividends when there is asymmetric information between firm mangers and capital providers.

24. We can use the supply relationship in (8.31) to write the after-tax return on dividends as $r_B(1 + \varphi_F)$ $(1 + \varphi_B^h)$, and it is less than the after-tax return on interest $r_B(1 + \varphi_B^h)$, and the after-tax return on capital gains $r_B(1 + \varphi_F)(1 + \varphi_E^h)$ since $|\varphi_E^h| < |\varphi_B^h| \; \forall_h$.

25. The tax rates for equity specialists are not implausible. For example, with a corporate tax rate of 30% and a marginal personal cash tax rate of 50% an equity specialist would need a marginal tax rate on capital gains of 28% or less.

26. It is unnecessary to stop consumers from borrowing altogether, but the borrowing has to be restricted to bound their security trades when they face exogenous marginal tax rates. Note that there are no restrictions on the security trades by firms, where this gives them, or perhaps more realistically their agents financial intermediaries, the ability to arbitrage away profits. This is important for preserving a competitive equilibrium. Another way to restrict tax arbitrage is to deny consumers tax deductions for returns paid on their security sales, but that is unsatisfactory because they are tax deductible expenses under most tax codes when the funds are used to purchase other securities.

27. By following Harberger, who returns tax revenue back to taxpayers as lump-sum transfers, we can write the aggregate budget constraint in (8.19), as:

$$px = p_0 \bar{x}_0 + p_0(y_{-k0} + z_{-k0}) + \sum_{G \in B,E} \frac{\rho_1^G(p_1' y_1 + p_{k0} y_{k0}(1 + r_G))}{1 + r_G(1 + \varphi_G)}$$

$$+ \frac{p_1' z_1}{1 + r_B(1 + \varphi_B)} + p_{k0} z_{k0}.$$

28. The tax wedges are defined here as specific tax equivalents.

29. Elton and Gruber (1995) provide a clear derivation of the CAPM equation when consumers face non-linear income taxes. Despite being slightly more complicated it has the same structure as the standard CAPM equation in (8.37), which is referred to as the security market line (SML).

30. Formal derivations of the Arrow–Lind Theorem are provided in Myles (1995) and Tresch (2002).

9

Optimal Commodity Taxation

A large literature looks at the most efficient way for governments to raise revenue with distorting taxes, including taxes on final consumption, turnover taxes, and taxes on income. Poll taxes are deemed inequitable, and there is limited scope to levy taxes on economic rent. Ramsey (1927) established rules for setting optimal commodity taxes on a subset of goods. Diamond and Mirrlees (1971) and Mirrlees (1976) extend them by including distributional effects and by allowing producer prices to change endogenously. Their results are summarized in Auerbach (1985). Commodity taxes are Ramsey optimal when they minimize the social cost of raising a given amount of revenue, and this is achieved by equating their marginal excess burdens. This chapter uses welfare decompositions in previous chapters to show why income effects play no role in setting Ramsey optimal taxes in single (aggregated) consumer economies.

When public and private firms use the same production technologies the resource movements from marginally raising a tax are equivalent to a small public sector project. That means we can compute its marginal excess burden by shadow pricing these changes in activity, and this conveniently provides a measure of the change in tax inefficiency with variable producer prices that coincides with the familiar measure with fixed producer prices in Diamond and Mirrlees. Their measure is the tax-weighted sum of the compensated changes in the demands for taxed activities, and is used to derive a number of the familiar Ramsey optimal tax rules.[1] Once producer prices change endogenously, however, the weights on the changes in the compensated demands are shadow consumer taxes, which measure the difference between the consumer and shadow prices of each good. This measure of the change in tax inefficiency is used to extend a number of the familiar optimal tax rules to economies with variable producer prices.

There are circumstances where policy evaluation is simplified considerably by adopting Ramsey optimal taxes. Diamond and Mirrlees (1976) and Stiglitz and Dasgupta (1971) find that producer prices can be used as shadow prices in project evaluation when there is:

(1) *Constant Returns to Scale (CRS) Production* which makes the ratio of the revised shadow prices of goods equal to the ratio of their respective producer prices that is, they are proportional. If aggregate marginal production costs are constant, as is the case in economies with linear production possibility frontiers, the compensated shadow prices of goods are equal to their producer prices; or,

(2) *Decreasing Returns and a 100% Profits Tax* that make the shadow and producer prices of goods proportional.

In both cases, consumers receive no profit from private production where this insulates their surplus from endogenous changes in producer prices. In such circumstances, optimal taxes are determined solely by their impact on consumer prices. They are very attractive results from a practical point of view because they simplify the task of computing shadow prices. In this chapter, the economic intuition will be explained by shadow pricing the changes in consumption demand that result from marginal tax changes. Then by using the generalized Hatta decomposition to isolate the income effects, we find the compensated shadow prices of goods are equal to their producer prices in these circumstances. Whenever the public sector marginally supplies more of a good it must adjust commodity taxes to stop consumer prices changing. This holds consumer utilities constant and preserves activity in every market by completely crowding out private production. The value of the resources released by the extra public output is equal to the market price of the good, and in the compensated equilibrium it is held as surplus revenue by the government. Once this revenue is transferred to the private economy it has income effects that will impact on private activity. However, by the Hatta decomposition, they are independent of the policy change and play no role in policy evaluation.

9.1 RAMSEY OPTIMAL TAXES

Ramsey finds the set of commodity taxes that will raise a given amount of revenue with the smallest cost to welfare in a single (aggregated) consumer economy. If all $N + 1$ commodities can be taxed a uniform tax on final consumption is Ramsey optimal, and each dollar of revenue reduces private surplus by a dollar because, in the absence of relative price changes, the tax has no excess burden.[2] However, a number of final consumption goods are difficult to tax, most notably leisure and home-produced consumption. Once taxes distort relative prices they are Ramsey optimal when the social cost of raising a given amount of revenue is minimized, and this occurs when they have the same marginal excess burden (meb). The proposition is confirmed by minimizing the change in social welfare from marginally raising one tax (m) and returning the extra revenue to taxpayers by lowering another tax (d), where from the conventional welfare equation in (2.7), we have:

$$(S_{t_m})_D = \left(\frac{dW}{dt_m} \right)_D \frac{1}{\beta} = \frac{\partial L}{\partial t_m} (\text{meb}_d - \text{meb}_m) = 0,[3] \qquad (9.1)$$

with:

$$\text{meb}_i = -\frac{(\partial W/\partial t_i)(1/\beta)}{\partial L/\partial t_i} \qquad \text{for } i \in d, m. \qquad (9.2)$$

Once taxes have the same marginal excess burden the marginal social cost of public funds (MCF) is independent of the tax the government uses to balance its budget. Diamond and Mirrlees (1971) decompose the welfare loss in (9.2) with *constant producer prices*, where the marginal excess burden for tax d is obtained using the welfare equation in (2.7) to compute the change in tax inefficiency, and (2.6) to solve the change in government revenue, as:

$$\text{meb}_d = \frac{\hat{\text{meb}}_d / (1 - \theta)}{1 - (\hat{\text{meb}}_d / (1 - \theta))}, \quad {}^4 \tag{9.3}$$

with:

$$\hat{\text{meb}}_d = -\sum_i t_i \frac{\partial \hat{x}_i(q)}{\partial q_d} \frac{1}{x_d - \bar{x}_d}$$

being the compensated marginal excess burden, and

$$\theta = \sum_i t_i \frac{\partial x_i(q, I)}{\partial I}$$

the revenue effect.

In public finance $\hat{\text{meb}}_d$ is referred to as the distortionary effect of taxation, and it is equated across taxes (with $\hat{\text{meb}}_d = \hat{\text{meb}}_m$) by the familiar optimal tax rule with constant producer prices in Diamond and Mirrlees (1971) and Diamond and McFadden (1974). It is clear from the welfare decomposition in (9.3) why the income effects, which are isolated in the Hatta coefficient $1 - \theta$, will play no role in setting Ramsey optimal taxes in single (aggregated) consumer economies. Since $1 - \theta$ is an independent scaling coefficient on the distortionary effects, each tax must have the same actual marginal excess burden (with $\text{meb}_d = \text{meb}_m$) when their distortionary effects are equal (with $\hat{\text{meb}}_d = \hat{\text{meb}}_m$).

This important result is extended to *variable producer prices* by decomposing the marginal excess burden for any tax d, as:

$$\text{meb}_d = (S_R)_D \hat{\text{meb}}_d, \quad {}^5 \tag{9.4}$$

where the optimal tax rule in (9.1), becomes:

$$(St_m)_D = \frac{\partial \hat{L}}{\partial t_m} (\hat{\text{meb}}_d - \hat{\text{meb}}_m)(S_R)_D = 0 \qquad \forall_{d, m}. \tag{9.5}$$

All the income effects are isolated in the revised shadow value of government revenue $(S_R)_D$. Since it is independent of the tax used to balance the government budget when taxes are Ramsey optimal, they must have the same distortionary effect. The intuition for this result is straightforward; at a social optimum (where $\hat{\text{meb}}_d = \hat{\text{meb}}_m$) there is no efficiency effect from marginally raising one tax and lowering another to balance the government budget, and without any efficiency effect there can be no income effect (which means $\text{meb}_d = \text{meb}_m$). Based on this result analysts can set Ramsey optimal taxes without computing the compensated welfare changes in (9.5). Instead, they can set them using the actual (observable) welfare changes in (9.2).

9.1.1 Ramsey Optimal Taxes with Distributional Effects

Governments are concerned about the distributional effects of taxes. In Australia, for example, fresh food is exempt from the uniform tax on final consumption demand in an attempt to lower the relative tax burden on low income consumers. Indeed, progressive marginal tax rates are applied to consumer incomes in most countries. Non-linear income taxes were examined in earlier chapters, so in this section optimal commodity tax rules will be extended to accommodate distributional effects. We do this using the conventional welfare equation in (3.4), with $dL = 0$, where optimally chosen commodity taxes (t_m and t_d), solve:

$$\left(\frac{\partial W}{\partial t_m}\right)_D \frac{1}{\bar{\beta}} = \frac{\partial L}{\partial t_m} (\text{mc\={f}}_d - \text{mc\={f}}_m) = 0, ^6 \tag{9.6}$$

with $\text{mc\={f}}_i$ being the marginal social cost of public funds in (7.22) for taxes $i \in d, m$. Consider the role played by distributional effects when *producer prices are constant*, where the MCF for tax d becomes:

$$\text{mc\={f}}_d = \frac{\text{DC}_{t_d}}{1 + [t(\partial x/\partial t_d)(1/(x_d - \bar{x}_d))]}. \tag{9.7}$$

Recall from the welfare equation in (3.4) that DC_{t_d} is the distributional characteristics from marginally raising tax d; it is unity when consumers are assigned the same welfare weights, and is larger than one when more private surplus is transferred from consumers with relatively low incomes. By separating the income and substitution effects, we have:

$$\text{mc\={f}}_d = \frac{\text{DC}_{t_d}}{1 - (\text{m\^{e}b}_d/(1 - \theta))}, \tag{9.8}$$

where for optimally chosen taxes:

$$\text{mc\={f}}_d = \frac{\text{DC}_{t_d}}{1 - (\text{m\^{e}b}_d/(1 - \theta))} = \frac{\text{DC}_{t_m}}{1 - (\text{m\^{e}b}_m/(1 - \theta))} = \text{mc\={f}}_d.$$

Now whenever taxes have different distributional effects (with $\text{DC}_{t_d} \neq \text{DC}_{t_m}$) they must have different distortionary effects (with $\text{m\^{e}b}_d \neq \text{m\^{e}b}_m$) to offset them. For example, there are higher taxes on goods with larger distortionary effects when they have favourable distributional characteristics (i.e. with relatively low values of DC_t). And this occurs if taxes take relatively more surplus from high income consumers (who have lower distributional weights). Further distributional effects arise when prices change endogenously, but they make the task of setting Ramsey optimal taxes much more complicated. In particular, they increase the data requirements.

Despite these optimal tax rules, however, many governments have adopted uniform taxes on final consumption demand. Harberger (1990) argues they are preferable to Ramsey optimal taxes due to the lower costs of administering them. Estimates of the own and cross-price elasticities of the demands and supplies of the taxed goods are costly to obtain, especially when they change over time, and these costs rise when distributional effects matter due to the large amount of information needed to compute them. There is also the unavoidable task of having to choose the distributional weights for consumers affected by the tax changes. Moreover, the process of setting Ramsey optimal taxes can politicize the tax system when affected parties, particularly producer groups who are usually smaller in size than consumers, lobby governments to have their taxes lowered.

9.1.2 Project Evaluation and Ramsey Optimal Taxes

Diamond and Mirrlees (1971) find, that with Ramsey optimal taxes, aggregate produc-tion efficiency is desirable when consumers receive no profit from private production. Since commodity taxes extract revenue from consumer surplus in these circumstances, they do not distort producer prices when they are optimally set. And production effi-ciency means producer prices can be used as shadow prices, where socially profitable projects are profitable at market prices. There are two ways to remove private profit from consumer budget constraints, Diamond and Mirrlees (1976) adopt CRS produc-tion, while Stiglitz and Dasgupta use a 100% profits tax. Both are demonstrated here using shadow prices to write the marginal excess burden for any tax d, as:

$$\text{meb}_d = \frac{(S_R)_D \sum_i ((\hat{S}_i)_D - p_i)(\partial y_i(p)/\partial p_d)}{(1 - \Phi)y_d},^7 \qquad (9.9)$$

with profit tax Φ. From the welfare decomposition in (9.4), where $\text{meb}_d = (S_R)_D \hat{\text{meb}}_d$, we have:

$$\sum_i ((\hat{S}_i)_D - p_i)\frac{\partial y_i(p)}{\partial p_d}\frac{1}{y_d} = \hat{\text{meb}}_d(1 - \Phi),^8 \qquad (9.10)$$

and with $\sum_i p_i(\partial y_i(p)/\partial p_d) = 0$ for competitive private firms, this becomes:

$$\sum_i (\hat{S}_i)_D \frac{\partial y_i(p)}{\partial p_d}\frac{1}{y_d} = \hat{\text{meb}}_d(1 - \Phi). \qquad (9.11)$$

Since tax changes move resources between markets in the same way public projects do, they can be replicated by combinations of tax changes when all but one good can be taxed. On this basis, the distortionary effect of the tax change in (9.11) is the sum of the shadow values of the resulting changes in activity. The decomposition in (9.10) is convenient because it relates the shadow and producer prices of goods through *shadow producer taxes*, $(\hat{S}_i)_D - p_i$, which are net social gains from expanding production of each good i. This relationship will now be used to demonstrate and explain the results of Diamond and Mirrlees and Stiglitz and Dasgupta.

(i) *CRS Production—Diamond and Mirrlees (1976)*. If firms use CRS production technologies there is production efficiency when taxes are Ramsey optimal. Two cases are considered.

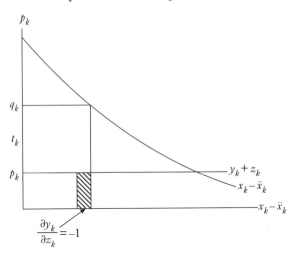

Figure 9.1 *The shadow price with CRS production*

1. *Constant Marginal Cost—Fixed Producer Prices.* Whenever firms produce output with a single input (or equivalently, the same constant input mix) the economy has a linear production frontier. In such circumstances, a marginal increase in public output will crowd out the same private output without changes in relative prices. When the government withdraws the resource cost saving to hold utility constant, the revised compensated shadow price of any good k will be equal to its producer price, with:

$$(\hat{S}_k)_D = p_k \qquad \forall_{d,k}.^9 \tag{9.12}$$

This result is illustrated in Figure 9.1 where an extra unit of good k increases government revenue by p_k. With constant marginal cost there is an equal fall in private production at the unchanged producer price, where the value of the resource cost saving (p_k) is retained by the government as surplus revenue to hold consumer utilities constant. This is the potential (compensated) revenue that extra output of good k will generate for the government budget.

   Once the government transfers the surplus revenue (p_k) to the private sector by lowering tax d there are income effects that will impact on taxed activities, where the uncompensated shadow price becomes:

$$(S_k)_D = (S_R)_D(\hat{S}_k)_D = (S_R)_D p_k. \tag{9.13}$$

Since all the income effects are isolated in the revised shadow value of government revenue $(S_R)_D$, they will play no role in project evaluation. This special case provides the intuition for the important Little and Mirrlees (1969) result for the shadow prices of fully traded goods in small open economies.[10] Since these goods are supplied to the economy at unchanged world prices they have relative shadow prices equal to their relative border prices (i.e. world prices measured in units of domestic currency).

2. *Increasing Marginal Cost—Variable Producer Prices.* When firms use CRS technologies and different input mixes, the production possibility frontier is non-linear. As resources move between activities producer prices change endogenously, but this will not affect consumers because they receive no profit from private production. Diamond and Mirrlees (1976) prove that the shadow and producer prices are proportional in these circumstances if taxes are Ramsey optimal.

Proof. Set the profit tax to zero (with $\Phi = 0$) and write (9.10), as:

$$\sum_i ((S_i)_D - (S_R)_D p_i)\, \omega_{id} = \frac{\text{meb}_d}{(\partial y_d(p)/\partial p_d)(1/y_d)} \qquad \forall_d, \qquad (9.14)$$

where:

$$\omega_{id} = \frac{\partial y_i(p)/\partial p_d}{\partial y_d(p)/\partial p_d}.$$

When price-taking firms have constant marginal costs their supply schedules are perfectly price elastic, with $\omega_{dd} = -1$, and $\omega_{id} = +1\ \forall_{i \neq d}$. With $\partial y_d(p)/\partial p_d = \infty$ the right-hand side of (9.14) is zero, where the relationship between the shadow and producer prices with Ramsey optimal taxes (with $\text{meb}_d = \text{meb}\ \forall_d$), becomes:

$$\sum_i ((\hat{S}_i)_D - p_i)\omega_{id} = 0 \qquad \forall_d. \qquad (9.15)$$

In competitive markets we have $\sum_i p_i(\partial y_i(p)/\partial p_d) = 0$ which means $\sum_i (\hat{S}_i)_D \omega_{id} = 0\ \forall_d$. This makes the shadow and producer prices proportional, where for any two goods k and j, we have $(\hat{S}_k)_D/(\hat{S}_j)_D = p_k/p_j$.[11] $\qquad \square$

Thus, by using the generalized Hatta decomposition in (6.9), we must also have: $(S_k)_D/(S_j)_D = p_k/p_j$.[12] In the absence of private profit consumers are insulated from the effects of producer price changes, so that Ramsey optimal taxes are determined solely by their impact on consumer prices.

(ii) *Decreasing Returns and a 100% Profits Tax—Stiglitz and Dasgupta (1971).* In economies with non-linear production frontiers producer prices change endogenously when resources are moved between markets. These price changes will impact on consumers through the profits they receive as shareholders in private firms. Stiglitz and Dasgupta find the shadow and producer prices are proportional if a 100% profit tax is used to remove this profit from consumers when commodity taxes are Ramsey optimal. This replicates the result in Diamond and Mirrlees with CRS production.

Proof. Set $\Phi = 1$ and use the symmetry of the cross-price supply substitution effects to write (9.10), as:

$$(S_R)_D \sum_i \varepsilon_{y_d p_i}((\hat{S}_i)_D - 1) = 0 \qquad \forall_d, \tag{9.16}$$

where $\varepsilon_{y_d p_i} = (\partial y_d(p)/\partial p_i)(p_i/y_d)$ is the supply elasticity for good d with respect to price i.

With Ramsey optimal taxes the revised shadow prices are independent of the tax used to balance the government budget, and with $\sum_i \varepsilon_{y_d p_i} = 0$, $\forall_d$ by profit maximization, the relationship in (9.14) collapses to:

$$\sum_i \varepsilon_{y_d p_i}(\hat{S}_i)_D = 0 \qquad \forall_d. \tag{9.17}$$

As was the case previously for constant returns to scale production, the shadow and producer prices are proportional, where for any two goods k and j:

$$\frac{(\hat{S}_k)_D}{(\hat{S}_j)_D} = \frac{(S_k)_D}{(S_j)_D} = \frac{p_k}{p_j}. {}^{13}$$

$\square$

The intuition for this result will be explained using Figure 9.2 where the supply of good k and its tax both rise. Assume initially there are only two goods, k and the

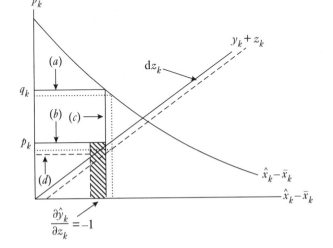

Figure 9.2 *Shadow prices with a 100% profits tax and Ramsey optimal taxes*

numeraire 0, and no initial public production. It is convenient to separate the welfare changes into two steps:

1. The equilibrium effects of the government selling another unit of good k are illustrated by the dotted lines. A lower market price raises commodity tax revenue by $(b) + (c) - (a) = (c)$, and consumer surplus by (a). None of the extra commodity tax revenue in (b) comes from private surplus because it is a transfer from profit tax revenue.

2. Next the government raises the tax to offset the change in consumer surplus in (a) and hold consumer utilities constant where the final equilibrium outcome is illustrated by the dashed lines. Since the tax change returns the consumer price to its initial level it also returns private demand to its initial level; all the tax change falls entirely on the producer price until the extra public output of good k crowds out the same private output. With unchanged supply there is no net change in total tax revenue, where the extra commodity tax revenue in $(b) + (d)$ is a transfer from profit tax revenue. All resources freed up by the fall in private production will flow into the market for the numeraire good which the government holds as surplus revenue. Thus, government revenue rises by the sales revenue (p_k) which is the cross-lined rectangle in Figure 9.2. It is the revised compensated shadow price of the good measured in units of the numeraire good 0. If there are cross-effects in other markets the extra good k will impact on their consumer prices, and they must be reversed by tax changes to hold consumer utilities constant. Once all consumer prices are returned to their initial levels the resources released from crowding out private production of good k are diverted into the numeraire good which the government holds as surplus revenue (p_k).

Whenever private profit is removed from consumer budget constraints, which is the case with a 100% profits tax or constant returns to scale production technologies, there is, in the terminology used by Tresch (2002), a disconnect between the consumer and producer prices. This can be confirmed by noting that the compensating transfers are solved using:

$$d\hat{L} = (x - \bar{x})\, d\hat{q}, \tag{9.18}$$

with $d\hat{q} = d\hat{p} + d\hat{t}$. The revised compensated shadow price of good k is obtained by using the conventional welfare equation in (2.9), and the transfer equation in (9.18), where:

$$(\hat{S}_k)_D = p_k + \left\{ t\frac{\partial \hat{x}}{\partial z_k} + \text{mêb}(x - \bar{x}) \right\} \frac{\partial \hat{q}}{\partial z_k}.^{[14]} \tag{9.19}$$

Once the tax changes reverse the consumer price changes to hold consumer utilities constant, we have $\partial \hat{q}_i / \partial z_k = 0 \,\forall_i$, where the shadow price becomes:

$$(\hat{S}_k)_D = p_k \qquad \forall_{d,k}.^{[15]} \tag{9.20}$$

If this surplus revenue is transferred to the private economy by changing commodity taxes, the dollar change in social welfare is obtained from the welfare decomposition in (6.9), as:

$$(S_k)_D = p_k(S_R)_D, \qquad (9.21)$$

where $(S_R)_D$ is derived in (6.10). It is a dollar measure of the change in social welfare from endowing a dollar of surplus revenue on the government who transfers it to consumers by adjusting commodity taxes. Recall from the welfare decomposition in (7.24) that $(S_R)_D$ is the distributional weighted sum of the personal shadow values of government revenue for each consumer. When commodity taxes change to make them positive for every consumer the welfare change in (9.21) is also a Pareto improvement.

All the income effects are isolated in $(S_R)_D$, and since it is independent of the tax used to balance the government budget when taxes are Ramsey optimal, the shadow prices of goods are proportional to their respective producer prices, where for any two goods k and j, we have:

$$\frac{(S_k)_D}{(S_j)_D} = \frac{p_k}{p_j}. \qquad (9.22)$$

The relationships between the shadow and producer prices for each case examined in this section are summarized in Table 9.1.

To see why removing profit from consumer budget constraints is important for these results reconsider the derivation of the shadow price illustrated in Figure 9.2 in the absence of the profit tax. When extra output drives down the market price of good k the additional commodity tax revenue in (b) comes from private profit. In the absence of public production it completely offsets the gain in consumer surplus in (a). Thus, there is no need to change the commodity tax to hold consumer utilities constant, and the surplus government revenue now exceeds the sales revenue (p_k) by the extra tax revenue in (c). There is no longer production efficiency when taxes are Ramsey optimal in these circumstances.

Table 9.1 *Shadow prices and producer prices*

	Compensated	Uncompensated
CRS Production		
Constant producer prices	$(\hat{S}_k)_D = \hat{S}_k = p_k$	$\dfrac{(S_k)_D}{(S_j)_D} = \dfrac{p_k}{p_j}$
Variable producer prices (and Ramsey optimal taxes)	$(\hat{S}_k)_D = p_k$	$\dfrac{(S_k)_D}{(S_j)_D} = \dfrac{p_k}{p_j}$
100 % Profits tax		
Variable producer prices (and Ramsey optimal taxes)	$(\hat{S}_k)_D = p_k$	$\dfrac{(S_k)_D}{(S_j)_D} = \dfrac{p_k}{p_j}$

Dixit (1985) makes the observation that when optimal taxes result in production efficiency it rules out taxes on international trade flows in small open economies. Tariffs on imports or taxes on exports are not optimal because they distort the relative producer prices of traded and non-traded goods. Instead, taxes and subsidies must be applied to the domestic consumer prices of traded goods.

9.1.3 Project Evaluation with Ramsey Optimal Taxes and Distributional Effects

Diamond and Mirrlees, and Stiglitz and Dasgupta obtain their shadow pricing rules in a more general setting where consumers have different distributional weights. This can be demonstrated by using the shadow prices with distributional effects in (7.21) to write the marginal excess burden for any tax d, as:

$$(\bar{S}_R)_D \sum_i \{(\hat{S}_i)_D - p_i\} \frac{\partial y_i(p)}{\partial p_d} \frac{1}{y_d} = \text{m\={e}b}_d(1 - \Phi), \text{[16]} \tag{9.23}$$

with $\text{m\={e}b}_d = \text{m\={c}f}_d - 1$ defined in (7.22). Ramsey optimal taxes will now have the same marginal excess burden of taxation with distributional effects, where $\text{m\={e}b}_i = \text{m\={e}b} \; \forall_i$. Once again, the shadow and producer prices are proportional if consumers do not receive profits from private production.[17] The proof is not provided here because it closely follows the analysis in the previous section. However, the basic intuition follows from the way compensating tax changes are used to stop consumer prices changing. Since this holds private demand constant extra public output must crowd out the same private output, where the value of the resources released are equal to the market price of the good, which the government holds as surplus revenue. Once this revenue is transferred to consumers by lowering any distorting tax d the additional welfare effects are independent of the tax used when taxes are Ramsey optimal. Thus, optimally chosen taxes do not distort relative producer prices, and can therefore be used as shadow prices in project evaluation.[18]

9.2 OPTIMAL TAX RULES AND PIECEMEAL TAX REFORM

It is convenient for policy analysts to have simple rules for setting optimal taxes, and a number apply in special circumstances. Equal *ad valorem* tax rates on final consumption demands are optimal if all commodities can be taxed, the inverse-elasticity rule applies in the absence of cross-price effects between consumer demands, and the Corlett and Hague (1953: 4) rule sets higher tax rates on goods that are complementary with untaxed goods. Tax reform is frequently undertaken as an incremental process when policy-makers do not have the information needed to make large discrete changes, or are constrained by public skepticism about the stated benefits from the reforms. Clearly, there is no guarantee in a second best setting that all incremental reforms are welfare improving. A number have been identified in the public finance literature, and they are examined in Section 9.2.2. The next section considers three familiar optimal tax rules and extends them, where possible, to variable producer prices.

9.2.1 Optimal Tax Rules

A large portion of government spending is financed from commodity tax revenue, and occasionally governments return surplus revenue to the private economy by reducing commodity taxes. Optimal tax rules are normally based on demand-side parameters because they are derived with *constant producer prices* where the marginal excess burden for each tax d is obtained from (9.3), as:

$$\text{mêb}_d = -\sum_i t_i \frac{\partial \hat{x}_i(q)}{\partial q_d} \frac{1}{x_d - \bar{x}_d} \qquad \forall_d. \qquad (9.24)$$

It is the familiar measure of the distortionary effect of taxation in Atkinson and Stern (1974), Auerbach, and Diamond and Mirrlees (1971). Fane (1991a) proves Ramsey optimal taxes will contract taxed activities by the same proportion in this setting. It is an appealing proposition because it finds efficient taxes raise a given amount of revenue by having the smallest impact on economic activity (i.e. on final consumption demand). The proposition is proved by demonstrating the marginal excess burden for any tax d in (9.24) is equal to the compensated radial elasticity (CRE) of its tax base (with fixed producer prices), where the CRE is the proportionate reduction in the tax base when all commodity taxes are raised by 1% with:

$$e_d = -\frac{\mu}{x_d - \bar{x}_d} \frac{\partial \hat{x}_d(q)}{\partial \mu}.^{19} \qquad (9.25)$$

Taxes are defined in specific terms, as $t_i = \mu \bar{t}_i \forall_i$, with $\bar{t}_i$ being the initial tax and μ a scaling factor, where a radial increase in commodity taxes is achieved by raising μ. By evaluating (9.25) at $\mu = 1$, we have:

$$e_d = -\sum_i \frac{\partial \hat{x}_d(q)}{\partial q_i} \frac{\partial q_i}{\partial \mu} \frac{1}{x_d - \bar{x}_d} = -\sum_i t_i \frac{\partial \hat{x}_i(q)}{\partial q_d} \frac{1}{x_d - \bar{x}_d} = \text{mêb}_d. \qquad (9.26)$$

Thus, Ramsey optimal taxes have the same CREs, which means taxed demands will contract by the same proportion when all taxes are raised by 1%.[20]

A convenient way to decompose the distortionary effect of taxation with *variable producer prices* uses consumer valuations of the changes in activity, as:

$$\text{meb}_d = -(S_R)_D \sum_i (q_i - (\hat{S}_i)_D) \frac{\partial \hat{x}_i(q)}{\partial q_d} \frac{1}{x_d - \bar{x}_d}.^{21} \qquad (9.27)$$

Income effects are removed by using the welfare decomposition in (9.4), where:

$$-\sum_i (q_i - (\hat{S}_i)_D) \frac{\partial \hat{x}_i(q)}{\partial q_d} \frac{1}{x_d - \bar{x}_d} = \text{mêb}_d. \qquad (9.28)$$

This measure of the change in tax inefficiency is independent of the profits tax, and it looks very similar to the familiar measure obtained with constant producer prices in (9.24), except that changes in demand are weighted by the *shadow consumer taxes*, $q_i - (\hat{S}_i)_D$, which are the net social benefit from expanding demand for each good i.[22] They account for endogenous changes in producer prices that shift the burden of taxation away from consumers when any tax d rises. By symmetry of the cross-price compensated changes in demand, and with compensated demands being homogenous of degree zero in consumer prices, the normalized change in tax inefficiency in (9.28) becomes:

$$\sum_i (\hat{S}_i)_D \frac{\partial \hat{x}_d(q)}{\partial q_i} \frac{1}{x_d - \bar{x}_d} = \hat{meb}_d.^{23}$$

As it should, the marginal excess burden in (9.28) collapses to the familiar measure in (9.24) when producer prices are constant. From the previous section recall that the shadow prices of goods are equal to their producer prices in economies with linear production frontiers, where this makes $q_i - (\hat{S}_i)_D = t_i \; \forall i$.[24] We will now use the welfare decompositions in (9.24) and (9.28) to demonstrate a number of familiar optimal tax rules.

A Uniform Ad Valorem Commodity Tax

A uniform *ad valorem* commodity tax is optimal when all final consumption goods can be taxed. In the absence of relative price changes there is no marginal excess burden, and this is confirmed by decomposing the marginal excess burden for the representative tax d, as:

$$\left\{ \frac{\varphi \sum_i q_i \sum_j (\partial \hat{x}_i(q)/\partial q_j) \sum_i \delta_{ji}(\partial y_i(p)/\partial p_d)}{(1 - \Phi)y_d - \sum_j (z_j + \Phi y_j) \sum_i \delta_{ji}(\partial y_i(p)/\partial p_d)} \right\} (S_R)_d = \hat{meb}_d, {}^{25} \qquad (9.29)$$

where φ is the uniform *ad valorem* tax, with $t_i = \varphi q_i \; \forall i$. By Euler's Theorem the numerator in (9.29) becomes:

$$\varphi \sum_i \sum_j \frac{\partial \hat{x}_j(q)}{\partial q_i} q_i \sum_i \delta_{ji} \frac{\partial y_i(p)}{\partial p_d} = 0.^{26}$$

However, this rule will not apply in the presence of distributional effects, unless the initial distribution of income is β *optimal*, that is, the initial distribution of income maximizes social welfare. Distorting taxes can raise welfare by *improving* the distribution of income when consumers have different distributional weights. This is demonstrated by using the MCF for tax d in (9.8) with constant producer prices. The distortionary effect of taxation is eliminated by a uniform *ad valorem* tax on all final consumption demand, with $\hat{meb}_d = 0 \; \forall d$, but that makes $\hat{mcf}_d = DC_d$. Thus, the condition for a social optimum in (9.6) cannot be satisfied unless the taxes have the same distributional characteristics, with $DC_d = 1 \; \forall d$, that is, they are β optimal.

There are practical reasons why a number of consumption goods cannot be taxed, where leisure and home produced consumption are perhaps the most widely cited examples. Also, governments exempt some goods from tax for political reasons.[27] The following tax rules apply when commodity taxes distort relative prices.

The Inverse Elasticity Rule

This rule finds Ramsey optimal commodity taxes are inversely related to the own-price elasticity of their compensated demands, and it applies when there are no cross-price effects in demand, with $\partial \hat{x}_i(q)/\partial q_j = 0 \, \forall_{i \neq j}$. It is normally obtained with constant producer prices where the marginal excess burden for Ramsey optimal taxes in (9.24), becomes:

$$-\varphi_d \hat{\varepsilon}_{x_d q_d} = \text{mêb} \qquad \forall_d, \tag{9.30}$$

with:

$$\hat{\varepsilon}_{x_d q_d} = \frac{\partial \hat{x}_d(q)}{\partial q_d} \frac{q_d}{x_d - \bar{x}_d}$$

being the compensated own-price elasticity of demand for good d. For any two taxes d and m, we have:

$$\frac{\varphi_d}{\varphi_m} = \frac{\hat{\varepsilon}_{x_m q_m}}{\hat{\varepsilon}_{x_d q_d}} \qquad \forall_{d,m}, \tag{9.31}$$

where goods with the relatively less elastic demands will be subject to higher tax rates. If there are cross-effects in demand the highest taxes are levied on commodities with relatively less elastic radial tax bases, as is confirmed by the relationship between the compensated radial elasticity of each tax base and the tax inefficiency in (9.26). While the standard way of demonstrating the inverse-elasticity rule uses compensated elasticities, it will also apply for the *uncompensated elasticities*. This is confirmed by using the welfare decomposition in (9.4) to write the marginal excess burden for Ramsey optimal taxes with fixed producer prices in (9.30), as:

$$-\varphi_d \hat{\varepsilon}_{x_d q_d}(S_R)_\text{D} = -\varphi_d \varepsilon_{x_d q_d} = \text{mêb}(S_R)_\text{D} = \text{meb}_d \qquad \forall_d,$$

where $\varepsilon_{x_d q_d} = (\partial x_d/\partial q_d)(q_d/(x_d - \bar{x}_d))$ is the own-price elasticity of the Bailey (1954) demand for good d.

Thus, for any taxes d and m, we must have:

$$\frac{\varphi_d}{\varphi_m} = \frac{\varepsilon_{x_m q_m}}{\varepsilon_{x_d q_d}} \qquad \forall_{d,m}. \tag{9.32}$$

Recall from Chapter 1 that Bailey demands are general equilibrium demands solved as functions of the endowments, preferences, and public policy choices. Even if producer prices are fixed by a linear production possibility frontier, income will change endogenously due to revenue transfers by the government to balance its budget. Thus, from (9.30) and (9.32) the inverse-elasticity rule applies for both compensated and uncompensated demand elasticities in economies with a single (aggregated) consumer. By the generalized Hatta decomposition, the income effects from the tax changes are independent scaling coefficients on the compensated changes in tax inefficiency and therefore play no role in the analysis.

The inverse-elasticity rule can be extended to *variable producer prices* if firms have CRS technologies, or there is a 100% profit tax. In these circumstances, the compensated shadow prices of goods are equal to their respective producer prices, with $(\hat{S}_i)_D = p_i \forall_i$, where this allows us to write the ratio of the marginal excess burden of taxation in (9.28) for any two Ramsey optimal taxes d and m, as:

$$\frac{\sum_i p_i (\partial \hat{x}_d(q)/\partial q_i)(1/(x_d - \bar{x}_d))}{\sum_i p_i (\partial \hat{x}_m(q)/\partial q_i)(1/(x_m - \bar{x}_m))} = 1.$$

By adding and subtracting the tax for each good to its producer price and using Euler's Theorem, we have:

$$\frac{\sum_i t_i (\partial \hat{x}_d(q)/\partial q_i)(1/(x_d - \bar{x}_d))}{\sum_i t_i (\partial \hat{x}_m(q)/\partial q_i)(1/(x_m - \bar{x}_m))} = 1.$$

Private surplus is unaffected by endogenous changes in producer prices in these circumstances, where in the absence of any cross-price effects in demand (with $\partial \hat{x}_d(q)/\partial q_i = 0 \; \forall_{d \neq i}$), the familiar inverse-elasticity rule in (9.30) applies. Indeed, by the welfare decomposition in (9.4), the rule in (9.32) also applies.

The Corlett and Hague (1953/4) rule

For Ramsey optimal taxes the Corlett and Hague (1953/4) rule finds higher taxes will apply to goods that are relatively complementary with untaxed goods. It is often presented as a piecemeal tax reform that begins with a uniform tax on a subset of the taxed goods. One tax is raised marginally and another lowered to hold consumer utilities constant. Auerbach (1985) demonstrates this rule with *constant producer prices*, and it is replicated here by writing the marginal excess burden of taxation in (9.24), as:

$$-\sum_i \varphi_i \hat{\varepsilon}_{x_d q_i} = \text{mêb} \qquad \forall_d, \tag{9.33}$$

where $\hat{\varepsilon}_{x_d q_i} = (\partial x_d(q)/\partial q_i)(q_i/(x_d - \bar{x}_d))$ is the compensated cross-price elasticity of demand for good d.

Auerbach examines a three good case with no tax on good 0 and taxes on goods 1 and 2. The two tax rates are solved using (9.33), with:

$$\frac{\varphi_1}{\varphi_2} = \frac{\varepsilon_{\hat{x}_2 q_0} + \varepsilon_{\hat{x}_2 q_1} + \varepsilon_{\hat{x}_1 q_2}}{\varepsilon_{\hat{x}_1 q_0} + \varepsilon_{\hat{x}_2 q_0} + \varepsilon_{\hat{x}_1 q_2}} \cdot \frac{28}{} \tag{9.34}$$

If the cross-price elasticities of the taxed goods 1 and 2 with respect to price q_1 are the same, with $\varepsilon_{\hat{x}_2 q_0} = \varepsilon_{\hat{x}_1 q_0}$, then the tax rates must be equal. However, when they differ the higher tax will apply to the good that is relatively more complementary with the untaxed good 0.

9.2.2 Piecemeal Tax Reform

As noted earlier, there are a variety of reasons why governments undertake tax reform as an incremental process. A number of welfare improving piecemeal reforms have been identified in the public finance literature for *constant producer prices*. Fane derives three of them using the relationship between the compensated radial elasticity (CRE) for each tax base and its marginal excess burden (meb) in (9.26). They are each summarized in turn.

1. A radial tax reduction financed from lump–sum taxation increases efficiency (see Foster and Sonnenschein (1970); Bruno (1972); Hatta (1977)). This is proved using the conventional welfare equation in (2.9) with specific taxes defined as $t_i = \mu \bar{t}_i \ \forall i$, where:

$$\frac{d\hat{R}}{d\mu} = \sum_d \frac{d\hat{R}}{dt_d} \frac{dt_d}{d\mu}.$$

   By evaluating the change around $\mu = 1$, we have from (9.26), that $\partial \hat{R}/\partial t_d = -e_d(x_d - \bar{x}_d)$, and with constant producer prices $dt_d/d\mu = dq_d/d\mu$. On this basis a radial tax reduction is welfare improving, since:

$$-\frac{d\hat{R}}{d\mu} = \sum_d e_d \frac{\partial q_d}{\partial \mu} > 0,$$

   with $e_d < 0$ by the fundamental property of compensated demands.

2. Marginal reductions (increases) in the highest (lowest) tax rate are welfare improving when the changes in tax revenue are returned to taxpayers as lump–sum transfers if the goods subject to the highest and lowest tax rates are net substitutes for all other goods (Hatta (1977)). Fane proves this by ordering goods so that t_1 is the smallest element and t_N the largest in the vector of taxes. (Recall that the numeraire good 0 is not subject to tax.) A radial increase in all taxes will raise the consumer price of every good relative to good 1 and lower the consumer price of every good relative to good N. If goods 1 and N are net substitutes for all other goods, the relative price changes must increase the compensated demand for good 1 and reduce the compensated demand for good N. This makes the CRE for good 1 negative and the CRE for good N positive which proves the result.

3. When taxable goods are subject to a uniform tax, welfare can be raised by marginally increasing the tax on a good that is more complementary with non-taxed goods than the good whose tax is lowered to hold tax revenue constant (the *Corlett and Hague rule*). Fane proves this by aggregating non-taxed goods into a single composite good,

leisure, and then raises the uniform tax to reduce the relative price of leisure without changing the relative prices of taxed goods. This makes the CRE for each taxable good directly proportional to the net elasticity of substitution between it and leisure, which proves the result.

All these results will apply when producer prices are variable if firms have CRS technologies or there is a 100% profit tax. As was demonstrated previously, consumers are not affected by changes in producer prices in these circumstances.

9.3 CONCLUDING REMARKS

Whenever governments can tax all final consumption demands at the same rate they will raise revenue without distorting economic activity. Unfortunately, however, not all final consumption demands can be taxed, where the most obvious examples are leisure and non-marketed consumption goods. Thus, commodity taxes distort economic activity by raising the prices of taxed goods relative to non-taxed goods. There are two schools of thought about the most efficient way to tax commodities in these circumstances. One argues tax rates should be set to minimize the excess burden of raising a given amount of tax revenue, that is, Ramsey optimal taxes, while the other school argues administrative costs of setting Ramsey optimal taxes are too great and broad-based taxes should be levied on all final consumption expenditure. In recent years, a number of countries have moved towards broadly based taxes on final consumption even though not all goods can be taxed, and they often do it by lowering income taxes and eliminating taxes in inputs to production.

Despite these reforms, however, there is considerable interest in knowing how to set Ramsey optimal taxes because it provides a benchmark measure of the welfare cost of taxation against which other taxes can be compared. It also allows us to establish optimal tax rules that will minimize the excess burden of taxation. These rules apply when administrative and other costs are included in the welfare analysis to justify the move towards a broad-based consumption tax. The generalized Hatta decomposition was used in this chapter to prove income effects play no role in setting Ramsey optimal taxes in single (aggregated) consumer economies, even when producer prices are variable. And this is useful from a practical point of view because it means analysts can set Ramsey optimal taxes by equating the uncompensated (or actual) marginal excess burden for each tax. There is no need for them to separately compute the compensated welfare changes. This decomposition was also used to generalize the familiar measure of the marginal excess burden of taxation in Diamond and Mirrlees (1971). Their measure is obtained with constant producer prices as the tax weighted sum of the changes in the compensated demands for taxed activities. Once producer prices change endogenously, the weights on the changes in the compensated demands are the shadow consumer taxes $q_i - (\hat{S}_i)_D$, which measure the net social benefit from increasing demand in each market in just the same way taxes do when producer prices are fixed. This measure of the marginal excess burden of taxation was used to extend the familiar inverse elasticity rule.

Finally, the revised shadow prices derived in Chapters 6 and 7 were used to confirm the important results established by Diamond and Mirrlees, and Stiglitz and Dasgupta where they find the shadow prices of goods are proportional to their producer prices if taxes are Ramsey optimal and consumers receive no profit from private production. Under these circumstances, there is production efficiency and Ramsey optimal taxes do not include taxes on production inputs. Indeed, when the Australian and New Zealand Governments adopted a broad-based consumption tax they also removed, where possible, taxes on production inputs as though they were setting non-distorting commodity taxes. This reflects a desire to move away from discriminatory taxes, which may violate Ramsey optimal tax rules, to avoid the higher administrative costs of implementing them.

NOTES

1. Strictly speaking it is the tax-weighted sum of the proportionate changes in the compensated demands.
2. Recall there are $N + 1$ goods. Good 0 is chosen as the numeraire and is not subject to tax.
3. The welfare effect of marginally raising one tax and lowering another to balance the government budget is derived in Appendix 9. It is the approach used by Ahmad and Stern (1984), Hatta (1986), and Hatta and Haltiwanger (1986) to identify welfare improving tax reforms.
4. A more general expression is obtained in Appendix 10 where producer prices can change endogenously in the presence of a profit tax Φ. The decomposition in (9.3) differs from that of Diamond and Mirrlees, who implicitly obtain:

$$\text{meb}_d = \frac{\text{m\^eb}_d + \theta}{1 - \text{m\^eb}_d - \theta}.$$

   While they do not identify the marginal excess burden, they derive the welfare effects of a tax change in their equation (37) on page 262, which is rearranged here as the meb for tax d. The reason this differs from (9.3) is due to the way the income effects are solved. This is explained in Chapter 4 where the approach of Hatta is used to show the income effects are a multiplicative scaling factor on the substitution effects once all changes in surplus are included through the economy's budget constraints. By using a Slutsky decomposition, Diamond and Mirrlees hold money income constant and do not therefore account for the transfer of surplus as tax revenue back to consumers in a conventional Harberger manner.
5. This result is derived as equation (A.21) in Appendix 6.
6. Using (3.4), with $dL = 0$, we have:

$$(\bar{S}_{t_m})_D = - \left\{ DC_p z \frac{\partial p}{\partial t_m} + DC_{t_m}(x_m - \bar{x}_m) \right\} - \left\{ DC_p z \frac{\partial p}{\partial t_d} + DC_{t_d}(x_d - \bar{x}_d) \right\} \left(\frac{dt_d}{dt_m} \right)_D,$$

   where the tax change to balance the government budget, is:

$$\left(\frac{dt_d}{dt_m} \right)_D = - \frac{\partial L/dt_m}{\partial L/dt_d}.$$

   Equation (9.6) is obtained using the MCF defined in (7.22).
7. Detailed workings are provided in Appendix 10.
8. Sieper (1994) obtains this relationship by decomposing the *compensated* marginal excess burden for the tax d.
9. A proof is provided in Appendix 11. This is also why the compensated shadow prices of fully traded goods are equal to their border prices in economies that are small in world markets when foreign exchange is chosen as numeraire. In effect, these goods are supplied to the economy at a constant

marginal cost equal to their border prices, which are c.i.f. prices for imports and f.o.b. prices for exports.

10. The Little–Mirrlees (1969) result is presented in Chapter 5 where internationally traded goods are included.

11. By stacking the relationships in (9.15) for all N goods whose prices change, and using matrix notation, we have $[(\tilde{S})_\mathrm{D}][\omega_y] = [\tilde{0}]$, with $[(\tilde{S})_\mathrm{D}]$ being the $(1 \times N)$ row vector of revised shadow prices, $[\omega_y]$ the $(N \times N)$ matrix comprising the ratios of supply substitution terms, and $[\tilde{0}]$ the $(1 \times N)$ row vector of zeros. By profit maximization $[\tilde{p}][\omega_y] = [0]$, where $[\tilde{p}]$ is the $(1 \times N)$ row vector of producer prices. Since the vectors of producer and shadow prices are orthogonal to all the columns in $[\omega_y]$, the shadow and producer prices must be proportional.

12. By using the generalized Hatta decomposition in (6.9), we have:

$$\frac{(S_R)_\mathrm{D}}{(S_R)_\mathrm{D}} \frac{(\hat{S}_k)_\mathrm{D}}{(\hat{S}_j)_\mathrm{D}} = \frac{P_k}{P_j}.$$

13. By stacking the relationships in (9.17) for all N goods whose price change, and using matrix notation, we have $[\varepsilon_y][(\tilde{S})_\mathrm{D}] = [\tilde{0}]$ with $[\varepsilon_y]$ the $(N \times N)$ matrix of supply substitution effects, $[(\tilde{S})_\mathrm{D}]$ the $(N \times 1)$ column vector of revised shadow prices, and $[\tilde{0}]$ the $(N \times 1)$ column vector of zeros. From profit maximization $[\varepsilon_y][\tilde{p}] = [0]$, where $[\tilde{p}]$ is the $(N \times 1)$ column vector of producer prices. Since the vectors of producer and shadow prices are orthogonal to all the rows in $[\varepsilon_y]$, the shadow and producer prices must be proportional. The generalized Hatta decomposition in (6.9) is used to derive the same relationship between the uncompensated shadow and producer prices.

14. Using the conventional welfare equation in (2.9), we have:

$$(\hat{S}_k)_\mathrm{D} = p_k + t\frac{\partial \hat{x}}{\partial q}\frac{\partial \hat{q}}{\partial z_k} - \sum_i \mathrm{m\hat{e}b}_i \frac{\partial \hat{L}}{\partial t_i}\left(\frac{\mathrm{d}\hat{t}_i}{\mathrm{d}z_k}\right)_\mathrm{D},$$

with:

$$\mathrm{m\hat{e}b}_i = -\frac{\partial \hat{R}/\partial t_i}{\partial \hat{L}/\partial t_i}.$$

The compensating tax changes solve:

$$\left(\frac{\mathrm{d}\hat{L}}{\mathrm{d}z_k}\right)_\mathrm{D} = \frac{\partial \hat{L}}{\partial z_k} + \sum_i \frac{\partial \hat{L}}{\partial t_i}\left(\frac{\mathrm{d}\hat{t}_i}{\mathrm{d}z_k}\right)_\mathrm{D} = 0,$$

and the compensating transfers are obtained using the transfer equation in (9.18), as:

$$\sum_i \frac{\partial \hat{L}}{\partial t_i}\left(\frac{\mathrm{d}\hat{t}_i}{\mathrm{d}z_k}\right)_\mathrm{D} = -\frac{\partial \hat{L}}{\partial z_k}.$$

When taxes are Ramsey optimal they will have the same compensated marginal excess burden, with $\mathrm{m\hat{e}b}_i = \mathrm{m\hat{e}b}\,\forall_i$, which leads to the revised shadow price in (9.19).

15. This is confirmed in Tresch (2002) who obtains the shadow profit for a public sector project that produces another unit of good k.

16. Detailed workings are provided in Appendix 12. Also, the welfare decomposition in (7.24) is used to separate the distributional effects from extra output of each good i in the revised shadow value of government revenue with distributional effects, $(\tilde{S}_R)_\mathrm{D}$, where:

$$(\tilde{S}_i)_\mathrm{D} = (\tilde{S}_R)_\mathrm{D}(\hat{S}_i)_\mathrm{D} \qquad \forall_i,$$

with

$$(\bar{S}_i)_D = \sum_h \beta^h (S_i^h)_D \quad \forall_i \qquad \text{and} \qquad (\bar{S}_R)_D = \sum_h \beta^h (S_R^h)_D.$$

17. When the taxes are set optimally they have the same marginal excess burden with $\text{mêb}_d = \text{mêb}$ for all taxes d, and the shadow prices are independent of the tax used to balance the government budget, with $(\bar{S}_i)_D$ and $(\bar{S}_R)_D$ being unaffected by the choice of tax.

18. Dasgupta and Stiglitz (1972) show that it may not be socially desirable to tax all private profit away when there are distributional effects. If some consumers derive a large proportion of their income from shareholdings in the profit of private firms a 100% profit tax will have a considerable impact on their consumption. Thus, at a social optimum the profit tax may be less than 100% with taxes on production inputs.

19. Fane defines x_d as the net demand for good d. It is defined here as $x_d - \bar{x}_d$.

20. With *variable producer prices* the compensated radial elasticity for any tax d becomes:

$$e_d = -\sum_i t_i \frac{\partial \hat{x}_i(q)}{\partial q_d} \frac{1}{x_d - \bar{x}_d} \left\{ 1 - \sum_i \delta_{ji} \frac{\partial \hat{x}_i(q)}{\partial q_j} \right\}.$$

It is no longer equal to the compensated marginal excess burden for tax d.

21. Detailed workings are provided in Appendix 13 where distributional effects are also included.

22. Drèze and Stern (1990) and Mirrlees (1971) define $q_i - (\hat{S}_i)_D$ as the shadow consumer tax for each good i.

23. By symmetry of the cross-price changes in compensated demands, we have:

$$\frac{\partial \hat{x}_i(q)}{\partial q_d} = \frac{\partial \hat{x}_d(q)}{\partial q_i} \qquad \forall_{i,d}.$$

Since compensated demands are homogeneous of degree zero in consumer prices, Euler's Theorem can be used to show that:

$$\sum_i q_i \frac{\partial \hat{x}_d(q)}{\partial q_i} = 0 \qquad \forall_d.$$

24. When $(\hat{S}_i)_D = p_i$ for all goods i it is possible to write (9.28), as:

$$-\sum_i (p_i + t_i) \frac{\partial \hat{x}_d(q)}{\partial q_i} \frac{1}{x_d - \bar{x}_d} + \sum_i p_i \frac{\partial \hat{x}_d(q)}{\partial q_i} \frac{1}{x_d - \bar{x}_d} = \text{mêb}_d.$$

25. This is derived as equation (A.32) in Appendix 10.

26. This follows from the fact that compensated demands are homogeneous of degree zero in consumer prices.

27. For example, food and other items are exempt from the goods and services tax in Australia.

28. By stacking the condition in (9.33) over all $N+1$ goods, and using matrix notation, we have $[\hat{\varepsilon}_x][\tilde{\varphi}] = -\text{mêb}[\tilde{1}]$, with $[\varepsilon_{\hat{x}}]$ the $(N+1) \times (N+1)$ matrix of compensated supply elasticities, $[\tilde{\varphi}]$ the $(N+1) \times 1$ column vector of *ad valorem* tax rates (with some being zero for untaxed goods), and mêb a constant scalar on the $(N+1) \times 1$ unit column vector. Since $[\varepsilon_{\hat{x}}]$ has full rank it can be inverted to solve the taxes, as $[\tilde{\varphi}] = -\text{mêb}[\hat{\varepsilon}_x]^{-1}[\tilde{1}]$.

10

The Optimal Provision of Public Goods

Government provision of a pure public good is a popular application in public economics because it combines public spending and taxation in a single project. Indeed, it provides an excellent opportunity to apply much of the welfare analysis developed in previous chapters. When a pure public good is optimally supplied the summed marginal consumption benefits ($\sum$ MRS) will be equal to the marginal resource cost (MRT) of producing it, with $\sum$ MRS = MRT.[1] This is the familiar Samuelson (1954) condition which holds in a general equilibrium setting with a single (aggregated) consumer and no market distortions. There are, however, additional welfare costs when the government uses distorting taxes to fund the project. Pigou (1947) recognized this and used the conventional marginal social cost of public funds (MCF) to account for the excess burden of taxation, where the revised Samuelson condition is $\sum$ MRS = mcf · MRT, with: mcf = 1 + meb. Pigou argued that the marginal excess burden of taxation (meb) would raise the MCF above unity and drive down the optimal supply of the good (with $\sum$ MRS > MRT), but subsequent studies are critical of this finding for two reasons:

1. In the presence of distorting taxes, Diamond and Mirrlees (1971) and Stiglitz and Dasgupta (1971) identify endogenous changes in tax revenue when the public good impacts on taxed activities. Snow and Warren (1996) refer to this as the spending effect, which reduces the budgetary cost of producing extra output of the public good when it is positive.
2. Atkinson and Stern (1974) also identify a revenue effect in the conventional MCF that can offset the distortionary effect of taxation and make mcf < 1. It is the income effect from marginally raising a tax, which is positive when taxed goods are inferior (and/or subsidized goods are normal).

Taken together, the spending and revenue effects can work to contradict Pigou's claim by making $\sum$ MRS < MRT when the good is optimally supplied.[2] A conventional cost–benefit analysis is used in the next section to isolate these effects. If, in the presence of distorting taxes, a marginal increase in the supply of a public good G is funded from lump–sum transfers, the Samuelson condition becomes $\sum$ MRS = MRT − dT/dG, where dT/dG is the so called spending effect; it is the change in tax revenue from the combined effects of the extra public good and the increase in lump–sum taxation.[3] Private surplus rises by the summed consumption benefits endowed on consumers ($\sum$ MRS), and falls by the surplus collected as tax revenue to fund the net increase in government spending (MRT − dT/dG). A positive spending effect will reduce the size of the budget deficit and, as a consequence, the cost to private surplus of funding the project. If government spending is funded with distorting tax d the revised Samuelson condition must be amended to account for its marginal excess burden, and this is achieved by using the conventional MCF in (7.2) to gross up the revenue transfers made to balance the government budget, where $\sum \text{MRS} = \text{mcf}_d(\text{MRT} - dT/dG)$. These welfare measures are formally derived in following sections, where the revenue effect identified by Atkinson and Stern in the conventional MCF (mcf_d) is isolated using the generalized Hatta decomposition in (2.12). It proves that the income effect, which can make $\text{mcf}_d < 1$, has no impact on the optimal supply of the public good in a single (aggregated) consumer economy.

A number of recent studies obtain the revised Samuelson condition by using a modified measure of the MCF. It is not the conventional MCF which returns tax revenue to taxpayers as lump-sum transfers. Instead, it returns tax revenue as extra government expenditure. Most empirical estimates of the modified MCF are for wage taxes in the United States where tax revenue is returned as extra output of a pure public good.[4] Snow and Warren (1996) and Mayshar (1990, 1991) derive it by writing the revised Samuelson condition as $\sum \text{MRS} = \text{mcf}_d^* \cdot \text{MRT}$, where:

$$\text{mcf}_d^* = \text{mcf}_d \left(1 - \frac{1}{\text{MRT}} \frac{dT}{dG} \right).$$

By including the spending effect in the MCF there are as many measures of the modified MCF for each tax as ways the revenue can be spent. Thus, by construction, it is a project specific measure of the cost of transferring a dollar of tax revenue between the private and public sectors of the economy.[5]

This chapter reconciles the modified MCF with the conventional Harberger (1964) measure. It also examines the role of income effects in the conventional MCF by using the generalized Hatta decomposition. The formal analysis begins by including the public good G in the utility function for each consumer h, as $u^h(x^h, G)$. We follow Atkinson and Stern, and Ballard and Fullerton, and assume the public good is produced solely by the government.[6] Now the private demands and supplies can be solved as functions of the exogenous policy variables G, z, t, and R, where dollar changes in social welfare are solved using the budget constraints in (2.2), as:

$$\frac{dW}{\beta} = \sum \text{MRS} \cdot dG - z \, dp - (x - \bar{x}) \, dt - dL, \tag{10.1}$$

with $\sum \text{MRS} = \sum_h (\partial u^h/\partial G)/\lambda^h$ being the summed marginal consumption benefits from the public good. Since these benefits are endowed on consumers they impact directly on private surplus, as distinct from private goods where the marginal consumption benefits are collected as sales revenue and transferred to consumers when the government balances its budget. These revenue transfers are solved using the government budget, as:

$$dL = dT + z \, dp + p \, dz - dR. \tag{10.2}$$

A *conventional welfare equation* is obtained by substituting (10.2) into (10.1), where:

$$\frac{\mathrm{d}W}{\beta} = \sum \mathrm{MRS} \cdot \mathrm{d}G + p\,\mathrm{d}z + t\,\mathrm{d}x - \mathrm{d}R. \tag{10.3}$$

Two further assumptions are frequently made to simplify the analysis. First, the public good is produced by a simple production technology that uses dollars of government revenue (R) as the sole input, with $\mathrm{d}R/\mathrm{d}G = \mathrm{MRT}$, and second, the public sector does not trade in private markets, with $z_i = 0\,\forall_i$.[7] The analysis begins by adopting these assumptions, and is extended in Section 10.2.3 where the public sector uses labour (n) to produce good G. Distributional effects are included in Section 10.3.

10.1 THE SAMUELSON CONDITION WITH LUMP-SUM TAXATION

A conventional Samuelson condition is obtained by deriving the shadow profit for a public sector project that produces another unit of good G with revenue raised by lump-sum taxation, where in the presence of distorting taxes, we have:

$$\pi_G^S = S_G - S_R \cdot \mathrm{MRT}. \tag{10.4}$$

The conventional shadow price of the public good is obtained from the welfare equation in (10.3) by endowing another unit of G on the economy, where:

$$S_G = \sum \mathrm{MRS} + \frac{\partial T}{\partial G}. \tag{10.5}$$

Ballard and Fullerton (1992) assume that the only tax is a single wage tax on labour (n) employed by firms ($t_n < 0$), and labour supply increases with extra output of the public good. The shadow price in (10.5) is illustrated under these circumstances in Figure 10.1 as the summed consumption benefits endowed on consumers ($\sum \mathrm{MRS}$) plus the extra tax revenue in (a) which they receive as a revenue transfer when the government balances its budget (with $\partial L/\partial G = (a)$).

The shadow value of government revenue in (10.4) is obtained from (10.3) by endowing a dollar of surplus revenue on the economy, as:

$$S_R = 1 - \frac{\partial T}{\partial R}. \tag{10.6}$$

It will exceed unity whenever wage tax revenue rises (with $-\partial T/\partial R > 0$), which is the case when leisure is an inferior good for consumers. However, it must be less than unity when leisure is a normal good. We use the shadow prices in (10.5) and (10.6) to write the shadow profit in (10.4), as:

$$\pi_G^S = \sum \mathrm{MRS} + \frac{\partial T}{\partial G} - \left(1 - \frac{\partial T}{\partial R}\right)\mathrm{MRT}. \tag{10.7}$$

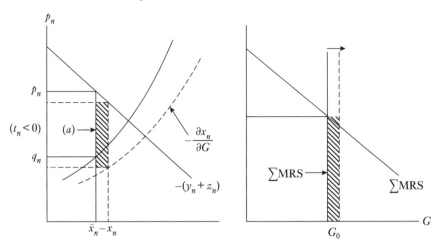

Figure 10.1 *The conventional shadow price of a public good*

The conventional Samuelson condition in the presence of distorting taxes is obtained by setting $\pi_G^S = 0$, where:

$$\sum \text{MRS} = \text{MRT} - \frac{dT}{dG},\tag{10.8}$$

with $dT/dG = (\partial T/\partial R)\text{MRT} + (\partial T/\partial G)$ being the spending effect identified by Diamond and Mirrlees, and Stiglitz and Dasgupta. Notice how a positive spending effect will drive the summed marginal consumption benefits below the marginal production cost at a social optimum (with $\sum \text{MRS} < \text{MRT}$). Kaplow (1996) argues this effect offsets the distortionary effect of taxation identified by Pigou thereby making the public good easier to fund. The Samuelson condition in (10.8) is illustrated in Figure 10.2 for the single tax on labour when leisure is a normal good. We follow Ballard and Fullerton and assume labour supply increases with extra output of the public good.

There is extra tax revenue in (*a*) when labour supply rises with good G, and a further increase in (*b*) when the lump-sum tax reduces the real income of consumers. These combined changes in tax revenue constitute the spending effect, which is $dT/dG = (a) + (b)$, where the Samuelson condition in (10.8), becomes:

$$\sum \text{MRS} = \text{MRT} - \{(a) + (b)\}.$$

At a social optimum, private surplus rises by the summed consumption benefits and falls by the revenue transfers to fund the government budget deficit in $\text{MRT} - \{(a) + (b)\}$.

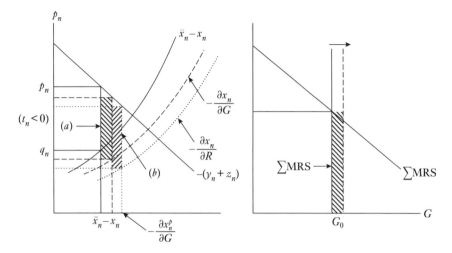

Figure 10.2 *The conventional Samuelson condition*

10.1.1 Income Effects and the Optimal Supply of Public Goods

Each component of the project examined in the previous section has income effects on consumers; extra output of the public good raises real income, while the lump–sum tax reduces it. However, at a social optimum, they will exactly offset each other and have no impact on the optimal supply of the public good in (10.8). This is confirmed by decomposing the income and substitution effects in the shadow prices in (10.5) and (10.6). For the shadow price of the public good in (10.5), we have:

$$S_G = \frac{\sum \mathrm{MRS} + (\partial \hat{T}/\partial G)}{1 - \theta}, \,{}^{8} \tag{10.9}$$

where θ isolates the income effects, and is defined earlier in (2.14).[9] A similar decomposition of the shadow value of government revenue in (10.6), yields:

$$S_R = \frac{1}{1 - \theta}. \tag{10.10}$$

It is based solely on income effects isolated in θ. We use the shadow prices in (10.9) and (10.10) to write the shadow profit for the project in (10.4), as:

$$\pi_G^S = S_R \left(\sum \mathrm{MRS} + \frac{\partial \hat{T}}{\partial G} - \mathrm{MRT} \right),$$

where it provides the Samuelson condition in the compensated equilibrium, of:

$$\sum \mathrm{MRS} = \mathrm{MRT} - \frac{\partial \hat{T}}{\partial G}.{}^{10} \tag{10.11}$$

All the income effects are isolated in S_R and they play no role in determining the optimal supply of the good in a single (aggregated) consumer economy. Indeed, at a social optimum there is no efficiency gain from producing more of the public good (with $\hat{\pi}_G^S = 0$), and with no surplus revenue to transfer to the private sector there can be no change in utility (with $\pi_G^S = 0$).

10.2 THE SAMUELSON CONDITION WITH DISTORTING TAXATION

Most studies focus on the optimal provision of public goods when they are funded with distorting taxes. By imposing an excess burden on private surplus they increase the social cost of financing government spending, where the revised shadow profit from producing an extra unit of good G, becomes:

$$(\pi_G^S)_D = (S_G)_D - (S_R)_D \cdot \text{MRT}. \tag{10.12}$$

Ballard and Fullerton (1992), Snow and Warren (1996), and Wildasin (1979, 1984) obtain a revised Samuelson condition in the presence of a wage tax on employment (n). We follow them by assuming it is the only distorting tax in the economy, where the revised shadow price of the public good G, is:

$$(S_G)_D = \sum \text{MRS} + \text{mcf}_n \frac{\partial T}{\partial G}.^{[11]} \tag{10.13}$$

Now the revenue transfer is grossed up by the conventional MCF to account for changes in the marginal excess burden of taxation in the second term of (10.13). The revised shadow value of government revenue is obtained in a similar manner, as:

$$(S_R)_D = \text{mcf}_n \left(1 - \frac{\partial T}{\partial R}\right).^{[12]} \tag{10.14}$$

We obtain the revised Samuelson condition by using the shadow prices in (10.13) and (10.14) to write the shadow profit in (10.12) at a social optimum (with $(\pi_G^S)_D = 0$), as:

$$\sum \text{MRS} = \text{mcf}_n \left(\text{MRT} - \frac{dT}{dG}\right). \tag{10.15}$$

Whenever the MCF exceeds unity (with $\text{mcf}_n > 1$) the project is more costly to fund, thereby reducing the optimal supply of the public good. For the special case considered by Ballard and Fullerton leisure and the public good are *ordinary independents*, where the combined effects of the increase in G and the wage tax (t_n) leave employment unchanged. The welfare changes are illustrated in Figure 10.3. For this special case the spending effect in $(a) + (b)$ offsets the distortionary effect from the tax in (c). Thus, $\sum \text{MRS} = \text{MRT}$ when the good is optimally supplied.[13] This is confirmed using a conventional cost–benefit analysis where extra output of the public good raises private

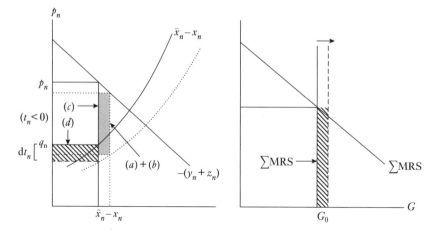

Figure 10.3 *The conventional shadow price of a public good*

surplus by $\sum MRS$ and reduces it by the revenue required to fund the net increase in government spending, $MRT - \{(a) + (b)\}$.

There is a larger reduction in private surplus when the revenue is collected with the wage tax because it has a marginal excess burden of $meb_n = (c)/[(d) - (c)]$, where the MCF is:

$$mcf_n = \frac{(d)}{(d) - (c)}.\,^{14}$$

Based on these changes, the revised Samuelson condition becomes:

$$\sum MRS = \frac{(d)}{(d) - (c)}\,(MRT - \{(a) + (b)\})\,.$$

With unchanged employment we have $(a) + (b) = (c)$ and $MRT = (d)$, where $\sum MRS = MRT = (d)$ at a social optimum. Once employment changes $(a) + (b) \neq (c)$ and $\sum MRS \neq MRT$. If the spending effect is positive and larger than the distortionary effect the project has a smaller impact on net public spending, where $\sum MRS < MRT$ at a social optimum. The reverse applies when the spending effect is smaller (or negative). Whenever the spending effect offsets the change in tax inefficiency the projects net impact on the government budget will be determined solely by the production cost (MRT), where this leads some analysts to conclude that the MCF is unity in these circumstances.

10.2.1 A Modified Measure of the MCF

Ballard and Fullerton obtain a revised Samuelson condition by using the MCF in Snow and Warren, and Mayshar, to write (10.15), as:

$$\sum MRS = mcf_n^* \cdot MRT, \tag{10.16}$$

where:

$$\mathrm{mcf}_n^* = \mathrm{mcf}_n \left(1 - \frac{1}{\mathrm{MRT}} \frac{\mathrm{d}T}{\mathrm{d}G} \right). \tag{10.17}$$

Notice how the spending effect is included in this modified measure of the MCF, which is why it differs from the conventional Harberger measure (mcf_n). It is illustrated in Figure 10.3 for the special case where the project leaves employment unchanged, as:

$$\mathrm{mcf}_n^* = \frac{(d)}{(d) - (c)} \left(1 - \frac{(a) + (b)}{\mathrm{MRT}} \right).$$

If the spending effect offsets the tax inefficiency, then $\mathrm{mcf}_n^* = 1$. Such a possibility seems counter-intuitive to anyone who is familiar with the conventional MCF which is always greater than unity for a single distorting tax. In a conventional cost–benefit analysis the spending effect is included in the welfare effects from changing the supply of the public good, and not in the welfare effects from the tax change. Indeed, Mayshar (1991) and Dahlby (1998) state a preference for this approach as a way to separate the welfare effects of policy changes. By doing so, any benefits from government expenditure are separated from the costs of raising the revenue to fund it.

A positive spending effect is the reason why Ballard and Fullerton obtain estimates of the MCF for lump-sum taxes that are less than unity. They are estimating the modified MCF and not the conventional measure which is always unity for a lump-sum tax (with $\mathrm{mcf}_L = 1$).[15] For the special case illustrated in Figure 10.3 the modified MCF in (10.17) for a lump-sum tax, is:

$$\mathrm{mcf}_L^* = 1 - \frac{(a) + (b)}{\mathrm{MRT}},$$

where the additional tax revenue in $(a) + (b)$ means $\mathrm{mcf}_L^* < 1$. Clearly, it is not incorrect to include the spending effect in the MCF, but when it is, policy analysts must know that they are using a modified measure of the MCF because it is project specific. However, these different approaches do not undermine the important point made by Diamond and Mirrlees, and Stiglitz and Dasgupta, and that is, in the presence of distorting taxes the spending effect is a welfare change that should be included in the revised Samuelson condition. It is a welfare change not included in the partial equilibrium analysis of Pigou, and can lead to $\sum \mathrm{MRS} < \mathrm{MRT}$ when the public good is optimally supplied.

10.2.2 Income Effects and the MCF

Atkinson and Stern identify a revenue effect in the conventional MCF and argue it can impact on the optimal provision of the public good. It is the change in tax revenue that can be attributed to the income effect from marginally raising taxes. Indeed, Atkinson and Stern identify circumstances where the revenue effect can drive the MCF below unity, which is the case when taxed goods are inferior. As real income falls the extra tax revenue will offset the distortionary effect of the tax change. For the single wage tax the revenue effect is isolated by separating the income and substitution effects in the conventional MCF. Following the analysis in Chapter 7, we have:

$$\text{mcf}_n = \frac{1}{1 - (\text{mêb}_n/(1-\theta))},$$ (10.18)

where $\theta = \sum t_i(\partial x_i(q, I, G)/\partial I)$ is the revenue effect; and, $\text{mêb}_n = -(t_n/(\bar{x}_n - x_n))(\partial \hat{x}_n(q)/\partial q_n)$ the distortionary effect.[16] While a positive revenue effect (with $-\theta > 0$) can reduce the MCF, it will not, however, impact on the optimal supply of the public good in the single (aggregated) consumer economy. This is confirmed by isolating all the income effects in the revised Samuelson condition in (10.15). By separating the income and substitution effects in the spending effect, we have:

$$\frac{dT}{dG} = \frac{-\theta \text{MRT} + \theta \sum \text{MRS} + (\partial \hat{T}/\partial G)}{1-\theta}.[17]$$ (10.19)

After substituting (10.18) and (10.19) into (10.15) we are left with the compensated revised Samuelson condition:

$$\sum \text{MRS} = \text{mĉf}_n \left(\text{MRT} - \frac{\partial \hat{T}}{\partial G} \right),[18]$$ (10.20)

with: $\text{mĉf}_n = 1/(1 - \text{mêb}_n)$. All the income effects, which are isolated in θ, will offset each other at a social optimum. Thus, while the revenue effect identified by Atkinson and Stern can raise or lower the conventional MCF in (10.18), it cannot affect the relationship between $\sum \text{MRS}$ and MRT in (10.20). There is an offsetting income effect from the extra output of the public good. Indeed, this confirms the generalized Hatta decomposition in (6.9). At a social optimum, there are no efficiency gains from the project to distribute to consumers (with $(\hat{\pi}_G^S)_\text{D} = 0$), and as a consequence, there cannot be changes in consumer utilities (with $(\pi_G^S)_\text{D} = 0$).

10.2.3 The Samuelson Condition with Production Inputs

A natural way to extend the previous analysis is to introduce a production input. Most public goods are produced using marketed goods and services, where, for example, defence and police services are produced by labour, capital, and other raw material inputs. To see how this changes the revised Samuelson condition, assume the public good G is produced using labour (n) as the sole input, where the revised shadow profit for the project becomes:

$$(\pi_G^S)_\text{D} = (S_G)_\text{D} - (S_n)_\text{D} \, a_{nG},$$ (10.21)

with $a_{nG} \equiv -\partial z_n/\partial G > 0$ being the input–output coefficient. In the absence of taxes and public sector trade in other private markets, the revised shadow wage is:

$$(S_n)_\text{D} = \text{mcf}_n \left(p_n + \frac{\partial T}{\partial z_n} \right) + \text{meb}_n \, z_n \frac{\partial p_n}{\partial z_n},$$ (10.22)

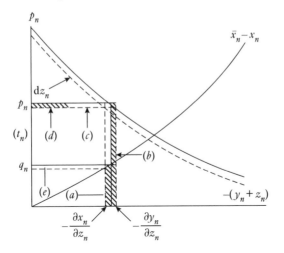

Figure 10.4 *The revised shadow wage rate*

where the last term is a welfare gain from a lower wage that reduces the public sector wage bill (with $z_n < 0$ for labour demand). Whenever the government trades in private markets it extracts surplus from the private economy which is returned when the budget is balanced. These surplus transfers play no role in the welfare analysis whenever they are made in a lump-sum fashion. However, they do play a role when they are made with distorting taxes. The shadow wage in (10.22) is illustrated in Figure 10.4 when the government initially employs half the labour supplied. It is computed by endowing a unit of labour on the government, which reduces its demand. The excess supply of labour drives down the wage to expand private employment $(-\partial y_n/\partial z_n > 0)$ and leisure $(-\partial x_n/\partial z_n > 0)$.

Welfare rises by the consumption benefits as leisure in (a) and the value of the marginal product of private employment in (b). Since this gain is collected as government revenue, private surplus rises by $\mathrm{mcf}_n[(a) + (b)]$, which is larger due to the reduction in tax inefficiency when the tax is lowered to make the revenue transfer. There is also a net loss in private surplus of $(e) - (c)$ due to the lower wage, but it matches the surplus government revenue from the lower wage bill in (d), with $(d) = (e) - (c)$. Thus, the welfare gain is confined to the reduction in tax inefficiency in $\mathrm{meb}_n(d)$. After summing these welfare changes, the shadow wage becomes:

$$(S_n)_\mathrm{D} = \mathrm{mcf}_n\{(a) + (b)\} + \mathrm{meb}_n(d).$$

The revised shadow price of the public good G is obtained in a similar fashion, as:

$$(S_G)_\mathrm{D} = \sum \mathrm{MRS} + \mathrm{mcf}_n\frac{\partial T}{\partial G} + \mathrm{meb}_n z_n\frac{\partial p_n}{\partial G}. \tag{10.23}$$

It is the revised shadow price in (10.13) plus the change in tax inefficiency on the surplus transfers when wage changes impact on the public sector wage bill. By using the shadow prices in (10.22) and (10.23) and the shadow profit in (10.21) we obtain the revised Samuelson condition:

$$\sum \text{MRS} = \text{mcf}_n \left(p_n a_{nG} - \frac{\mathrm{d}T}{\mathrm{d}G} \right) - \text{meb}_n z_n \frac{\mathrm{d}p_n}{\mathrm{d}G}. \quad [19] \tag{10.24}$$

If the project bids up the market wage (with $\partial p_n / \partial G > 0$) the increase in the public sector wage bill drives down the optimal supply of the public good due to the additional tax inefficiency incurred (when $-\text{meb}_n z_n (\partial p_n / \partial G) > 0$). This welfare change was absent in the Samuelson condition in (10.20) because the government did not trade in any private market.

Another way to extend the standard analysis is to look at public sector employment in the presence of *a minimum wage*. They are common in unionized segments of the labour market, which is much more likely when employers have the ability to pass on higher wages in their product prices. When the government employs a relatively large proportion of workers in any given segment of the labour market it is more likely to be unionized and subject to a minimum wage. Indeed, it is easier for the government to fund higher wages from general tax revenue than it is for private firms to raise their prices, especially when there is competition in product markets.

Once again, effects in related markets are restricted by assuming a single tax on employment, and the labour market is the only private market where the government trades. If the budget is balanced using lump-sum taxes, the Samuelson condition is obtained using the shadow wage rate in (4.8), as:

$$\sum \text{MRS} = \bar{p}_n a_{nG} + \left(t_n - \frac{\delta_n}{\lambda} \right) \frac{\mathrm{d}x_n}{\mathrm{d}G}, \quad [20] \tag{10.25}$$

where $\delta_n / \lambda > 0$ is the welfare gain from marginally relaxing the constraint on employment in the presence of the minimum wage. The first term is the wage payment by the government when it produces one extra unit of the public good, while the second term measures the net welfare loss from exacerbating the constraint on labour supply when leisure increases. If the increase in public sector demand for labour is matched by an equal reduction in private demand (with $\partial y_n / \partial z_n = -1$ and $\partial x_n / \partial z_n = 0$) the shadow wage is the market wage; it is the value of the marginal product of labour crowded out by extra public employment. However, if there is no change in private employment and all extra labour supply comes from reducing leisure (with $\partial y_n / \partial z_n = 0$ and $\partial x_n / \partial z_n = -1$) the shadow wage is the marginal value of the foregone consumption benefits as leisure (with $S_n = \bar{p}_n + t_n - \delta_n / \lambda$).[21] For this latter case the Samuelson condition in (10.25) is:

$$\sum \text{MRS} = (\bar{p}_n + t_n - \delta_n / \lambda) a_{nG} = q_n a_{nG}. \tag{10.26}$$

The welfare effects are illustrated in Figure 10.5. After the government increases output of good G it draws labour from leisure with a social cost equal to the foregone consumption benefits in (*a*). The public good is optimally supplied when this shadow

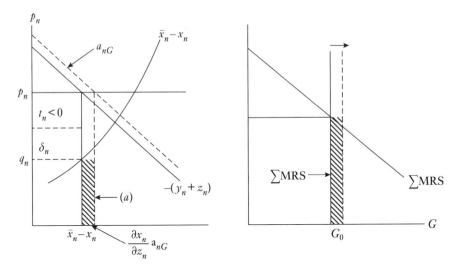

Figure 10.5 *The Samuelson condition with a minimum wage*

wage is equal to the summed marginal consumption benefits from the public good ($\sum$ MRS). There is no spending effect here because private demand for labour is unchanged by the project.

When the government balances its budget using the wage tax the social cost of the project is higher by the change in tax inefficiency on the revenue transfers, where the extra cost, is:

$$\text{meb}_n \left(\bar{p}_n + t_n \frac{\mathrm{d}x_n}{\mathrm{d}G} \right). \tag{10.27}$$

The revised Samuelson condition is obtained by adding this cost to the right-hand side of (10.26). Note that there is no excess burden on the summed consumption benefits from the extra public good or from relaxing the constraint multiplier because they have direct welfare effects on consumers.

10.3 DISTRIBUTIONAL EFFECTS

A number of studies look at the way distributional effects change the optimal supply of a pure public good. Stiglitz and Dasgupta, and Diamond and Mirrlees do so in a general equilibrium setting where the government raises revenue with distorting taxes. Slemrod and Yitzhaki (2001) obtain similar results using distributional characteristics in Boadway (1976) for the policy variables when producer prices are fixed. The Samuelson condition is now derived with distributional effects and variable producer prices.

A welfare equation with distributional effects is obtained using the approach demonstrated in Chapter 3, as:

$$\frac{dW}{\bar{\beta}} = DC_G \sum MRS\, dG + DC_p(\bar{x} + y - x)\, dp - DC_t(x - \bar{x})\, dt + dL,$$

(10.28)

where the distributional characteristics are:

$\bar{\beta} = \sum_h \beta^h g^h$ for lump-sum revenue transfers to consumers;

$DC_G = \dfrac{\sum_h \beta^h MRS^h}{\bar{\beta} \sum MRS}$ for extra output of the public good;

$DC_{p_i} = \dfrac{\sum_h \beta^h DE^h_{p_i}}{\bar{\beta}(\bar{x}_i - x_i + \rho^h_i y_i)}$ for a marginal increase in each producer price i; and,

$DC_{t_i} = \dfrac{\sum_h \beta^h DE^h_{t_i}}{\bar{\beta}(\bar{x}_i - x_i)}$ for a marginal increase in the tax on each good i.

The distributional effects from government transfer policy choices are summarized in $\bar{\beta}$, while those arising from extra output of the public good are determined by the marginal benefits each consumer receives. The remaining distributional effects result from price changes, where higher producer prices make net sellers better off (with $\bar{x}_i + \rho^h_i y_i - x_i > 0$), while higher taxes make net consumers worse off (with $x_i - \bar{x}_i > 0$). In the absence of public sector trade in private markets the revenue transfers are solved using the government budget constraint, with:

$$dL = dT - dR.$$

(10.29)

A conventional welfare equation with distributional effects and public production is obtained by substituting (10.2) into (10.28), as:

$$\frac{dW}{\bar{\beta}} = DC_G \sum MRS\, dG + (1 - DC_p)z\, dp$$

$$+ (1 - DC_t)(x - \bar{x})\, dt + p\, dz + t\, dx - dR.$$

(10.30)

Whenever consumers have the same welfare weights (with $\beta^h = \beta\ \forall_h$) we have $\bar{\beta} = \beta$ and $DC_G = DC_p = DC_t = 1$, where (10.30) collapses to the welfare equation without distributional effects in (10.3). Any transfers of private surplus resulting from endogenous price and tax changes must sum to zero. While the government cannot alter the pattern of consumption benefits from extra output of the public good it can affect the distribution of income through its transfer policy choice (in $\bar{\beta}$). Lindahl (1919) prices collect revenue from consumers to fund the cost of producing the public good, and they undo its marginal distributional effects. Indeed, they are personalized prices that are equal to the marginal consumption benefit each consumer gets from the public good. We examine the Lindahl prices later in Section 10.4. Before doing so, however, we derive the Samuelson condition with distributional effects when revenue is raised with lump-sum transfers and then distorting taxes.

10.3.1 The Samuelson Condition with Lump-sum Taxation

If the government balances its budget using lump-sum transfers the public good will be optimally supplied when:

$$\bar{\pi}_G^S = \bar{S}_G - \bar{S}_R \, \text{MRT} = 0, \tag{10.31}$$

where $\bar{S}_G$ and $\bar{S}_R$ are, respectively, the shadow prices of the public good and government revenue with distributional effects. They are obtained using the welfare equation in (10.30), where for the public good G, we have:

$$\bar{S}_G = \text{DC}_G \sum \text{MRS} + \frac{\partial T}{\partial G} + (1 - \text{DC}_p)z\frac{\partial p}{\partial G}, \tag{10.32}$$

and for the shadow value of government revenue:

$$\bar{S}_R = 1 - \frac{\partial T}{\partial R} - (1 - \text{DC}_p)z\frac{\partial p}{\partial R}. \tag{10.33}$$

The Samuelson condition with distributional effects is obtained by using these shadow prices to rewrite the shadow profit in (10.31), where:

$$\text{DC}_G \sum \text{MRS} = \text{MRT} - \frac{dT}{dG} - (1 - \text{DC}_p)z\frac{dp}{dR}, \tag{10.34}$$

with: $dp/dG = \text{MRT}(\partial p/\partial R) + (\partial p/\partial G)$—being the aggregated changes in producer prices; $dT/dG = \text{MRT}(\partial T/\partial R) + (\partial T/\partial G)$—the spending effect.

Clearly, the distributional effects and the resulting price changes can alter the optimal supply of the public good. Whether it is higher or lower will depend on the marginal benefits consumers get and how they are affected by the price changes. If low income consumers benefit most from the public good their larger distributional weights will make DC_G bigger. However, the distributional effects from the price changes are less certain without knowing the shareholdings of consumers and their net demands for private goods. Also, prices may rise or fall. Indeed, the distributional effects from the price changes could offset the distributional effects from the extra supply of the good, but it is equally plausible that they could augment them. The computational task is much simpler when producer prices are fixed, which is the case in economies with linear aggregate production frontiers, because the distributional effects are confined to those arising from extra output of the public good and the pattern of revenue transfers. This reinforces the important role the transfer policy choices play in project evaluation, especially when governments make lump-sum transfers, as is the case in a conventional Harberger analysis. Even when consumers are assigned the same welfare weights, the equilibrium outcomes are determined by their transfer shares when they have different marginal propensities to consume income.

10.3.2 The Samuelson Condition with Distorting Taxation

There is considerable interest in finding the optimal supply of public goods when governments raise revenue with distorting taxes. After all, that is what generally happens in practice. Ballard and Fullerton provide an excellent summary of the literature for the single consumer economy where distributional effects play no role in determining the optimal supply of the public good.[22] Gaube (2000), Pirttila and Tuomala (2001), Sandmo (1998), and Wildasin (1984) extend these results by including distributional effects. They do so for a range of different types of taxes, particularly with respect to income.

Welfare changes in the absence of lump-sum taxation are isolated using (10.28), with $dL = 0$. We assume the government balances its budget using the tax on labour (n), where the tax changes are solved using (10.2). When the public good is optimally supplied, we have:

$$(\bar{\pi}_G^S) = (\bar{S}_G) - (\bar{S}_R)\text{MRT} = 0, \tag{10.35}$$

where the revised shadow price of the public good, is:

$$(\bar{S}_G)_D = \text{DC}_G \sum \text{MRS} + \text{m}\bar{\text{c}}\text{f}_n \left(\frac{\partial T}{\partial G} + z\frac{\partial p}{\partial G} \right) - \text{DC}_p z \frac{\partial p}{\partial G},^{23} \tag{10.36}$$

and the revised shadow value of government revenue:

$$(\bar{S}_R)_D = \text{m}\bar{\text{c}}\text{f}_n \left(1 - \frac{\partial T}{\partial R} - z\frac{\partial p}{\partial R} \right) + \text{DC}_p z \frac{\partial p}{\partial R}. \tag{10.37}$$

A revised Samuelson condition with distributional effects is obtained by using these shadow prices to write the shadow profit in (10.35), as:

$$\text{DC}_G \sum \text{MRS} = \text{m}\bar{\text{c}}\text{f}_n \left(\text{MRT} - \frac{dT}{dG} - z\frac{dp}{dG} \right) + \text{DC}_p z \frac{dp}{dG}. \tag{10.38}$$

While this is a seemingly complex expression, the welfare changes are relatively straightforward to explain. On the left-hand side, the summed marginal consumption benefits are weighted by their distributional characteristics. These social benefits are higher when consumers with relatively low incomes and high distributional weights get more of the consumption benefits (with $\text{DC}_G > 1$). The first term on the right-hand side of (10.38) is the direct cost to private surplus of funding the budget deficit with the wage tax. Government spending rises by the input cost (MRT) less the spending effect and the increase in public profit when producer prices rise endogenously. Finally, the last term is the distributional effects from endogenous prices changes, and there are also distributional effects from the tax change inside the MCF. It is clear from (10.38) that considerable extra information is required to compute the distributional effects for the project, in particular, the shareholdings of each consumer and their net consumption demand for each good whose price changes. If the wage tax is non-distorting (with $\bar{\text{mcf}}_n = 1$) then (10.38) collapses to the revised Samuelson condition with distributional effects in (10.34), and if consumers are assigned the same distributional weights it collapses to the revised Samuelson condition in (10.15).

10.3.3 A Modified Measure of the MCF with Distributional Effects

Previously in Section 10.2.1 the revised Samuelson condition was rearranged using a modified measure of the MCF in Ballard and Fullerton, Snow and Warren, and Wildasin. By adopting their approach, the Samuelson condition in (10.38) can be rearranged, as:

$$\text{DC}_G \sum \text{MRS} = \bar{\text{mcf}}_n^* \cdot \text{MRT}, \tag{10.39}$$

where the modified MCF with distributional effects becomes:

$$\bar{\text{mcf}}_n^* = \bar{\text{mcf}}_n \left(1 - \frac{1}{\text{MRT}} \frac{dT}{dG} - \frac{z}{\text{MRT}} \frac{dp}{dG} \right) + \frac{\text{DC}_p}{\text{MRT}} z \frac{dp}{dG}. \tag{10.40}$$

If consumers have the same distributional weights this measure of the modified MCF collapses to the measure obtained previously in (10.17). Once again, it differs from the conventional MCF by including welfare effects attributable to extra output of the public good, which means it cannot be used to evaluate other public spending.

10.3.4 The Revised Samuelson Condition in Slemrod and Yitzhaki (2001)

Slemrod and Yitzhaki choose to rearrange the revised Samuelson condition in (10.38), with fixed producer prices, as:

$$\left(\frac{\sum_h \beta^h \text{MRS}^h}{\sum \text{MRS}} \right) \frac{\sum \text{MRS}}{\text{MRT} - (dT/dG)} = \left(\frac{\sum_h \beta^h (x_n^h - \bar{x}_n^h)}{x_n - \bar{x}_n} \right) \text{mcf}_n, \tag{10.41}$$

where the terms inside the brackets are their definitions of the distributional characteristics for the public good G and tax n, respectively. They also define the marginal efficiency benefit from the public good, as:

$$\text{mb}_G = \frac{\sum \text{MRS}}{\text{MRT} - (dT/dG)}.$$

It is the summed marginal consumption benefits per dollar change in government spending, which is consistent with the normalization for the conventional MCF. Thus, in the absence of distributional effects the public good is optimally supplied when $\text{mb}_G = \text{mcf}_n$. The distributional characteristics weight these efficiency effects, where $\text{mb}_G < \text{mcf}_n$ when low income consumers receive relatively more of the consumption benefits and bear less of the tax burden for the project. Clearly, the distributional effects from endogenous price changes in the last term of (10.38) can overturn this result.

10.4 LINDAHL PRICES

Prior to the work of Bergson (1938) and Samuelson (1954), who formalized social welfare functions, Lindahl looked at ways to distribute the tax burden imposed on consumers to fund government spending. One important goal was to levy *just* or *fair* taxes which would, at least in part, be based on the benefits each consumer receives from government spending. Lindahl prices for a pure public good reflect this philosophy. They are personalized prices that are set at the marginal consumption benefit each consumer gets from the public good when it is optimally supplied. Consumers make a payment (or pay a tax) equal to their Lindahl price times the quantity of the good supplied, but this fee plays no allocative role when the good is publicly provided. Instead, it divides the cost of supplying the good over consumers based on their marginal consumption benefits.[24]

Consider the simple example illustrated in Figure 10.6 of a pure public good that is consumed by two individuals A and B, and supplied at constant marginal production cost (MRT). Each consumer pays a Lindahl price equal to their marginal consumption benefit at the optimal supply G^*, with $q_G^A = \text{MRS}^A(G^*)$ and $q_G^B = \text{MRS}^B(G^*)$, where total revenue is equal to the cost of supplying the good, with: $(q_G^A + q_G^B)G^* = \text{MRT} \cdot G^*$.

In a general equilibrium setting there are additional welfare effects in the Lindahl prices (q_G^h). At a social optimum they are the compensating transfers that will hold consumer utilities constant, and are solved using the welfare equation in (10.1), as:

$$\frac{dW}{dG} = \sum_h \beta^h \left\{ \text{MRS}^h + (\bar{x}^h + \rho^h y - \bar{x}^h) \frac{dp}{dG} - q_G^h \right\} = 0, \qquad (10.42)$$

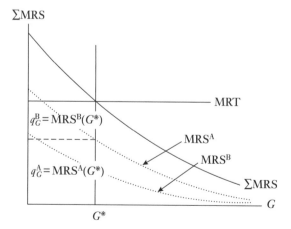

Figure 10.6 *Conventional Lindahl prices*

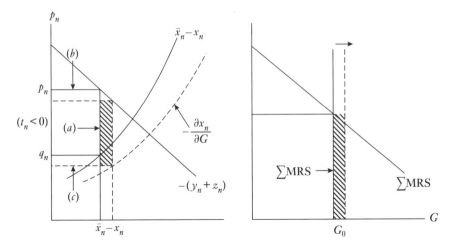

Figure 10.7 *Lindahl prices with welfare effects in related markets*

subject to the summed marginal contributions from consumers being equal to the marginal cost of supplying the public good, with:

$$\sum_h q_G^h + \frac{dT}{dG} - MRT + z\frac{dp}{dG} = 0. \tag{10.43}$$

For each consumer h, the Lindahl price is:

$$q_G^h = MRS^h + (\bar{x}^h + \rho^h y - x^h)\frac{dp}{dG}, \tag{10.44}$$

when: $\sum_h q_G^h = MRT - (dT/dG) - z(dp/dG)$.

With constant producer prices and no distortions in related markets, (10.44) collapses to the classic textbook Lindahl prices illustrated in Figure 10.7, with:

$$q_G^h = MRS^h, \tag{10.45}$$

when: $\sum_h q_G^h = MRT$.

For the more general analysis in (10.44) there are three amendments:

1. Endogenous prices changes transfer surplus between consumers, where higher prices make net consumers worse off (with $\bar{x}^h + \rho^h y - x^h < 0$), and net producers better off (with $\bar{x}^h + \rho^h y - x^h > 0$). Those who lose surplus pay lower Lindahl prices, while those who gain surplus pay higher Lindahl prices;
2. A positive spending effect from extra output of the public good (with $dT/dG > 0$) lowers the Lindahl prices for all consumers. It does this by expanding taxed activities, which reduces the amount of revenue the government needs to balance its budget; and,

3. An increase in public profit (with $z(dp/dG) > 0$) will lower the Lindahl prices for all consumers by generating extra revenue for the government budget.

Consider the example used in previous sections with a single wage tax on employment and no initial public sector demand for labour. The Lindahl prices are illustrated in Figure 10.7 when extra output of the public good increases labour supply that is, the spending effect is positive.

Consumers receive the consumption benefits in $\sum \text{MRS}$ and experience surplus transfers from the lower wage; suppliers of labour lose (c) while shareholders gain (b), with $(c) = (b)$. These transfers reduce the Lindahl prices for net labour suppliers and raise the Lindahl prices for net shareholders through the second term in (10.44). The positive spending effect in (a) reduces the Lindahl prices for all consumers, with $\sum_h q^h_G = \text{MRT} - (a)$.

10.5 CONCLUDING REMARKS

There is a large literature on the optimal provision of pure public goods. Some of it looks at the way government provision affects private supply, but this important issue was set to one side to focus on modifications to the Samuelson condition in a general equilibrium setting with distorting taxes. It is a popular application in public economics because it demonstrates the role of the MCF in project evaluation. At times it is difficult to reconcile results presented in the literature. For example, Ballard and Fullerton, and Atkinson and Stern argue the MCF can be less than unity, even in economies with a single distorting tax, thereby making the public good less costly to fund at the margin than a lump-sum tax. However, this appears to contradict the claim by Pigou that distorting taxes lower the optimal level of government spending.

These opposing views were reconciled in this chapter by using a conventional Harberger analysis to isolate all the welfare effects in the Samuelson condition. The following provides a summary of the main findings:

1. Ballard and Fullerton use a modified measure of the MCF that differs from the conventional Harberger measure. It includes a spending effect identified by Diamond and Mirrlees, and Stiglitz and Dasgupta that depends on the way government spending affects taxed activities. When it is positive the modified MCF can fall below the conventional measure. Indeed, the modified MCF can be less than unity when the conventional measure exceeds unity. This spending effect is not ignored in a conventional cost–benefit analysis. Rather, it is included in the welfare effects from the extra output of the public good, and not the welfare effects from the tax change. A number of empirical studies estimate the MCF for a range of different taxes. Some estimate the modified MCF and others the conventional Harberger measure. It is important for analysts to know which measure of the MCF is being estimated because the modified measure is project specific.

2. Atkinson and Stern examine the role of income effects in the conventional MCF. They identify circumstances where it can drive the MCF below unity, thereby making

the public good less costly to fund at the margin. The generalized Hatta decomposition was used to show the income effects are irrelevant to the optimal supply of a public good in single (aggregated) consumer economies. While the income effects from the tax change can lower the MCF below unity, which is the case when tax activities are inferior, they are offset by the income effects from extra output of the public good. At a social optimum there are no efficiency gains or losses from marginal increases in the public good and hence no income effects.

3. Lindahl prices distribute the cost of producing a public good across consumers on the basis of the marginal benefits they receive. They are affected by the spending effect identified by Diamond and Mirrlees, and Stiglitz and Dasgupta, and the distributional effects from endogenous price changes. When the public good expands taxed activities it will generate additional tax revenue that reduces the social cost of providing it. This lowers the Lindahl price for every consumer who benefits from extra output of the public good. The distributional effects from endogenous price changes will lower the Lindahl prices for consumers who lose private surplus and raises the Lindahl prices for those who gain surplus. In effect, Lindahl prices are compensating transfers for a marginal increase in the public good at the social optimum that undo any distributional effects.

NOTES

1. We define a pure public good as one that is perfectly non-rivalrous and non-excludable. Once supplied it can be consumed by every consumer, and there are no congestion costs. In practice, goods lie somewhere between being purely private, in that they are perfectly rivalrous and excludable, and purely public. The extreme case is adopted to illustrate the important difference between private and public goods.
2. Atkinson and Stern correctly observe the need to define a benchmark for determining the way distorting taxes affect the optimal supply of a public good. One benchmark is optimal supply in the absence of distorting taxes as a first-best solution. Another is optimal supply in the presence of distorting taxes when marginal output is funded from lump-sum taxation.
3. The spending effect is the combination of two conventional Harberger terms. This is formalized in the next section.
4. The estimates in these studies are summarized in Chapter 7.
5. This is the measure of the MCF used by Ballard and Fullerton (1992) when they obtain empirical estimates of the MCF for lump-sum taxes that are not unity.
6. It is possible for public output to completely crowd out private output in a Nash–Cournot equilibrium. This invariance result is demonstrated in Bergstrom, Blume and Varian (1986), Kirchsteiger and Puppe (1997) and Warr (1983). We rule it out by assuming the public sector is the sole provider of good G.
7. In Section 10.2.3 the analysis will be extended by making labour the sole input used to produce the public good.
8. The change in tax revenue is decomposed as:

$$\frac{\partial T}{\partial G} = \frac{\theta \sum MRS + (\partial \hat{T}/\partial G)}{1 - \theta},$$

where (10.9) is obtained by substituting this into (10.5). Detailed workings are provided in Appendix 14.
9. For the single wage tax, we have: $\theta = t_n \sum_j (\partial y_n(p)/\partial p_j)\alpha_j$, with:

$$\alpha_j = -\sum_i \delta_{ji} \frac{\partial x_i(q, I)}{\partial I}, \text{ and } |\delta_{ji}| = \left| \frac{\partial \hat{x}_i(q)}{\partial q_j} - \frac{\partial y_i(p)}{\partial p_j} \right|^{-1}.$$

10. This Samuelson condition is obtained by computing the compensated marginal shadow profit for the project, where:

$$\hat{\pi}_G^S = \hat{S}_G - \hat{S}_R \cdot \text{MRT} = 0,$$

with: $\hat{S}_R = 1$ and $\hat{S}_G = \sum \text{MRS} + (\partial \hat{T}/\partial G)$.

11. Using the welfare equation in (10.3), we have:

$$(S_G)_D = S_G + \text{meb}_n \frac{\partial L}{\partial G},$$

where the revenue transfer is solved using (10.2), with $z_i = 0\ \forall_i$, as $\partial L/\partial G = \partial T/\partial G$.

12. This obtained by writing the revised shadow value of government revenue in (10.14), as:

$$(S_R)_D = S_R + \text{meb}_n \frac{\partial L}{\partial R},$$

and then solving the (notional) lump-sum transfers using (10.2), with $z_i = 0\ \forall_i$, where:

$$\frac{\partial L}{\partial R} = 1 - \frac{\partial T}{\partial R}.$$

13. Wildasin uses the terminology *ordinary independents* to describe this special case, and considers *compensated independents* as a separate case.

14. This is solved using: $\text{mcf}_n = 1 + \text{meb}_n = 1 + [(c)/((d) - (c))]$.

15. A number of studies argue the conventional MCF for a lump-sum tax can differ from unity, but they are actually referring to the shadow value of government revenue. This is examined in detail in Section 7.5 of Chapter 7.

16. It is derived in equation (7.11).

17. Workings are provided in Appendix 15.

18. When (10.18) and (10.19) are substituted into (10.15), we have:

$$\sum \text{MRS} = \frac{1 - \theta}{1 - \theta + (t_n/(\bar{x}_n - x_n))((\partial \hat{x}_n(q, G))/\partial t_n)} \left(\frac{\text{MRT} - \theta \sum \text{MRS} - (\partial \hat{T}/\partial G)}{1 - \theta} \right),$$

where it is rearranged as the revised Samuelson condition in (10.20).

19. The aggregate change in tax revenue for the project is defined as:

$$\frac{dT}{dz_n} = \frac{\partial T}{\partial G} - \frac{\partial T}{\partial z_n} a_{nG},$$

and the aggregate change in public profit as:

$$z_n \frac{dp_n}{dz_n} = z_n \frac{\partial p_n}{\partial G} - z_n \frac{\partial p_n}{\partial z_n} a_{nG}.$$

20. By using the labour market clearing condition, $x_n = \bar{x}_n + y_n + z_n$, it is possible to write the shadow wage in (10.25), as:

$$\sum \text{MRS} = \bar{p}_n a_{nG} + \left(t_n - \frac{\delta_n}{\lambda} \right) \left(\frac{\partial y_n}{\partial z_n} + 1 \right) a_{nG} - t_n \frac{\partial y_n}{\partial G}.$$

Using the notation in Chapter 4 we write the aggregate change in leisure, as:

$$\frac{dx_n}{dG} = \frac{\partial x_n}{\partial z_n} a_{nG} + \frac{\partial x_n}{\partial G}.$$

21. This is the shadow wage illustrated in Figure 4.4.
22. Clearly, even when consumers have the same welfare weights, the distributional effects of the governments transfer policy choices will affect the final welfare changes when consumers have different marginal propensities to consume income.
23. The conventional MCF with distributional effects ($\text{m}\bar{\text{c}}\text{f}_n$) is defined in (7.22). For the wage tax it is:

$$\text{m}\bar{\text{c}}\text{f}_n = \frac{\text{DC}_{t_n}(x_n - \bar{x}_n) + \text{DC}_p z \partial p / \partial t_n}{\partial L / \partial t_n}.$$

24. When a public good is privately provided in a Nash–Cournot equilibrium it is optimally supplied if consumers pay Lindahl prices for their private contributions. The Lindahl price incorporates a subsidy that internalizes the external benefit from these private contributions. Roberts (1987) and Boadway, Pestieau and Wildasin (1989) show how the subsidies will support the full set of (Pareto) efficient allocations when they are funded from lump-sum taxes.

11

Problems

The following problems cover most of the important material covered in previous chapters of the book. Some of them are larger take-home assignments where welfare measures are derived in simple general equilibrium economies to provide hands-on experience of the formal analysis. They establish a general framework for developing economic intuition for applied welfare analysis.

CHAPTER 1

1. An individual consumes two goods x_1 and x_2 taking their respective prices, q_1 and q_2, as given. At initial prices $q^0 = \{q_1 = 2, q_2 = 4\}$ the individual consumes the bundle $x^0 = \{x_1 = 5, x_2 = 10\}$. Use the Laspeyres and Paasche quantity indexes to rank (P) the following bundles that are chosen when $q^1 = \{1, 4\}$ with the initial bundle x^0. Is $x^1 P x^0$ for $x^1 = \{6, 10\}$; $x^1 = \{10, 8\}$; $x^1 = \{25, 5\}$; $x^1 = \{6, 12\}$; $x^1 = \{15, 5\}$; $x^1 = \{18, 2\}$; and, $x^1 = \{2, 14\}$. Illustrate your answers in the following diagram, and provide explanations for the rankings.

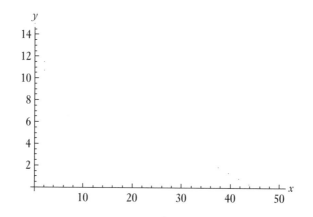

2. David consumes bread and wine from fixed money income. Use the Laspeyres and Paasche price indexes to compute the welfare loss for him when the price of bread rises from $1.00 to $1.20 per loaf, and his ordinary demand for bread falls from 20 to

15 loaves per month. (Let the price of wine be $1 per litre.) Compare these measures to the compensated welfare measures when bread is a normal good. Illustrate your answers in the bread–wine commodity space and the bread commodity–price space. (Repeat these comparisons when bread is inferior for David.) Use the diagram to show that bread must be inferior for $L_P = \text{EV}$.

3.   Consider the following price–quantity combinations for a single consumer who consumes the three goods x, y, and z. Derive the welfare change from the price increases in the markets for good x and good y using the price and quantity indexes. (Price p_x is raised first.) Compare these welfare measures when expenditure is held constant. How are they related when expenditure also changes?

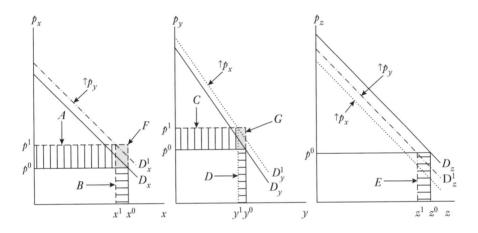

4.   Use the Samuelson criterion to show that:

(1) growth (1) is socially preferred (by the Samuelson criterion) to no growth (0) in a small open economy under free trade, that is, $1\text{SP}^{\text{SAM}}0$;
(2) free trade (1) is socially preferred (by the Samuelson criterion) to distorted trade (0) in a small economy; and
(3) trade restricted by (trade) taxes (1) is socially preferred (by the Samuelson criterion) to autarky (0).

5.   This question looks at aggregating compensated welfare effects when prices change endogenously. In a two-good two-person endowment economy use an Edgeworth box diagram to compute the sum of the compensating variations for a policy that moves the endowment of a good from one consumer to the other. (Do this for a non-linear contract curve, then repeat the exercise with a linear contract curve. Assume they trade in a competitive equilibrium where all trades occur at the market clearing prices set by a Walrasian auctioneer.) Illustrate the Boadway paradox and show how it can be avoided by allowing prices to change endogenously with the compensating transfers.

6. Derive the ordinary demand functions for the following utility function $U = \sqrt{X}\sqrt{Y}$.

1. Are these demand functions path independent, and is the utility function homogeneous? Derive the income elasticity of demand for each good.
2. Derive an expression for the marginal utility of income. Show that it is:

   (a) homogeneous of degree -1 in prices and money income; and
   (b) independent of the relative price ratio.

   Provide an explanation for these results.
3. Redo parts 1 and 2 above when $U = XY + X^2 Y^2$. Show that this utility function is a monotonic transformation of $U = \sqrt{X}\sqrt{Y}$.

7. Derive the ordinary demand functions for the following utility function $U = Y + \ln X$.

1. Are these demand functions path independent, and is the utility function homogeneous? Derive the income elasticity of demand for each good.
2. Derive an expression for the marginal utility of income. Show that it is:

   (a) homogeneous of degree -1 in prices and money income; and
   (b) independent of the relative price ratio.

   Provide an explanation for these results.

8. Consider a price-taking consumer who purchases quantities of the two goods x and y from initial money income of $1800 to maximize utility $u = \sqrt{x}\sqrt{y}$.

1. Derive the ordinary demand functions for the two goods and solve them for the dollar prices $p_x = 25$ and $p_y = 36$.
2. Use the compensating variation to obtain a measure of the inefficiency from a constant per unit tax on good x of $11.
3. Use the equivalent variation to obtain a measure of the inefficiency from the tax.
4. Compute the consumption bundle when the tax revenue is returned lump–sum to the consumer without any further compensation. Compare the tax revenue in this equilibrium to the revenue raised in parts 2 and 3 above.
5. Illustrate your answers to parts 2, 3, and 4 above in the x–y commodity space.
6. How would your answers above be changed when the two goods are perfect complements?

9. William consumes whiskey (w) and bread (b) as a price taker from fixed money income (m) to maximize utility $u = u(w, b)$. (Assume he has standard preferences.) Draw his budget constraint in the $\{b, w\}$ commodity space when he receives a 100% subsidy on each loaf of bread consumed up to (and including) $m/2p_b$ loaves. (He receives no subsidy on any additional loaves of bread consumed above $m/2p_b$, and the subsidy is independent of m.) Identify the inefficiency (in litres of whiskey) using the compensating variation when, prior to the subsidy, William consumes less than $m/2p_b$ loaves of bread. Now identify the inefficiency using the equivalent variation. Will he ever consume less than $m/2p_b$ loaves of bread in the presence of the subsidy?

10. Explain why the Hatta decomposition finds income effects from marginal policy changes are an independent scaling coefficient on any substitution effects. How does this decomposition relate to the Slutsky equation for a price change? What role does the Hatta decomposition play in conventional welfare analysis?

11. A number of analysts measure the marginal excess burden for a tax as the compensated change in tax inefficiency divided by the actual (uncompensated) change in government revenue. Illustrate this measure for a commodity tax in an economy with a single (aggregated) consumer and constant producer prices.

CHAPTER 2

12. Interpret the welfare change isolated by the compensated shadow price of a good. How is this gain related to the conventional shadow price which is a dollar measure of the change in social welfare?

13. Consider the relationship between the marginal utility of income and the shadow value of government revenue for a price-taking consumer when commodities are subject to tax. (Assume the economy has a linear production possibility frontier.)

14. This question uses the Hatta (1977) decomposition to separate the income and substitution effects for a marginal policy change. Constantine is a price-taking consumer who chooses two goods, x_1 and x_2, to maximize utility maximize $u = \sqrt{x_1}\sqrt{x_2}$ subject to the budget constraint

$$I = M + R = x_1 + (p + t)x_2,$$

where I is money income (measured in units of good 1, i.e., good 1 is numeraire), M is a fixed sum of money (in units of good 1), q is the relative consumer price of good 2 with $q = p + t$, t is the specific tax on good 2 (in units of good 1), and $R = tx_2$ is the tax revenue returned to her as a lump-sum transfer. (NB. She does not relate the lump-sum transfer directly to the tax she pays on good 2, that is, the tax distorts the relative price q.)

1. Derive expressions for Constantine's 'Bailey' demands for the two goods. These are her demands when the change in tax revenue affects her money income. Derive an expression for the welfare cost of marginally raising tax t. (Measure the change in utility in units of good 1.)
2. Compute the 'Bailey' demands in part 1 when $M = 100$, $p = 1$, and $t = 0.5$. Also, compute the welfare cost (in units of good 1) of marginally raising tax t.
3. Derive expressions for her 'Ordinary' demands for the two goods. These are her demands when the change in tax revenue does not affect her money income. Use this to derive an expression for change in the demand for good 2 when income is raised marginally. This is the income effect used in the Slutsky decomposition of a price change.

4. Derive expressions for her compensated demands for the two goods at initial utility u_0, and an expression for the compensated welfare cost (in units of good 1) of marginally raising tax t. Compute this welfare cost for $M = 100$, $p = 1$, and $t = 0.5$.

5. Use your answer in part 3 to compute the shadow value of government revenue (S_R), where

$$S_R = \frac{1}{1 - t(\partial x_2/\partial I)}.$$

6. Now use your answers in parts 2, 4, and 5 to confirm the Hatta decomposition, which says:

$$t\frac{\partial x_2}{\partial t} = S_R \cdot t\frac{\partial \hat{x}_2}{\partial q}.$$

Provide the economic intuition for this decomposition, and explain what the implications are for project evaluation.

15. Wooden bench seats are a non-traded good subject to a production tax (t). Six hundred seats are produced in the presence of this tax, where the producer price (p) is \$5 per seat, the own price elasticity of demand (η_{cq}) is -1.2, and the own-price elasticity of supply (η_{yp}) is 0.8. Use a partial equilibrium analysis to answer the following questions. (You should examine the relationship between the shadow and market prices in each question, and use a diagram to illustrate your answers. Set out detailed workings for your calculations.)

1. Calculate the shadow price (S) of wooden bench seats when the tax is a \$5 specific tax on each seat produced (i.e. $q = p + t$).
2. Recalculate the shadow price in part 1 for a 100% *ad valorem* tax on producers (i.e. $p(1 + t) = q$).
3. What is the shadow price of wooden bench seats when $\eta_{yp} = \infty$? Provide an intuitive explanation for your answer.
4. What is the shadow price of wooden bench seats when $\eta_{yp} = 0$? Once again, provide an intuitive explanation for your answer.

16. The shadow value of government revenue is the Hatta coefficient. It converts compensated shadow prices into dollar changes in utility. Consider a closed economy that produces two goods, X and Y, with a single price-taking consumer, who maximizes social welfare $W(X, Y)$, subject to:

$$E \equiv (p + t)X + Y = w\bar{N} + \pi_X + \pi_Y + L \equiv I,$$

where p is the relative price of X (with Y as numeraire), t a consumption tax, w the wage rate, $\pi_X = pF(N_X) - N_X$ profit from private production of good X, where $F(N_X)$ is a concave technology that uses labour input N_X, $\pi = H(N_Y) - wN_Y$ profit from private production of good Y, where $H(N_Y)$ is a concave technology that uses labour input N_Y, L is a lump-sum transfer from the government, and $\bar{N} = N_X + N_Y + N_G$ the fixed supply of labour, with N_G being public sector demand.

The government budget surplus is:

$$R = \pi_G + tX - L,$$

where $\pi_G = pG(N_G) - wN_G$ is profit from public production of good X, with $G(N_G)$ being a concave technology that uses labour input N_G.

Use this model to answer the following questions. (Assume government production, tax t, and labour demand N_G are exogenous variables. All markets are competitive.)

1. Derive a structural form expression for the compensated shadow price of good X.
2. Derive a structural form expression for the shadow value of government revenue.
3. Derive a structural form expression for the uncompensated shadow price of good X to verify the proposition by Sieper (1981) that:

$$S_G = S_R \hat{S}_G.$$

CHAPTER 3

17. Provide a summary of the implications of distributional weights for optimal commodity taxation, investment in projects, and marginal tax rates on personal income in the paper by Harberger (1978). How would you account for distributional considerations in cost–benefit analysis? (Refer also to the reference by Parish (1976).) How does the inability to make lump-sum transfers affect your answer?

18. Use a partial equilibrium analysis to identify the distributional effects from marginally increasing production quota in a competitive market when the government collects all the quota rent as sales revenue. Assume there are three separate groups—consumers, producers, and the government—where all individuals within each group have the same distributional weight. Consider circumstances where distributional effects offset the efficiency gains.

19. In your opinion, what role should distributional effects play in policy evaluation? Some argue distributional considerations should not be included in the evaluation of individual policy changes. Instead, they should be addressed as a separate issue. Critically evaluate this idea.

20. Summarize the basic needs approach in Harberger (1984) and compare it to the distributional weights approach.

21. When public policy redistributes income there are additional welfare effects to those obtained using a conventional Harberger analysis if consumers have different distributional weights. Consider a good X that is produced by a single-price monopolist. There is one price-taking consumer of the good and another single shareholder in the monopoly firm. (Assume initially there is no government production of good X and the marginal cost of private production increases over output. Ignore effects in related markets.)

1. Use a quantity–price diagram to illustrate the shadow price of good X when the consumer and shareholder have the same distributional weight. (Endow a unit of the good on the government who sells it and transfers the revenue to the consumer in a lump-sum.) Explain the difference between the shadow and market prices of the good.

2. Identify the areas in your diagram in part 1 where the distributional effects arise and isolate the shadow price when the consumer and shareholder have different distributional weights. Do so by writing down the distributional weighted welfare changes for the areas you isolate in the diagram and show that this shadow price collapses to the shadow price in part 1 above when the consumer and shareholder have the same welfare weight. Explain each component of the welfare changes and consider whether giving the consumer and shareholder an equal share of the surplus government revenue would lead to a Pareto improvement based solely on the welfare changes in the market for good X. (Use the distributional weights defined for an individualistic social welfare function. These are the weights defined for equation (1.23).

CHAPTER 4

22.   Wooden bench seats are a non-traded good subject to *production quota* that restricts output to 600 seats, where the producer price (p) is \$5 per seat, the own price elasticity of demand (η_{cq}) is -1.2, and the own-price elasticity of supply (η_{yp}) is 0.8. Use a partial equilibrium analysis to answer the following questions. (You should examine the relationship between the shadow and market prices in each question, and use a diagram to illustrate your answers. Set out detailed workings for your calculations.)

1. Calculate the shadow price of wooden bench seats when the production quota are not increased with project output.

2. Calculate the shadow price of wooden bench seats when the production quota are increased with project output.

23.   Explain how the answers to the previous question would change when there are taxes on inputs used to produce each seat. Assume there are two normal inputs, k and l, with respective (specific) taxes τ and θ. Derive an expression which captures the change in the shadow price derived in part 1. Would these taxes raise or lower the shadow prices you computed in question 22? How would the answers be changed when there are subsidies instead of taxes on the inputs?

24.   Show diagrammatically how you would derive the (compensated) shadow price of a commodity whose private production is undertaken by a *profit maximizing* *(single-price) monopolist.* Then consider the specific example of a monopolist facing the (compensated) demand curve $D = 400 - 0.2P$ (where D is demand and P the price of the good in cents) with total costs (also expressed in cents) equal to $C = 25,000 + 5y^2$.

1. Find the numerical value of the shadow price of the commodity for this case. Interpret the shadow price as a Harberger weighted average (i.e. identify the margins of adjustment to consumption and private production and the valuation of the good at these margins).
2. Confirm that the shadow price you obtain in part 1 measures the increase in the government budget surplus at constant utility, then compare this shadow price to the market price of the good and provide an intuitive explanation for the difference in these prices.
3. Rework your answer in part 1 when total cost is $C = 25,000 + 1000y$. Explain why the shadow price for this cost function is different to the shadow price obtained for the cost function in part 1.

25. In a cost–benefit analysis shadow prices of goods will, in general, differ from their corresponding market prices when there are distortions in markets. While taxes are the most widely examined distortions to economic activity, externalities are also important, particularly in economies where private property rights are poorly defined or are inadequately protected under law. In the following questions use a partial equilibrium analysis in quantity–price diagrams to illustrate the conventional shadow price of cement when production generates *a constant marginal external cost* (c) from polluting the air. (Assume cement is produced in a competitive market with increasing marginal production cost and is consumed by a large number of identical consumers.)

1. Illustrate the shadow price of cement for a public sector project when government production generates the same externality as private production. Carefully explain the welfare changes and compare the shadow and market prices.
2. Redo part 1 when government production is free of the external cost that arises from private production. Explain the welfare changes and compare this shadow price to the shadow price obtained in part 1.
3. Redo part 1 when there is a constant unit tax (t) on cement production that is half the size of the externality (with $c = 2t$). Once again, explain the welfare changes and compare this shadow price to the shadow price obtained in part 1.

26. Good k is produced by two firms in a Cournot duopoly. They face no threat of entry, and have the same constant marginal production cost of $30. Use a partial equilibrium analysis to compute the shadow price of the good when market demand is $D_k = 120 - p_k$. (There is no initial public production.) Compare this to the shadow price when the two firms form a cartel.

27. The *shadow wage* is derived here using the Harris and Todaro (1970) model with a minimum wage, differential employment costs and taxes. Lakeland is a large island economy with a fixed supply of labour ($\bar{N}$) which is employed by competitive firms who produce coal (C) and mangoes (M). Labour is homogenous and perfectly mobile between both sectors of production. (Assume all markets are competitive and consumers are identical.)

1. Use the quantity–price diagram to isolate the conventional shadow wage of labour in each sector when there is a minimum wage paid to coal workers which holds it above the unrestricted market clearing wage. (Hint: The shadow wage is the social cost (measured in dollars) of an exogenous unit increase in the demand for labour by the government.) Compare the shadow and market wages in each sector and explain what the shadow wages measure. (Assume there are no distortions in other markets.)

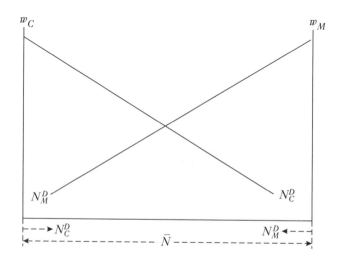

2. Now suppose coal producers are located inland where workers incur a constant marginal cost to utility (measured in dollars) per unit of labour supplied due to the hot and dusty conditions. This cost is not incurred by workers employed by mango producers who are located by the sea. Use a quantity–price diagram like the one above to isolate the conventional shadow wage in each sector (in the absence of the minimum wage). Compare the shadow and market wages in each sector and explain what the shadow wages measure. (Once again assume there are no distortions in any other markets.)

3. Would your answer in part 2 be changed if the differential employment cost was replaced by an equal size constant per unit tax on labour supplied to the coal sector?

28. A monopolist supplies electricity to two consumers with a constant marginal cost (MC) of 40 cents per unit. The linear demand schedules are illustrated below where income effects from any price changes will spill onto other goods. (Assume the

monopolist knows these demand schedules and faces no threat of entry. All the fixed costs are sunk.)

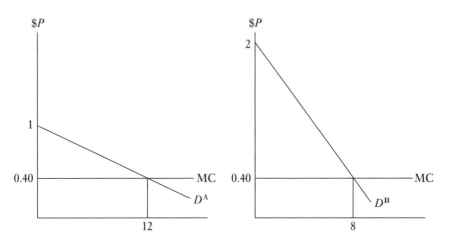

1. Solve the pricing policy that will maximize profit when the monopolist uses access fees and prices each unit of electricity traded. What are the efficiency and equity effects of this policy?
2. Solve the pricing policy when the monopolist is constrained to set uniform access fees and the same price per unit. (Assume the monopolist cannot set prices to exclude a consumer.) What are the efficiency and equity effects of this policy?

29. Pay TV services are provided by a single-price monopolist with no threat of entry. It sets a dollar price of $P = 800 - 2Q$, where Q is measured in hours, and has constant marginal cost of $300 per hour of service provided. Compute the shadow price of the service when the monopolist has a fixed cost of $31,250.

30. In some countries governments set *price caps (ceilings)* on selected commodities like bread, sugar, petrol, and rice and on services like rental accommodation. There is, however, the problem of excess demand at the capped price, where activity is constrained by supply in these markets.

Answer the following questions in a closed economy with a single (price-taking) consumer who purchases private goods X and Y to maximize $u(X, Y)$, subject to:

$p_X X + p_Y Y = \eta_X + \eta_Y + w(N_X + N_Y) + L$—consumer budget constraint;
$\eta_X = p_X F(N_X) - w N_X$—profit from private production of good X;
$\eta_Y = p_Y H(N_Y) - w N_Y$—profit from private production of good Y; and
$\bar{N} = N_X + N_Y$—fixed supply of labour.

Competitive private firms produce both goods using labour (N) that has diminishing marginal productivity (i.e. both goods are produced with increasing marginal costs). Consumer expenditure is funded from private profits (η), wage income on a fixed supply of labour ($\bar{N}$), and lump-sum transfers (L) from the government. (This makes the government budget surplus: $R = -L$.)

1. Use a price–quantity diagram to isolate the *compensated* welfare effects of introducing a binding price ceiling on good Y. Then introduce a consumption tax t on good X and isolate its welfare effects in the presence of the price ceiling. (Formal derivations of the welfare changes are not required.)
2. Derive a conventional welfare equation in the presence of the price ceiling and consumption tax in part 1. Use it to measure the *compensated* welfare effects from marginally raising the consumption tax. Illustrate the answer in price–quantity diagrams and provide economic intuition for the welfare changes.

31.   Welfare measures are obtained here in the presence of a *single-price monopolist.* Consider an economy with a single price-taking consumer who chooses consumption of good X and leisure (H), to maximize $u(X, H)$, subject to the budget constraint:

$$pX = \pi + wN + L,$$

where $\pi = pF(N) - wN$ is profit from private production of good X, w the wage rate per unit labour supply, N labour employed in the production of good X, L a lump-sum transfer from the government to the consumer, p the market price (in dollars) of good X, pX the private expenditure on good X, $F(N)$ the concave production technology the monopolist uses to produce good X, and $\bar{N} = N + H$ the time constraint.

1. Use a conventional welfare equation to derive an expression for the conventional shadow price of good X when it is produced by a single-price monopolist who maximizes profit. Identify the lump-sum transfers that isolate this shadow price. (Assume the government does not initially produce good X. Show your workings.)
2. Illustrate your answers to part 1 above in a quantity–price diagram and explain the economic intuition for the areas you identify. In particular, isolate the shadow price by areas over changes in activity.
3. Derive the conventional shadow price of good X when the consumer, as shareholder, votes on the firm's production choice. Compare this to the shadow price in part 1 above and explain the reasons for any difference.

CHAPTER 5

32.   Explain why fully traded goods in small countries have compensated shadow prices equal to their border prices when the official exchange rate is fixed. How does this shadow price change when the exchange rate is flexible? (Assume there are no quantity restrictions on internationally traded goods.)

33.   Explain the role the shadow exchange rate plays in policy evaluation. In particular, explain its role when the official exchange rate is the numeraire good. How do trade taxes affect the relationship between the shadow and the official exchange rates?

34. What is the value of the domestic resource cost ratio (DRCR) for traded goods when market prices are used to value the outputs and inputs in a competitive equilibrium? Explain what the DRCR measures when inputs and outputs are valued using shadow prices.

35. There are different welfare effects from extra output of imported goods when they are subject to *tariff and quota restrictions*. This question obtains the shadow prices of traded goods under these different distortions. Sundials are an importable good (under small country assumptions) with a compensated domestic demand schedule, $c = 1000 - 10q$, and a domestic supply schedule, $y = 15p$. Imports are restricted by (volume) quota to 200 sundials, with a per unit world price (in domestic currency) of $20. Use this information to answer the following questions. (Ignore any welfare effects in related markets, that is, use a partial equilibrium analysis.)

1. Calculate the shadow value of the quota (Q_k) on imports of sundials, when:

   – there are no taxes or subsidies;
   – there is a $5 tariff on each imported sundial; and
   – there is a $12 tariff on each imported sundial.

   (Derive expressions for these shadow prices and illustrate them in quantity–price diagrams. Explain each component of the shadow price.)
2. Calculate the shadow price of sundials, when:

   – there are no taxes or subsidies;
   – there is a $5 tariff on each imported sundial; and
   – there is a $12 tariff on each imported sundial.

(Once again, derive expressions for these shadow prices and illustrate them in quantity–price diagrams.)

36. The *Little and Mirrlees (1969) result* proves the ratio of the shadow prices of fully traded goods in small open economies is equal to the ratio of their border prices. Explain why this result holds and examine whether or not it requires a fixed official exchange rate. Show why in small open economies with fixed official exchange rates the ratio of the conventional shadow price of any fully traded good T to the conventional shadow price of any non-traded good N, is:

$$\frac{S_T}{S_N} = \frac{p_T^W}{\hat{S}_N},$$

where p_T^W is the border price of the fully traded good and $\hat{S}_N$ the compensated shadow price of the non-traded good. Why is the shadow value of foreign exchange irrelevant in this case? Is the shadow value of foreign exchange irrelevant when there is a floating exchange rate? Use your answers to explain what difference the choice of numeraire makes to welfare measures in project evaluation.

37. In project evaluation the *shadow exchange rate* can be used to compute the shadow prices of fully traded goods in a small open economy. Angara is a small open economy that exports 40 metric tons of rubber at a world price (measured in domestic currency) of $3/k, and imports 60,000 L of milk at a world price (measured in domestic currency) of $2/L. This trade takes place in the presence of taxes and subsidies; domestic rubber producers receive a subsidy of 60 cents/k, domestic rubber consumers a subsidy of 20 cents/k, and domestic milk consumers pay a tax of 20 cents/L. There are also a large number of non-traded goods in Angara whose prices are determined in competitive markets. (Assume there are no taxes or other distortions in any of these markets.)

1. Use diagrams to illustrate the equilibrium outcomes in the domestic markets for rubber and milk if domestic production of rubber is 60 metric tons and milk 160,000 L. Identify the consumer and producer prices in each market. (Assume marginal production cost increases over output in each market.)

2. Calculate the shadow price of foreign exchange by endowing US$1 on the economy. You discover that in the new full equilibrium this extra foreign exchange raises domestic milk production by $\frac{1}{2}$ kg, domestic rubber production by $\frac{2}{3}$ kg, and domestic rubber demand by 1 kg. The fixed official exchange rate converts one Angara dollar into 50 US cents. Use diagrams to illustrate and explain your calculation.

3. Use the shadow exchange rate you calculate in part 2 above to compute the conventional shadow price of the exportable good. Compare this to its compensated shadow price and explain why the two shadow prices differ.

38. Australis exports butter as a small country at the world price (p^w) of $20 per carton (measured in domestic currency). Domestic butter demand is determined by $Q_D = 75 - 1.2p$, while domestic supply is produced competitively with $Q_S = 4p$. Undertake a partial equilibrium analysis to answer the following questions. Illustrate your answers in price–quantity diagrams. (When doing so assume the official exchange rate is fixed and domestic consumers have the same distributional weights.)

1. Identify the free trade level of butter exports and compute a dollar measure of the welfare gains from international free trade. Explain the source of these gains.

2. The Australis Government introduces a *home-price consumption scheme* to raise butter exports. It does this by taxing domestic butter consumption to fund a subsidy to domestic butter producers. Find the per carton tax that will fund the largest per unit production subsidy and illustrate the welfare effects of the scheme. Compute the welfare cost of the scheme in dollars.

3. Isolate the conventional shadow price of butter as project output in the presence of the home-price consumption scheme. Consider if it makes any difference whether or not the extra project output receives the production subsidy. Explain the welfare changes and compare them to the world price of butter.

4. Isolate the conventional shadow price of butter as project input in the presence of the home-price consumption scheme. Consider if it makes any difference whether or not the extra project demand is subject to the consumption tax. Explain the welfare changes and compare them to the world price of butter. (Assume the tax rate does not change with the extra project demand.)

CHAPTER 6

39. Use a partial equilibrium analysis to compute the marginal excess burden of a 30 cents tax on each loaf of bread which is produced at constant marginal cost of $1.50 per loaf when demand (D) at each dollar price (P) per loaf, is $D = 10 - 2P$. (Assume there is a single (aggregated) consumer in the market for bread.)

40. Derive an expression for the compensated marginal excess burden of taxation. Explain what it measures and how it is used in policy evaluation. Compute the compensated marginal excess burden for the tax on bread in question 39 by assuming the demand schedule is unaffected by changes in income.

41. In this question the *revised shadow price* of a good is computed using a partial equilibrium analysis. When governments make revenue transfers with distorting taxes the revised welfare effects are obtained by adding changes in tax inefficiency to the conventional (lump-sum) welfare changes. Let the uncompensated demand for a non-traded good X be:

$$D_X = 2000 - 2(p_X + t_X),$$

where p_X is the producer price (in dollars), and t_X a specific consumption tax. Private supply of the good is:

$$S_X = 3p_X.$$

The government initially produces 400 units of this good, and the consumption tax is set at $100 per unit X.

1. Calculate the conventional uncompensated shadow price of good X. (Assume any related effects are confined to non-distorted markets.)
2. Derive an expression for the lump-sum transfers that arise from the extra unit of good X in part 1 above. Calculate the dollar value of these transfers, and use a quantity–price diagram to illustrate your answer to this question and your answer to part 1 above.
3. Now suppose it is not possible to make lump-sum transfers to balance the government budget. Instead, the transfers are made using the (specific) consumption tax on another non-traded good Y. The uncompensated demand for this good is:

$$D_Y = 3500 - 10(p_Y + t_Y),$$

and marginal production cost is constant at $200. Derive an expression for the cost to utility (measured in dollars) from marginally raising this tax, and calculate its value when the tax is initially $50 per unit. (Once again, assume there are no cross-price effects between the two goods X and Y.)
4. Derive an expression for the lump-sum transfers that arise from a marginal increase in the tax on good Y in part 3 above. Calculate the dollar value of these transfers, and use a quantity–price diagram to illustrate your answer to this question and your answer to part 3 above.

5. Obtain an expression for the revised shadow price of good X when the consumption tax on good Y is used to balance the government budget. Calculate the dollar value of this shadow price and use your previous diagrams to illustrate your answer. (Assume good X is the only good that the government produces.)

42. This question computes the *revised compensated shadow price* of a good. The conventional (lump-sum) shadow price is computed, then the change in tax inefficiency on the compensating transfers is added to it. Let the compensated demand for a non-traded good X be:

$$D_X = 2000 - 2(p_X + t_X),$$

where p_X is the producer price (in dollars), and t_X a specific consumption tax. Private supply of the good is:

$$S_X = 3p_X.$$

The government initially produces 400 units of the good (it is the only good it produces) and the consumption tax is set at $100 per unit X. All the welfare changes below are computed in the compensated equilibrium.

1. Calculate the conventional shadow price of good X. (Assume any related effects are confined to non-distorted markets.)
2. Derive an expression for the compensating transfers for the extra unit of good X in part 1 above. Calculate the dollar value of these transfers, and use a quantity–price diagram to illustrate your answer to this question and your answer to part 1 above.
3. Now suppose it is not possible to make these transfers in a lump-sum manner. Instead, they are made using the (specific) consumption tax on another non-traded good Y. The compensated demand for this good is:

$$D_Y = 3500 - 10(p_Y + t_Y),$$

and marginal production cost is constant at $200. Derive an expression for the marginal deadweight loss from this tax, and calculate its dollar value when the tax is initially $50 per unit. (Once again, assume there are no cross-price effects between the two goods X and Y.)
4. Derive an expression for the compensating transfers for a marginal increase in the tax on good Y in part 3 above. Calculate the dollar value of these transfers, and use a quantity–price diagram to illustrate your answer to this question and your answer to part 3 above.
5. Obtain an expression for the revised shadow price for good X when the consumption tax on good Y is used to make any compensating transfers. Calculate a dollar value for this shadow price and use diagrams to illustrate your answer.
6. Compute the shadow price in part 5 using the marginal cost of funds for t_Y. Illustrate your answer in the quantity–price diagrams.

43. Consider a small open economy that produces two fully traded goods, X and Y, using a fixed supply of labour $\bar{N}$ in competitive markets. Labour is perfectly mobile between the two sectors, where good X is produced by private firms using technology $F(N_X)$, and by the public sector using technology $G(N_G)$, while good Y is produced solely by private firms using technology $H(N_Y)$. They are strictly concave technologies (i.e. $F'' < 0$ and $H'' < 0$). There are a large number of identical price-taking consumers in the economy who maximize social welfare $W(X, Y)$, subject to the budget constraint:

$$E \equiv (p + t)X + Y = w\bar{N} + \pi_X + \pi_Y + L \equiv I,$$

where $\pi_X = pF - wN_X$ is the profit from private production of good X, $\pi_Y = H - wN_Y$ the profit from private production of good Y, and $\bar{N} = N_X + N_Y + N_G$ the endowment of time.

Good X is subject to a specific consumption tax and has a producer price p. Good Y is chosen as the numeraire and w is wage per unit of labour supply. The *government budget surplus* (in units of good Y) is:

$$R = \pi_G + tX - L,$$

where profit from public production of good X is: $\pi_G = pG - wN_G$. (When answering the following questions assume government production is exogenously determined, that is, the variable N_G is exogenous. Calculate the conventional welfare equation using the first-order conditions to the consumer and firm problems, and then totally differentiate it for the policy variables G, t, and $\bar{N}$.)

1. In the shadow pricing literature there is considerable interest in computing the shadow wage rates for labour, where in most economies, the labour market is segmented by minimum wages in one sector and not others. Compute the compensated shadow wage rate in the absence of minimum wage regulations (i.e. $d\bar{N}$). (Hint: Substitute the hours constraint into profit from producing good Y, where $\pi_Y = H(\bar{N} - N_X - N_G) - w(\bar{N} - N_X - N_G)$, and note $dN_G = 0$); illustrate the answer in the following diagram. Compare this to the uncompensated shadow wage rate.

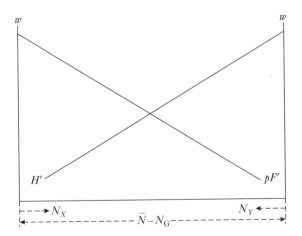

2. Suppose there is a minimum wage of $\bar{w}$ in sector X which is higher than the market clearing wage in its absence. Harberger argues that in these circumstances the binding minimum wage is the social opportunity cost of employing labour. Calculate the compensated shadow wage rate on the assumption that all the labour that leaves sector X as a result of the high minimum wage is absorbed in sector Y where the wage is flexible. Does this coincide with Harberger's shadow wage? Illustrate the answer in the following diagram. Compare this to the uncompensated shadow wage rate.

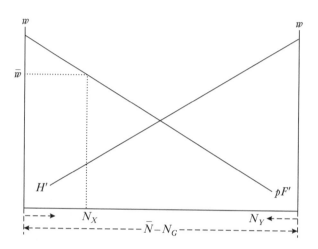

3. Now suppose the probabiity (π) of gaining employment in sector X at the minimum wage $\bar{w}$ is equal to those employed over the total workforce in that sector. This encourages workers to migrate from sector Y until the wage in that sector is driven up to the expected wage $(\pi\bar{w})$ in sector X, and creates a pool of unemployed workers (U_X), where the total labour supplied in sector X is equal to: $N_X + U_X + N_G$. (Total hours is now equal to: $\bar{N} = N_X + U_X + N_G + N_Y$.) Thus, the probability of obtaining work in sector X is:

$$\pi = \frac{N_X}{N_X + U_X} = \frac{N_X}{\bar{N} - N_G - N_Y}.$$

Calculate the compensated shadow wage rate (i.e. derive $d\hat{R}/d\bar{N}$). Illustrate your answer in the diagram below. Compare this to the uncompensated shadow wage rate. (This case is presented in Srinivasan and Bhagwati (1978: 109.)

CHAPTER 7

44. Derive an expression for the conventional marginal social cost of public funds (MCF). Explain how it is used in policy evaluation. Examine the relationship between

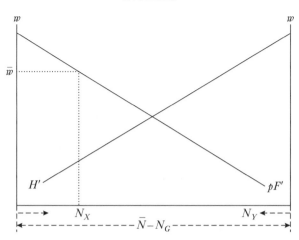

this conventional measure and the modified MCF in Ballard and Fullerton (1992), Mayshar (1990), and Snow and Warren (1996).

45. Explain why the conventional measure of the marginal social cost of public funds for a lump-sum tax must always be unity, even when it is computed in the presence of distorting taxes.

46. In project evaluation the shadow value of government revenue and the MCF play distinctly separate, but related roles. They are derived in this question and the relationship between them is formalized.

Answer the following questions in a closed economy with a single (price-taking) consumer who chooses private good X and leisure H, to maximize $u(X, H, G)$, subject to:

$X = \eta + (w - \tau)N + L$—consumer budget constraint;
$\eta = F(N) - wN$—private profits from production by competitive firms;
$R \equiv \tau N = C(G) + L$—government budget constraint; and
$\bar{N} = N + H$—time constraint.

The public good G is not privately supplied and the variables take the definitions used in Chapter 10. Derive the following welfare changes in full equilibrium, that is, where the government balances its budget and utility changes.

1. Obtain a conventional welfare equation and use it to derive the conventional Harberger measure of the MCF for a lump-sum tax. Explain what this MCF measures and how it is used in project evaluation.
2. Derive the shadow value of government revenue when the government balances its budget using lump-sum transfers. Explain what this shadow price measures and how it is used in project evaluation.
3. Use the answers in parts 1 and 2 to demonstrate the relationship between the shadow value of government revenue and the MCF.

CHAPTER 8

47. Examine the role of the shadow discount rate in policy evaluation. Consider circumstances where it will differ from the weighted average formula of Harberger (1969) and Sandmo and Dréze (1971). What are the arguments for making the shadow discount rate lower on public sector projects?

48. There is a single individual in a closed economy who consumes leisure H in the current period and good x in the second period to maximize utility $u(x, H)$. Consumption expenditure in the second period is funded by saving all wage income earned from supplying labour $(T - H)$ in the first period, with T being an endowment of time, where:

$$\frac{(p+t)x}{1+r-\tau} = (w - \tau)(T - H) + \pi + L,$$

where p is the price of good x in the second period, t a specific consumption tax on good x, r the market rate of interest, τ a specific tax on labour supply and saving, where the tax on labour is collected in the first period and the tax on saving in the second period, w the wage per unit of labour supplied, and $\pi = (py(N) - (1+r)wN)/(1+r-\tau)$ the present value of profit from producing good x, where $y(N) = x$ is a strictly concave production technology with N being labour demand. In effect, the firm borrows wN from the consumer in the first period to produce output of good x in the second period; and $L = (tx/(1+r-\tau)) + (\tau wN/(1+r-\tau)) + \tau(T - H)$ is a lump-sum transfer from the government budget.

Assume the consumer and firm are price takers, where r changes endogenously to equate borrowing and saving, price p to equate the demand and supply of good x, and w to equate the demand and supply of labour. Labour is essentially a capital good in this setting. By allocating time to employment the consumer is saving for future consumption of good x.

1. Derive a conventional welfare equation for exogenous changes in τ, t, T, and R. (Hint: You should substitute the transfer L directly into the consumer's budget constraint and cancel a number of the terms. Then totally differentiate the Lagrange function for the consumer problem using this aggregate budget constraint. Use the market clearing conditions and the first-order conditions for consumers and firms to eliminate a number of terms.)
2. Obtain an expression for the shadow value of government revenue. Explain why in general it differs from unity.
3. Derive an expression for the welfare loss from marginally raising the consumption tax (t) when it is the only tax. Repeat the exercise for the income tax on labour and saving (τ) when it is the only tax. Compare the marginal welfare loss for each tax when they are initially set at the same rate.
4. Compute the shadow price of capital (S_k) in the absence of the consumption tax and the tax on labour. Use this shadow price to isolate the shadow discount rate (S_r),

and then illustrate the welfare changes in a diagram to explain why it differs from the market rate of interest.

CHAPTER 9

49. Diamond and Mirrlees (1976) and Stiglitz and Dasgupta (1971) find that producer prices can be used as shadow prices in economies where taxes are Ramsey optimal and there is no private profit in consumer budget constraints. Illustrate this result in a price–quantity diagram by deriving the compensated shadow price of a good produced at constant marginal cost, then repeat the exercise for increasing marginal cost with a 100% profits tax. Do taxes need to be Ramsey optimal in both cases?

50. Explain the logic of the 'Ramsey Rule' of efficient commodity taxation. Define the marginal excess burden of a tax and show its relationship to the Ramsey Theorem that in an efficient tax system a (small) equi-proportional compensated increase in all tax wedges will reduce all tax bases by the same proportion. Finally, indicate the conditions under which uniform commodity taxation is Ramsey optimal and the circumstances under which the simple inverse elasticity rule, which says that each tax should be proportional to the reciprocal of a commodity's compensated elasticity of demand, applies. (Assume the producer prices stay constant.)

CHAPTER 10

51. The government is the sole supplier of defence which it funds with revenue from distorting taxes. If defence and taxed goods are ordinary independents the combined change in public production and taxes to fund it will leave taxed activities unchanged. Explain why the conventional measure of the marginal social cost of public funds (MCF) must exceed unity. (Assume the taxes are Ramsey optimal, or there is a single distorting tax in the economy.) Reconcile this with the finding in Ballard and Fullerton (1992) that the MCF is unity in these circumstances.

52. Examine the role of the revenue effect identified by Atkinson and Stern (1974) in the MCF. Consider circumstances where it drives the MCF below unity. Does the revenue effect have any impact on the revised Samuelson condition for the optimal supply of a public good?

53. How does the spending effect identified by Diamond and Mirrlees (1971) and Stiglitz and Dasgupta (1971) impact on the Samuelson condition for the optimal supply of a public good? Explain what it measures and consider how it is included in a conventional cost–benefit analysis for a marginal increase in the supply of a public good. Does the spending effect vanish when taxes are Ramsey optimal?

54. Consider an economy with a single (price-taking) consumer who maximizes $u(X, H, G)$, subject to the budget constraint on the consumption of good X (which is the numeraire good):

$$X = \pi + (w - \tau)(N_X + N_G) + L,$$

where $\pi = F(N_X) - wN_X$ is profit from private production of good X, $F(N_X)$ a concave production technology, w the wage paid to labour employed to produce good $X(N_X)$ and labour employed by the government (N_G) to produce a pure public good G, τ a specific tax on labour, and L a lump-sum transfer from the government.

Government expenditure is constrained by wage tax revenue, with $wN_G + L = \tau(N_X + N_G)$, and labour supply plus leisure (H) is constrained by a fixed endowment of time, with $\bar{N} = N_X + N_G + H$.

1. Use conventional shadow prices to obtain a Samuelson condition for the optimal provision of the public good.
2. Use the revised shadow prices to obtain a revised Samuelson condition for the optimal provision of the public good. Carefully explain why this condition differs from the one you obtained in part 1. Identify the factors that determine the amount of tax inefficiency that arises from the marginal increase in production of the public good.

55. This question derives the Samuelson condition for the optimal provision of a pure public good when it is funded from revenue raised with a distorting tax. Consider an economy with a single price-taking consumer who chooses a private good X and leisure H to maximize utility $u(X, H, G)$, where G is output of a pure public good supplied solely by the government. The private budget constraint (with good X chosen as numeraire) is:

$$X = (w - \tau)N + \pi - cN + L,$$

where N is the labour supply which is constrained by an endowment of time $\bar{N} = N + H$, w the relative wage per unit N, τ a constant tax per unit N, $c > 0$ a constant external cost per unit N (which is not internalized by employers), $\pi = F(N) - wN$ profit from private production of good X with $F(N)$ being a strictly concave production technology, and L a lump-sum transfer from the government.

Output of the public good G is produced by the government using good X as an input (with MRT $= \partial R/\partial G$) where the public sector budget constraint, is: $T = \tau N = R + L$.

1. Derive a conventional welfare equation for changes in the exogenous policy variables G, τ, and R, and then use it to obtain the Samuelson condition for the optimal supply of good G (with $c > \tau > 0$) when the government balances its budget using lump-sum transfers. What impact does the externality have on the optimal supply of the public good when extra output raises employment?
2. Compute an expression for the welfare loss from raising the tax on labour supply in the presence of the externality with $c > \tau > 0$. Use this to derive an expression for the MCFs for tax τ. What is the MCF when the tax is set to internalize the

externality, that is, a Pigouvian tax? Derive the MCF for a lump-sum tax in the presence of the externality. Is it the same as the conventional shadow value of government revenue when $\tau = c$?

3. Obtain a revised Samuelson condition in the presence of the externality (with $c > \tau > 0$). Explain how the optimal supply of the public good is affected, relative to the output obtained in part 1, when the distorting tax is used to balance the government budget. Identify the factors that determine the amount of tax inefficiency.

Appendix

1 DECOMPOSING THE CONVENTIONAL SHADOW PRICES

This section confirms the Sieper welfare decomposition in (2.12) by decomposing the actual and compensated shadow prices over endogenous changes in prices and income.

1.1 *Actual (Uncompensated) Shadow Prices*

The shadow price in (2.8) can be decomposed, as:

$$S_k = \frac{p_k + t_k + \sum_i t_i \sum_j (\partial y_i(p)/\partial p_j)\delta_{jk}}{1 - \theta},\tag{A.1}$$

with:

$$\theta = \sum_i t_i \sum_j \frac{\partial y_i(p)}{\partial p_j}\alpha_j.\tag{A.2}$$

Proof. Since private production is a function of market prices, we can write (2.8), as:

$$S_k = p_k + \frac{\partial T}{\partial z_k} = p_k + t_k + \sum_i t_i \sum_j \frac{\partial y_i(p)}{\partial p_j}\frac{\partial p_j}{\partial z_k}.\tag{A.3}$$

The relative price changes must satisfy the market clearing conditions for the N markets, and they are solved using the following system of equations:

$$\left|\frac{\partial x_i(q,I)}{\partial q_j} - \frac{\partial y_i(p)}{\partial p_j}\right|\left|\frac{\partial p_j}{\partial z_k}\right| + \left|\frac{\partial x_i(q,I)}{\partial I}\right|\frac{\partial I}{\partial z_k} = |\epsilon_i|,$$

with $\epsilon_k = 1$, and $\epsilon_i = 0 \; \forall_{i\neq k}$, where aggregate consumer income changes by:

$$\frac{\partial I}{\partial z_k} = \sum_j x_j \frac{\partial p_j}{\partial z_k} + S_k.^1$$

After substitution, the price changes, are:

$$\frac{\partial p_j}{\partial z_k} = \delta_{jk} + \alpha_j S_k \qquad \forall_j.^2\tag{A.4}$$

Equation (A.1) is obtained by using (A.4) to rewrite (A.3). $\qquad\qquad\square$

1.2 Compensated Shadow Prices

The compensated shadow price in (2.11) can be decomposed, as:

$$\hat{S}_k = p_k + t_k + \sum_i t_i \sum_j \frac{\partial y_i(p)}{\partial p_j} \delta_{jk}, \tag{A.5}$$

where δ_{jk} is the compensated price change for each good j.

Proof. In the compensated equilibrium the shadow price in (2.11) expands to:

$$\hat{S}_k = p_k + \frac{\partial \hat{T}}{\partial z_k} = p_k + t_k + \sum_i t_i \sum_j \frac{\partial y_i(p)}{\partial p_j} \frac{\partial \hat{p}_j}{\partial z_k}. \tag{A.6}$$

The equilibrium price changes will satisfy the N market clearing conditions, where:

$$\left| \frac{\partial \hat{x}_i(q, I)}{\partial q_j} - \frac{\partial y_i(p)}{\partial p_j} \right| \left| \frac{\partial \hat{p}_j}{\partial z_k} \right| = |\epsilon_i|,$$

with $\epsilon_k = 1$ and $\epsilon_i = 0 \; \forall_{i \neq k}$. For each good j, we therefore have:

$$\frac{\partial \hat{p}_j}{\partial z_k} = \delta_{jk}, \tag{A.7}$$

which is used to rewrite (A.6) as the shadow price in (A.5). The generalized Hatta decomposition in (2.12) is confirmed by multiplying this shadow price in (A.5) by the revised shadow value of government revenue in (2.14) to obtain the uncompensated shadow price in (A.1). □

2 DERIVING THE CONVENTIONAL WELFARE EQUATION WHEN THERE ARE EXTERNALITIES

After totally differentiating the private sector budget constraint, and using the first-order conditions for price-taking consumers and firms, the dollar change in social welfare becomes:

$$\frac{dW}{\beta} = -z \, dp - (y + z) \, dt - (1 - g_k) c_k (dy_k + \epsilon_k \, dz_k) + dL, \tag{A.8}$$

where $1 - g_k$ is the share of the externality that falls on the private sector. The net change in government revenue is determined by:

$$dR = dT + z \, dp + p \, dz - g_k c_k (dy_k + \epsilon_k \, dz_k) - dL. \tag{A.9}$$

We obtain the conventional welfare equation in (4.20) by solving the revenue transfers dL using (A.9), and substituting them into (A.8).

3 EFFECTIVE RATES OF PROTECTION AND DOMESTIC RESOURCE COST RATIOS

The relationship between the ERP (effective rate of protection) and the DRCR (domestic resource cost ratio) is obtained using the conventional shadow price in (5.6) and the price–tax relationships in (5.1) and (5.2) to write the shadow profit in (5.41), as:

$$
\pi_j^S = p_j^w + \tau_j - t_j + \frac{\partial T}{\partial z_j} - a_{mj}\left(p_m^w + \tau_m - t_m + \frac{\partial T}{\partial z_m}\right) - a_{kj}S_k - a_{nj}S_n.
$$

(A.10)

After rearranging terms, we have:

$$
\pi_j^S = (p_j^w - a_{mj}p_m^w) - p_m^w(a_{mj} - a_{mj}^*) - (t_j - a_{mj}t_m) + (\tau_j - a_{mj}\tau_m)
$$
$$
+ \left(\frac{\partial T}{\partial z_j} - a_{mj}\frac{\partial T}{\partial z_j}\right) - a_{kj}S_k - a_{nj}S_n,
$$

(A.11)

where:

$$
\pi_j^S = (p_j^w - a_{mj}p_m^w)\left\{1 + \frac{(\tau_j - a_{mj}\tau_m) - (t_j - a_{mj}t_m) - p_m^w(a_{mj} - a_{mj}^*)}{(p_j^w - a_{mj}p_m^w)}\right.
$$
$$
\left. - \frac{(a_{kj}S_k + a_{nj}S_n)S_e}{(p_j^{w*} - a_{mj}p_m^{w*})e}\right\} + \left(\frac{\partial T}{\partial z_j} - a_{mj}\frac{\partial T}{\partial z_j}\right).
$$

(A.12)

This becomes equation (5.44) by using the ERP$_j$ in (5.40) and the DRCR$_j$ in (5.43).

4 ACTUAL WELFARE CHANGES IN THE ABSENCE OF (HYPOTHETICAL) LUMP-SUM TRANSFERS

The revised shadow price of any good k in (6.1) is obtained using the conventional welfare equation in (2.7), as:

$$
(S_k)_D = \left(\frac{dW}{dz_k}\right)_D \frac{1}{\beta} = \frac{\partial W}{\partial z_k}\frac{1}{\beta} + \sum_i \frac{\partial W}{\partial t_i}\frac{1}{\beta}\left(\frac{dt_i}{dz_k}\right)_D.
$$

(A.13)

These are conventional Harberger terms isolated using (notional) lump-sum transfers to balance the government budget. The first term is the conventional shadow price of good k (S_k) while the second term in (6.1) is obtained by dividing and multiplying the last term in (A.13) by the revenue transfers from the tax changes ($\partial L/\partial t_i$) and using the marginal excess burden of taxation defined in (6.2).

It is also possible to derive this revised shadow price as direct changes in private surplus by ruling out lump-sum transfers to balance the government budget and relying instead on endogenous changes in distorting taxes, where dollar changes in utility are obtained using (2.5) with $dL = 0$, as:

$$\frac{dW_D}{\beta} = -z\, dp_D - (y + z)\, dt_D.$$

By using this welfare equation we can derive the revised shadow price, as:

$$(S_k)_D = \left(\frac{dW}{dz_k}\right)_D \frac{1}{\beta} = \left(\frac{\partial W}{\partial z_k}\right)_D \frac{1}{\beta} + \sum_i \left(\frac{\partial W}{\partial t_i}\right)_D \frac{1}{\beta} \left(\frac{dt_i}{dz_k}\right)_D.$$

The endogenous tax changes balance the government budget and are solved using (6.3). It is the same change in welfare as (A.13), which is confirmed by adding and subtracting the notional lump-sum transfers for good k $(\partial L/\partial z_k)$, where:

$$(S_k)_D = \left(\frac{\partial W}{\partial z_k}\right)_D \frac{1}{\beta} + \frac{\partial L}{\partial z_k} + \sum_i \left(\left(\frac{\partial W}{\partial t_j}\right)_D \frac{1}{\beta} - \frac{\partial L}{\partial t_i}\right)\left(\frac{dt_i}{dz_k}\right)_D.$$

This is the same welfare change as the shadow price in (A.13) because the Harberger terms are derived as:

$$\frac{\partial W}{\partial z_k}\frac{1}{\beta} = \left(\frac{\partial W}{\partial z_k}\right)_D \frac{1}{\beta} + \frac{\partial L}{\partial z_k} \quad \text{and} \quad \frac{\partial W}{\partial t_i}\frac{1}{\beta} = \left(\frac{\partial W}{\partial t_i}\right)_D \frac{1}{\beta} + \frac{\partial L}{\partial t_i}\ \forall_i.$$

5 COMPENSATED WELFARE CHANGES IN THE ABSENCE OF (HYPOTHETICAL) LUMP-SUM TRANSFERS

The compensated revised shadow price of any good k in (6.5) is obtained from the conventional welfare equation in (2.9), as:

$$(\hat{S}_k)_D = \left(\frac{d\hat{R}}{dz_k}\right)_D = \frac{\partial \hat{R}}{\partial z_k} + \sum_i \frac{\partial \hat{R}}{\partial t_i}\left(\frac{d\hat{t}_i}{dz_k}\right)_D. \tag{A.14}$$

These are conventional Harberger terms isolated using (notional) lump-sum to hold consumer utilities constant. The first term is the conventional shadow price of good k $(\hat{S}_k)$, while the second term in (6.5) is obtained by dividing and multiplying the last term in (A.14) by the compensating transfers for each tax $(\partial \hat{L}/\partial t_i)$, and using the marginal excess burden of taxation defined in (6.6).

This welfare change can also be obtained by measuring the direct changes in net government revenue when notional lump-sum transfers are ruled out (with $d\hat{L} = 0$), where:

$$d\hat{R}_D = d\hat{T}_D + z\, d\hat{p}_D + p\, d\hat{z}_D.$$

The revised compensated shadow price of good k becomes:

$$(\hat{S}_K)_D = \left(\frac{d\hat{R}}{dz_k}\right)_D = \left(\frac{\partial\hat{R}}{\partial z_k}\right)_D + \sum_i \left(\frac{\partial\hat{R}}{\partial t_i}\right)_D \left(\frac{d\hat{t}_i}{dz_k}\right)_D,$$

where the welfare changes are no longer conventional Harberger terms. Instead, they are direct changes in net government revenue. The compensating tax changes are solved using (6.7), and as confirmation this provides the same welfare change in (A.14), we subtract and add the notional lump-sum transfers for good k ($\partial L/\partial z_k$), where:

$$(\hat{S}_k)_D = \left(\frac{\partial\hat{R}}{\partial z_k}\right)_D - \frac{\partial\hat{L}}{\partial z_k} + \sum_i \left(\left(\frac{\partial\hat{R}}{\partial t_i}\right)_D - \frac{\partial\hat{L}}{\partial t_i}\right)\left(\frac{d\hat{t}_i}{dz_k}\right)_D.$$

The conventional welfare changes are derived as:

$$\frac{\partial\hat{R}}{\partial z_k} = \left(\frac{\partial\hat{R}}{\partial z_k}\right)_D - \frac{\partial\hat{L}}{\partial z_k} \qquad \text{and} \qquad \frac{\partial\hat{R}}{\partial t_i} = \left(\frac{\partial\hat{R}}{\partial t_i}\right)_D - \frac{\partial\hat{L}}{\partial t_i}\,\forall_i.$$

6 DECOMPOSING THE REVISED SHADOW PRICES

The generalized Hatta decomposition in (6.9) can be confirmed by decomposing the shadow prices as functions of prices and money income when taxes have the same marginal excess burden, with $meb_i = meb_d\,\forall_i$.

6.1 Conventional Shadow Prices

The revised shadow price of any good k in (6.4) becomes:

$$(S_k)_D = \left(\hat{S}_k + m\hat{e}b_d \sum_i z_i\delta_{ik}\right)(S_R)_D, \tag{A.15}$$

with:

$$(S_R)_D = \frac{1 + meb_d\left(1 + \sum_i \alpha_i z_i\right)}{1 - \theta}\,3. \tag{A.16}$$

Proof. By solving partial $\partial L/\partial z_k$ using (2.6), we can write the *revised shadow price* in (6.4), as:

$$(S_k)_D = S_k + meb_d\left(S_k + \sum_i z_i\frac{\partial p_i}{\partial z_k}\right), \tag{A.17}$$

where the price changes in (A.4), and the welfare decomposition in (2.12) and (2.14), makes this:

$$(S_k)_D = \hat{S}_k (S_R)_D + \text{meb}_d \sum_i z_i \delta_{ik}, \tag{A.18}$$

with:

$$\text{meb}_d = \frac{-\sum_i t_i \sum_j (\partial y_i(p)/\partial p_j)(\partial p_j/\partial t_d)}{\sum_i t_i \sum_j (\partial y_i(p)/\partial p_j)(\partial p_j/\partial t_d) + (y_d + z_d) + \sum_j z_j (\partial p_j/\partial t_d)}. \tag{A.19}$$

The price changes are solved using the goods market clearing conditions, as:

$$\frac{\partial p_j}{\partial t_d} = \alpha_j \sum_i t_i \frac{\partial y_i}{\partial t_d} - \sum_i \delta_{ji} \frac{\partial \hat{x}_i(q)}{\partial q_d} \qquad \forall j,^4 \tag{A.20}$$

where this allows us to write the marginal excess burden for tax d in (A.19), as:

$$\text{meb}_d = (S_R)_D \, \hat{\text{meb}}_d,^5 \tag{A.21}$$

with:

$$\hat{\text{meb}}_d = \frac{\sum_i t_i \sum_j (\partial y_i(p)/\partial p_j) \sum_i \delta_{ji}(\partial \hat{x}_i(q)/\partial q_d)}{(y_d + z_d) - \sum_i z_i \sum_j \delta_{ji}(\partial \hat{x}_i(q)/\partial q_d)}. \tag{A.22}$$

The revised shadow price in (A.15) is obtained by using the price changes in (A.20) and the welfare decomposition of the meb in (A.21) to rewrite (A.17). □

6.2 Compensated Shadow Prices

When taxes have the same marginal excess burden, with $\hat{\text{meb}}_i = \hat{\text{meb}}_d \,\forall_i$, the compensated shadow price in (6.8) can be decomposed as:

$$(\hat{S}_k)_D = \hat{S}_k + \hat{\text{meb}}_d \sum_i z_i \delta_{ik}. \tag{A.23}$$

Proof. By using (2.10) to solve the compensating transfers for extra output of good k we can write the revised shadow price in (6.8), as:

$$(\hat{S}_k)_D = \hat{S}_k + \hat{\text{meb}}_d \left(\hat{S}_k + \sum_i z_i \frac{\partial \hat{p}_i}{\partial z_k} \right). \tag{A.24}$$

The shadow price in (A.23) is obtained by using the compensated price changes in (A.7), and the welfare decomposition in (6.9) is confirmed by using the compensated shadow price for good k in (A.23) to rewrite its uncompensated shadow price in (A.15). □

7 DECOMPOSING THE MCF

Using the measure of the marginal excess burden in (A.19) and the price changes in (A.20), we can write the conventional MCF, as:

$$
\mathrm{mcf}_d = \left[\left(\frac{\sum_i \alpha_i z_i \sum_i t_i \sum_j (\partial y_i(p)/\partial p_j) \sum_i \delta_{ji}(\partial \hat{x}_i(q)/\partial q_d)}{1 - \theta} \right) \right.
$$

$$
\left. -(y_d + z_d) + \sum_i z_i \sum_j \delta_{ji} \frac{\partial \hat{x}_i(q)}{\partial q_d} \right]
$$

$$
\times \left[\left(1 + \sum_i \alpha_i z_i \right) \left(\frac{\sum_i t_i \sum_j (\partial y_i(p)/\partial p_j) \sum_i \delta_{ji}(\partial \hat{x}_i(q)/\partial q_d)}{1 - \theta} \right) \right.
$$

$$
\left. -(y_d + z_d) + \sum_i z_i \sum_j \delta_{ji} \frac{\partial \hat{x}_i(q)}{\partial q_d} \right]^{-1}. \tag{A.25}
$$

This collapses to the MCF in (7.9) when producer prices are constant and there is no public production.

8 PROJECT SHADOW PROFITS WITH PUBLIC PRODUCTION

In the presence of public production the revised shadow profit for the project in (7.13) is obtained using the revised shadow prices in (7.5), as:

$$
\left(\pi_k^S \right)_D = \mathrm{mcf}_d (S_k - S_R \mathrm{MRT}) + \mathrm{meb}_d z \frac{dp}{dz_k},
$$

where $z(dp/dz_k) = z(\partial p/\partial z_k) + z(\partial p/\partial R)\mathrm{MRT}$ is the total change in public profit due to endogenous price changes from the project. The second term is the tax inefficiency when the change in profit is transferred to the private economy with distorting tax d. Since this exactly offsets direct changes in private surplus, only the tax inefficiency from making these transfers will impact on social welfare. By using the generalized Hatta decomposition in (7.15) the revised shadow profit becomes:

$$
\left(\pi_k^S \right)_D = (S_R)_D ((\hat{S}_k)_D - \mathrm{MRT}),
$$

where $(\hat{\pi}_k^S)_D = (\hat{S}_k)_D - \mathrm{MRT}$ is the compensated revised shadow profit for the project. All the income effects are isolated in $(S_R)_D$.

9 THE MARGINAL SOCIAL COST OF DISTORTING TAXATION

The welfare loss from marginally raising tax m and using tax d to balance the government budget, is:

$$\left(\frac{dW}{dt_m}\right)_D \frac{1}{\beta} = \frac{\partial W}{\partial t_m} + \frac{\partial W}{\partial t_d}\left(\frac{dt_d}{dt_m}\right)_D.$$

The change in tax d solves:

$$\left(\frac{dL}{dt_m}\right)_D = \frac{\partial L}{\partial t_m} + \frac{\partial L}{\partial t_d}\left(\frac{dt_d}{dt_m}\right)_D = 0,$$

with: $dt_d/dt_m = -(\partial L/\partial t_m)/(\partial L/\partial t_d)$. After substitution we obtain the revised welfare change in (9.1).

10 THE RELATIONSHIP BETWEEN SHADOW AND PRODUCER PRICES

With a profit tax Φ the government budget constraint in (2.4) becomes:

$$R = t(y + z) + \Phi py + pz - L. \tag{A.26}$$

There is no change in the conventional welfare equation in (2.7) because revenue from the profit tax has been transferred back to the private sector as a lump-sum payment. The new transfer equation is obtained from (A.26), as:

$$dL = dT + \Phi y\,dp + py\,d\Phi + p\,dz + z\,dp. \tag{A.27}$$

The relationships between the revised shadow prices of goods and their corresponding producer and consumer prices is obtained by solving changes in activity using demand and supply responses, respectively.

By solving changes in activity over demand responses the marginal excess burden for the representative tax d in (9.2) becomes:

$$meb_d = \frac{-\sum_i t_i(\partial x_i/\partial t_d)}{\sum_i t_i(\partial x_i/\partial t_d) + (1-\Phi)y_d + \sum_j(z_j + \Phi y_j)(\partial q_j/\partial t_d)}.^6 \tag{A.28}$$

The change in tax revenue can be decomposed as:

$$\sum_i t_i\frac{\partial x_i}{\partial t_d} = \sum_i t_i \sum_j \frac{\partial x_i(q, I)}{\partial q_j}\frac{\partial q_j}{\partial t_d} + \sum_i t_i\frac{\partial x_i(q, I)}{\partial I}\frac{\partial I}{\partial t_d}, \tag{A.29}$$

where the income effect is:

$$\frac{\partial I}{\partial t_d} = \sum_i t_i \frac{\partial x_i}{\partial t_d} + \sum_j x_j \frac{\partial q_j}{\partial t_d}, \tag{A.30}$$

and the price changes are:

$$\frac{\partial q_j}{\partial t_d} = \alpha_j \sum_i t_i \frac{\partial x_i}{\partial t_d} - \sum_i \delta_{ji} \frac{\partial y_i(p)}{\partial p_d}] \qquad \forall_j.^7 \tag{A.31}$$

After rewriting the change in tax revenue in (A.29) using the income effect in (A.30) and the price changes in (A.31) the marginal excess burden in (A.28) becomes:

$$\text{meb}_d = \left\{ \frac{\sum_i t_i \sum_j (\partial \hat{x}_i(q)/\partial q_j) \sum_i \delta_{ji}(\partial y_i(p)/\partial p_d)}{(1-\Phi)y_d - \sum_j (z_j + \Phi y_j) \sum_i \delta_{ji}(\partial y_i(p)/\partial p_d)} \right\} (S_R)_D, \tag{A.32}$$

where the term inside the brackets is the compensated marginal excess burden for tax d which is also solved using demand-side responses. This can be rearranged as:

$$(1-\Phi)y_d\text{meb}_d = \sum_i t_i \sum_j \frac{\partial \hat{x}_i(q)}{\partial q_j}(S_R)_D \sum_i \delta_{ji}\frac{\partial y_i(p)}{\partial p_d}$$

$$+\text{meb}_d \sum_j (z_j + \Phi y_j) \sum_i \delta_{ji}\frac{\partial y_i(p)}{\partial p_d}. \tag{A.33}$$

By following the same approach we can decompose the revised shadow price of good k in (6.4), as:

$$(S_k)_D = \hat{S}_k(S_R)_D + \text{meb}_d \sum_j (z_j + \Phi y_j)\delta_{jk}, \tag{A.34}$$

where:

$$\hat{S}_k = p_k + \sum_i t_i \sum_j \frac{\partial \hat{x}_i(q)}{\partial q_j}\delta_{jk}. \tag{A.35}$$

After rearranging terms this becomes:

$$(S_k)_D - p_k(S_R)_D = \sum_i t_i \sum_j \frac{\partial \hat{x}_i(q)}{\partial q_j}\delta_{jk}(S_R)_D + \text{meb}_d \sum_j (z_j + \Phi y_j)\delta_{jk}. \tag{A.36}$$

By using (A.36) it is possible to write the welfare change in (A.33) as:

$$(1-\Phi)y_d\text{meb}_d = (S_R)_D \sum_i \{(\hat{S}_i)_D - p_i\}\frac{\partial y_i(p)}{\partial p_d}, \tag{A.37}$$

which is the welfare change in (9.9).

11 WHY SHADOW AND PRODUCER PRICES ARE EQUAL WHEN AGGREGATE MARGINAL COSTS ARE CONSTANT

From (6.8) the revised compensated shadow price of any good k, is:

$$(\hat{S}_k)_D = \hat{S}_k + \text{mêb}_d \frac{\partial \hat{L}}{\partial z_k}.$$

Since producer prices do not change endogenously in economies with linear production possibility frontiers there are no compensating transfers from extra output of good k, where the compensating transfers are solved using (2.10) as $\partial \hat{L}/\partial z_k = 0$. This means that the revised shadow price is equal to the conventional shadow price, with:

$$(\hat{S}_k)_D = \hat{S}_k = p_k + t_k + \sum_i t_i \frac{\partial \hat{y}_i}{\partial z_k}.^8$$

In constant cost economies, extra public output will crowd out the same private output, where the change in tax revenue becomes:

$$\sum_i t_i \frac{\partial \hat{y}_i}{\partial z_k} = -t_k.$$

On this basis the compensated shadow price of good k is equal to its producer price, with:

$$(\hat{S}_k)_D = \hat{S}_k = p_k.$$

12 THE RELATIONSHIP BETWEEN SHADOW AND PRODUCER PRICES WITH DISTRIBUTIONAL EFFECTS

In the presence of distributional effects and the profit tax Φ the revised welfare equation becomes:

$$\frac{dW_D}{\bar{\beta}} = -DC_p(z + \Phi y) \, dp - DC_t(y + z) \, dt, \tag{A.38}$$

where the change in the distorting tax(es) to balance the government solves:

$$dL = dT + \Phi y \, dp + py \, d\Phi + p \, dz + z \, dp. \tag{A.39}$$

By decomposing changes in activity using demand responses we can write the marginal social cost of public funds for tax d, as:

$$\text{mĉf}_d = 1 + \text{mēb}_d = \frac{DC_{t_d}(y_d + z_d) + DC_p z(\partial p/\partial t_d)}{\sum_i t_i (\partial x_i/\partial t_d) + (1 - \Phi y_d) + \sum_j (z_j + \Phi y_j)(\partial q_j/\partial t_d)}, \tag{A.40}$$

where the marginal excess burden with distributional effects in (9.23), is:

$$\mathrm{m\bar{e}b}_d = \left[-\sum_i t_i\left(\frac{\partial x_i}{\partial t_d}\right) - (1-\Phi)y_d\right]$$

$$\times \left[\sum_i t_i\left(\frac{\partial x_i}{\partial t_d}\right) + (1-\Phi y_d) + \sum_j (z_j + \Phi y_j)\left(\frac{\partial q_j}{\partial t_d}\right)\right]^{-1}$$

$$+ \left[\sum_i (\mathrm{DC}_{p_i}-1)(z_i+\Phi y_i)\left(\frac{\partial q_i}{\partial t_d}\right) + \mathrm{DC}_{t_d}(y_d + z_d) - \mathrm{DC}_{p_d}(z_d + \Phi y_d)\right]$$

$$\times \left[\sum_i t_i\left(\frac{\partial x_i}{\partial t_d}\right) + (1-\Phi y_d) + \sum_j (z_j + \Phi y_j)\left(\frac{\partial q_j}{\partial t_d}\right)\right]^{-1}. \tag{A.41}$$

The change in tax revenue in (A.41) solves:

$$\sum_i t_i \frac{\partial x_i}{\partial t_d} = \sum_i t_i \sum_j \frac{\partial x_i(q,I)}{\partial q_j}\frac{\partial q_j}{\partial t_d} + \sum_i t_i \frac{\partial x_i(q,I)}{\partial I}\frac{\partial I}{\partial t_d}, \tag{A.42}$$

with income effect:

$$\frac{\partial I}{\partial t_d} = \sum_i t_i \frac{\partial x_i}{\partial t_d} + \sum_j x_j \frac{\partial q_j}{\partial t_d}, \tag{A.43}$$

and price changes:

$$\frac{\partial q_j}{\partial t_d} = \alpha_j \sum_i t_i \frac{\partial x_i}{\partial t_d} - \sum_i \delta_{ji}\frac{\partial y_i(p)}{\partial p_d} \qquad \forall j. \tag{A.44}$$

By using (A.43) and (A.44) we can write (A.41), as:

$$\mathrm{m\bar{e}b}_d = \frac{\sum_i t_i \sum_j (\partial \hat{x}_i(q)/\partial q_j)\sum_i \delta_{ji}(\partial y_i(p)/\partial p_d)(\bar{S}_R)_D}{(1-\Phi)y_d}$$

$$+ \frac{\sum_j \left\{\mathrm{m\bar{c}f}_d(z_j + \Phi y_j) - \mathrm{DC}_{p_j}(z_j + \Phi y_j)\right\}\sum_i \delta_{ji}(\partial y_i(p)/\partial p_d)}{(1-\Phi)y_d}, \tag{A.45}$$

with:

$$(\bar{S}_R)_D = \frac{\sum_j \left\{[1 + \alpha_j(z_j + \Phi y_j)]\mathrm{m\bar{c}f}_d - \mathrm{DC}_{p_j}(z_j + \Phi y_j)\right\}}{1-\theta}. \tag{A.46}$$

By following the same approach we can decompose the revised shadow price of good k with distributional effects in (7.21), as:

$$(\bar{S}_k)_D = \hat{S}_k(\bar{S}_R)_D + \sum_j \left(\text{mcf}_d(z_j + \Phi y_j) - \text{DC}_{p_j}(z_i + \Phi y_j) \right) \delta_{jk}, \qquad \text{(A.47)}$$

where:

$$\hat{S}_k = p_k + \sum_i t_i \sum_j \frac{\partial \hat{x}_i(q)}{\partial q_j} \delta_{jk}. \qquad \text{(A.48)}$$

Using (A.47) and (A.48), we have:

$$(\bar{S}_k)_D - p_k(\bar{S}_R)_D = \sum_i t_i \sum_j \frac{\partial \hat{x}_i(q)}{\partial q_j} \delta_{jk}(\bar{S}_R)_D + \sum_j (\text{mc}\bar{f}_d(z_j + \Phi y_j) \delta_{jk}$$

$$- \text{DC}_{p_j}(z_j + \Phi y_j)) \delta_{jk}, \qquad \text{(A.49)}$$

where the welfare change in (A.45) becomes:

$$(1 - \Phi) y_d \, \bar{\text{meb}}_d = \sum_i \{ (\bar{S}_i)_D - (\bar{S}_R)_D p_i \} \frac{\partial y_i(p)}{\partial p_d}. \qquad \text{(A.50)}$$

By using the generalized Hatta decomposition in (7.24), with $(\bar{S}_i)_D = (\bar{S}_R)_D (\hat{S}_i)_D \; \forall i$, we obtain the welfare change in (9.23).

13 THE RELATIONSHIP BETWEEN SHADOW AND CONSUMER PRICES

When changes in activity are solved using supply responses the marginal excess burden for the representative tax d in (6.2), becomes:

$$\text{meb}_d = \frac{-\sum_i t_i(\partial y_i / \partial t_d)}{\sum_i t_i(\partial y_i / \partial t_d) + (y_d + z_d) + \sum_j (z_j + \Phi y_j)(\partial p_j / \partial t_d)}. \qquad \text{(A.51)}$$

The change in tax revenue can be decomposed as:

$$\sum_i t_i \frac{\partial y_i}{\partial t_d} = \sum_i t_i \sum_j \frac{\partial y_i(p)}{\partial p_j} \frac{\partial p_j}{\partial t_d}, \qquad \text{(A.52)}$$

where the price changes are:

$$\frac{\partial p_j}{\partial t_d} = \alpha_j \sum_i t_i \frac{\partial y_i}{\partial t_d} - \sum_i \delta_{ji} \frac{\partial \hat{x}_i(q)}{\partial q_d} \qquad \forall j. \qquad \text{(A.53)}$$

By using (A.52) and (A.53), we are able to write (A.51), as:

$$
\text{meb}_d = \left\{ \frac{\sum_i t_i \sum_j (\partial y_i(p)/\partial p_j) \sum_i \delta_{ji}(\partial \hat{x}_i(q)/\partial q_d)}{(y_d + z_d) - \sum_j (z_j + \Phi y_j) \sum_i \delta_{ji}(\partial \hat{x}_i(q)/\partial q_d)} \right\} (S_R)_D, \qquad (A.54)
$$

where the term inside the brackets is the compensated marginal excess burden for tax d solved using supply responses. This can be rearranged as:

$$
\text{meb}_d = \sum_i t_i \sum_j \frac{\partial y_i(p)}{\partial p_j} (S_R)_D \delta_{ji} \frac{\partial \hat{x}_i(q)}{\partial q_d} \frac{1}{y_d + z_d}
$$

$$
+ \text{meb}_d \sum_j (z_j + \Phi y_j) \sum_i \delta_{ji} \frac{\partial \hat{x}_i(q)}{\partial q_d} \frac{1}{y_d + z_d}. \qquad (A.55)
$$

We can decompose the compensated shadow price of good k in (A.34) by following the same approach, as:

$$
\hat{S}_k = q_k + \sum_i t_i \sum_j \frac{\partial y_i(p)}{\partial p_j} \delta_{jk}, \qquad (A.56)
$$

where:

$$
(S_k)_D - q_k(S_R)_D = \sum_i t_i \sum_j \frac{\partial y_i(p)}{\partial p_j} \delta_{jk}(S_R)_D + \text{meb}_d \sum_j (z_j + \Phi y_j) \delta_{jk}. \qquad (A.57)
$$

Using (A.57) allows us to write the welfare change in (A.55), as:

$$
\text{meb}_d = (S_R)_D \sum_i \left\{ (\hat{S}_i)_D - q_i \right\} \frac{\partial \hat{x}_i(q)}{\partial q_d} \frac{1}{y_d + z_d}. \qquad (A.58)
$$

The welfare change in (9.27) is obtained using the market clearing condition $y_d + z_d = x_d - \bar{x}_d$.

Distributional Effects are included by using the conventional welfare equation in (3.4) with $dL = 0$ and including the profit tax Φ to write the marginal excess burden for the representative tax d, as:

$$
\bar{\text{meb}}_d =
$$

$$
\left[-\sum_i t_i \left(\frac{\partial y_i}{\partial t_d} \right) + \sum_i (\text{DC}_{p_i} - 1) (z_i + \Phi y_i) \left(\frac{\partial p_i}{\partial t_d} \right) + (\text{DC}_{t_d} - 1) (y_d + z_d) \right]
$$

$$
\times \left[\sum_i t_i \left(\frac{\partial y_i}{\partial t_d} \right) + (z_d + y_d) + \sum_j (z_j + \Phi y_j) \left(\frac{\partial q_j}{\partial t_d} \right) \right]^{-1} {}^{.10} \qquad (A.59)
$$

The change in tax revenue in (A.59) becomes:

$$\sum_i t_i \frac{\partial y_i}{\partial t_d} = \sum_i t_i \sum_j \frac{\partial y_i(p)}{\partial p_j} \frac{\partial p_j}{\partial t_d}, \tag{A.60}$$

where the price changes are:

$$\frac{\partial p_j}{\partial t_d} = \alpha_j \sum_i t_i \frac{\partial y_i}{\partial t_d} - \sum_i \delta_{ji} \frac{\partial \hat{x}_i(q)}{\partial q_d} \qquad \forall j. \tag{A.61}$$

By using (A.60) and (A.61) the welfare change in (A.59) expands as:

$$\bar{\mathrm{meb}}_d = (\mathrm{DC}_{t_d} - 1) + \sum_i t_i \sum_j \frac{\partial y_i(p)}{\partial q_j} \sum_i \delta_{ji} \frac{\partial \hat{x}_i(q)}{\partial q_d} \frac{1}{x_d - \bar{x}_d}(\bar{S}_R)_{\mathrm{D}}$$

$$+ \sum_j \{\bar{\mathrm{mcf}}_d(z_j + \Phi y_j) - \mathrm{DC}_{p_j}(z_j + \Phi y_j)\} \sum_i \delta_{ji} \frac{\partial \hat{x}_i(q)}{\partial q_d}. \tag{A.62}$$

The revised shadow price of good k can be decomposed using the same approach, as:

$$(\bar{S}_k)_{\mathrm{D}} = \hat{S}_k(\bar{S}_R)_{\mathrm{D}} + \sum_j (\bar{\mathrm{mcf}}_d(z_j + \Phi y_j) - \mathrm{DC}_{p_j}(z_j + \Phi y_j))\delta_{jk}, \tag{A.63}$$

where:

$$\hat{S}_k = p_k + \sum_i t_i \sum_j \frac{\partial \hat{x}_i(q)}{\partial q_j}\delta_{jk}. \tag{A.64}$$

This allows us to write the revised shadow price with distributional effects in (A.63), as:

$$(\bar{S}_k)_{\mathrm{D}} - q_k(\bar{S}_R)_{\mathrm{D}} = \sum_i t_i \sum_j \frac{\partial y_i(p)}{\partial p_j}\delta_{jk}(\bar{S}_R)_{\mathrm{D}}$$

$$+ \sum_j (\bar{\mathrm{mcf}}_d(z_j + \Phi y_j) - \mathrm{DC}_{p_j}(z_j + \Phi y_j))\delta_{jk}. \tag{A.65}$$

By using (A.65), the welfare change in (A.62) becomes:

$$\bar{\mathrm{med}}_d = (\mathrm{DC}_{t_d} - 1) + \sum_i \{(\bar{S}_i)_{\mathrm{D}} - q_i(\bar{S}_R)_{\mathrm{D}}\}\frac{\partial \hat{x}_i(q)}{\partial q_d} \frac{1}{x_d - \bar{x}_d}. \tag{A.66}$$

This extends the welfare decomposition of the marginal excess burden of taxation in (9.28) by including distributional effects.

14 DECOMPOSING THE SAMUELSON CONDITION

The change in tax revenue in the shadow price of the public good in (10.5) can be decomposed, as:

$$\frac{\partial T}{\partial G} = \sum_i t_i \sum_j \frac{\partial y_i(p)}{\partial p_j} \frac{\partial p_j}{\partial G}, \tag{A.67}$$

where the price changes are solved using the market clearing conditions for the private goods markets, as:

$$\frac{\partial q_j}{\partial G} = \alpha_j \frac{\partial T}{\partial G} - \sum_i \delta_{ji} \frac{\partial x_i(q, I, G)}{\partial G} \qquad \forall_j.^{11} \tag{A.68}$$

By using (A.68) the change in tax revenue in (A.67) becomes:

$$\frac{\partial T}{\partial G} = \frac{\sum_i t_i \sum_j (\partial y_i(p)/\partial p_j) \sum_i \delta_{ji}(\partial x_i(q, I, G)/\partial G)}{1 - \theta}, \tag{A.69}$$

with: $\theta = \sum_i t_i \sum_j (\partial y_i(p)/\partial p_j)\alpha_j$ and $\alpha_j = -\sum_i \delta_{ji}(\partial x_i(q, I, G)/\partial I)$.
Using the Slutsky decomposition, we have:

$$\frac{\partial x_i(q, I, G)}{\partial G} = \frac{\partial \hat{x}_i(q, G)}{\partial G} - \frac{\partial x_i(q, I, G)}{\partial I} \frac{\partial I(q, I, G)}{\partial G}, \tag{A.70}$$

with: $(\partial I(q, I, G)/\partial G) = -\sum \text{MRS}$, where this makes the change in tax revenue in (A.69):

$$\frac{\partial T}{\partial G} = \frac{\sum_i t_i \sum_j (\partial y_i(p)/\partial p_j) \sum_i \delta_{ji} \left(\partial \hat{x}_i(q, G)/\partial G + (\partial x_i(q, I, G)/\partial I) \sum \text{MRS} \right)}{1 - \theta}. \tag{A.71}$$

After substituting (A.71) into (10.5) we obtain the welfare decomposition in (10.9).

15 DECOMPOSING THE REVISED SAMUELSON CONDITION

The spending effect is defined in (10.8) as the total change in tax revenue for the project, with:

$$\frac{dT}{dG} = \frac{\partial T}{\partial G} + \frac{\partial T}{\partial R}\text{MRT}. \tag{A.72}$$

From (A.71), we have:

$$\frac{\partial T}{\partial G} = \frac{\theta \sum \text{MRS} + (\partial \hat{T}/\partial G)}{1 - \theta}, \tag{A.73}$$

and using the decomposition in (2.14), we have:

$$\frac{\partial T}{\partial R} = \frac{-\theta}{1-\theta}.$$
(A.74)

After substituting (A.73) and (A.74) into (A.72) we obtain the welfare decomposition for the spending effect in (10.19).

NOTES

1. In general equilibrium aggregate consumer income is:

$$I = q\bar{x} + py + T + pz = px + tx.$$

2. This is obtained using the Slutsky decomposition, where δ_{ji} is defined in Chapter 2 as the element of matrix:: $|\delta_{ji}| = |\partial \hat{x}_i(q)/\partial q_j - \partial y_i(p)/\partial p_j|^{-1}$, and $\alpha_i = -\sum_j \delta_{ij}(\partial x_i(q, I)/\partial I)$.

3. Using (2.6) to solve the lump-sum transfers allows us to write the shadow value of government revenue in (6.10), as:

$$(S_R)_D = S_R(1 + meb_d) - meb_d \sum_i z_i \frac{\partial p_i}{\partial R},$$

where: $\partial p_i/\partial R = -\alpha_i S_R$. The revised shadow value of government revenue in (A.16) is obtained using the welfare decomposition in (2.14).

4. These price changes are solved using the approach employed in the Appendix 1 where the change in income is:

$$\frac{\partial I}{\partial t_d} = \sum_j x_j \frac{\partial p_d}{\partial t_d} + \frac{\partial T}{\partial t_d}.$$

5. Using the price changes in (A.20) allows us to write (A.19) as:

$$meb_d = \left[\frac{\sum_i t_i \sum_j (\partial y_i(p)/\partial p_j) \sum_i \delta_{ji}(\partial \hat{x}_i(q)/\partial q_d)}{1-\theta}\right]$$

$$\times \left[-\left(1 + \sum_i \alpha_i z_i\right)\left(\frac{\sum_i t_i \sum_j (\partial y_i(p)/\partial p_j) \sum_i \delta_{ji}(\partial \hat{x}_i(q)/\partial q_d)}{1-\theta}\right)\right.$$

$$\left. +(y_d + z_d) - \sum_i z_i \sum_j \delta_{ji}\left(\frac{\partial \hat{x}_i(q)}{\partial q_d}\right)\right]^{-1}.$$

The decomposition in (A.21) is obtained by using the revised shadow value of government revenue in (A.16).

6. We use the conventional welfare equation in (2.7) and the transfer equation in (A.27) to solve the marginal excess burden for tax d in (9.2). Also, from the market clearing conditions we have:

$$\sum_i t_i \frac{\partial y_i}{\partial t_d} = \sum_i t_i \frac{\partial x_i}{\partial t_d}.$$

7. The price changes are solved using the market clearing conditions, and this is demonstrated in the Appendix 1. We also use the price–tax relationships in (2.3), where:

$$\frac{\partial q_d}{\partial t_d} = \frac{\partial p_d}{\partial t_d} + 1 \quad \text{and} \quad \frac{\partial q_j}{\partial t_d} = \frac{\partial p_j}{\partial t_d} \qquad \forall_{j \neq d}.$$

8. With constant marginal production cost, we have: $\partial \hat{y}_k / \partial z_k = -1$ and $\partial \hat{y}_i / \partial z_k = 0 \ \forall_{i \neq k}$.
9. When consumers have the same distributional weights this collapses to the marginal excess burden in (A.28).
10. When consumers have the same distributional weights this collapses to the marginal excess burden in (A.51).
11. The price changes are solved using the approach demonstrated in the Appendix 1 and using the income effects obtained from the economy's budget constraint, as:

$$\frac{\partial I}{\partial G} = \frac{\partial T}{\partial G} + \sum_j x_j \frac{\partial q_j}{\partial G}.$$

Bibliography

Ahmad, E. and N. Stern (1984), 'The Theory of Reform and Indian Indirect Taxes', *Journal of Public Economics* 25(3): 259–98.

Arrow, K. J. (1950), 'A Difficulty in the Concept of Social Welfare', *Journal of Political Economy* 58: 328–46.

—— (1951), *Social Choice and Individual Values*, Wiley, New York.

—— and R. C. Lind (1970), 'Uncertainty and the Evaluation of Public Investment Decisions', *American Economic Review* 60: 364–78.

Atkinson, A. B. (1973), 'How Progressive Should the Income Tax Be?', in *Essays on Modern Economics*, edited by M. Parkin, Longman Group Ltd, London.

—— and N. H. Stern (1974), 'Pigou, Taxation and Public Goods', *The Review of Economic Studies* 41(1): 117–27.

Auerbach, A. J. (1979), 'Share Valuation and Corporate Equity Finance', *Journal of Public Economics* 11: 291–305.

—— (1985), 'The Theory of Excess Burden and Optimal Taxation', in *Handbook of Public Economics*, edited by A. J. Auerbach and M. Feldstein, Elsevier Science Publishers, New York, Vol. 1, pp. 61–127.

—— and J. R. Hines (2002), 'Taxation and Economic Efficiency', in *Handbook of Public Economics*, edited by A. J. Auerbach and M. Feldstein, Elsevier Science Publishers, New York, Vol. 4.

—— and M. A. King (1983), 'Taxation, Portfolio Choice, and Debt-Equity Ratios: A General Equilibrium Model', *Quarterly Journal of Economics* 48: 587–609.

Bailey, M. J. (1954), 'The Marshallian Demand Curve', *Journal of Political Economy* 62(3): 255–61.

—— and M. C. Jensen (1972), 'Risk and the Discount Rate for Public Investment', in *Studies in the Theory of Capital Markets*, edited by M. C. Jensen, Praeger, New York, pp. 269–93.

Balassa, B. and D. M. Schydlowsky (1972), 'Domestic Resource Costs and Effective Protection Once Again', *Journal of Political Economy* 80 (January/February): 63–9.

Ballard, C. L. (1988), 'The Marginal Efficiency Cost of Redistribution', *American Economic Review* 78(5): 1019–33.

—— and D. Fullerton (1992), 'Distortionary Taxes and the Provision of Public Goods', *Journal of Economic Perspectives* 6(3): 117–31.

Ballard, C. L., J. B. Shoven, and J. Whalley (1985), 'General Equilibrium Computations of the Marginal Welfare Costs of Taxes in the United States', *American Economic Review* 75: 128–38.

Baumol, W. J. and B. G. Malkiel (1967), 'The Firm's Optimal Debt–Equity Ratio and the Cost of Capital', *Quarterly Journal of Economics* 81(4): 547–8.

Bergson, A. (1938), 'A Reformulation of Certain Aspects of Welfare Economics', *Quarterly Journal of Economics* 68: 233–52.

Bergstrom, T. C., L. Blume, and H. Varian (1986), 'On the Private Provision of Public Goods', *Journal of Public Economics* 29: 25–49.

Bhattacharya, S. (1979), 'Imperfect Information, Dividend Policy, and the Bird in the Hand Fallacy', *Bell Journal of Economics* 10: 259–70.

Blackorby, C. and D. Donaldson (1990), A Review Article: The Case against the Use of the Sum of Compensating Variations in Cost–Benefit Analysis', *Canadian Journal of Economics* 23(3): 471–94 (review).

Boadway, R. W. (1974), 'The Welfare Foundations of Cost–Benefit Analysis', *Economic Journal:* 926–39.

——(1976), 'Integrating Equity and Efficiency in Applied Welfare Economics', *Quarterly Journal of Economics* 90(4): 541–56.

——(1978), 'A Note on the Treatment of Foreign Exchange in Project Evaluation', *Economica* 45(180): 391–9.

——and N. Bruce (1984), *Welfare Economics*, Basil Blackman, Oxford.

Boadway, R., P. Pestieau, and D. E. Wildasin (1989), 'Tax–Transfer Policies and the Voluntary Provision of Public Goods', *Journal of Public Economics* 39: 157–76.

——and D. E. Wildasin (1984), *Public Sector Economics*, Little, Brown and Co., Boston, MA.

Bradford, D. F. (1975), 'Constraints on Government Investment Opportunities and the Choice of Discount Rate', *American Economic Review* 65(5): 887–99.

——(1981), 'The Incidence and Allocative Effects of Tax on Corporate Distributions', *Journal of Political Economy* 15: 1–22.

Brekke, K. A. (1997), 'The Numeraire Matters in Cost–Benefit Analysis', *Journal of Public Economics* 64: 117–23.

Browning, E. K. (1976), 'The Marginal Cost of Public Funds', *Journal of Political Economy* 84(2): 283–98.

——(1987), 'On the Marginal Welfare Cost of Taxation', *American Economic Review* 77: 11–23.

Bruce, N. and R. G. Harris (1981), *The Compensation Principle: Reversal and Bias in Cost–Benefit Tests*, Discussion Paper No. 422, Queen's University, Kingston, Ontario.

——, ——(1982), 'Cost–Benefit Criteria and the Compensation Principle in Evaluating Small Projects', *Journal of Political Economy* 90(4): 755–76.

Bruno, M. (1972), 'Market Distortions and Gradual Reform', *Review of Economic Studies* 39: 373–83.

Campbell, H. F. (1975), 'Deadweight Loss and Commodity Taxation in Canada', *Canadian Journal of Economics* 8: 441–7.

——and K. A. Bond (1997), 'The Cost of Public Funds in Australia', *Economic Record* 73(220): 22–34.

Coates, S. (2000), 'An Efficiency Approach to the Evaluation of Policy Changes', *Economic Journal* 110: 437–55.

Corden, W. M. (1974), *Trade Policy and Economic Welfare*, Oxford University Press, London.

Corlett, W. J. and Hague, D. C. (1953/4), 'Complementarity and the Excess Burden of Taxation', *The Review of Economic Studies* 21(1): 21–30.

Cornes, R. C. and T. Sandler (1985), 'The Simple Analytics of Pure Public Good Provision', *Economica* 52: 103–16.

Cox, C. C. (1980), 'The Enforcement of Public Price Controls', *Journal of Political Economy* 88(5): 887–916.

Dahlby, B. (1994), 'The Distortionary Effect of Raising Taxes', in *Deficit Reduction: What Pain, What Gain?*, edited by W. B. P. Robson and W. M. Scarth, Howe Institute, Toronto, pp. 44–72.

——(1998), 'Progressive Taxation and the Social Marginal Cost of Public Funds', *Journal of Public Economics* 67(1): 105–22.

Dammon, R. M. and R. C. Green (1987), 'Tax Arbitrage and the Existence of Equilibrium Prices for Financial Assets', *Journal of Finance* 42: 1143–66.

Dasgupta, P., S. Marglin, and A. Sen (1972), *Guidelines for Project Evaluation*, UNIDO: United Nations, New York.

—— and J. E. Stiglitz (1972), 'On Optimal Taxation and Public Production', *Review of Economic Studies* 39(1): 87–103.

DeAngelo, H. and R. W. Masulis (1980), 'Optimal Capital Structure Under Corporate and Personal Taxation', *Journal of Financial Economics* 8: 3–29.

Deaton, A. S. and J. Muellbauer (1980), *Economics and Consumer Behaviour*, Cambridge University Press, Cambridge.

Diamond, P. A. and D. L. McFadden (1974), 'Some Uses of the Expenditure Function in Public Economics', *Journal of Public Economics* 77: 3–21.

—— and J. A. Mirrlees (1971), 'Optimal Taxation and Public Production I and II', *American Economic Review* (March) 61(1): 8–27; (June) 61(3): 261–78.

——,—— (1976), 'Private Constant Returns and Public Shadow Prices', *Review of Economic Studies* 43(133): 41–7.

Diewert, W. E. (1983), 'Cost–Benefit Analysis and Project Evaluation: A Comparison of Alternative Approaches', *Journal of Public Economics* 22: 265–302.

—— and D. E. Lawrence (1996), 'The Deadweight Costs of Taxation in New Zealand', *Canadian Journal of Economics* 29(0), Special Issue Part 2: S658–73.

Dixit, A. (1975), 'Welfare Effects of Tax and Price Changes', *Journal of Public Economics* 4: 103–23.

—— (1985), 'Tax Policy in Open Economies', in *Handbook of Public Economics*, edited by A. J. Auerbach and M. Feldstein, Elsevier Science Publishers, Amsterdam, Vol. I, Ch. 6, pp. 313–74.

—— (1987), 'Trade and Insurance with Moral Hazard', *Journal of International Economics* 23: 201–20.

—— (1989), 'Trade and Insurance with Adverse Selection', *Review of Economic Studies* 56: 235–48.

Dréze, J. (1998), 'Distribution Matters in Cost–Benefit Analysis: Comment', *Journal of Public Economics* 70(3): 485–8.

—— and N. Stern (1985), 'The Theory of Cost–Benefit Analysis', in *Handbook of Public Economics*, edited by A. J. Auerbach and M. Feldstein, North Holland, Vol. II.

——,—— (1990), 'Policy Reform, Shadow Prices and Market Prices', *Journal of Public Economics* 42(1): 1–45.

Elton, E. J. and M. J. Gruber (1995), *Modern Portfolio Theory and Investment Analysis*, John-Wiley and Sons, New York.

Fane, C. G. (1991*a*), 'Piecemeal Tax Reforms and the Compensated Radial Elasticities of Tax Bases', *Journal of Public Economics* 45(2): 263–70.

—— (1991*b*), 'The Social Opportunity Cost of Foreign Exchange: A Partial Defence of Harberger et al.,', *The Economic Record* 67(199): 307–16.

Farrar, D. E. and L. L. Selwyn (1967), 'Taxes, Corporate Financial Policy and Returns to Investors', *National Tax Journal* 20(4): 444–54.

Feldstein, M. (1973), 'On the Optimal Progressivity of the Income Tax', *Journal of Public Economics* 2(2): 159–71.

Findlay, C. C. and R. L. Jones (1982), 'The Marginal Cost of Australian Income Taxation', *Economic Record* 58(162): 253–62.

Findlay, R. and S. Wellisz (1976), 'Project Evaluation, Shadow Prices and Trade Policy', *Journal of Political Economy* 84(3): 543–52.

Fontaine, E. R. (1969), 'El Precio sombra de las divisas en evaluación social de proyectos', Universidad Católica de Chile, Santiago.

Foster, E. and H. Sonnenschein (1970), 'Price Distortion and Economic Welfare', *Econometrica* 38: 281–97.

Fullerton, D. (1991), 'Reconciling Recent Estimates of the Marginal Welfare Cost of Taxation', *American Economic Review* 81(1): 302–8.

Gaube, T. (2000), 'When do Distortionary Taxes Reduce the Optimal Supply of Public Goods?', *Journal of Public Economics* 76: 151–80.

Goulder, H. L. and R. C. Williams III (2003), 'The Substantial Bias from Ignoring General Equilibrium Effects in Estimating Excess Burden, and a Practical Solution', *Journal of Political Economy* 111(4): 898–927.

Green, J. H. A. (1976), *Consumer Theory*, MacMillan Press Ltd, London, 2nd edn.

Håkonsen, L. (1998), 'An Investigation into Alternative Representations of the Marginal Cost of Public Funds', *International Tax and Public Finance* 5: 329–43.

Harberger, A. C. (1964), 'The Measurement of Waste', *American Economic Review* 54(3): 58–76.

—— (1968), 'Survey of Literature on Cost–Benefit Analysis for Industrial Project Evaluation', in *Manual for the Evaluation of Industrial Projects*, edited, UNIDO, United Nations, New York.

—— (1969), 'Professor Arrow on the Social Discount Rate', in *Cost–Benefit Analysis of Manpower Policies*, edited by G. G. Somers and W. D. Wood, Queens University, Industrial Relations Centre, Kingston, Ontario, Canada: 76–88.

—— (1971), 'Three Basic Postulates for Applied Welfare Economics: An Interpretive Essay', *Journal of Economic Literature* 9: 785–97.

—— (1978), 'On the Use of Distributional Weights in Social Cost-Benefit Analysis', *Journal of Political Economy* 86(2): 87–120.

—— (1984), 'Basic Needs Versus Distributional Weights in Social Cost–Benefit Analysis', *Economic Development and Cultural Change* 32(3): 455–74.

—— (1990), 'Reflections on Uniform Taxation', in *The Political Economy of International Trade: Essays in Honor of Robert E. Baldwin*, edited by R. W. Jones and A. O. Kruger, Oxford and Cambridge, Blackwell, Massachusetts.

Harris, J. R. and M. P. Todaro (1970), 'Migration, Unemployment and Development: A Two-Sector Analysis', *American Economic Review* 60(1): 126–42.

Harris, M. and A. Raviv (1991), 'The Theory of Capital Structure', *Journal of Finance* 46: 297–355.

Hatta, T. (1977), 'A Theory of Piecemeal Policy Recommendations', *Review of Economic Studies* 44: 1–21.

—— (1986), 'Welfare Effects of Changing Commodity Tax Rates Toward Uniformity', *Journal of Public Economics* 29: 99–112.

—— and J. Haltiwanger (1986), 'Tax Reform and Strong Substitutes', *International Economic Review* 27: 303–15.

Hicks, J. R. (1939), 'The Foundations of Welfare Economics', *Economic Journal* 49(196): 696–712.

—— (1940), 'The Valuation of Social Income', *Economica* 7(26): 105–24.

—— (1954), *A Revision of Demand Theory*, Oxford University Press.

Hines, J. J. R. (1999), 'Three Sides of Harberger Triangles', *Journal of Economic Perspectives* 13(2): 167–88.

Johansson, P. O. (1998), 'Does the Choice of Numeraire Matter in Cost–Benefit Analysis', *Journal of Public Economics* 70: 489–93.

Jones, C. M. (2000), 'A Correction to: The Structure of General Equilibrium Shadow Pricing Rules for a Tax-Distorted Economy', ANU Working Papers in Economics and Econometrics No. 386.

—— (2001), 'Conventional Cost–Benefit Analysis with Distorting Taxes and the Revised Samuelson Condition', ANU Working Papers in Economics and Econometrics No. 398.

—— and F. Milne (1992), 'Tax Arbitrage, Existence of Equilibrium and Bounded Tax Rebates', *Mathematical Finance* 2(3): 189–96.

Kaldor, N. (1939), 'Welfare Propositions of Economics and Interpersonal Comparisons of Utility', *Economic Journal* 49(195): 549–52.

Kaplow, L. (1996), 'The Optimal Supply of Public Goods and the Distortionary Cost of Taxation', *National Tax Policy* 49: 523–33.

Kawamata, K. (1974), 'Price Distortion and Potential Welfare', *Econometrica* 42: 435–60.

Kay, J. A. (1980), 'The Deadweight Loss from a Tax System', *Journal of Public Economics* 13: 111–19.

Kim, E. H. (1982), 'Miller's Equilibrium, Shareholder Leverage Clienteles, and Optimal Capital Structure', *Journal of Finance* 37: 301–23.

Kirchsteiger, G. and C. Puppe (1997), 'On the Possibility of Efficient Private Provision of Public Goods through Government Subsidies', *Journal of Public Economics* 66: 489–504.

Kuznets, S. (1948), 'On the Valuation of Social Income—Reflections on Professor Hicks' Article', *Economica* 15: 1–16.

Lerner, A. P. (1936), 'The Symmetry Between Import and Export Taxes', *Economica* 11: 306–13.

Lindahl, E. (1919), 'Die gerechtigkeit der Besteverung', reprinted in part as 'Just Taxation—a Positive Solution' in *Classics in the Theory of Public Finance*, edited by R. A. Musgrave and R. A. Peacock, Macmillan (1958), London.

Little, I. M. D. (1949), 'The Valuation of the Social Income', *Econometrica* 16: 11–26.

—— and J. A. Mirrlees (1969), *Manual of Industrial Project Analysis in Developing Countries*, OECD.

—— (1972), 'A Reply to Some Criticisms of the O.E.C.D. Manual', *Bulletin of the Oxford University Institute of Economics and Statistics* 34(1): 551–82.

Marglin, S. A. (1963*a*), 'The Social Rate of Discount and the Optimal Rate of Investment', *Quarterly Journal of Economics* 77(1): 95–111.

—— (1963*b*), 'The Opportunity Costs of Public Investment', *Quarterly Journal of Economics* 77(2): 274–89.

Mayshar, J. (1990), 'On Measures of Excess Burden and Their Application', *Journal of Public Economics* 43(3): 263–89.

—— (1991), 'On Measuring the Marginal Cost of Funds Analytically', *American Economic Review* 81(5): 1329–35.

Miller, M. H. (1977), 'Debt and Taxes', *Journal of Finance* 32: 261–75.

—— (1988), 'Modigliani–Miller Propositions After Thirty Years', *The Journal of Economic Perspectives* 2(4): 99–120.

Mirrlees, J. A. (1971), 'An Exploration in the Theory of Optimal Income Taxation', *The Review of Economic Studies* 38 (April): 175–208.

—— (1976), 'Optimal Taxation: A Synthesis', *Journal of Public Economics* 6(4): 327–58.

Modigliani, F. and M. H. Miller (1958), 'The Cost of Capital, Corporate Finance, and the Theory of Investment', *American Economic Review* 48: 261–97.

—,—— (1963), 'Corporate Income Taxes and the Cost of Capital: A Correction', *American Economic Review* 53: 433–43.

Musgrave, R. A. and T. Thin (1948), 'Income Tax Progression', *Journal of Political Economy* 56(6): 498–514.

Myles, G. G. (1995), *Public Economics*, Cambridge University Press, Cambridge.

Papps, I. (1993), 'Shadow Pricing with Price Controls', *Scottish Journal of Political Economy* 40(2): 199–209.

Parish, R. M. (1972), 'On How to Interpret Ambiguous Market Signals when Appraising Investment Projects', mimeo, IBRD.

—— (1973), 'Shadow Prices for Factors and Non-Traded Goods in a Tax-Distorted Economy', mimeo, Monash University.

—— (1976), 'The Scope of Cost–Benefit Analysis', *The Economic Record* 52(139): 302–14.

Peck, R. M. (1998), 'The Inefficiency of the Poll Tax', *Journal of Public Economics* 67: 241–52.

Pigou, A. C. (1932), *The Economics of Welfare*, MacMillan Press Ltd, 4th Edn.

—— (1947), *A Study in Public Finance*, MacMillan Press Ltd, 3rd Edn.

Pirttila, J. and M. Tuomala (2001), 'On Optimal Non-Linear Taxation and Public Good Provision in an Overlapping Generations Economy', *Journal of Public Economics* 79: 485–501.

Ramsey, F. P. (1927), 'A Contribution to the Theory of Taxation', *Economic Journal* 37: 47–61.

Rawls, J. (1971), *A Theory of Justice*, Harvard University Press, Cambridge, MA.

Roberts, R. D. (1987), 'Financing Public Goods', *Journal of Political Economy* 95: 420–37.

Samuelson, P. A. (1948), *Foundations of Economic Analysis*, Harvard University Press, Cambridge, MA.

—— (1950), 'Evaluation of Real National Income', *Oxford Economic Papers* 2: 1–29.

—— (1954), 'The Pure Theory of Public Expenditure', *Review of Economic and Statistics* 36: 387–9.

—— (1962), 'The Gains from International Trade Once Again', *Economic Journal* 72: 820–9.

—— (1964), 'Principles of Efficiency: Discussion', *American Economic Review* 54: 93–6.

Sandmo, A. (1998), 'Redistribution and the Marginal Social Cost of Public Funds', *Journal of Public Economics* 70: 365–82.

—— and J. H. Dréze (1971), 'Discount Rates for Public Investment in Closed and Open Economies', *Economica* 38: 396–412.

Sarig, O. and J. Scott (1985), 'The Puzzle of Financial Leverage Clienteles', *Journal of Finance* 40(5): 1459–67.

Schydlowsky, D. M. (1968), 'On the Choice of a Shadow Price for Foreign Exchange', Harvard University Development Advisory Service, Economic Development Report No. 108.

Scitovsky, T. (1941), 'A Note on Welfare Propositions in Economics', *Review of Economic Studies* 9(1): 77–88.

Sen, A. K. (1977), 'On Weights and Measures', *Econometrica* 45: 1539–72.

Sheshinski, E. (1989), 'Note on the Shape of the Optimum Income Tax Schedule', *Journal of Public Economics* 40: 201–15.

Shoven, J. B. (1974), 'A Proof of the Existence of a General Equilibrium with ad Valorem Commodity Taxes', *Journal of Economic Theory* 8(1): 475–89.

Sieper, E. (1981), 'The Structure of General Equilibrium Shadow Pricing Rules for a Tax-Distorted Economy', Discussion Paper No. 4, Centre of Policy Studies, Monash University.

—— (1982), *Rationalising Rustic Regulation*, The Centre for Independent Studies, Sydney, Australia.

——(1994), 'Shadow Prices and the Marginal Excess Burden of Taxation: Reconciling Harberger and Diamond and Mirrlees', mimeo, ANU.

Silberberg, E. (1972), 'Duality and the Many Consumer's Surpluses', *American Economic Review* 62: 942–52.

——and W. C. Suen (2001), *The Structure of Economics: A Mathematical Analysis*, McGraw Hill, New York, 3rd edn.

Sjaastad, L. A. and D. L. Wisecarver (1977), 'The Social Cost of Public Finance', *Journal of Political Economy* 85(3): 513–47.

Slemrod, J. and S. Yitzhaki (2001), 'Integrating Expenditure and Tax Decisions: The Marginal Cost of Funds and the Marginal Benefit of Projects', *National Tax Journal* 54(2): 189–201.

——S. Yitzhaki, J. Mayshar, and M. Lundholm (1994), 'The Optimal Two-Bracket Linear Income Tax', *Journal of Public Economics* 53: 269–90.

Snow, A. and R. S. Warren, Jr. (1996), 'The Marginal Welfare Cost of Public Funds: Theory and Estimates', *Journal of Public Economics* 61(2): 289–305.

Squire, L., (1989), 'Project Evaluation in Theory and Practice', in *Handbook of Development Economics*, edited by H. Chenery and T. N. Srinivasan, Elsevier Science Publishers, Amsterdam, II: 1093–137.

Srinivasan, T. N. and J. N. Bhagwati (1978), 'Shadow Prices for Project Selection in the Presence of Distortions: Effective Rates of Protection and Domestic Resource Costs', *Journal of Political Economy* 86(1): 97–116.

Stiglitz, J. E. and P. Dasgupta (1971), 'Differential Taxation, Public Goods and Economic Efficiency', *Review of Economic Studies* 38: 151–74.

Stuart, C. (1984), 'Welfare Costs Per Dollar of Additional Tax Revenue in the United States', *American Economic Review* 74: 352–62.

Tresch, R. W. (2002), *Public Finance: A Normative Theory*, Elsevier Science/Academic Press, San Diego and London, 2nd Edn.

Triest, R. K. (1990), 'The Relationship between the Marginal Cost of Public Funds and Marginal Excess Burden', *American Economic Review* 80(3): 557–66.

Vickery, W. (1964), 'Principles of Efficiency: Discussion', *American Economic Review* 54: 88–92.

Warr, P. G. (1982), 'Shadow Pricing Rules for Non-Traded Commodities', *Oxford Economic Papers* 34: 305–25.

——(1983), 'The Private Provision of a Public Good is Independent of the Distribution of Income', *Economics Letters* 13: 207–11.

Wildasin, D. E. (1979), 'Public Good Provision with Optimal and Non-Optimal Commodity Taxation', *Economics Letters* 4: 59–64.

——(1984), 'On Public Good Provision with Distortionary Taxation', *Economic Inquiry* 22: 227–43.

Williams, J. (1988), 'Efficient Signalling with Dividends, Investment, and Stock Repurchases', *Journal of Finance* 43: 737–47.

Willig, R. (1976), 'Consumer's Surplus without Apology', *American Economic Review* 66(4): 589–97.

Author Index

Subject Index